THE WOODEN SPOON

Patricia Mandronico Cerjan

Claire,
Enjoy!
Patricia

2016

To my parents

Mary and Barney Mandronico

For handing down their "love of cooking" and for developing my skills to follow my dreams.

THE WOODEN SPOON

"There is no love sincerer than the love of food."

-George Bernard Shaw

Patty's Cooking Journal

Patricia Mandronico Cerjan
Copyright © 2016

Contents

INTRODUCTION	6
A LITTLE GIRL GROWING UP IN A COOKING ENVIRONMENT	9
COOKING WITH MOM	13
GRANDMA ROSARIA MANDRONICO'S KITCHEN	43
COOKING AND PREPPING AT BARNEY'S RESTAURANT	50
PIES, PIES, PIES	58
A NEW BRIDE LIVING IN GERMANY	70
OFFICER'S WIFE	98
LIVING IN NEW ENGLAND	119
THE ART OF BREAD MAKING	136
GAINESVILLE, GEORGIA	148
ROCKY MOUNT, NC THE LEAN YEARS	165
ROCKY MOUNT, NC THE GOURMET YEARS	222
ROCKY MOUNT, NC DINNER PARTIES AND COFFEES	277
MY TYPICAL ITALIAN DINNER PARTY	292
COCKTAIL PARTIES	297
NORTHERN CHICAGO	299
EL SABOR DE COSTA RICA	344
PARADISE IN FLORIDA	358
GRILLING WITH STEVE	415

THANKSGIVING MENU	429
CHRISTMAS MENU	435
SAUCES	437
SUGGESTED MENUS	461
DINNER PARTIES FOR 8-10	468
ACKNOWLEDGEMENTS	469

The Wooden Spoon

This is not the typical cookbook. Within these pages you won't find instructions on how to whip meringues to their fluffiest potential or hidden secrets for creating a classic, easy-bake cake. Instead, I invite you to share the journey of my life through good food. These are the types of nibbles and noshes that require fifty-five years and multiple geographical locations to perfect. Each "pinch of this" marks a different point in my life and every "dash of that" reminisces another adventure. Be that as it may, they all originated from the same place, a dream I had as a young girl and my Grandma's curious wooden spoon.

My father, Angelo "Barney" Mandronico, owned and operated a small-scale diner tucked away on Dominick Street in the modest town of Rome, New York. Day in and day out, my parents stood shoulder to shoulder thoughtfully preparing classic, American fare along with my Italian family's favorites. Barney's Restaurant served more than flavorful meals and a way to make a livelihood, it was our home. For eight years we occupied the dimly lit flat situated above the restaurant. Often there were evenings when my brother and I were left alone upstairs while my parent's put forth late dinners to hungry customers eagerly waiting in the dining room below. On these nights, I'd pass time staring through my bedroom window studying the rhythmic flashes coming from the electric sign as it squiggled out B-A-R-N-E-Y-'S R-E-S-T-A-U-R-A-N-T in neon ink. While observing the diner's activities by night, I'd conjure up images of myself running a restaurant just like my Dad.

The insatiable buzz of living in and above a restaurant stirred a desire in me to cook and cook more. Whenever the stove was lit, I was by my mother's side shadowing her handiwork. Whether watching the careful preparation of pies and pastries as they made their way atop the craving plates of patron's or helping prepare meals for our family, hours were spent in the kitchen with my Mom baking, chopping, and tasting.

Besides Barney's Restaurant and my parents, there were others provoking the chef in me. Perhaps it's an Italian birthright, but all of my relatives had the gift of bringing soul to a recipe. Yet, Grandma Rosaria's talents surpassed them all. Decades before anyone thought farm to table a trend, Grandma nurtured a vast garden and used its offerings to characterize the dishes she created. She dried her own cayenne pepper, made pastas from scratch and perfected the Rosette wedding cookie.

Anything culinary my Grandmother could accomplish and she did so without ever following a single recipe. When cooking, she simply summonsed her instincts and the aid of a trusted wooden spoon. Other than being antiqued and aged with use, there was nothing remarkable about the design of this gadget. Solid wood with an oversized dip and elongated handle, this was the type of tool typically used for stirring. Intended for this purpose, added to the fact that this one in particular didn't have metric markings, I found it an odd choice for measuring ingredients. Grandma's creative use of cookware and my curiosity would soon prove useful partners.

At twenty-one, I was newly engaged and ready to leave the comforts of family and Barney's Restaurant. In preparation, I took on the immense task of squeezing a lifetime's worth of my family's culinary creations onto what seemed like infinitesimally small recipe cards. Without Grandma's recipes recorded in writing, there was only one way for me to understand her approach. It started with a semi-productive conversation with Grandma who at 70 years old, still spoke broken English. Next, I laid out every ingredient I could find from liquids to powders to crumbs, and measured exactly how much that dutiful spoon of hers held. With the secrets of the wooden spoon revealed and recipe cards complete, I was about to spin my journey with food in a new direction.

Throughout our marriage, I was fortunate enough to zigzag up and down the eastern United States and live overseas twice. Each jaunt brought another culture to learn and a new way of cooking to experience. Germany shared the Wiener Schnitzel, Georgia the art of southern fried, New England the succulence of seafood, and Costa Rica the fiery passion of Latin cuisine. Unexpectedly, two French chefs in Midwestern Chicago educated me on the importance of a good stock and exactly what goes into cooking for an upscale restaurant. Along the way, I met and enjoyed the ride with other inquisitive galloping gourmets. Although, to speak of it as a pilgrimage of privilege would be an inaccurate interpretation of my story. Many nights were spent serving comfort foods to get us through the financially lean years. These were the times when one chicken made two casseroles and the kids begged to eat dinner at a friend's house.

Regardless the geographical location, my culinary compass never pointed towards a restaurant of my own. At one juncture, while living in a rural city in North Carolina, I thought it would happen as I envisioned opening a bistro. Weeks were spent carefully constructing menus and composing courses. When finished, I called Daddy. His words made me reflect back on Barney's Restaurant and the family sacrifices my parents made to ensure the prosperity of their establishment. In a caring way, Dad explained the challenges our location would have for an accomplished business and the difficulties between succeeding and keeping my family happy. The conversation made me pause and shuffle my ambitions elsewhere.

Today, I live in Florida and enjoy life as a retiree. My relationship with the preparation of delectable food still beats on with an enthusiasm to excel at all I've learned. I'm constantly reading cookbooks and scouring the internet for recipes. Appetizing plates I dreamt up years ago with friends from another place and time, I relive with those I know today.

In writing this book, I was reminded of the many treasured moments and joyful memories I've had throughout my life. In completing these recipes, I realized the dream I had as a little girl did come true. Each time I prepare a family meal or host a dinner party, I share a portion of my adventure with food amongst friends and loved ones. It's gratifying to witness their smiles as they eat and to listen to their stories recanting the last time they had such a dish. In the end, isn't that what being a successful chef and restaurateur is all about?

It's my wish that you enjoy using this book as much as I have enjoyed writing it. Thank you for allowing me to pass along the inspirations that sparked my dreams and the magic of the wooden spoon.

May you eat well and laugh often,

Patricia

My talented daughter Mary Cerjan wrote this beautiful introduction.

A LITTLE GIRL GROWING UP IN A COOKING ENVIRONMENT

My childhood dream was cooking. I never remember not being around a cooking environment either at home, in my relatives' kitchens or in our family restaurant.

I recall getting very anxious before my dance recitals, but not nearly as nervous as when I made my first cake. I made that cake to earn my Girl Scout cooking badge in 1952.

While most of my girlfriends in the Girl Scout troop made Rice Krispies bars or simple recipes, my mom convinced me to make Boston Cream Cake. Making that cake was the start of my love for cooking and baking.

MY FIRST RECIPE
BOSTON CRÈME CAKE
Girl Scout Cooking Badge Age 9

When I retrieved this old recipe from my archives, I found it very yellow with age. I also noticed the old cooking methods of that era. I attempted to update the methods and some of the ingredients.

1½ cups flour	6 tablespoons butter
1½ teaspoons baking powder	1½ cups sugar
1½ teaspoons vanilla	Lemon zest about 1 teaspoon
¾ teaspoon salt	Cream filling
3 large eggs	Chocolate Glaze
¾ cup whole milk	

- Preheat oven to 325°. Adjust the oven rack to a medium position
- Lightly grease two 9-inch cake pans with nonstick spray and line with parchment or waxed paper
- Whisk flour, baking powder and salt into a small bowl
- Heat milk and butter in small saucepan; remove from heat and add vanilla; cover
- In electric mixer using the whisk attachment; beat together the eggs, zest and sugar on high speed about 5 minutes; add the milk mixture and whisk by hand until incorporated
- Add dry ingredients and whisk again until all is incorporated
- Quickly turn into prepared pans
- Bake until a cake tester inserted in center comes out clean; 20-22 minutes
- Place pans on wire rack and cool completely about 2 hours
- Run small knife around edges of pans, then invert onto wire rack; remove parchment; invert cakes again
- At this point you can put the cakes on a cookie sheet and freeze firmly and then wrap for future use or begin to make the filling and assemble the cake

CREAM FILLING:

2 cups half and half	¼ cup flour
6 large egg yolks	4 tablespoons cold butter, cut into pieces
½ cup sugar	1½ teaspoons vanilla extract
Pinch salt	

- Heat the half and half in saucepan until just simmering.
- Whisk yolks, sugar and salt in bowl until smooth.
- Add flour to yolk mixture and whisk.
- Remove half and half from heat and whisking constantly, slowly add ½ cup of the half and half to the yolk mixture to temper. Whisking constantly, return tempered yolk mixture to half and half in saucepan.

- Return to heat and cook, whisking constantly until the mixture thickens slightly about 1 minute.
- Reduce heat and continue to simmer whisking constantly for another 8 minutes.
- Increase heat and cook whisking constantly until the pudding bubbles and burst on the surface (1-2 minutes).
- Remove from heat and whisk in butter and vanilla.
- Place a sheet of saran wrap or greased waxed paper over the filling to keep a "skin" from forming making sure the wrap touches all of the filling.
- Refrigerate for at least 2 hours or up to 24 hours before assembling cake.

CHOCOLATE GLAZE

½ cup heavy cream
2 tablespoons light corn syrup
4 ounces bittersweet chocolate chopped finely

- Bring cream and syrup to simmer
- Remove from heat and add chocolate
- Whisk until smooth
- Let stand, whisking occasionally until thickened (5 minutes)

ASSEMBLY:

- Put one cake layer on cake dish
- Spread with filling
- Put second layer over filling
- Pour glaze onto the center of the cake
- With long handled spatula, smooth to edges of cake allowing the glaze to fall off sides of cake
- Chill the finished cake for at least 3 hours before slicing
- Can make and assemble cake a day in advance

Yield: 8-10

FRESH SCRAMBLED EGGS

What can be difficult about scrambling a few eggs? To an inexperienced 9-year old it can be a big deal. I still remember serving these eggs to my brother Ronnie for the first time. I felt so grown up. Mom told me the secret to the eggs is the splash of cream. In those days we got fresh cream from the top of the milk bottles. The milkman delivered fresh milk to our home daily and we would shake the bottle to mix the cream into the milk.

8 large eggs mixed with a wire whisk
Salt and pepper to taste
Splash of fresh cream

- Whisk together all ingredients
- Melt fresh butter in skillet
- Add eggs and stir gently until eggs are cooked

Serves: 6

MILLION DOLLAR FUDGE
1956

I learned to make this wonderful fudge as a Girl Scout. My scout leader, Mrs. Rysinski, gave the recipe to me when I became a senior scout.

4½ cups sugar
2 tablespoons butter
1 tall can evaporated milk
Pinch of salt

12 ounces semi-sweet chocolate morsels
12 ounces German sweet chocolate
1 pint marshmallow cream
2 cups chopped walnuts

- Bring sugar, butter, milk and salt to a boil stirring constantly
- Boil for 6 minutes
- Pour over the chocolate and marshmallow cream and nuts
- Beat all in a mixer until all chocolate is melted
- Immediately pour into greased 9x13 inch pan or two square pans
- Let cool in refrigerator for 2 hours
- Store in a metal box

COOKING WITH MOM

A mother's kitchen is the center of family life.

In my childhood it was the social hub of our family and our extended families. It was an extension of our family restaurant.

Mom cooked for work and for pleasure. Her favorite was baking. She loved to bake hot sweet breads and deliver them to friends and family. She found joy in their delight of her sweet gifts.

Italian dishes were served at least four times a week in our household. Mom made a pot of her spaghetti sauce every week. This sauce became the basis for her pastas, vegetable dishes and pizzas.

I spent countless hours in her kitchen soaking up her skills. We made everything from stuffed artichokes to her famous pineapple upside down cake. While I was always her helper, as I got closer to age 13 she allowed me to take the helm.

The recipes from mom's kitchen are still used today in my kitchen.

BAKED LASAGNA
CIRCA 1954

I made this Italian dish hundreds of times over the years and many times when I worked at Barney's Restaurant. My version is slightly different from mom's. I do not use sliced hard-boiled eggs as one of the layers.

1 pound lasagna noodles
1 pound hamburger meat or Italian sausage casings removed or combo of each
Recipe for spaghetti sauce
1 pound shredded or sliced mozzarella

1 pound ricotta cheese
1 egg
Salt and pepper
Minced fresh parsley
Freshly grated Parmigiano-Reggiano cheese
Lasagna pan greased with cooking spray

- Prepare spaghetti sauce per recipe.
- Boil large pot of water. Add salt and oil to prevent noodles from sticking.
- When water comes to boil, add noodles, bring to boil and simmer 8 minutes.
- Drain noodles and rinse with cold water.
- Separate the noodles and place each in a row on waxed paper to cool.
- Add 1 egg, salt, pepper, and parsley to ricotta cheese and set aside.
- Shred or slice mozzarella cheese, grate the Parmesan cheese and set both aside.
- Sauté hamburger, or sausage meat in a bit of olive oil, and set aside.
- Spoon a large ladleful of sauce on bottom of lasagna pan.
- Place noodles side by side to fill bottom of pan.
- Sprinkle a layer of hamburger/sausage meat for first layer.
- Spread a layer of ricotta cheese mixture.
- Sprinkle a layer of mozzarella cheese.
- Sprinkle layer of Parmigiano-Reggiano cheese.
- Add another layer of noodles, spoon layer of spaghetti sauce over noodles.
- Continue layering until you end with noodles.
- Spread sauce over the top layer.
- Sprinkle lots of Parmigiano-Reggiano cheese over top.
- Cover with foil and bake 375° for 45-50 minutes.
- Uncover and bake another 10-15 minutes or until bubbling.
- Let stand 15 minutes to set before cutting and serving.

I sometimes freeze the lasagna making sure I have added ample amount of sauce on top. You can bake for 30 minutes, cool in refrigerator and then freeze or freeze without baking.

- Cover the lasagna with a sheet of plastic wrap and a sheet of foil. Place in large freezer bag.
- To thaw lasagna, place it in the refrigerator the day before you plan to serve it. Remove the plastic wrap and bake with foil covering for 40-50 minutes.
- Remove the foil and bake an additional 15 minutes, let stand 15 minutes before cutting.

SPAGHETTI ALL'OLIO E AGLIO
1949

This is a traditional Christmas Eve dish in the Cerjan home passed down from my mom and my grandmother Rosaria Mandronico. Both my mom and my grandmothers served this every Christmas Eve as part of the Italian Catholic Vigilia or Feast of the Seven Fishes. I serve this as a side dish with my Seafood Ramekins.

- Heat ½ cup olive oil in a skillet
- Add 4 cloves of garlic, sliced thinly
- Slowly cook garlic just until very lightly browned
- Slowly add:
    - ½ cup water
    - 1 tablespoon chopped fresh Italian parsley
    - ⅛ teaspoon pepper
    - Anchovy paste or can of anchovy filets minced
- Simmer 10 minutes
- Toss sauce with 8 ounces of cooked angel hair pasta
- If dry add a bit of pasta water

Serves: 4 nice side dishes

ITALIAN SPAGHETTI SAUCE
1965

This is my mom's basic sauce. After watching her make this sauce every week, I decided to write out her recipe the year I got married. The secret to this sauce is the long slow simmering and stirring. My kids remember me saying, "Stir the sauce". We took turns stirring the sauce so it would not stick to the bottom of the pot. I added or omitted a few extra ingredients to suit my taste.

4	(28-ounce) cans of high quality Italian imported whole peeled tomatoes -- the higher quality of tomatoes, the better the flavor. You can rinse the cans with a bit of water and use the water in the sauce.
2-3	boneless pork chops, omit if making a marinara
¼-½	cup extra virgin olive oil for browning
8	cloves whole garlic
	Pinch of hot pepper flakes
2	teaspoons salt or to taste
	Freshly ground pepper
	Splash of red wine (optional)
2	tablespoons chopped fresh basil
2	tablespoons chopped fresh Italian parsley
2	tablespoons chopped fresh oregano
1	can tomato paste (I no longer use paste in my sauce)*

- Squeeze the tomatoes with your hands or smash through a colander (sometimes to save time I swirl the tomatoes in my processor)
- Preheat a large Dutch oven
- Swirl olive oil into preheated pot
- Brown meat set aside (can also brown the meat in the oven)
- Add garlic, sauté slowly until lightly browned
- Add hot pepper flakes and sauté a few seconds
- Add all tomatoes and browned meat
- If desired you can add some dried Italian herbs
- Add salt and pepper and wine
- Stir and cover pot, bring to slight boil
- Lower heat to LOW and simmer for about 3½-4 hours: covered for 2 hours and uncovered for 1½ hours to thicken
- STIR FREQUENTLY throughout the cooking time
- During the last 30 minutes add browned meatballs, browned chicken parts, or browned Italian sausage and simmer stirring often
- Add fresh herbs
- Simmer for 10 minutes
- Cool and refrigerate, use next day to allow flavors to meld

If you decide to use Braciole, I recommend making a separate marinara sauce and simmer the Braciole for 2 hours (see Braciole recipe).

Yield: 2 quarts

ITALIAN MEATBALLS
1961

1 pound hamburger meat
  Handful of freshly grated Parmesan cheese
1 teaspoon salt
  Freshly ground pepper
2 tablespoons fresh Italian parsley chopped
2 tablespoons fresh basil chopped
1 egg beaten
2 cloves garlic minced
2 slices bread soaked in water and then hand squeezed. Crumble into pieces
¼ cup dried breadcrumbs
  Toasted pinenuts and raisins (variation)

- Place all ingredients in bowl and mix with hands
- Roll into meatballs
- Preheat skillet, add olive oil, brown meatballs
  OR
- Preheat cast iron skillet and add olive oil and bake in oven until just browned
- Add to sauce and simmer in the sauce for the last 30 minutes of cooking time

Either method there is no need to worry if the meatballs are not completely cooked…simmering in the sauce will complete the cooking…you want them just browned to create the browned bits at the bottom of the pan/skillet. I usually take a scoopful of my sauce and deglaze those wonderful flavor bits from sautéing the meatballs and then add to my sauce to enhance the flavor of the sauce.

ITALIAN SAUSAGE AND PEPPERS
1955

My mom's kitchen was never complete without a platter of sausage and peppers. It was a family favorite. She served it with Italian bread or hard crusted Italian rolls. I wrote this recipe from memory after watching her make it almost every week along with her spaghetti sauce.

2 pounds of Italian sweet sausage or a mix of sweet and hot
3 cloves of cracked garlic
4 red long Italian peppers
4 green long Italian peppers
1 large onion preferable Vidalia
½ cup extra virgin olive oil
½ teaspoon salt

- Preheat oven to 350°
- Slice the red and green peppers and onions
- Season with ⅓ cup oil and the salt and toss
- Place the sausages into a 3-inch deep baking pan
- Add the garlic and drizzle with ¼ cup oil
- Bake for 45 minutes
- Place the seasoned sliced peppers and onions on top of the sausages
- Cover with foil and cook for 1 more hour
- Mix thoroughly and serve

FRYING METHOD:

- Spray a large frying skillet with PAM and add ¼ cup olive oil
- Place sausages and garlic in skillet and fry for 30-35 minutes
- Add seasoned peppers and onions on top of sausages
- Cover with lid and cook on medium-low for 45 minutes

ITALIAN STUFFED ARTICHOKES
1955

Mom made these artichokes for every holiday meal. She did not remove the prickly part of the choke. I choose to remove this section from the heart of the choke for a more pleasant taste. As children, this was one of our favorite holiday foods.

2 medium artichokes or 1 large choke	¼ cup minced parsley
1½ cups soft breadcrumbs	¼ cup hot water
¾ cup grated Parmesan cheese	¼ cup oil
½ teaspoon salt	Boiling water
½ teaspoon pepper	1 clove garlic, sliced
1 small onion minced (optional)	2 teaspoons salt

- Wash chokes thoroughly, cut off one third of the artichoke
- Trim stems and cut off tip of leaves
- Spread leaves open by placing upside down and pressing down firmly
- With a teaspoon dig out the center to remove the prickly choke
- Mix crumbs, cheese, salt, pepper, onion, parsley and water
- Fill center and individual leaves with mixture
- Stand filled chokes in deep saucepan just big enough to fit the artichokes in snuggly
- Pour boiling water in pan to about 1-2 inches
- Pour 1 tablespoon oil over each choke
- Add garlic and 2 teaspoon salt to water
- Cover and cook for 45-60 minutes
- Lift out carefully and serve with melted butter

This recipe will heavily stuff two small artichokes or one large choke. If lightly stuffed, it will yield more chokes.

DO NOT DISCARD THE ARTICHOKE LEAVES OR RAW CENTER LEAVES IN GARBAGE DISPOSAL.

BRACIOLE
1958

I was not fond of this dish while growing up in my Italian family, but grew to like it as an adult. Today I use lean pork in place of the beef.

- 1½ pounds of beef flank steak, round steak thinly sliced, or boneless pork chops pounded to ¼ inch thick
- ½ teaspoon coarse salt and ½ teaspoon freshly ground pepper
- ½ cup Italian-style bread crumbs
- ⅔ cup Parmigiano-Reggiano
- ½ cup Italian parsley chopped
- 1 cup white wine or beef stock
- Plain round toothpicks
- 2 tablespoons olive oil
- 2 cloves garlic minced
- Marinara sauce

- Stir together cheese, bread crumbs, parsley and garlic
- Season meat with ½ teaspoon salt and ½ teaspoon pepper
- Sprinkle, cheese, parsley, garlic crumb mixture over steak or pork
- Start at short end and roll up and fasten with toothpick
- Tie the steak roll with twine; sprinkle with remaining salt and pepper
- Heat skillet and add oil
- Brown meat on all sides, 6 minutes
- Remove meat and deglaze the pan with wine or beef stock
- Put meat back in pan, add sauce and simmer covered for 20 minutes
- Heat oven to 350°
- Place meat roll in covered pan and bake
- Bake for about 1½ hours basting with sauce
- Uncover and bake another 30 minutes or until tender
- Transfer meat roll to platter, remove toothpicks
- Slice on serve with sauce
- You can also simmer the meat roll in your marinara sauce instead of baking in oven

Serves: 4

RATATOUILLE "Kagoots"
1957

Catholics were not allowed to eat meat on Fridays in the 50's and 60's. Mom prepared this vegetable dish nearly every Friday accompanied by fried haddock. She referred to the dish as "kagoots". Ratatouille is a French dish, but is widely used in the Italian culture. I have adjusted mom's recipe over the years. I like baking it with cheese on top. That is my touch.

	Good quality olive oil
3-4	cloves of garlic, minced
1	onion, chopped
2-3	cups chopped zucchini
2	cups chopped yellow squash
	Fresh mushrooms
1	large green pepper
	Fresh and dried basil
	Fresh chopped Italian parsley
1	can (15-ounce) diced tomatoes OR fresh tomatoes peeled and chopped, OR leftover spaghetti sauce. I use whatever I have on hand.
	Salt and pepper to taste
1	cup shredded mozzarella cheese
	Handful Parmesan cheese

- Preheat oven to 350°
- Spray a baking dish with cooking spray (PAM)
- Heat oil in large skillet; cook garlic and onion till soft
- Add zucchini, squash, bell pepper, mushroom, herbs, salt and pepper
- Cook mixture for about 5-7 minutes and then add the tomatoes or sauce
- Cook covered, until vegetables are soft
- Transfer to casserole
- Sprinkle both cheeses on top
- Bake for about 20 minutes or until bubbling and cheese is melted

Serves: 6-8

Can be made ahead, refrigerated and then baked.

CHEESE STUFFED MANICOTTI
OR PASTA SHELLS
1965

- 1 (12-ounce) box Jumbo shells or manicotti tubes
- 2 eggs
- 1 large container (2 pounds) Ricotta cheese
- 2 cups (8 ounces) shredded mozzarella cheese
- 1½ cups grated Parmigiano-Reggiano cheese divided
- ½ cup chopped fresh parsley
- ¼ cup fresh basil
- 1 teaspoon salt
- 3 cups marinara sauce (recipe follows)

- Preheat oven to 350°
- Cook shells in boiling salted water for 9-10 minutes
- Drain, cover and set aside
- In medium bowl, beat eggs, stir in ricotta, mozzarella and ¾ cup of the Parmesan cheese
- Add parsley, basil and salt
- Grease a 13x9-inch baking dish with cooking spray
- Spoon a little sauce into bottom of baking dish
- Spoon about one tablespoon of cheese mixture into each shell
- Arrange filled shells in greased baking dish
- Top with spaghetti sauce
- Sprinkle with remaining Parmesan cheese
- Bake 25-30 minutes or until heated through
- Let rest for about 10 minutes
- Serve with a sprig of fresh basil

You can freeze after filling.

- The day before baking, thaw in refrigerator
- The next day bake 45 minutes covered at 350°
- Bake another 5-10 minutes uncovered
- Let rest for 10 minutes

Serves: 6-8

MARINARA SAUCE

Marinara sauce is a meatless sauce used with baked vegetables, seafood or for topping casserole dishes.

- 1 tablespoon olive oil
- 2 large diced onions
- 1½ teaspoons salt
- freshly-ground pepper to taste
- 2-4 cloves garlic finely chopped
- 1 tablespoon dried oregano
- ½ teaspoon crushed red pepper (optional)
- Small bunch fresh basil
- ¼ cup white wine
- 1 (28-ounce) can crushed tomatoes
- 1 (28-ounce) can whole tomatoes-- diced
- ½ teaspoon sugar (optional)

- Heat oil in large saucepan and add onions salt and pepper
- Cook until onions are translucent
- Add garlic, when onions start to brown, add oregano, red pepper, basil, salt and pepper to taste
- Cook over medium heat, stirring occasionally, until onions caramelize
- Add the wine and turn up the heat to medium-high
- Cook stirring until most of the liquid has evaporated
- Add the tomatoes and bring to a boil
- Reduce heat to low
- Cover and simmer 20-30 minutes stirring occasionally

ITALIAN SAUTÉED
ESCAROLE GREENS

Rome, NY

I grew up in a small upstate town of Rome, NY where sautéed greens are the local Italian dish. Back in 1980 my husband and I would go to the Hollywood Restaurant in East Rome with my sister Marie and her husband Bert. After a movie or a night at a local bar, we would savor over "greens" at the Hollywood. The greens recipe comes in many versions, but this one is my favorite. Simple, nutritious, and delicious.

2 pounds or 2 heads of escarole, cored and coarsely chopped	¼ teaspoon crushed hot pepper flakes, or to taste
2-4 tablespoons high quality olive oil	Italian breadcrumbs
2 cloves garlic, thinly sliced	Parmigiano-Reggiano freshly grated

- Wash escarole and drain
- Cook in large pot of boiling salted water until tender (10 minutes)
- Drain in colander
- Heat oil and sauté garlic until lightly golden brown…do not overcook garlic as it will produce a bitter flavor
- Add red pepper flakes, sauté 10 seconds to bring out the sweet flavor
- Add escarole, stirring to coat with the oil; increase heat and cook uncovered until most of the liquid is evaporated 8-10 minutes
- Season with sea salt
- Spoon onto platter and drizzle with more oil, breadcrumbs and cheese to taste

VARIATIONS:

- This version uses Italian hot peppers seeded and sliced thinly with chopped prosciutto. Follow basic recipe and sauté garlic, peppers and prosciutto in oil; add escarole with 2 tablespoons chicken broth; cook uncovered until liquid is evaporated.
- Another small upstate town of Utica serves a version of greens as an entrée adding roasted sweet or hot long Italian cherry pepper slices, fried potatoes, and fried Italian sausage cut into small pieces. Italian hot ham and prosciutto are also added to the mix with the chicken broth.

CHICKEN CACCIATORE
1968

My mom made this dish often when I was growing up in Rome, NY. She used lots of mushrooms and green peppers. Over the years I have added more spices and use the shitake mushroom, olives and anchovy for more flavor. I also use wine where my mom used chicken broth.

- 3 pounds chicken thighs and drumsticks. You can use bone-in breasts, but they do not have the rich and moist flavor of the thighs and drumsticks. I use whole leg quarters.
- ½ cup flour
- Creole seasoning or combination of oregano and cayenne. I use Emeril's original seasoning—gives a nice spicy flavor
- Olive oil as needed to brown the chicken
- 1 large onion chopped
- 1-2 tablespoons anchovy paste or 2 filets (optional)
- Salt and fresh ground pepper
- 1 pound shitake mushrooms or mushrooms of choice, cleaned, stemmed and sliced
- 3 cloves garlic sliced
- 1 cup or so of Chianti wine or 1 cup dry white wine
- 1 bay leaf
- 4 sprigs fresh thyme
- Chopped fresh rosemary (optional)
- ¼ cup basil chopped Chiffonade style
- Handful of pitted green or black Italian olives
- 2-3 cups chopped fresh tomatoes, peeled and seeded and 1 cup tomato sauce Or you can use 1 large can crushed or diced Italian tomatoes in juice
- 1 tablespoon finely chopped fresh parsley leaves for finishing
- Parmesan cheese grated for finishing
- ½ pound cooked fettuccine, spaghetti or any tubular pasta (I use Penne pasta)

- Preheat oven to 350°
- Wash the chicken
- Season the chicken with just a light sprinkle of the Creole seasoning
- Season the flour with Creole seasoning
- Dredge the chicken in the flour, coating completely and shaking off the excess
- In a large Dutch oven, over medium heat, add the oil
- When the oil is hot, add the chicken and brown for 3-4 minutes on each side
- Remove the chicken and set aside
- Add the mushrooms, onions, garlic, and anchovy, salt and pepper
- Sauté for 2 minutes
- Stir in the wine, tomatoes, olives and chicken
- Bring to a boil; add the thyme, bay leaf and basil
- Cover pot and bake for 1 hour or 1 hour 15 minutes

- Mound the pasta in the center of each plate
- Lay the chicken over the pasta
- Spoon the sauce over the chicken; garnish with cheese and parsley
- If made ahead; bring out of the refrigerator one hour before reheating
- Bake at 350° for 30-40 minutes stirring mid-way through the cooking time

You may sauté green or red peppers along with the onions. You may also use anchovy fillets as part of the seasoning. If you prefer, serve with a salad or cannelloni beans instead of pasta. Serve with Chianti wine.

Yield: 4

CHEESE RAVIOLI
1950

When mom made her ravioli she fretted. She never felt they were as good as grandma Rosaria's ravioli. I could never tell the difference.

3 cups flour	⅓ cup water
3 eggs	½ teaspoon salt
2 tablespoons oil	2 egg whites whisked

- Combine flour and salt; mix well
- Make a hole in the center of the flour
- Combine eggs, water and oil; mix well
- Pour into the center of the flour
- Mix with hands until a dough forms
- Knead
- Roll out very thin
- Drop a dollop of filling about 2 inches apart
- Brush whisked egg whites around edges
- Place another sheet of dough
- Press down around each ravioli
- With a ravioli cutter, cut each ravioli
- Using a fork seal edges
- Dust with flour to prevent sticking
- Place in boiling salted water and cook until they float to the top (3-4 minutes)
- Drain and serve with pasta sauce

FILLING:

One (16-ounce) carton of ricotta cheese
1 cup grated Parmesan cheese
   Salt and pepper to taste
2 egg yolks

STUFFED EGGPLANT

1960

This is another "Friday night" meal that mom prepared for our family. She often served pasta as a side dish.

Marinara Sauce recipe - about 2 cups
1 large eggplant
Salt and pepper
Fresh basil chopped
Fresh oregano chopped
Fresh parsley chopped

1 stalk celery minced
½ onion minced
¼ cup of grated Parmesan cheese or to desired taste
2 slices of stale bread soaked in water or milk (I now use 1 pkg. of seasoned bread stuffing mix)

- Preheat oven to 375°
- Wash eggplant and cut in half lengthwise; remove pulp, but not too close to the skin
- Cut pulp of the eggplant into chunks and sprinkle with salt; press with a plate to remove water (10-15 minutes)
- Soak bread for at least 10 minutes, then squeeze out liquid with hands
- Add seasonings and fresh herbs
- Sauté celery, onion, and eggplant chunks in 1 tablespoon olive oil
- Add all together for stuffing; set aside
- Place eggplant shells cut side down, in a shallow baking dish with ½ inch of water; bake for 10 minutes or until shells are tender
- Drain turn eggplant to cut side up and stuff with bread mixture
- Cover with sauce and cheese
- Bake for 20 minutes or until nicely browned

Serves: 4

EGGPLANT PARMIGIANO
1960

Mom sliced the eggplant and fried each slice before assembling this dish. I bake the slices for a lower fat version. Both are delicious.

One (2-pound) eggplant	Salt and pepper
2 eggs, slightly beaten	2 cups marinara sauce
¼ cup milk	Bunch of fresh basil chopped
Olive oil	1 pound fresh mozzarella, sliced
⅔ cups fine dry bread crumbs	½ cup freshly grated Parmesan cheese

- Preheat oven to 350°
- Slice eggplant into about 6-7 pieces, lightly season with salt and pepper
- Whisk the eggs with the milk
- Dip eggplant slices into egg mixture, then into bread crumbs
- Slowly brown both sides of eggplant slices in olive oil
- Line the bottom of a greased baking pan with a layer of sauce
- Place a layer of eggplant slices, followed by mozzarella slices, grated cheese and basil
- Add a layer of sauce
- Repeat layers
- Top with mozzarella cheese, toasted breadcrumbs, and chopped basil
- Bake uncovered for about 20 minutes or until cheese is lightly browned
- Serve with remaining sauce

BAKED VERSION:

- Preheat oven to 450°
- Season slices with salt and pepper
- Spray olive oil on baking sheet
- Bake in 450° oven for 15 minutes or until deep brown on top turning at halfway point
- Cool and assembly as above*

LINGUINE WITH CLAM SAUCE
1983

This linguine dish is another Friday meal at the Mandronico household. My mother often substituted shrimp for the clams or used a marinara sauce. In the 80's, I added a bit to her recipe. I like the fresh lemon zest and the wine. As we became adults, I discovered that this seafood dish is my sister Marie's favorite.

- 1 pound linguine
- ½ cup olive oil
- 1 shallot finely minced or onion
- 6 cloves garlic, finely chopped
- ½ cup dry white wine
- 18 littleneck clams (about 2-2½ pounds) scrubbed clean
- Fresh parsley
- Salt and pepper to taste
- 1-2 tablespoons butter

- Bring a large pot of salted water to a boil and cook the pasta (do not rinse after draining)
- Meanwhile warm ½ cup of the olive oil in skillet
- Add the garlic and shallots cook until softened but not browned (2 minutes)
- Add the wine and allow to simmer for 2 minutes
- Add the clams, salt, pepper and cover the skillet
- Cook until the clams open (5-8 minutes) or until clams are all opened*
- Add parsley and if desired add the butter for thickening
- Add the pasta and mix
- Serve in a pasta bowl with a sprinkle of parsley and a bit of lemon zest

Serves: 4

*Discard any unopened clams

STROMBOLI
1950

Mom made Stromboli to have on hand for lunches or later for a snack when Steve and I came home from a date.

- 1 pound Basic Pizza Dough, can purchase at bakery or supermarket
- ¼ pound Italian sausage, removed from casings and crumbled
- 1 onion sliced
- ¼ pound sliced Italian hot ham
- ¼ pound thinly sliced pepperoni or salami
- ¼ cup black olives
- 6 ounces grated mozzarella
- 6 ounces grated provolone
- 1 large egg, beaten with 1 tablespoon of water for egg wash
- 1 cup finely grated Parmesan

- Allow dough to thaw for about 8 hours in refrigerator
- Once thawed or if purchased fresh, place dough in a large greased bowl
- Dough should rise until doubled about 2 or more hours
- Punch down
- Preheat oven to 350°, grease a large baking sheet
- Cook sausage and onion
- On a floured board, roll out the dough into a large rectangle 12x18
- Spread the sausage mixture to within an inch of the border
- Layer ham, pepperoni, olives and cheeses
- Brush the edges of the border with egg wash
- Starting at the long end rollup the dough into a cylinder, inching the edges to seal
- Place on baking sheet
- Let the dough rise for 30 minutes
- Brush top of each Stromboli with egg wash
- Bake till brown and crisp about 30 minutes
- Sprinkle with the Parmesan cheese and return to the oven until the cheese is melted (5 minutes)
- Remove and let stand 20 minutes; slice thickly and serve with warm spaghetti

VEAL OR CHICKEN PARMESAN
1965

From the time I was a little girl my mom made this dish with breaded veal cutlets. I make it breaded and have adopted a lighter version without the breadcrumbs. Both versions are wonderful, although, in our later years Steve and I prefer the lighter version.

1½ - 2 pounds chicken cutlets or veal cutlets	Pepper to taste
1½ cups fine breadcrumbs	⅓ cup olive oil
¾ cup Parmesan cheese	2 cups spaghetti sauce marinara or meat sauce
3 eggs beaten	6 slices Mozzarella cheese
1 teaspoon salt	

- Grease an 11x7 inch baking dish
- Preheat oven to 350°
- Wipe chicken or veal with a clean cloth or paper towel
- Place a piece of plastic wrap over each cutlet and pound cutlets
- Mix in a shallow pie dish the bread crumbs with the Parmesan cheese
- Combine in another shallow pie dish the eggs, salt and pepper
- Dip the cutlets into the egg mix and then into crumb mixture
- Add cutlets to skillet and slowly brown on both sides
- Arrange browned cutlets in baking dish
- Pour sauce over cutlets
- Place one piece of Mozzarella cheese atop each cutlet
- Bake in oven for 15-20 minutes or until cheese is melted and lightly browned

Serves: 6

LIGHT VERSION:

- Brush both sides of the cutlets with olive oil, a bit of finely chopped rosemary, parsley and thyme; sprinkle with salt and pepper
- Add the cutlets to a heavy skillet on high
- Cook just until brown about 1-2 minutes per side
- Arrange cutlets in prepared baking dish
- Spoon the sauce over the cutlets
- Place one piece of Mozzarella cheese atop each cutlet
- Sprinkle 2-3 teaspoons of freshly grated Parmigiano-Reggiano cheese atop each cutlet
- Bake in hot (450°) oven until the cheese melts and the cutlets are cooked through (about 5 minutes)

PINEAPPLE SQUARES
CIRCA 1952

These squares were served when mom's friends came to the house to play card games or when the extended families visited.

FILLING:

1 large can crushed pineapple
¾ cup sugar
2 eggs
1 teaspoon vanilla
3 tablespoons cornstarch
1 tablespoon butter

- Preheat oven to 350°
- Combine pineapple, sugar, eggs, vanilla, cornstarch and butter
- Cook until thick stirring constantly

CRUST:

Combine and mix well
3 cups flour
½ cup sugar
½ teaspoon baking soda
½ teaspoon salt
2½ teaspoons baking powder

MIX:

¾ cup shortening
2 eggs
¼ cup milk
1 teaspoon vanilla

- Mix all ingredients together to form a dough
- Chill dough for 30 minutes
- Roll half of dough out and place onto a greased cookie sheet with 1-inch sides
- Cover with the filling
- Make a lattice top with the remaining dough
- Bake at 350° for 20 minutes
- Cool; dust with confectioners sugar and cut into squares

ITALIAN ALMOND COOKIES
1950

As a kid, I loved these cookies. When I visited my aunts or grandmothers as a child, I remember these cookies served with coffee or weak hot tea and milk.

2 cups sugar
2 cups almond paste
1 cup fine breadcrumbs
5 egg whites (slightly beaten)

- Preheat oven to 375°
- Mix all together and put a very small spoonful onto a lightly greased cookie sheet
- Bake at 375° for 8-10 minutes

Yield: 5 dozen

ITALIAN PIGNOLI COOKIES

I use my food processor today, but my aunts mixed the mixture by hand.

8 ounces can almond paste
¾-1 cup sugar (natural sugar is best)
Pinch of salt
2 egg whites
Bowl of pine nuts

- Preheat oven to 350°
- Cover cookie sheet with parchment paper
- Place almond paste into food processor and pulse until mixture is like bread crumbs
- Add sugar and salt, process
- Add egg whites, process
- With wet hands roll dough into small balls
- Place top of each ball into the bowl of pine nuts
- Bake 15 minutes
- Cool on wire rack

PINEAPPLE UPSIDE-DOWN CAKE
1950

This was my very favorite cake when I was growing up.

BOTTOM OF CAKE

- 3 tablespoons butter
- ¾ cup packed dark brown sugar
- 6 slices drained pineapple slices
- Maraschino cherries
- Cake batter

CAKE

- ½ cup butter
- ½ cup sugar
- 1 egg
- 1½ cups sifted flour
- 1½ teaspoons baking powder
- ½ teaspoon salt
- ½ cup milk

CAKE BATTER:

- Cream butter; add sugar gradually and beat until light and fluffy
- Add egg and beat well
- Sift dry ingredients
- Add sifted dry ingredients alternately with milk and beat until smooth, beginning and ending with dry ingredients

ASSEMBLY:

- Preheat oven to 375°
- In a 9-inch square cake pan, melt butter and sprinkle with brown sugar
- Arrange pineapple slices and cherries on sugar mixture in a design
- Cover with cake batter
- Bake in 375° oven for 35 minutes
- Let cake stand for about 5 minutes before turning out on serving plate
- Serve warm with whipped cream

Serves: 9

ANISE-ALMOND BISCOTTI
1957

This easy Italian cookie uses a large wooden spoon and a whisk to beat the wet ingredients.

My mom and I made biscotti every Christmas and Easter. They are delicious with hot coffee laced with Anisette! I tweaked the recipe a bit adding freshly ground aniseed instead of the extract my mom used in the 50's. I also use unsalted butter instead of mom's salted butter for a more subtle taste. I use parchment paper for the cookie sheets for easy clean up.

3¼ cups all-purpose flour
1 tablespoon baking powder
Pinch of salt
1½ cups sugar
10 tablespoons unsalted butter melted
3 large eggs
1 tablespoon vanilla extract (I use a good quality extract or vanilla bean paste)
2 teaspoons freshly ground aniseed
1 cup whole almonds, toasted and coarsely chopped in food processor
1 large egg white whisked until foamy

- Preheat oven to 350° and position rack in center position.
- Line baking sheet with parchment paper.
- Sift flour, baking powder and salt into bowl.
- Mix sugar, melted butter, eggs, vanilla extract and aniseed in another large bowl.
- Add flour mixture to egg mixture and stir with wooden spoon until blended.
- Mix in almonds blending well.
- Divide dough in half.
- On floured board, shape each dough half into a 13 in x 3 inch log.
- Transfer to prepared baking sheet, spacing about 3 inches apart.
- Brush over the tops and sides with the beaten egg white.
- Bake logs about 30 minutes or until golden brown.
- Cool completely in baking sheet on a wire rack for about 25 minutes. Maintain the oven temperature.
- Transfer logs to wooden board and discard the parchment paper.
- Using a serrated knife, cut logs on the diagonal into ½-inch wide slices.
- Arrange slices, cut side down, on same baking sheet.
- Bake 12 minutes at 350°.
- Turn biscotti over and bake until just beginning to color about 8 minutes.
- Transfer to rack and cool.

Yield: 3 dozen

Store in airtight container or freeze

BANANA NUT BREAD
1962

I changed this recipe using butter instead of shortening.

- 1 cup sugar
- 8 tablespoons (1 stick) unsalted butter, room temperature
- 2 large eggs
- 3 ripe bananas, coarsely mashed with a fork
- 1 teaspoon vanilla
- 1 tablespoon milk
- 1 teaspoon ground cinnamon
- 2 cups all-purpose flour
- 1 teaspoon baking powder
- 1 teaspoon baking soda
- 1 teaspoon salt
- ½ cup broken walnuts

- Preheat the oven to 325°
- Grease a 9 x 5 x 3 inch loaf pan
- Cream the sugar and butter in a large mixing bowl until light and fluffy
- Add the eggs one at a time, beating well after each addition
- In a small bowl, mash the bananas with a fork
- Mix in the milk and cinnamon, and vanilla
- In another bowl, mix together the flour, baking powder, baking soda and salt
- Add the banana mixture and nuts to the creamed mixture and stir until combined
- Add dry ingredients, mixing just until flour disappears
- Pour batter into prepared pan and bake 1 hour or until a toothpick inserted in the center comes out clean
- Set aside to cool on a rack for 15 minutes
- Remove bread from pan, invert onto wire rack and cool completely before slicing

Makes one large loaf or 4 mini loaves

MOM'S CHEESECAKE
1959

CRUST:

2¼ cups graham cracker crumbs or Zwieback baby cookie crumbs
¼ pound melted butter or margarine (1 stick)
1 tablespoon sugar
   Pinch of cinnamon
   Mix together and press on bottom and up sides of a large spring form pan

FILLING:

3 (8-ounce) packages of cream cheese
1 cup sugar
4 eggs
1 teaspoon vanilla
- Preheat oven to 350°
- Cream the cheese and add the sugar
- Add eggs one at a time
- Bake at 350° for 35 minutes

SOUR CREAM LAYER OF FILLING:

1 pint sour cream
2 tablespoons sugar

- Blend together and spread over the above filling after the 35 minutes…then bake an additional 5 minutes with this second layer on

TOPPING:

1 can of blueberry, strawberry, or cherry pie filling.

Chill in refrigerator for at least 24 hours before putting topping on and before cutting.

Serves: 12

MOM'S
COFFEE CAKE

1951

- 1 stick butter
- 1 cup sugar
- 2 eggs
- 1 teaspoon vanilla
- 2 cups flour
- 1 teaspoon baking powder
- 1 teaspoon baking soda
- 1 cup sour cream

FILLING MIXTURE:

- ¼ cup sugar
- 1-2 teaspoon cinnamon depending on taste
- ½-1 cup chopped walnuts

- Preheat oven to 375°
- Butter and flour a tube or Bundt pan
- Combine flour, baking powder and baking soda in bowl, mix with whisk or sift in a sifter
- Cream butter and sugar
- Add eggs one at a time
- Add ⅓ of the flour and mix
- Then add ⅓ of the sour cream and mix
- Continue alternating with flour and sour cream until completely mixed
- Add vanilla
- Put half of the cake mixture in pan
- Sprinkle with half of the filling mixture
- Put last of cake mixture over the filling
- Sprinkle with remaining filling mixture
- Bake 35 minutes or until cake tester comes out clean
- Cool in pan on rack for 10 minutes remove from pan

PIZZA FRITTA

1957

Whenever Steve and I returned from a date, we found mom whipping up a batch of these tasty frittas for Steve. Ah, what memories.

DOUGH:

You can use this recipe or buy a pound of dough in the bakery section of your local supermarket or bakery.

- 2 packages dry yeast
- 1½ cups lukewarm water (80-100°)
- 4 cups flour
- 1 teaspoon salt
- ½ teaspoon sugar
- 1 tablespoon olive oil
- Heavy skillet with two inches of vegetable oil. Do not use olive oil because it will burn and smoke.

- Dissolve yeast in water and set aside for 5 minutes, stirring occasionally.
- Combine flour, salt, sugar and oil in bowl.
- Make a well in the center.
- When water/yeast mixture is bubbly, pour mixture into center of the well.
- Start kneading dough, bringing flour toward center of the bowl, gradually increase kneading motion. If dough feels dry, add a little more water. If it feels sticky, add more flour.
- Knead vigorously until dough is smooth and elastic.
- Roll into ball.
- Cover with a damp cloth. Let rest for about 20 minutes in warm place.
- Beat dough with your palm to expel gas formed while fermenting.
- Roll dough again into ball and place in greased bowl. Baste with oil.
- Cover with plastic wrap and store in the refrigerator.
  When ready to use, place dough on floured counter top or table.
- Cut off a handful of dough and stretch with hands until very thin.
- Heat vegetable oil in very heavy skillet (cast iron).
- Put stretched dough into VERY HOT OIL...brown, turn.
- Dust immediately with sugar.
- Serve immediately.

Serves: 4

MINUTE RICE PUDDING
1957

I loved this dessert as a kid growing up.

⅔ cup Minute Rice
2¾ cups milk
⅓ cup sugar

½ teaspoon salt
⅓ cup raisins
2 eggs slightly beaten

1 teaspoon vanilla extract
¼ teaspoon nutmeg

- Preheat oven to 375°
- Combine rice, milk, sugar and raisins in saucepan
- Bring to boil, stirring frequently
- Reduce heat; simmer 10 minutes stirring often
- Mix 2 slightly beaten eggs, vanilla and nutmeg in 1 quart casserole
- Slowly stir in rice mixture mixing well
- Place the casserole pan in a larger pan of hot water
- Bake at 375° for 20-30 minutes or until center is set
- Cool at least 1 hour before serving

Serves: 6-8

GRANDMA ROSARIA MANDRONICO'S KITCHEN

Grandma Rosaria Mandronico was my cooking idol. As a child I followed her around her huge kitchen and watched her every move. She started her day in her garden picking herbs and vegetables for the day's meal. Then she prepared her harvest either to cook or to hang in her pantry to dry.

July 1954

Grandma's pantry was adorned with long strings of hot peppers, oregano, basil, parsley and sage. Freshly picked herbs and vegetables hung on strings until dried to her satisfaction. At the front of the pantry noodle racks were found dripping with her homemade noodles awaiting the pot of boiling water. Further back in the pantry were shelves lined with her freshly canned tomatoes and green beans. When she canned the tomatoes she always added one or two fresh basil leaves just before she screwed the tops on the bottles.

The kitchen itself consisted of a large enamel-topped table, a huge black wood stove, a small icebox, grandpa's wooden chair aside the wood stove and a small mirror attached to the far wall for shaving and primping. In the old homes of the 30's and early 40's the kitchen was the catchall room of the home. It was the social hub where the family ate, played cards, drank, and just sat and socialized.

ITALIAN CHERRY COOKIES
1964

This is one of the traditional Italian wedding and Christmas cookies.

- ½ cup shortening
- 2 eggs
- 1 cup sugar
- ½ teaspoon vanilla
- 1 teaspoon almond extract
- ½ cup milk
- 2½ teaspoons baking powder
- 4 ounces drained maraschino cherries minced
- ¼ cup chopped nuts usually walnuts
- 4 cups flour or as needed for a soft dough
- Dashes of red food coloring

- Preheat oven to 350° or convection oven to 325°.
- Mix the vegetable shortening and sugar until fluffy.
- Add eggs, ¼ cup of the milk, the baking powder, red food coloring, and almond and vanilla flavorings.
- Add the remainder of the milk and enough flour to form a soft dough.
- Add the cherries and nuts.
- Refrigerate for several hours.
- Roll into small balls and place 2" apart on a baking sheet. If you line the cookie sheet with parchment paper, you will have better results.
- Bake for about 12 minutes.
- Cool on wire rack.

GLAZE:

- 1 cup of confectioner's sugar
- Almond flavoring
- Milk
- A bit of juice from cherries

- This should be a thin glaze not a thick frosting.
- After the cookies are cooled completely, toss or dip in the glaze and dry on a wire rack until hardened.

Yield: 4 dozen

ROSETTE COOKIES
1964

The "Wooden Spoon" is created from this special recipe. It is one of my favorite cookies and I carefully watched grandma use her large wooden spoon to measure all the flour, sugar and oil. Then she took smaller wooden spoons to measure the remainder of the ingredients. This is her signature wedding cookie.

My mom made many varieties of Italian cookies every Christmas and gave them as gifts. I gleaned this recipe and all of my grandma's cookie recipes a few weeks before our wedding. In an attempt to achieve an accurate recipe, I measured the capacity of each of grandma's wooden spoons and then converted the amounts into cups, teaspoons, and tablespoons.

Steve and I now work as a team and carry out this gift-giving tradition during the Christmas season.

Dough:
- 6 eggs
- 6 teaspoons baking powder
- 6 teaspoons vanilla
- 1 cup sugar
- 1 cup oil
- Salt
- About 4½ - 5½ cups of flour to form a stiff dough

Filling:
- 1 cup crushed walnuts
- 1½ teaspoons cloves
- 2 cups sugar
- 2 teaspoons cinnamon

- Take a large bowl and mix eggs, baking powder, vanilla, sugar and oil.
- Mix well with a good electric mixer and add enough flour so that it can easily be handled.
- Put dough in the refrigerator for a few hours before rolling out.
- Preheat the oven to 350°.
- Dust a wooden board with flour and roll out a small portion of the dough at a time into a rectangle. USE A WOODEN BOARD TO ROLL THIS DOUGH OUT.
- The dough is very touchy so you need to be sure you have enough flour to handle well, but not so much as to ruin the taste of the cookie. I gently knead the dough with flour before rolling it out.
- Brush the rolled out dough with oil and then sprinkle the nut/spice filling over the dough almost to the edges. Roll up like a jellyroll starting at the longest edge. It is a little difficult to handle so be careful not to break the roll. Cut into one-inch pieces and pinch in the middle to form a rosette.
- Bake at 350° for 15 minutes.

Hint: It is easier to use a heavy-duty electric mixer...roll out on a **wooden** board for easier handling. Use parchment paper on your cookie sheets for ease and even baking.

CHOCOLATE
ITALIAN WEDDING COOKIE
1964

This recipe is one of the traditional wedding and Christmas cookies. Over the years I have added an orange with rind to improve the texture and taste.

CREAM TOGETHER:

- ½ cup shortening or margarine
- 2 eggs
- 1¼ cups sugar

ADD:

- ½ cup milk
- 2 teaspoons baking powder
- ½ teaspoon cinnamon
- ¼ teaspoon ground cloves
- ½ orange blended in food processor, rind and juice (seeds removed)
- 1½ teaspoons vanilla
- ¾ cup cocoa
- Chocolate chips (about ½ cup or to your liking)
- 3-4 cups flour to make stiff dough
- Chopped walnuts (enough to suit your taste)

- Chill until firm enough to form balls
- Preheat the oven to 350°
- Place balls on greased cookie sheet and bake for 10-12 minutes at 350°
- Use parchment paper on cookie sheets for better results

FROST:

- When cookies are cool, frost
- Use confectioners sugar, milk, and powdered cocoa to make a very <u>thin</u> glaze
- Toss the cookies in the glaze, then place frosted cookies on a wired rack to harden
- If you wish you can roll in confectioners sugar <u>prior</u> to baking for a different type of covering

Yield: 5 dozen

GNOCCHI
1955

In 1955-58 I lived with grandma for 6 weeks each year while my parents vacationed in Florida. We made these delicate gnocchi every week and served them with meatballs.

3 medium potatoes about 3 pounds	1 egg
2 cups sifted flour	Pinch of salt

- Boil the potatoes until they are soft
- Drain and put back on the stove to dry over low heat
- Mash or rice and put on a floured pastry board
- Make a well in the center of the mashed potatoes and sprinkle with flour, using all of the flour
- Place egg and salt in the center of the well
- Using a fork, stir the egg and salt into the flour and potatoes, just like normal pasta
- Once the egg is mixed in, bring dough together, kneading gently until a ball is formed
- Knead gently about 4 minutes until ball is dry
- Roll baseball-sized ball of dough into ¾-inch diameter logs and cut logs into 1-inch long pieces
- On floured board using a floured fork, flick pieces off to form the gnocchi
- Continue with this method until all dough is used
- Drop the little gnocchi into boiling salted water and cook until they float (about 1 minute)
- Meanwhile continue with the remaining dough, forming logs, cutting 1-inch pieces and forming gnocchi
- Serve hot with spaghetti sauce and freshly grated Parmesan cheese

The secret to a light textured Gnocchi is to be sure the potatoes are dry

If using the gnocchi at a later time, make an ice bath:

- As gnocchi float to top of water, remove them to an ice bath
- Continue until all have been cooled
- Let sit several minutes in bath and drain from ice water
- Toss with ½ cup oil and store covered in refrigerator up to 48 hours until ready to use

SPICY MARINARA SAUCE
FOR SEAFOOD OR SNAILS
1955

No matter how hard I try I cannot replicate the spicy taste of grandma's marinara sauce. It may be the lack of her hand crushed hot peppers or her hand canned fresh tomatoes. However, this is close. She simmered fresh snails in the sauce as one of the entrees on Christmas Eve. She called this dish "chamaroogs".

1 tablespoon olive oil	1 tablespoon dried oregano
2 large diced onions (optional)	½-¾ teaspoon crushed red pepper
½ teaspoon salt	Small bunch fresh basil
Salt and pepper to taste	¼ cup white wine or red wine
2-4 cloves garlic finely chopped	2 (28-ounce) cans crushed tomatoes

- Heat oil in large saucepan and add onions salt and pepper
- Cook until onions are translucent
- Add garlic, when onions start to brown, add oregano, red pepper, basil and salt and pepper to taste
- Cook over medium heat, stirring occasionally, until onions caramelize
- Add the wine and turn up the heat to medium-high
- Cook stirring until most of the liquid is gone
- Add the tomatoes and bring to a boil
- Reduce heat to low
- Cover and simmer 20-30 minutes
- Add fresh shrimp and simmer until shrimp is cooked
- Serve with linguine

POLENTA
WITH SAUCE AND MEAT
1956

Grandma and I made this polenta every week during my stays with her. Once the polenta was cooked and thick, she poured portions into bowls. Grandpa Dominick had an enormous appetite so we made a huge plate for him.

- 2 cups water
- 2 cups corn meal
- 3 tablespoons butter
- 4 cups boiling water
- 1 teaspoon salt

- In large heavy pot boil 4 cups water with salt
- Place 2 cups cold water and 2 cups corn meal in a bowl and mix well
- Slowly add the corn meal mix into the boiling water
- Stir constantly and simmer for 20-30 minutes until thick
- Add butter
- Pour into a greased serving bowl
- Cool slightly then turn out onto a plate
- Slice and top with spaghetti sauce and freshly grated Parmesan cheese
- Top with meatballs, Italian sausage or roasted chicken

Grandma did not plate the polenta…everyone got their own bowl.

She simmered sautéed chicken parts and mild Italian sausage into her tomato sauce for a hearty dinner.

Thanksgiving Day - 1948

COOKING AND PREPPING AT BARNEY'S RESTAURANT
1954

Barney's Restaurant originated circa: 1947 as a seafood raw bar. Dad shucked dozens of clams for customers and served them with cocktail sauce, crackers and beer. He later expanded to raw oysters and shrimp. In the 1950's my parents expanded the restaurant to a "mom and pop" family restaurant featuring Italian foods and homemade pies. They continued to offer steamed and raw clams on the menus.

As the restaurant developed, they added daily features.   A fried haddock dinner with fresh French Fries and Cole Slaw was featured every Friday.   Since most of the community is Catholic, our fish fare attracted many of the locals.

In the "back" kitchen of Barney's I learned to chop vegetables and assist my parents in the preparation of the daily foods featured for the day. Once the salads were made and refrigerated, they began to cook the daily specials for the steam table located in the front of the restaurant. Of course, I had to start off at age 9 as the inventory girl, cashier and dishwasher before I graduated to the chopping board and stove areas of the restaurant. I have included some of Barney's signature dishes for your enjoyment.

MANHATTAN CLAM CHOWDER
CIRCA 1947

There is no better chowder than what we experienced at Barney's Restaurant. Unfortunately my dad never left us the recipe. I developed this recipe from memory. I would help chop the vegetables while my eyes were on daddy as he made his chowder.

- 4 pounds (2-3 dozen) cherrystone clams, scrubbed and rinsed
- 2 slices bacon, cut into ½-inch lengths
- 1 cup chopped onion
- ½ cup finely chopped celery
- 1 cup finely diced carrots
- 1 teaspoon garlic minced and 1 bay leaf
- 2 sprigs fresh thyme
- 4–6 cups clam juice; chicken broth as needed to bring liquid to desired amount
- 3 potatoes diced
- ¼–½ teaspoon red pepper flakes crushed
- One (16-ounce or 28-ounce) can chopped or diced tomatoes (juice reserved)
- 1½ teaspoons salt, fresh ground pepper, and fresh chopped parsley

- Bring 1 cup water to a boil. Add clams and cook for 5-10 minutes.
- Uncover, quickly stir clams well and put lid on.
- Allow clams to cook 5-10 more minutes or until most of the clams are opened. Discard any unopened clams.
- Transfer clams to a large bowl and strain broth through a fine-meshed sieve (you should have about 4 cups broth). If not add enough chicken broth to bring the volume up to the 4 cups. You can also use bottled clam juice.
- When clams are cool, remove from shells and chop into ½- inch pieces; set aside
- In heavy pot, add bacon and render. Pour off fat and leave 2 tablespoons to sauté the onions, celery and carrots. Sauté the celery and carrots for about 10 minutes. Add garlic, bay leaves, thyme and red pepper.
- Increase heat to high and add potatoes, clam broth and chicken stock; bring to boil covered.
- Cook for 20 minutes or until potatoes are tender.
- Add tomatoes and continue to cook for 10-15 more minutes.
- Remove the pot from heat and add clams and parsley; season with salt and pepper.
- Allow chowder to sit for at least 1 hour to allow flavors to meld.
- Reheat slowly...do not boil.

BARNEY'S
NAVY HAM AND BEAN SOUP
CIRCA 1948

My dad had a saying; leftovers in a Restaurant are a good part of the bottom line profit. This soup uses the leftover ham bone from the huge hams he would prepare each week. This recipe has been reduced to accommodate 6 servings.

1 pound dry navy beans, soaked overnight in water
Leftover ham bone with meat attached
1 onion diced
2 carrots, diced
2 stalks celery, diced
Sautéed fresh garlic
Salt and pepper to taste
1 quart water

- Rinse beans and put into large stock pot; cover with water
- Soak beans overnight and drain
- In stockpot add beans, 1 quart of water, ham bone and simmer until beans are almost soft
- Remove bone and cut off meat
- Remove beans and mash about ½ of the beans
- Return the ham and beans back to the stockpot and add the onion, carrots, celery, garlic, pepper and salt
- Simmer until all vegetables are tender

BARNEY'S
OYSTER STEW
1950

Dad made this stew to order. He did not have a huge pot of oyster stew in the kitchen, but he would make one or two servings at customers' requests.

THIS RECIPE SERVES 6

- 2 pints (24 ounces) raw shucked oysters with liquor
- 4 tablespoons of butter
- 1 quart of half and half
- Dash Tabasco

- Salt and pepper to taste
- Minced chive or parsley
- Butter
- Oyster liquor strained

- Drain the oysters, reserving liquor
- In large pan melt butter and add the oysters and simmer very gently for 2-4 minutes
- In separate pan, slowly heat the milk and cream and the oyster liquor (you should strain the liquor to remove all the sand)
- When oysters are cooked, slowly add the hot milk; season with Tabasco, salt and pepper
- Serve in warm soup bowl and garnish with parsley or chives
- Top with a generous pat of butter

BARNEY'S
MACARONI SALAD
1950

- 3 cups elbow macaroni
- 1½ cups mayo
- Minced onion
- 2 tablespoons carrots finely chopped

- 1 teaspoon white vinegar
- Stalk celery finely chopped
- Salt, pepper
- 2 hard cooked eggs, chopped

- Bring large pot salted water to a boil
- Cook macaroni for 8 minutes
- Drain and rinse in cold water until cool
- Toss with remainder ingredients
- Chill for 30 minutes

Serves 6

BARNEY'S
SCALLOPED POTATOES
LAYERED METHOD
1965

Mom made these potatoes for the restaurant to accompany meatloaf, Swiss steak, stuffed pork chops or ham steak. She also made this dish for the family. It was my favorite dish to make when helping her in the kitchen.

- 2 pounds potatoes (about 6 medium)
- 3 tablespoons butter
- 3 tablespoons flour (or as needed)
- Salt and pepper
- 2½ cups scalded milk
- ¼ cup finely chopped onion or onion slices
- 1 tablespoon butter
- Cheddar cheese (optional)

- In greased 2-qt. casserole, arrange potatoes in 4 layers, sprinkling each of the first 3 layers with some of the flour, sliced onion, salt and pepper and 1 T. butter. You can add cheese here if desired
- Heat milk just to scalding
- Pour over potatoes almost to cover potato
- Cover and bake 45 minutes
- Uncover and bake 15–30 minutes longer
- Let stand 5-10 minutes before serving

Serves: 4-6

POTATO SALAD
1965-2010

Over the years I have tweaked the restaurant recipe many times, thus, creating this recipe. I made tons of potato salad for Barney's Restaurant and took one thing away from that old recipe. Mom seasoned the potatoes while they were piping hot. She peeled the hot potatoes carefully, diced them, and then added the seasonings. I decided to peel the potatoes before boiling and reduce the pain of handling hot potatoes. I also switched out yellow mustard for the dry mustard and added the celery seed.

- 2 pounds potatoes, peeled and cut into cubes
- Salt
- 2 tablespoons white vinegar
- 2 tablespoons shallots or red onion diced
- ½ cup finely chopped celery
- ½ cup mayo or to taste
- ¾ teaspoon mustard powder
- Black pepper
- ¾ teaspoon celery seed
- 3 tablespoons sweet pickle relish (optional)
- 2 hard cooked eggs, chopped
- Freshly minced parsley

- Make sure water is above the potatoes; add salt to the cooking water
- Boil potatoes for about 8-10 minutes or until tender
- Drain potatoes
- Transfer to a large bowl
- Add vinegar and toss
- Let potatoes stand for about 20 minutes to cool
- Make dressing in small bowl: celery, relish, mayo, mustard, celery seed, parsley, pepper and onion
- Add about ½ teaspoon salt
- Gently fold dressing into potatoes
- Fold in the chopped eggs
- Cover and refrigerate until chilled about 1-2 hours so the flavors meld together

Yield: 4 servings

BARNEY'S
BAKED BEANS
CIRCA 1948-50

I remember helping my mom sort and wash the beans. They were delivered to the restaurant kitchen in large burlap sacks. We sorted them to pull out tiny stones and then washed them thoroughly.

4 slices bacon
½ cup chopped onion
2 cups navy beans
3 tablespoons molasses
2 teaspoons salt
Black pepper

¼ cup brown sugar or to taste
1 tablespoon Worcestershire sauce
1 teaspoon mustard
¼ cup of your favorite barbeque sauce or to taste
½ cup ketchup

- Soak beans overnight in water
- Simmer beans in same water until tender, 1-2 hours
- Drain beans and reserve liquid
- Spray a casserole dish with cooking spray
- Preheat oven to 325°
- Cook bacon until crisp reserving bacon drippings
- Crumble bacon
- Cook onion in reserved drippings till tender but not brown
- Add onions with the bacon and the remaining ingredients
- Mix well and turn into casserole dish
- Pour just enough reserved bean water to cover beans
- Bake covered for 3-4 hours
- Half way through cooking, check and add more liquid if necessary

Serves 6

PIES, PIES, PIES

Mom began making pies very early in the morning in her small apartment kitchen above the restaurant. On weekends and throughout the summer months I was in charge of stirring the cream fillings. After the puddings were diligently spooned into the baked pie shells, I would sit and lick the spoons and pans until they were clean. Needless to say, I was a pudgy little girl.

Mom's pies were the specialty of Barney's Restaurant. On average she would make between 15-20 pies per day. Graham cracker cream pie was the best seller and her signature pie.

She cooled the pies on the windowsills in her tiny kitchen. At 11 a.m. she carefully carried the pies downstairs to the restaurant. My brother, Ronnie, has a story to tell about her pies cooling on the windowsills. The steam from all the fruit pies attracted a neighbor's attention. He called the fire department because he thought mom's kitchen was on fire.

These are very dear memories of those old days in the late 40's.

In the early 1950's, the restaurant was expanded to include a larger kitchen area. It meant mom was able to cook and bake with commercial ovens, stoves and mixers. I remember her mixer well because it was nearly as tall as I was. The favorite part of her new kitchen was the huge butcher-block counter she used to rollout her pastry.

MOM'S
BASIC VANILLA CREAM
1947

Imagine a saucepot measuring 16 inches high. That is the pot that my mom used each morning to prepare her vanilla cream for all her cream pies. Somehow I managed to adjust her recipe down to yield enough cream for one or two pies.

2 cups half and half or whole milk	¼ cup flour
6 large egg yolks	4 tablespoons cold butter, cut into pieces
½ cup sugar	1½ teaspoon vanilla
Pinch of salt	

- Heat the half and half just until it is simmering
- Whisk yolks, sugar and salt in bowl
- Add flour to yolk mixture and whisk thoroughly
- Add a bit of warm half and half to temper this mixture
- Remove the half and half from stove and while whisking constantly add the tempered yolk mixture to the half and half, return to the stove and cook, whisking constantly until it bubbles and thickens
- Reduce the heat and continue to cook for about 8 minutes whisking constantly
- Then bring the heat up and cook until the pudding bubbles
- Remove from heat and whisk in the butter and vanilla
- In order to keep the cream from forming a film, put a piece of greased waxed paper or saran wrap over the top making sure the paper is touching the pudding
- Cool to room temperature or pour into baked pastry pie shell or graham cracker shell

GRAHAM CRACKER
CREAM PIE
Barney's Restaurant, Rome, NY
CIRCA 1948

Mom made at least 2-3 graham cracker cream pies each day because it not only was her signature pie known by all her customers, but the specialty of the restaurant known throughout the town.

1½ cups graham cracker crumbs
¼ cup sugar
½ cup melted butter

1 recipe vanilla cream
1 recipe mom's meringue

- Mix crumbs, sugar and butter together and press into an 8 or 9-inch pie pan
- Bake at 375° for approximately 8 minutes
- Cool to room temperature
- Add vanilla cream
- Top with mom's meringue
- Sprinkle with extra graham cracker crumbs
- Bake in 350° oven for about 12 minutes or until meringue is golden brown
- Cool on wire rack

MERINGUE TOPPING
1947

Mom beat approximately two dozen or more egg whites in her huge mixer for her meringue. She topped all her cream pies and then browned the meringues in her baker's oven. The following recipe yields enough meringue for one pie.

3-4 egg whites room temperature. The whites must be at room temperature for optimal performance
¼ teaspoon cream of tartar
Scant (½ teaspoon) vanilla or lemon extract
6 tablespoons extra-fine sugar

- With wire whisk attachment, beat egg whites, and cream of tartar until soft peaks form
- Gradually add the sugar and beat until stiff peaks form
- Add extract of choice
- Spread on top of the hot/warm cream pie filling making sure meringue is touching the edge of the pie pastry
- Bake in 425° oven for 4-5 minutes or until golden brown, then cool on wire rack

PIE PASTRY
MOM'S RECIPE
CIRCA 1947

This recipe is truly a guess. I watched her every morning pile a 5-pound bag of flour onto a wooden butcher-block counter. She then sprinkled the flour with salt and tossed with her hands until blended just right. Next she added shortening from a huge wooden tub that I now guess was probably a blend of vegetable shortening and lard.

She crushed the mixture between her hands until the entire lot looked like tiny peas. Carefully she sprinkled iced water and continued to toss until she formed several balls of dough. Finally, she flawlessly rolled out her pastry.

Needless to say, I had to adjust the quantities in this pastry recipe. I also use the food processor or a pastry blender instead of mom's hands because it works for me.

Makes enough for a two-crust 9-inch pie or one 10-inch quiche.

- 2 cups flour
- 1 teaspoon salt
- ¾ cup chilled shortening
- 4-8 tablespoons iced cold water

IN FOOD PROCESSOR:

- Add flour, salt, shortening, cut into pieces if using a pastry blender
- Rapid pulse 15 times
- Add 4 tablespoons water and pulse 5 times
- Add 2 tablespoons water and pulse 3 times

Dough should be just damp enough to mass together. Can add more water 1 teaspoon at a time. Chill for 10 minutes and roll out.

**To blind bake pastry for cream pies, roll out dough and fit into a 9-inch pie pan. Crimp edges and line the bottom with foil and fill with beans. Bake at 425° for about 15–20 minutes. Remove beans and foil and prick the bottom and sides of the pie shell. Bake until golden brown.

ASSORTED CREAM PIES
Barney's Restaurant, Rome, NY
CIRCA 1948

1 recipe mom's basic vanilla cream (p.59)
1 recipe mom's meringue (p. 60)

PINEAPPLE CREAM PIE

- Add 1 cup drained crushed pineapple to vanilla cream
- Put cream into a baked 9-inch pie shell and top with meringue forming peaks with a spoon
- Brown in 350° oven until brown, cool on rack

BANANA CREAM PIE

- Slice 2 or 3 bananas and place onto the bottom of a baked 9-inch cooked pastry shell
- Top with mom's vanilla cream (can use banana extract instead of vanilla in the cream)
- Top with meringue
- Bake as above and cool

COCONUT CREAM PIE

- Add 1 cup flaked sweetened coconut to mom's vanilla cream
- Put cream into a baked 9-inch pastry shell
- Top with meringue
- Sprinkle ⅓ cup coconut over meringue
- Brown in oven and cool

CHOCOLATE CREAM PIE

- Prepare mom's vanilla cream filling but increase the sugar to 1 cup
- Add 2-3 ounces melted unsweetened chocolate to the whole milk before cooking the cream
- Put into a baked 9-inch pastry shell
- Top with meringue
- Brown in oven and cool

LEMON MERINGUE PIE
CIRCA 1947

I have to admit that I have days that I crave this luscious pie. I made this for my father-in-law many times. It was his very favorite dessert.

1¼-1½	cups sugar (depending on taste)
3	tablespoons cornstarch
3	tablespoons flour
	Dash salt
1½	cups hot water
3	beaten egg yolks
½-1	teaspoon grated lemon zest
2	tablespoons butter
⅓-½	cup fresh lemon juice depending on how tart you like your pie
1	blind crust baked until golden brown (see Pie Pastry)

- Combine sugar, flour, cornstarch and salt
- Gradually blend in water
- Bring to boil stirring constantly, cook and stir another few minutes
- Remove from heat and stir in a small amount of the hot mixture into the egg yolks
- Return remaining egg yolks to the hot mixture and bring to a boil stirring constantly
- Cook and stir for a few more minutes to cook the yolks
- Add butter, lemon zest and lemon juice
- Cover with waxed paper while you make the meringue
- Make meringue adding vanilla extract or lemon juice
- Put hot lemon pudding into cooked cooled pastry
- Spread meringue over top of hot pudding to prevent meringue from weeping (make sure you bring the meringue all the way to the edges of the crust)
- Bake at 425° for 4-5 minutes or until golden brown and cool on wire rack for about an hour
- Refrigerate for at least 3 hours and cut with a knife dipped in hot water
- After 3 hours in refrigerator, wrap pie

MERINGUE:

3-4	egg whites room temperature
¼	teaspoon cream of tartar
½	teaspoon vanilla or lemon extract
6	tablespoons extra-fine sugar

APPLE PIE
CIRCA 1947

This pie was one of the favorites among the customers. Often it was served a la mode (with a scoop of vanilla ice cream) or with a slice of cheddar cheese.

Pastry for 2-crust pie	Dash nutmeg
6 or 7 tart apples, Granny Smith	Dash salt
¾-1 cup sugar	Butter
2 tablespoons flour	2 tablespoons freshly squeezed lemon juice
½-1 teaspoon cinnamon	

- Preheat oven to 425°
- Roll out pastry for bottom of pie
- Pare apples and slice thinly
- Combine flour, sugar, lemon juice and spices and salt and add to apples
- Arrange filling in pie shell
- Dot with butter
- Top with second pastry
- Crimp edges and make tiny slits with sharp knife to allow steam to escape
- Sprinkle with cinnamon sugar
- Bake for 20 minutes then reduce heat to 350° for another 20 minutes or until golden brown

ALTERNATE: APPLE CRUMB TOPPING:

1 cup flour	¼ teaspoon salt
½ cup sugar	6 tablespoons butter

- Crumble together and sprinkle over apples
- Bake as usual

BLUEBERRY PIE
CIRCA 1947

The freshly picked blueberries were delivered to Barney's kitchen in small wooden crates. My dad purchased the blueberries from Maine or from local farmers.

- 1 (9-inch) pastry for double crust
- 4 cups fresh blueberries
- ¾-1 cup sugar
- ½ teaspoon lemon zest
- Dash salt
- Spices optional (cinnamon and or nutmeg)
- 2 teaspoons freshly squeezed lemon juice
- Butter

- Preheat oven to 400°
- Prepare pie pastry and roll out
- Line pie plate with pastry
- Fill with blueberry mixture
- Dot with butter
- Add top pastry
- Crimp edges and make tiny slits on top (to release steam)
- Sprinkle with sugar if desired
- Bake for 35-40 minutes
- Cool completely

MOM'S PECAN PIE
CIRCA 1957

This pie is not one that mom made often for the restaurant. My dad had a passion for pecans so she made this pie for him during the holidays.

- 1 (9-inch) unbaked pie shell
- ⅓ cup butter
- ⅔ cup sugar
- 1 cup dark or light corn syrup
- ½ teaspoon salt
- 3 eggs
- 1 cup toasted pecan halves

- Preheat oven to 375°
- Cream the butter with sugar until very fluffy
- Beat in syrup and salt
- Add eggs one at a time beating after each
- Stir in pecans
- Pour into pie shell
- Bake for 40-50 minutes or until filling is set
- Cool

CHERRY PIE
CIRCA 1947

This is the only pie that mom took a short cut and use canned cherries. If the cherries had a dull color to them, she added a few drops of red food coloring to brighten them to a rich cherry red. Often she created a lattice top for this pie.

Pastry for two-crust pie
3 cups drained canned pitted tart red cherries
1 cup sugar
¼ cup flour
¼ teaspoon salt
½ cup juice from drained cherries
1 tablespoon butter
¼ teaspoon almond extract

- Preheat oven to 450°
- Roll out pastry; line pie plate with bottom pastry
- Combine the cherry juice, sugar, flour and salt in saucepan
- Cook until thick; cook a minute longer
- Add cherries, butter, almond extract, and food coloring; cool
- Pour into pastry lined pie plate
- Add top pastry, crimp edges and cut a few slits in top to allow steam to escape
- Bake for 10 minutes at 450° and then reduce the oven to 350° and bake another 45 minutes or until golden

MINCEMEAT PIE
CIRCA 1947

It was fascinating to watch the small wooden barrel of mincemeat appear in Barney's kitchen. When we opened the barrel, it smelled very rich. I suspect there may have been some alcohol in the mix. This pie was served a la mode at the customer's request.

This is one of the few pies that mom would meticulously create a crisscross or lattice pastry top.

Pastry for two-crust 8- inch pie
2 cups of prepared mincemeat
¼ teaspoon lemon zest

- Preheat oven to 400°
- Prepare pastry and line pie plate
- Combine mincemeat and lemon zest
- Pour into a pastry lined pie pan
- Create a lattice top, crimp the edges, and sprinkle with sugar
- Bake for 35 minutes, serve warm

Sometimes mom added 1-2 thinly sliced apples to the mincemeat to cut down the sweetness.

PEACH PIE
CIRCA 1947

The peaches were delivered to the kitchen during the summer months only. Peach pie was not offered during the winter months.

Pastry for a two-crust pie
5 cups pared and sliced fresh peaches
¾ cup sugar
Dash salt

3 tablespoons flour
¼ teaspoon nutmeg or cinnamon
2 tablespoons butter
1 tablespoon freshly squeezed lemon juice

- Preheat oven to 400°
- Combine the sugar, salt, flour, and cinnamon or nutmeg
- Add to peaches and mix together
- Fill pie shell with peach mixture
- Dot with butter
- Add top pastry; crimp edges and sprinkle with sugar
- Bake for 40 minutes or until golden
- Serve warm with ice cream

This pie, as with the cherry pie, had a lattice top pastry. As a variation, mom added a dash of almond extract for a different flavor.

FRESH RHUBARB PIE
CIRCA 1950

Barney's Restaurant offered this pie during the summer season when the rhubarb was the sweetest. Mom made a lattice crust for the top of the pie.

Pastry for a two-crust pie
3 cups sliced rhubarb cut into 1-inch slices
1 cup sugar
½ teaspoon orange zest

3 tablespoons flour
Dash salt

- Preheat oven to 400°
- Combine sugar, orange zest, flour, and salt
- Add to rhubarb and mix lightly
- Arrange mixture in pie shell and dot with butter
- Prepare a lattice top, bake for 40-50 minutes or until golden and done

Variation: When strawberries were in season, mom added a cup of fresh sliced strawberries; increased the flour to 4-5 Tablespoons and a bit more sugar with a pinch of nutmeg.

MOM'S PUMPKIN PIE
CIRCA 1947

During the Halloween season mom boiled fresh pumpkins and mashed them in her mixer to make her pumpkin pies. She would also adorn the tops of the pies with Halloween figures cut out of her pastry dough. I mashed fresh pumpkins just one time in my life when my girls were very young. As a modern mom, I decided it was too much trouble and have used canned pumpkin ever since.

- 1 9-inch unbaked pastry shell
- 1½ cups canned cooked pumpkin
- ¾ cup sugar (I use about ½ cup sugar and ¼ cup brown sugar)
- ½ teaspoon salt
- 1 teaspoon cinnamon
- ½ teaspoon ginger
- ¼ teaspoon nutmeg
- ¼ teaspoon cloves
- 2-3 beaten eggs
- 1½ cups heavy cream, half and half or a 12-ounce can of evaporated milk

- Preheat oven to 400°
- Combine pumpkin, sugar, salt and spices
- Add beaten eggs
- Gradually blend in your choice of cream of milk
- Pour into pie shell
- Bake for about 50 minutes or until knife inserted in middle comes out clean
- Cool completely

MOM'S
CUSTARD PIE
CIRCA 1947

This was my favorite pie when I was a little girl.

4 beaten eggs
½ cup sugar
¼ teaspoon salt
1 teaspoon pure vanilla extract

⅛ teaspoon almond extract
2½ cups whole milk, scalded
Freshly grated nutmeg

- Scald the milk and set aside.
- Whisk together eggs, sugar, salt, vanilla, and almond extracts.
- Gradually stir in scalded milk.
- Brush bottom of pie shell with egg white to prevent sogginess.
- Put foil around edges of pie to prevent edges from getting too brown. You can remove the foil 10 minutes before pie is done to brown edges.
- Pour egg mixture into pie shell.
- Sprinkle with freshly grated nutmeg.
- Bake in 400° oven for 40-50 minutes or until a knife inserted comes out clean.
- Cool on rack for about 30 minutes before refrigerating.

COCONUT CUSTARD PIE
- Add one cup of sweet-flaked coconut with milk

A NEW BRIDE LIVING IN GERMANY
1965

A few months after our wedding I packed my wooden spoons and we moved to Fuerth, Germany. Fuerth is a small village outside of Nuremberg. We had a very tiny German apartment with an oven that had no temperature reading on the dial. Steve bought me an oven thermometer and I took it from there.

I took all the recipes that I gathered from my grandma and mom and reduced them down from six servings to two. Then I read all the cookbooks I received as gifts from friends and family. After a while I became comfortable cooking in the tiny German kitchen and my dinners took on a young bride's culinary beginning.

Nearly half of my husband's ancestry is Polish. As a new bride I certainly had to impress him with learning to make his favorite Polish dishes. I was able to take

his mom's recipe for Polish Golabki and later researched a good recipe for Polish Pierogi. Soon I was appealing to his Polish taste buds.

What I liked most about living in the Bavarian area of Germany was the opportunity I had to experience and prepare good everyday German foods and visiting the open markets.

In the city of Nuremberg there were many open vegetable markets that I frequented. During the Christmas season, the Christkindesmarkt (Christ-Child Market) opened. We purchased our first fresh Christmas tree and German wax ornaments at this Mart. We often walked to the food area and sampled the wonderful German Nuremberg brats as well as special German breads and rolls.

There was a small Kuken shop (pastry shop) at the market area that was our favorite. I was awe struck to see the samples of many wonderful German pastries including my favorite Black Forest Cake.

The recipes in this section include the German food we experienced, Steve's favorite Polish foods, and the International Fondues and recipes I made as a new bride living in Germany.

WIENER SCHNITZEL
1965

This is a typical everyday meal in Germany. It was served with a sweet and sour shredded red cabbage (Rotkohl) or potato pancakes.

4 veal cutlets pounded	1 teaspoon salt
2 eggs	1 cup fine breadcrumbs
5 tablespoons flour	½ cup oil or as needed

- Pound meat as thinly as possible
- Sprinkle with salt, dredge in flour
- Beat eggs with 3 tablespoons cold water
- Dip meat in egg and then in breadcrumbs or cracker crumbs
- Fry quickly in hot oil, 2 minutes each side till golden brown

At this point you can serve with the cabbage and slices of lemon.

SCHNITZEL ALTERNATIVE:

- Keep the schnitzels warm while you melt 2½ tablespoons butter and add 2 tablespoons capers to butter
- Swirl and add chopped fresh parsley
- Serve this dish with spaetzles

Serves: 4   Wine pairing: German Riesling or German Pinot Noir

MAY WINE
1966

Germans celebrate spring in May with this low alcohol drink. The Maypole is erected and Germans folk dance around it. The main ingredient is Woodruff, a special German plant, which is hard to come by. We made this wine for our Gourmet group just once and found the woodruff on Amazon.

½ cup dried Woodruff herb	1 bottle sparkling wine or champagne
1 bottle Riesling wine	2 quarts fresh strawberries

- Infusion process begins by placing the bottle of Riesling wine and woodruff in a large bowl or pitcher…let stand 1 hour
- Add sparkling wine or champagne
- Mix and float strawberries on top

FONDUE
1965

Fondue was very popular when we lived in Germany. Many of our friends shared this wonderful International supper. I served the cheese fondue as an appetizer.

Our favorite was the beef fondue for the main entrée. Over the years we added chicken and shrimp using a broth base, Fondue Court Bouillon.

Fondue turned out to be our daughter Janet's favorite dish and is her favorite to this day. It was her dinner choice for all of her birthdays.

BEEF FONDUE
(Fondue Bourguignonne)

The history of meat fondue dates back to the middle ages in Burgundy France. The pot of oil was placed out in the fields of the vineyards so that the workers were able to enjoy a meal without having to interrupt their work.

1½ pounds Beef tenderloin or top sirloin cut into ¾-inch cubes
Vegetable oil or Peanut oil
Dipping sauces
French rolls, sliced

- Arrange meat on a platter.
- Meanwhile heat oil to 400°. You can use an electric fondue pot or a copper fondue pot. Put the copper pot on the stove and heat until a thermometer reads 400°, and then carefully bring to table and place over a heating unit using Sterno or denatured alcohol.
- Each guest is given a long fondue fork to use to pierce the meat and cook as desired.
- Fondue plates are available with sections for the various sauces used to flavor the cooked beef.

FONDUE COURT BOUILLON

This version of The Fondue uses a boiled broth to cook meats instead of the hot oil. Its history is interesting in that it originally came from China. A man from Switzerland was visiting China and was served this type of fondue using broth to dunk meat. He reported back to Swiss chefs and the Court Bouillon was born.

FONDUE SAUCES
1965

TOMATO STEAK SAUCE

1 (8-ounce) can tomato sauce
⅓ cup bottled steak sauce
2 tablespoons brown sugar
2 tablespoons canola oil

- Mix ingredients. Bring to boil. Serve hot

Yield: 1 ½ cups

HORSERADISH CREAM

Combine 1 cup sour cream or ½ cup sour cream and ½ cup crème fraiche
3 tablespoons drained prepared hot horseradish
¼ teaspoon salt
Dash paprika
Dash dry mustard

- Chill before serving

GARLIC BUTTER

- Whip ½ cup soft butter and one clove minced garlic until fluffy

ANCHOVY BUTTER

1 (2-ounce) can anchovy fillets or anchovy paste
½ cup butter, softened
2 tablespoons olive oil
½ teaspoon paprika
½ teaspoon fresh pepper

- Drain anchovies; place in mixer bowl with remaining ingredients
- Beat until smooth

FONDUE
1965

Fondue was very popular when we lived in Germany. Many of our friends shared this wonderful International supper. I served the cheese fondue as an appetizer.

Our favorite was the beef fondue for the main entrée. Over the years we added chicken and shrimp using a broth base, Fondue Court Bouillon.

Fondue turned out to be our daughter Janet's favorite dish and is her favorite to this day. It was her dinner choice for all of her birthdays.

BEEF FONDUE
(Fondue Bourguignonne)

The history of meat fondue dates back to the middle ages in Burgundy France. The pot of oil was placed out in the fields of the vineyards so that the workers were able to enjoy a meal without having to interrupt their work.

1½ pounds Beef tenderloin or top sirloin cut into ¾-inch cubes
Vegetable oil or Peanut oil
Dipping sauces
French rolls, sliced

- Arrange meat on a platter.
- Meanwhile heat oil to 400°. You can use an electric fondue pot or a copper fondue pot. Put the copper pot on the stove and heat until a thermometer reads 400°, and then carefully bring to table and place over a heating unit using Sterno or denatured alcohol.
- Each guest is given a long fondue fork to use to pierce the meat and cook as desired.
- Fondue plates are available with sections for the various sauces used to flavor the cooked beef.

FONDUE COURT BOUILLON

This version of The Fondue uses a boiled broth to cook meats instead of the hot oil. Its history is interesting in that it originally came from China. A man from Switzerland was visiting China and was served this type of fondue using broth to dunk meat. He reported back to Swiss chefs and the Court Bouillon was born.

FONDUE SAUCES
1965

TOMATO STEAK SAUCE

1 (8-ounce) can tomato sauce
⅓ cup bottled steak sauce
2 tablespoons brown sugar
2 tablespoons canola oil

- Mix ingredients. Bring to boil. Serve hot

Yield: 1 ½ cups

HORSERADISH CREAM

Combine 1 cup sour cream or ½ cup sour cream and ½ cup crème fraiche
3 tablespoons drained prepared hot horseradish
¼ teaspoon salt
Dash paprika
Dash dry mustard

- Chill before serving

GARLIC BUTTER

- Whip ½ cup soft butter and one clove minced garlic until fluffy

ANCHOVY BUTTER

1 (2-ounce) can anchovy fillets or anchovy paste
½ cup butter, softened
2 tablespoons olive oil
½ teaspoon paprika
½ teaspoon fresh pepper

- Drain anchovies; place in mixer bowl with remaining ingredients
- Beat until smooth

CAPER SAUCE

- ¼ cup drained chopped sour pickle
- 2 tablespoons drained finely chopped capers
- 1 cup mayonnaise
- 1 teaspoon Dijon mustard

- Dry on paper towels chopped sour pickle and drained capers
- Add mayonnaise, stir in mustard and parsley
- Mix all together

CHANTILLY SAUCE

- Fold 1 tablespoon stiffly beaten whipped cream into 2 tablespoons mayonnaise
- Season with a tiny bit of lemon juice and a touch of paprika
- Add 1 tablespoon chopped parsley

CHEESE FONDUE
1965

The cheese fondue originated in Switzerland in the 18th century. The Swiss used aged cheeses to feed families who did not have adequate access to fresh foods during the cold winter months.

- 1 garlic clove
- 2 cups of dry white wine
- 1 pound Swiss cheese or ½ pound Gruyere and ½ pound Emmentaler
- 1 teaspoon butter
- Salt, pepper, grated nutmeg
- 2 tablespoons *Kirsch
- Bite size pieces of fresh French bread

- Rub garlic over the inside of an earthenware casserole or fondue pot.
- Add the butter and pour in the wine.
- Place the casserole over a moderate flame and stir the wine and butter with a wooden spoon.
- Add the cheese and continue to stir until the cheese is melted.
- As soon as the mixture begins to bubble, stir in the *Kirsch.
- Add salt and pepper and nutmeg.
- Add a pinch of baking soda at the last minute to make the Fondue lighter.
- Place the casserole on a Sterno burner. Adjust the flame to keep the Fondue cooking gently throughout the meal.
- Dip the bread cubes into the fondue and enjoy, serve with a dry white wine.

    * Cognac can be used instead of Kirsch.

Emmentaler cheese creates the mildest flavor whereas Gruyere creates a stronger flavor.

CHOCOLATE FONDUE
1965

The Chocolate Fondue originated in America during the mid-20th century.

¾ cup heavy cream
12 ounces high quality bittersweet or semi-sweet chocolate
1 tablespoon cognac, brandy or chocolate liqueur

Pineapple cubes
Strawberries
Mango cubes
Banana chucks
Pound cake cut into cubes

- Heat cream to simmer on medium flame
- Lower heat and add chocolate (melts in about 3 minutes)
- Add cognac or liqueur
- Transfer to fondue ceramic pot
- Arrange cups of different fruits or cakes
- Dip fruits and cakes into fondue with long fondue forks
- ENJOY

SPITZBUDEN URCHIN COOKIES
1965

⅔ cup softened butter
¼ teaspoon salt
2 cups sifted flour
1 cup sugar
2 tablespoons heavy cream
½ teaspoon vanilla
½ cup ground nuts
Currant jelly or vanilla sugar optional

- With hands, mix first 7 ingredients and form a smooth dough ball
- Chill for several hours
- Roll ⅛ in thickness and cut with floured 2-inch scalloped cutter or other fancy cutter
- Bake in preheated oven 375° for about 12 minutes
- Watch carefully; burns easily

These cookies can be served as is or put together in pairs with jelly or sprinkle with vanilla sugar.

GERMAN POTATO SALAD

1965

3 cups potatoes, peeled and diced
1 whole onion
1 small onion diced
1 teaspoon salt
Chopped fresh parsley

Pepper to taste
2-3 tablespoons sugar
3-4 slices bacon
¼ cup white vinegar

- Put potatoes and whole onion in pan and cover with water
- Boil and cook until tender but still firm
- Drain and remove onion
- Cook bacon until crisp; then crumble
- Cook diced onion in bacon fat until just browned
- Add the vinegar, salt, pepper and sugar to the pan with the onion
- Add the potatoes and half the bacon bits
- Toss lightly
- Spoon into bowl and garnish with remainder of bacon and parsley
- Let stand until cool
- Serve on a bed of lettuce

Serves: 6

ORIGINAL GERMAN
BLACK FOREST CAKE
1965

This is Josef Keller's original recipe. We went to the Christkindlesmarkt square every weekend to sample this cake and others in our favorite little cake shop. In German cake is called Kuchen. The history of this cake dates back to the 16th century in the Black forest region of Germany. The region is noted for its sour dark cherries and Kirsch (a double distilled, clear cherry brandy made from the sour Morella cherry).

CAKE:

This cake has a very dense texture. You can use a box of Duncan Hines dark chocolate cake—however, the texture is not as dense. I sometimes use both the dense hazelnut cake and the Duncan Hines cake for a diverse texture: 1-2 layers of the hazelnut version and 1 or 2 layers of the box cake.

- 4 eggs
- ¼ cup sugar
- 7 tablespoons unsalted butter, room temperature
- 5 ounces dark chocolate, melted
- 3 tablespoons Kirsch
- 7 tablespoons flour
- 1 teaspoon baking powder
- Pinch of salt
- 5 ounces ground roasted hazelnuts

- Preheat oven to 375°
- Spray and flour a 9-in spring form pan
- Grind nuts and roast in pan until light brown
- Stir eggs and sugar well
- Add the butter and the melted chocolate
- Mix flour, baking powder, and salt
- Sift or stir with a wire whisk
- Gently mix flour and hazelnuts into the egg-sugar mixture and pour all into the spring form pan
- Bake for about 35-45 minutes
- After the cake has cooled, cut horizontally to make **three** layers

CHERRY FILLING:

- 1 pound can of sour cherries (drained)
- 7 ounces cherry juice (reserved from the drained cherries)
- 1 ounce sugar
- 3 tablespoons cornstarch
- 5 tablespoons Kirsch

WHIPPED CREAM:

- 30 ounces whipping cream
- 2 ounces confectioner's sugar
- 1 teaspoon vanilla
- 4 tablespoons Kirsch (optional)
- ⅛ teaspoon cream of tartar (optional) if used it will hold the cream longer

- Mix the sugar and cream of tartar
- Beat the cream for a few seconds and then add the sugar mixture slowly while continuously beating the cream until it is quite stiff
- Then mix in the kirsch if desired

DECORATION

- 10 cherries
- 3-4 ounces of very dark chocolate shaved

ASSEMBLING THE CAKE:

- Brush the cakes with Kirsch
- Put 2 tablespoons of the cherry sauce (without cherries) evenly on the bottom layer
- Place the next cake layer on top and cover with the remaining cherry filling, to include the cherries, and then spread on one quarter of the whipped cream on top of the cherry filling
- On the next layer spread more cream
- Top with the last layer
- Put a bit of cream in a pastry bag with star tip attached
- Frost the entire cake with the whipped cream
- Garnish the top and the sides with the shaved chocolate
- With pastry bag pipe 10 rosettes on the top of the cake and top the rosettes with a cherry

Refrigerate at least 2-4 hours before serving; slice while well chilled for better results

Serves: 12

GERMAN RUMTOPF
(Rum Pot)
1965

I loved making this pot of fermented fruit. I kept it on my counter. Whenever we had ice cream, we would cover it with this tasty fruit compote.

1 pound fresh fruit washed, dried, pitted (see fruits below)
1 cup sugar
Good quality of dark rum

- Peel all the fruits except the plums.
- Put fruit into a large jar with a good sealing cover.
- Add sugar and mix.
- Add enough rum to cover fruit by one inch.
- Each month add an addition 1 pound fruit, sugar and rum.
- Allow to sit 4-6 weeks.
- If you see bubbles, it indicates fermentation. You do not want fermentation. If you see bubbles, add rum.
- Cover very tightly and store in a cool place or in the refrigerator.
- Serve over ice cream, cake, pudding or cheesecake.

RECOMMENDED FRUITS:

Pineapple (cored and cut into large cubes)
Cherries (stemmed and pitted)
Apricots (halved and pitted)
Peaches (halved or sliced and pitted)
Pears (cored peeled and sliced)

Plums (remove pit and quarter or halve)
Grapes (seedless)
Strawberries (do not wash; remove stem
Raspberries (do not wash)
Red currants (remove stem)
Gooseberries (remove stems)

DO NOT USE THE FOLLOWING:

Blackberries, watermelon, rhubarb, bananas, citrus fruit or apples

SPAETZLES
AND PAPRIKA SAUCE
1965

Great with Weiner Schnitzel.

SPAETZLES:

- 1 cup flour
- ¼ cup milk
- 2 eggs
- ½ teaspoon ground nutmeg
- Dash white pepper
- ½ teaspoon salt
- 1 gallon hot water
- 2 tablespoons butter
- 2 tablespoons freshly chopped parsley

- Boil the water
- Mix flour, salt, pepper and nutmeg
- Beat eggs well and add alternately with the milk to the dry ingredients
- Mix until smooth
- Press dough through a spaetzle maker, or a large holed sieve
- Drop a few at a time into simmering liquid
- Cook 5-8 minutes
- Drain well
- Sauté cooked spaetzle in butter; sprinkle with parsley and serve or mix with paprika sauce

PAPRIKA SAUCE

- 2 shallots, chopped
- 1 clove garlic, minced
- 4 tablespoons butter
- 3 tablespoons flour
- 1 teaspoon paprika
- 2 cups stock
- ⅓ cup dry white wine
- 2 tablespoons sour cream
- 1 teaspoon lemon juice

- Melt butter
- Sauté shallots and garlic (5 min); stir in flour and paprika to make a roux
- Blend well
- Add stock and wine stirring constantly
- Cook until thick; add sour cream and lemon juice

OLD FASHIONED
SPLIT PEA SOUP
1965

This is the first soup I prepared for Steve. It is his absolute favorite.

2½ cups green split peas	½ teaspoon pepper
1 meaty ham bone	¼ teaspoon marjoram
1½ cups diced onion	1 cup diced celery
1 teaspoon salt	1 cup diced carrots

- Cover peas with 2 quarts cold water and soak overnight OR simmer gently for 2 minutes and soak one hour
- Add ham bone, onion and seasonings
- Bring to boil; cover, reduce heat and simmer 1½ hours
- Stir occasionally
- Remove bone and cut off the meat and dice
- Return meat to soup
- Add vegetables
- Cook slowly, uncovered, 30-40 minutes
- Salt to taste

Serves 6-8

PICKLED BEETS
1966

2 cans sliced beets	¾ cup vinegar
1 cup sugar	2 cinnamon sticks

- Drain beets, reserving liquid in small saucepan
- Add sugar, vinegar and cinnamon sticks to reserved liquid
- Heat to boiling, stirring
- Pour over beets
- Cool
- Cover and refrigerate at least 8 hours
- Serve; remove beets with slotted spoon

Yield: 3 cups   Accompaniment for pork and veal. Excellent in salads.

POLISH GOLABKI
1965

A favorite family meal passed down from my mother- in-law, Betty Cerjan. This is a comfort food that was served at Steve's home frequently. Golabki (go wompki) stands for tiny pigeons and is served throughout the Slovak nations.

- 1 cup rice cooked in 2 cups water or chicken broth
- 1 pound hamburger meat
- ½ pound veal (optional)
- 1 or 2 eggs
- 3 tablespoons oil
- 1 medium onion chopped
- 1 garlic clove minced
- 1½ teaspoons salt or to taste
- ½ teaspoon pepper
- ½ teaspoon celery salt
- 1 Head of cabbage (choose cabbage with large loose leaves.
- 2 cans tomato sauce
- 2 cans tomato soup

- Preheat oven to 325°
- Mix tomato sauce and tomato soup together
- Wash out cans with chicken broth or water and add to sauce
- Cook rice in water
- Core out the cabbage and steam whole in a large pot until the leaves are soft enough to roll
- Sauté onion and garlic in oil
- Mix raw hamburger and veal mixture, rice, eggs, onions and seasonings in large bowl
- Lay leaves from cabbage on counter
- Put about 2 tablespoons mixture into each cabbage leaf and roll up starting at thickest part of the leaf bringing in sides and then rolling up
- Line a casserole dish with a few cabbage leaves that cannot be used
- Place rolled cabbage into casserole dish
- Cover with any other remaining leaves
- Pour sauce over all
- Cover and bake in 325° oven for 3 hours

POLISH PIEROGI
1965

Polish stuffed tiny pies.

DOUGH: MIX TOGETHER

1 cup milk   1 egg   ½ teaspoon salt

Make one filling…this dough recipe is enough for one filling or 2 cups of a filling. If you want a variety, double the dough recipe, or make ½ of each filling.

- Mix together the dough ingredients and add enough flour to make a soft dough. Dough should be pliable but not sticky.
- On floured surface knead gently 15-20 strokes.
- Cover and let rest 10 minutes.
- Divide dough in half.
- On floured surface roll half the dough at a time to a 12-inch circle, about ⅛ inch thick.
- With a 3-inch round cookie cutter, cut out circles of dough.
- Place 1 heaping teaspoon filling on one-half of the circle.
- Fold other half of circle over, making half-moon shape.
- Pinch edges together well to seal.
- Dip a fork into flour and crimp the edges.
- Place on kitchen towel or floured board.
- Cover while making remaining Pierogi.
- In a large saucepan boil the water.
- Gently slide some of the Pierogi into boiling water, stirring with a spoon to keep them from sticking together.
- Do not crowd. Boil gentle uncovered 4 minutes or until Pierogi float.
- Remove with slotted spoon, turn into shallow ovenproof bowl.
- Gently stir in a little melted butter.
- Keep in warm oven while cooking remaining Pierogi.
- To serve, top with a little sour cream or additional melted butter.
- Sprinkle with fresh or frozen snipped dill.

Makes about 30

Note: any leftover Pierogi can be chilled and reheated. To reheat, melt a little butter **in a** skillet, add Pierogi, cover. Cook over low heat till golden, turning once.

POTATO-COTTAGE CHEESE FILLING:

⅓ cup chopped onion
1 teaspoon fresh dill or ½ t. dried dill
¼ teaspoon salt
⅔ cup dry-curd cottage cheese
1½ cups mashed potatoes. Do not add milk or seasoning when you mash the potatoes

- Cook onion in butter till tender
- Combine with potatoes, dill, salt and dash pepper
- Stir in cottage cheese

Makes 2 cups

SAUERKRAUT FILLING:

2 tablespoons cooking oil
1 cup chopped onion
1 cup fresh mushrooms, finely chopped
1 (14-ounce) can sauerkraut, drained, rinsed and chopped fine
¼ teaspoon salt
¼ teaspoon pepper
2 tablespoons sour cream

- Heat oil and add onion and mushrooms
- Cook until tender but not brown
- Stir in sauerkraut, salt and pepper
- Cook 8-10 minutes, stirring occasionally
- Remove from heat, stir in sour cream
- Cool

Makes 2 cups

2014 Sarasota, Florida

POLISH POPPY SEED
COFFEE SWIRL
1968

This is Steve's favorite Polish dessert. I could never replicate his Aunt Nellie's recipe, but this one comes close.

- ½ butter
- ¼ cup sugar
- ½ teaspoon salt
- 2 packages Dry yeast
- ¾ cup warm water (110°)
- 2 teaspoons grated lemon rind
- 3 cups sifted flour

FILLING:

- 1 cup poppy seeds
- ½ cup raisins
- ¾ cup sugar
- ½ cup milk
- 2 teaspoons grated lemon rind

- Combine; bring to boil; stir and cook for 5 minutes and cool

BREAD:

- Combine butter, sugar and salt in pan; heat until the butter melts; cool
- Dissolve yeast and 1 teaspoon sugar in warm water
- Stir until well blended, and let stand 10 minutes or till bubbly
- Stir in cooled butter and mix
- Beat in enough flour to make a soft dough
- Knead for 5 minutes
- Place in greased bowl, turning once
- Cover with cloth and let rise for 1 hour
- Punch down; knead a few times
- Roll out to a 20x16 rectangle
- Spread with filling
- Roll up jelly roll fashion, starting with long end
- Seam side down onto a greased sheet
- Shape into a horseshoe
- Make cuts 1 inch apart to within ½ inch of center
- Twist pieces outward
- Cover, rise for 45 minutes
- Brush with beaten egg wash
- Bake at 350° for 40 minutes
- Cool and decorate with tiny swirls of confectioner's icing

ROCK CORNISH HENS
WITH RICE MINGLE
1965

As a new bride this was one of my first meals. I found the recipe and decided it would be our first Christmas dinner. We served this dish for many Christmases thereafter. At one point Steve grilled the hens. Serves: 8

8 frozen Cornish hens thawed (about 1 pound each)
Salt and pepper
Soft butter
Paprika
¼ cup melted butter
1 jar Red currant jelly melted

- Preheat oven to 425°
- Remove giblets, wash hens and dry with paper towels
- Sprinkle hens with salt and pepper
- Tie legs together with twine
- Rub hens with soft butter
- Sprinkle with paprika
- Place in roasting pan
- Roast hens for 45-55 minutes, 1 hour for 1½ pound birds—basting with melted butter
- Begin making the Rice Mingle and melt the currant jelly
- When the hens are done, remove strings and arrange on heated platter, spoon melted jelly over hens and let rest

RICE MINGLE

1 cup wild rice
½ teaspoon salt
3 cups boiling water
Butter
2 medium onions, minced
4 cups beef or chicken stock
Dash pepper
2 cups uncooked white or brown grain rice

- Wash wild rice.
- In medium pan add the wild rice, ½ teaspoon salt and the 3 cups of water. Bring to boil and simmer 45-60 minutes. Fluff with fork and simmer 5 more minutes. Drain well.
- In another saucepot add.
- 2 tablespoons butter and sauté onions.
- Stir in the chicken or beef stock and white rice.
- Cover and bring mixture to boil, reduce heat, and simmer 20 minutes.
- Add 1 tablespoon butter.
- Mix the cooked wild rice and cooked white rice together and fluff with fork.
- Can add sautéed mushrooms and/or caramelized onions at this point.

ROAST PORK
WITH CUMBERLAND GLAZE
1966

This is another one of my first recipes as a new bride. The glaze compliments this roast. I have used this glaze as a sauce for pork chops and chicken to jazz them up a bit. I simply mix the glaze ingredients and heat for a few minutes. This makes a nice meal to serve with guests.

Prepare one pork loin roast with salt and pepper: a 5 pound roast will take about 2¼ hours or 145° internal temperature.

GLAZE:

Combine and heat:
- ½ cup currant or apple jelly
- 2 tablespoons port wine
- 3 tablespoons fresh lemon juice
- ¼ cup raisins
- 1 teaspoon dry mustard
- 1 teaspoon paprika
- ½ teaspoon ground ginger
- 3 tablespoons thinly slivered orange rind

- Preheat oven to 325°
- One hour before the roast is done brush with glaze
- Add ½ cup water to pan to prevent raisins from sticking
- BASTE FREQUENTLY
- Let roast rest for 10 minutes before carving
- Serve with crab apples

Serve with a Beaujolais or Red Zinfandel

ROCK CORNISH HENS
WITH RICE MINGLE
1965

As a new bride this was one of my first meals. I found the recipe and decided it would be our first Christmas dinner. We served this dish for many Christmases thereafter. At one point Steve grilled the hens. Serves: 8

8 frozen Cornish hens thawed (about 1 pound each)
Salt and pepper
Soft butter
Paprika
¼ cup melted butter
1 jar Red currant jelly melted

- Preheat oven to 425°
- Remove giblets, wash hens and dry with paper towels
- Sprinkle hens with salt and pepper
- Tie legs together with twine
- Rub hens with soft butter
- Sprinkle with paprika
- Place in roasting pan
- Roast hens for 45-55 minutes, 1 hour for 1½ pound birds—basting with melted butter
- Begin making the Rice Mingle and melt the currant jelly
- When the hens are done, remove strings and arrange on heated platter, spoon melted jelly over hens and let rest

RICE MINGLE

1 cup wild rice
½ teaspoon salt
3 cups boiling water
Butter
2 medium onions, minced
4 cups beef or chicken stock
Dash pepper
2 cups uncooked white or brown grain rice

- Wash wild rice.
- In medium pan add the wild rice, ½ teaspoon salt and the 3 cups of water. Bring to boil and simmer 45-60 minutes. Fluff with fork and simmer 5 more minutes. Drain well.
- In another saucepot add.
- 2 tablespoons butter and sauté onions.
- Stir in the chicken or beef stock and white rice.
- Cover and bring mixture to boil, reduce heat, and simmer 20 minutes.
- Add 1 tablespoon butter.
- Mix the cooked wild rice and cooked white rice together and fluff with fork.
- Can add sautéed mushrooms and/or caramelized onions at this point.

ROAST PORK
WITH CUMBERLAND GLAZE
1966

This is another one of my first recipes as a new bride. The glaze compliments this roast. I have used this glaze as a sauce for pork chops and chicken to jazz them up a bit. I simply mix the glaze ingredients and heat for a few minutes. This makes a nice meal to serve with guests.

Prepare one pork loin roast with salt and pepper: a 5 pound roast will take about 2¼ hours or 145° internal temperature.

GLAZE:

Combine and heat:
- ½ cup currant or apple jelly
- 2 tablespoons port wine
- 3 tablespoons fresh lemon juice
- ¼ cup raisins
- 1 teaspoon dry mustard
- 1 teaspoon paprika
- ½ teaspoon ground ginger
- 3 tablespoons thinly slivered orange rind

- Preheat oven to 325°
- One hour before the roast is done brush with glaze
- Add ½ cup water to pan to prevent raisins from sticking
- BASTE FREQUENTLY
- Let roast rest for 10 minutes before carving
- Serve with crab apples

Serve with a Beaujolais or Red Zinfandel

GOLDEN CRUMB
BROCCOLI CASSEROLE
1965

This is one of my very first recipes. It became our family's favorite broccoli casserole. We enjoyed it with many of our holiday meals. Today it is my "go to" recipe.

- 2 (10-ounce) packages frozen chopped broccoli florets cooked until just crisp
- 1 can cream of mushroom soup
- ¼ cup mayonnaise
- ¼ cup sour cream
- ½ - ¾ cup shredded sharp cheese
- 1 tablespoon pimento
- 1 tablespoon fresh lemon juice
- 1 cup crushed cheese cracker crumbs (golf fish crackers)
- ¼ cup slivered almonds

- Preheat oven to 350°
- Mix all ingredients except cracker crumbs
- Spray a casserole dish with PAM
- Turn mixture into a casserole dish
- Sprinkle crumbs on top of dish
- Bake 30 minutes or until bubbly around the edges

Yield: 6-8

TRADITIONAL
GREEN BEAN CASSEROLE
1965

I was first introduced to this recipe from my father-in-law George. When I was a young 16-year old dating Steve, George invited me to Sunday afternoon dinners where we enjoyed a roast beef dinner with mashed potatoes, gravy, and this bean casserole. Dad Cerjan was the chief cook in the Cerjan household.

- 1 (10¾ -ounce) can Cream of Mushroom Soup
- ½ cup milk
- 1 teaspoon soy sauce
- Dash ground black pepper
- 4 cups French cut green beans, cooked and drained
- 1 and ⅓ cups French Fried Onions

- Preheat oven to 350°
- Spray casserole dish with PAM
- Mix soup, milk, soy, black pepper, beans and ⅔-cup onions in 1½ -quart casserole
- Bake at 350° for 25 minutes or until hot
- Stir contents of casserole
- Sprinkle with remaining onions and bake 5 minutes more

Makes 6 servings

CHILI CON CARNE
1965

I started making my chili with just a basic recipe. It became a developing recipe as I later added the cumin, cayenne and salsa.

- 1 pound ground beef
- 1 large onion, chopped
- 1 clove garlic minced
- 1 chopped green pepper
- 1 (28-ounce) can crushed tomatoes
- 1 (8-ounce) can tomato sauce or salsa*
- 1½ tablespoons chili powder or to taste
- 1½ teaspoons salt or to taste
- ½ teaspoon cumin powder
- ⅛ teaspoon cayenne red pepper
- ⅛ teaspoon paprika
- 1 bay leaf
- 2 cans kidney beans, drained (I use red kidney beans and black beans)

- Cook and stir ground beef, onion and green pepper in large skillet until meat is brown and onion is tender
- Drain off fat
- Stir in remaining ingredients except beans
- Heat to boiling
- Reduce heat, cover and simmer for 40 minutes, stirring occasionally
- Add beans and simmer another 20 minutes
- Remove bay leaf and serve with shredded sharp cheddar cheese, corn muffins or cheese straws

*For stronger flavor substitute the tomato sauce for a jar of salsa.

Yield: 6 servings

MY FAVORITE
PANCAKE RECIPE
1965

I have used this recipe for many years. Today I make these pancakes for my granddaughters, Thia and Avery.

1¼ cups sifted flour	½ teaspoon salt	2 tablespoons salad oil
3 teaspoons baking powder	1 beaten egg	
1 tablespoon sugar	1 cup milk	

- Preheat griddle and spray with PAM
- Stir together flour, baking powder, sugar and salt
- Stir with a wire whisk to sift further
- Combine egg, milk and oil
- Add to dry ingredients all at once; stirring just until the flour is moistened (batter will be lumpy)
- Bake on hot griddle

Makes eight 4-inch pancakes or 12 dollar size pancakes

VARIATIONS:

- Blueberry Pancakes: add blueberries to each pancake while on the griddle
- Buttermilk Pancakes: substitute buttermilk or sour milk for a sweet milk and add ½ teaspoon baking soda and only 2 teaspoons baking powder
- Chocolate Chip Pancakes: add chocolate chips to batter before baking

NOT SO SWEET
PECAN PIE
1965

I made this pie on our first Thanksgiving together as husband and wife and have made it every Thanksgiving since. It is not as sweet as my mom's version.

¼ cup butter
½ cup sugar
1 cup dark corn syrup
¼ teaspoon salt

3 eggs
1 cup pecan halves
1 (9-inch) unbaked pastry shell

- Preheat oven to 350°
- Cream butter to soften
- Add sugar gradually and cream until fluffy
- Add syrup and salt then beat well
- Add eggs one at a time, beating thoroughly after each
- Stir in pecans
- Pour into unbaked pastry shell
- Bake for 50 minutes or until knife comes out clean
- Cool

OFFICER'S WIFE
1967 Fort Benning, Georgia

My wooden spoons are on the road again as we moved to Fort Benning, Georgia in 1967.

As an officer's wife at Fort Benning, I became very active in teas and socials. In those days, officer's wives had many "white glove and hat" teas and coffees. While playing bridge or attending the big teas, we swapped recipes. Some of the recipes were luscious desserts and many were Southern based indigenous to the Georgia or Alabama culture where many of my closest friends originated.

MARY'S OLD FASHIONED
SOUTHERN POUND CAKE

1967

My Alabama friend, Mary Vice, taught me my first chapter in southern cooking. This is a sample.

- 1 stick of margarine
- 1 stick of butter
- 2 cups sifted flour (sift before measuring)
- ¼ teaspoon salt
- 5 eggs
- 1⅔ cup sugar
- 1 teaspoon vanilla extract

- Preheat oven to 325°
- Allow butter to soften
- Grease and flour a 9-inch tube pan or Bundt pan
- Sift flour and salt and set aside
- Cream butter and margarine
- Add sugar and beat until very fluffy
- Add small amount of flour, then one egg, beating about one minute at a medium speed
- Continue in this manner until all flour and eggs are used
- Add 1 teaspoon vanilla
- Bake in tube or Bundt pan (greased and floured) for 1 hour or until tester comes out clean
- Allow to sit for 5-10 minutes
- Invert onto a cake rack

FOR A CHOCOLATE VERSION:

- Add 3 squares melted unsweetened chocolate and increase the sugar to 2 cups.

CORN PUDDING
1967

2 tablespoons butter
1 medium onion minced
1 (16-ounce) bag of frozen corn kernels thawed
3 tablespoons masa harina or corn meal
4 eggs

1 tablespoon sugar
1½ teaspoons salt
   Dash hot pepper sauce
1 cup sour cream
½ cup milk
4 strips bacon cooked crisp and crumbled

- Preheat oven to 350°
- Grease casserole dish
- Melt 2 tablespoons butter in small skillet and sauté onion
- Divide corn in half and place one half in food processor
- Add onion and process with steel knife 10 seconds
- Add cornmeal, eggs, sugar, salt and hot pepper sauce
- Pulse for 10 seconds
- Add sour cream and ½ cup milk
- Stir in remaining half of corn
- Adjust seasoning
- Ladle into dish and sprinkle with bacon
- Bake until puffy (50 minutes)

This can be assembled several hours ahead. Cover lightly; do not refrigerate.

Serves: 8

YELLOW SQUASH CASSEROLE
1970

We first sampled this at a friend's home in Alabama. Steve loves this dish.

2 cups cooked yellow crookneck squash	1 cup breadcrumbs
1 large onion chopped	½ cup milk
1 cup sharp cheddar cheese	Pinch garlic salt or grated fresh garlic
1 cup sour cream	Salt and pepper to taste
2 eggs beaten	2 tablespoons butter

- Preheat oven to 350°
- Spray a casserole dish with PAM
- Cook onion in butter
- Mix all remaining ingredients
- Bake till bubbling

Yield: 6 servings

SAUSAGE CHEESE BALLS
1968

This popular recipe makes a wonderful breakfast item or appetizer.

- 1 pound Jimmy Dean's pork sausage mild or ½ pound mild and ½ pound hot
- 12 ounces shredded sharp cheddar cheese
- 3 cups Bisquick

- Preheat oven to 350°
- Mix sausage, Bisquick and cheese
- Roll into about 60 balls
- Bake on ungreased cookie sheet until bottoms are brown about 20 minutes

Yield: 3 dozen balls

BANANA NUT CAKE
WITH COCOA WHIPPED CREAM
1969

- ⅔ cup margarine
- 2½ cup sifted flour
- 1⅔ cups sugar
- 1¼ teaspoons baking powder
- 1 teaspoon baking soda
- 1 teaspoon salt
- 1¼ cup mashed fully ripe bananas
- ⅔ cup buttermilk
- 2 eggs
- ⅔ cup chopped toasted walnuts
- Chocolate chips (optional)
- Cocoa Whipped Cream OR Chocolate Frosting
- 2 bananas sliced

- Preheat oven to 350°.
- Prepare two 9-inch round cake pans. Spray with PAM, line with waxed or parchment paper, spray again with PAM.
- Stir margarine to soften.
- Sift in dry ingredients.
- Add bananas and half the buttermilk.
- Mix until all flour is dampened.
- Beat vigorously for 2 minutes.
- Add remaining buttermilk and the eggs.
- Beat 2 minutes then fold in nuts and chocolate chips.
- Bake about 35 minutes.
- Cool 10 minutes in pans on wire rack.
- Remove from pans and cool completely.
- Spread layer with ⅓ of Cocoa Whipped Cream.
- Top with two bananas sliced.
- Add second layer.
- Frost the top and sides with the remainder of the Cocoa Whipped Cream.
- An alternate to the Whipped Cream and bananas is to simply frost the cake with regular chocolate frosting.

COCOA WHIPPED CREAM:

- Combine ½ cup sugar, ⅓ cup cocoa and 1½ cups of heavy cream.
- Chill for 1 hour.
- Beat until stiff.

GRASSHOPPER PIE
1968

This is a simple but elegant dessert! My friend, Diane Eck, gave this recipe to me. We shared many dinners together at Fort Benning, GA.

24 chocolate filled chocolate cookies finely crushed (I use Oreo cookies)*
¼ cup melted butter
¼ cup green Crème de Menthe
1 (7-ounce) jar marshmallow cream
2 cups whipping cream, whipped.

- Finely crush Oreo cookies in food processor or blender
- In medium bowl toss cookie crumbs with butter mixing well
- Reserve ½ cup for the top
- Press remaining crumbs on bottom of 9-inch spring form pan
- Gradually add Crème de Menthe to marshmallow cream, mixing until well blended
- Whip cream until it holds it shape
- Fold into marshmallow mixture
- Pour into crumb lined pan
- Sprinkle with reserved crumbs
- Freeze until firm (overnight)

*For a lighter crust, use plain chocolate thin wafers and add some sugar.

Serves: 8-10

BLITZ TORTE
1968

CAKE:

4 eggs yolks
½ cup butter
¾ cup confectioners' sugar
1 cup flour
1 teaspoon baking powder
¼ teaspoon salt
6 tablespoons milk
1 teaspoon almond extract

- Preheat oven to 325°.
- Grease and flour two 8-inch round cake pans.
- Cream butter and sugar. Beat in egg yolks.
- Mix flour, baking powder and salt with wire whisk.
- Add flour mix to butter mixture. Add milk and almond extract, mix well.
- Spread batter into pans. Prepare Meringue and continue.

MERINGUE:

4 egg whites room temperature
½ cup confectioners' sugar
½ cup granulated sugar
½ cup slivered blanched almonds
2 tablespoons sugar

- Beat egg whites in a clean dry bowl until foamy.
- Beat in ½ cup each granulated and confectioners' sugar 1 tablespoon at a time.
- Continue beating until stiff and glossy.
- Spread half of meringue over batter in each pan.
- Sprinkle each pan with almonds and 1 tablespoon sugar over each pan.
- Bake 35-40 minutes or until meringue is set and cake is done.
- Prepare cream filling (see below) while cake is baking.
- When cake is done, cool on rack for 10 minutes, then with spatulas carefully remove first layer from pan and place on serving plate meringue side UP.
- Spread with filling.
- Arrange some strawberries over cream (optional).
- Remove second layer from pan and place over cream with meringue side UP.
- Chill at least one hour before serving.

FILLING:

- ⅓ cup sugar
- 2 tablespoons cornstarch
- ⅛ teaspoon salt
- 1½ cups milk
- 2 egg yolks, slightly beaten
- 1 teaspoon vanilla or almond extract
- 1 tablespoon butter

- Mix thoroughly sugar, cornstarch and salt in a saucepan.
- Stir milk into egg yolks, gradually stir egg mixture into dry ingredients.
- Cook over medium heat, stirring constantly until mixture thickens and boils.
- Boil and stir one minute, remove from heat, add butter and flavoring.

BELGUIM WAFFLES
1967

Weekend breakfast was always a treat for our family. I developed this recipe back in the 60's and it is a mainstay in my breakfast menus. Today my granddaughters love these waffles. They come out high and fluffy.

- 1¾ cups sifted flour
- 3 teaspoons baking powder
- ½ teaspoon salt
- 2 beaten egg yolks
- 1¼ cups milk
- ½ cup vegetable oil
- 2 stiff-beaten egg whites

- Preheat waffle iron
- When heated spray with PAM
- Sift dry ingredients into a bowl: I whisk the flour before measuring as a sifting technique; then whisk again with all the remaining dry ingredients
- Combine yolks and milk
- Stir into the dry ingredients
- Stir in oil
- Fold egg whites into batter leaving a few little fluffs—do not over mix
- Bake in preheated waffle iron

Makes eight 6-inch square waffles

LEMON CHESS PIE
1967

This is one of my favorites. It is very easy to make and it creates a pretty presentation on a dessert table.

1 9-inch deep-dish pie shell Juice of 3 lemons	2 cups sugar (may want to use less sugar)
Grated zest of 3 lemons	5 eggs
3 tablespoons flour	½ cup melted butter
Juice of 3 lemons	Confectioner's sugar for dusting

- Preheat oven 350°
- Combine lemon zest, lemon juice, flour and sugar
- Add eggs one at a time beating well after each egg
- Pour butter in steady stream while beating
- Pour filling into pie shell and bake at 350° for 45 minutes or until pie is set and top is golden brown
- Cool completely
- Sprinkle top with confectioner's sugar if desired.
- Serve with freshly whipped cream

I use my vodka piecrust for the pie shell.

MEXICAN WEDDING COOKIES
1968

We make these cookies every Christmas for holiday gifts.

- 1 cup unsalted butter, at room temperature
- ½ cup confectioners' sugar, plus more for coating baked cookies
- 1 teaspoon vanilla extract
- 1¾ cups all-purpose flour, plus more for dusting hands
- 1 cup pecans, chopped into very small pieces

- Using an electric mixer, cream the butter and the sugar at low speed until it is smooth.
- Beat in the vanilla.
- At low speed, gradually add the flour.
- Mix in the pecans with a spatula.
- At this point, refrigerate the dough for about 1-2 hours.
- Preheat oven to 275°.
- Line cookie sheets with parchment paper.
- With floured hands, take out about 1 tablespoon of dough and shape into a ball. Continue to dust hands with flour as you make more cookies.
- Place onto prepared cookie sheets.
- Bake for 40 minutes.
- When cool enough to handle, but still warm, roll in additional confectioners' sugar.
- Cool on wire racks.

I usually freeze these and later add them to my Christmas cookie tray. I freshen them **up** by popping them in confectioners' sugar before adding them to my tray.

BEEF STROGANOFF
1967

The first time I had this dish was at my sister-in-law Pat's home. She served it often with spaetzles, a salad and her famous Fudge Cake. I tried many recipes and found this to be the best. I have been making it for over 40 years. Stroganoff originates in Russia.

- 1 pound beef tenderloin or sirloin steak, about ½ inch thick
- 1 tablespoon oil
- 6 tablespoons unsalted butter
- Salt and pepper
- 12 ounces mushrooms, cleaned, trimmed and sliced
- 1 medium onion, minced or sliced thinly
- 1 can condensed beef broth; or 2 cups **rich** beef stock
- 2 tablespoons tomato paste
- 1 small clove garlic, minced
- 3 tablespoons flour
- 2 teaspoons dry mustard or Dijon mustard
- 1 cup sour cream
- 3 tablespoons dry sherry
- 1 tablespoon flat-leaf parsley leaves chopped
- 3-4 cups hot cooked noodles or cooked spaetzles

- Cut meat across the grain into ½ inch strips about 1½ inches long; season with salt and pepper
- Preheat skillet and add oil
- Brown beef and transfer to plate and set aside
- Melt 2 tablespoons butter in large skillet
- Add mushrooms and cook until browned, transfer to plate and set aside
- Heat 4 tablespoons butter in same skillet and add the onion and garlic, cook about 5 minutes
- Add the tomato paste and cook about a minute
- Whisk in the flour and cook a minute
- Pour in beef stock whisking and bring to a full boil
- Remove from heat and whisk in the sour cream, mustard, and sherry
- Season with salt and pepper and set aside
- Cook noodles, drain and toss with butter, salt, and pepper
- Add the beef and mushrooms with all juices to the sour cream sauce; add parsley
- Heat over medium heat until hot but do not boil
- Serve stroganoff over noodles

Serves: 4

SAVORY TURKISH LAMB PILAF
1968

You can use leftover lamb in this dish.

¼ cup butter
½ pound boneless lamb, cut into julienne strips
2 medium onions, chopped fine
¼ cup toasted pine nuts or walnuts
1 cup uncooked rice
1 large fresh tomato, peeled, seeded and chopped or 1 large can chopped tomatoes
¼ cup raisins
2 teaspoons salt
½ teaspoon pepper
½ teaspoon ground sage
¼ teaspoon ground allspice
2 cups boiling chicken stock or water
Chopped parsley or chopped mint

- In large skillet heat butter and sauté lamb strips until golden brown
- Remove and keep hot on a separate plate
- In same skillet melt butter and cook onion until soft
- Add nuts and rice and cook over medium heat for 5 minutes
- Add tomato, raisins, salt, pepper, spices and chicken stock
- Cover and cook 30 minutes
- Return lamb to rice and heat
- Recover and let stand for 15 minutes before serving
- Sprinkle with parsley or mint

MEAT LOAF
1966

My first meatloaf mimicked my mom's version. I have changed a few things about my meatloaf over the years to improve the taste. I still add some chopped carrot as mom did years ago. I found that if I shape my loaf and bake it on a foil lined rack it comes out with a crispier top and the juices fall away from the meat instead of sitting in the juices during cooking. Although the pork and veal add a different flavor to the loaf, it is optional.

- 2 eggs slightly beaten
- 2 pounds meat (75% ground beef, 25% ground pork and veal mix)
- ⅔ cups bread crumbs, or crushed saltine crackers, or instant oatmeal
- 2 tablespoons finely chopped fresh parsley
- 1 teaspoon salt
- ½ teaspoon pepper

- 1 tablespoon Worcestershire sauce
- 2 teaspoons mustard
- ½ cup milk
- ½ teaspoon dried thyme crushed
- 1 onion finely chopped
- 1 carrot finely chopped
- 1 clove garlic minced
- Oil for sautéing vegetables

TOPPING:

- ¼–½ cup ketchup
- 3 tablespoons brown sugar
- 1 teaspoon ground mustard

- Preheat oven to 350°
- Prepare a loaf pan or place foil on a wire rack over a baking sheet
- Poke some holes in the foil to allow juices to drip down
- Sauté onion, carrot and garlic in oil
- In large bowl mix the eggs, milk, seasonings, Worcestershire sauce, mustard, bread crumbs and meat
- Mix with fork or hands until completed combined
- Place meat into loaf pan or gently shape loaf for baking sheet
- Spread topping over meat loaf
- Bake for 1–1¼ hours or until internal temperature is 160°
- Let stand for 15-20 minutes before slicing

SOUTHERN STYLE
BLACK EYED PEAS
1966

When our Alabama friends invited us to supper, they served these peas with Southern corn bread. Dessert was homemade ice cream.

Black-eyed peas are often called Crowder peas. The Crowder pea is a bit different in color and taste.

Southerners eat the black-eyed peas on New Year's Day. It is a tradition that brings good luck for the New Year.

¾	pound ham hocks, my friend also used fat back
1	quart water
4	cups fresh black eyed peas, shelled (if you use dried, soak overnight in water and then drain well
1	onion, minced
¼	teaspoon pepper

- In a 3-quart Dutch oven, place ham hocks; add water and bring to boil
- Reduce heat cover and simmer for 30-40 or until meat is tender
- Remove ham hocks and discard
- Strain broth, chill until fat rises to the surface and hardens
- Remove the hardened fat
- Place broth, peas, onion and pepper in a Dutch oven
- Bring to boil, reduce heat, cover and simmer 30-40 minutes or until peas are tender
- Add more water if necessary

Serves: 6

Serve with corn bread or corn sticks.

BROWNIES BY THE DOZEN

Brownies are easy to make and fun to serve because everyone likes brownies. They are a perfect dessert at a picnic or with a fancy meal topped off with gelato and chocolate sauce. When I make brownies, I make many varieties at one time, and then freeze them for later use. The following brownie recipes are my absolute favorite.

CHOCOLATE SYRUP BROWNIES
1988

These brownies are cakelike.

½ cup butter
1 cup sugar
3 eggs
1 cup flour
¾ cup canned chocolate syrup

1 teaspoon vanilla
1 cup chopped nuts
   Cocoa Frosting (below)
   Nut Halves

- Preheat oven to 350°
- Grease a 9" square pan
- Cream butter and sugar
- Add eggs one at a time, beating after each addition
- Add remaining ingredients
- Bake about 40 minutes
- Cool in pan on cake rack
- Spread with frosting
- When firm, cut into squares
- Press a nut half in center of each brownie

Makes 16 brownies

FROSTING

1 teaspoon butter
3 teaspoons milk
1½ cups confectioner's sugar

Dash of salt
¼ cup unsweetened cocoa
½ teaspoon vanilla

- Heat butter and milk until butter is melted
- Mix next 3 ingredients
- Add milk, stirring to blend
- Then add vanilla and beat with spoon for a minute or until smooth

CHOCOLATE CHIP BROWNIES
BEST BROWNIE RECIPE
1969

¼ cup butter softened
¾ cup sugar
¼ cup light corn syrup
2 beaten eggs
1 teaspoon vanilla
2 ounces unsweetened chocolate melted

1 cup flour
½ teaspoon baking powder
½ teaspoon salt
½ cup semisweet chocolate morsels
½ cup chopped walnuts

- Preheat oven to 350°
- Lightly grease a 9-inch square pan
- Combine flour, baking powder and salt in small bowl
- Cream butter, gradually add sugar and beat until light and fluffy
- Add corn syrup, eggs, vanilla and beat well
- Stir in chocolate
- Stir flour mixture into creamed mixture
- Stir in chocolate morsels and walnuts
- Spread into lightly greased 9-inch square pan
- Bake for 25–30 minutes; do not over bake
- Cool and cut into squares

Yield: about 25 small squares

GANACHE FOR FROSTING BROWNIES

This Ganache can also be used as a dessert filling in small tarts

6 ounces semisweet chocolate chopped
3 tablespoons unsalted butter, room temperature
2 tablespoons whipping cream

- Whisk all ingredients in small saucepan
- Heat until melted and smooth, cool
- Pour evenly over brownies while in pan
- Chill brownies until the Ganache is set (2 hours)
- Serve at room temperature

MARBLED BROWNIES
1988

These brownies are cakelike.

1 cup butter softened
1½ teaspoons vanilla
2 cups sugar
4 eggs
1¾ cups flour
½ teaspoon salt
2 cups unsweetened chocolate melted and cooled
½ cup chopped nuts of choice
Velvety Chocolate Frosting

- Preheat oven to 350°
- Grease and line the bottom of a 13x9x2 baking dish with waxed paper
- Cream first 3 ingredients together until light and fluffy
- Add eggs one at a time, beating well after each
- Add flour and salt and mix until blended
- Stir in nuts
- Divide batter in half and add the melted chocolate to one half of the batter
- Drop the two batters alternately by heaping spoonful's into prepared pan
- Press down with spoon to smooth top of the batters and then run a knife through the batters several times to marbleize
- Bake for 45 minutes
- Turn out on cake rack and peel off the paper
- When cold, spread with frosting
- Cut into 2" squares

Makes 24 squares

VELVETY CHOCOLATE FROSTING

1¼ cups confectioners' sugar
4 squares unsweetened chocolate melted
4 egg yolks
¼ cup butter, melted
1 teaspoon vanilla extract

- Add ¼ cup hot water and the sugar to chocolate and mix well
- Add yolks one at a time, beating well after each
- Slowly add butter, then vanilla and beat until smooth

BLOND BROWNIES

1988

These brownies are chewy with a butterscotch flavor.

- ¼ cup butter
- 1 cup packed light brown sugar
- 1 egg
- ¾ cup flour
- 1 teaspoon baking powder
- ½ teaspoon salt
- ½ teaspoon vanilla extract
- ½ cup coarsely chopped nuts (pecans)

- Preheat oven to 350°
- Grease an 8" square pan
- In bowl, whisk flour with baking powder and salt, set aside
- Melt butter over low heat or in microwave
- Remove and add brown sugar and stir until well blended; cool
- Add egg and mix well
- Stir in dry ingredients, then add vanilla and nuts
- Spread in pan
- Bake for 25 minutes
- Cool in pan on cake rack
- Cut into 2" squares

Makes 16 squares

SAUCEPAN BROWNIES
1988

These brownies are chewy.

⅓ cup butter
½ cup sugar
2 tablespoons water
1 (6-ounce) package semisweet chocolate pieces
1 teaspoon vanilla

2 eggs
¾ cup flour
¼ teaspoon baking soda
¼ teaspoon salt
½ cup coarsely chopped nuts

- Preheat oven to 325°
- Grease an 8" square pan
- Whisk together flour, baking soda and salt in a small bowl; set aside
- Put first 2 ingredients, butter and sugar, and 2 tablespoons water into a saucepan
- Stir and bring just to a boil over medium heat
- Remove from heat and add the chocolate and vanilla
- Stir until blended and smooth
- Beat in the eggs one at a time
- Mix in the dry ingredients and stir well
- Add nuts and spread into prepared pan
- Bake for 25 minutes
- Cool in pan on cake rack
- Cut into 2" squares

Makes 16 squares

COFFEE BROWNIES
2006

Easy recipe but truly a five-star taste.

PAM cooking spray
⅓ cup water
⅓ cup vegetable oil
2 eggs
2 tablespoons coffee powder or as desired
1 (19.8-ounce) box brownie mix (recommended: Duncan Hines)
¾ cup semisweet chocolate chips

- Preheat oven to 350°
- Spray a 9x13-inch pan with PAM
- Whisk ⅓ cup water, oil, eggs and 2 tablespoons coffee powder in a large bowl to blend
- Add the brownie mix
- Stir until well blended
- Stir in chocolate chips
- Transfer batter to baking pan
- Bake until a toothpick inserted into the center comes out with a few moist crumbs attached, about 35 minutes
- Cool completely

GLAZE:

2 teaspoons coffee powder
2 tablespoons water
1 teaspoon vanilla
1½ cups powdered sugar
1 tablespoon unsalted butter, room temperature

- Dissolve 2 teaspoon coffee powder in 2 tablespoons water
- Whisk in the vanilla and add the powdered sugar and butter
- Whisk until smooth
- Pour over the brownies
- Refrigerate until the glaze is set
- Cut into bite-size pieces
- If you prefer, you can dispense with the glaze and simply sprinkle powdered sugar over the cut brownies and serve

Yield: 36 bite-size brownies

HOMEMADE CHURNED ICE CREAM
1966

I learned to make this from my friend, Mary Vice. She served this after her wonderful Southern suppers.

- 6 eggs
- 3 cans evaporated milk (chilled)
- 2 cups sugar
- 1 tablespoon vanilla
- 2½ cups chopped fruit

- Separate eggs;
- Beat yolks and sugar until creamy
- Continue beating and add chilled milk, add fruit and vanilla
- Beat egg whites until peaks form (not too stiff)
- Fold into mixture and pour into ice cream freezer or ice cream maker
- Make sure the beater in the ice cream freezer is chilled before pouring in mixture; put top on the can and place into ice cream bucket filled with an ice and rock salt mixture
- Plug in and run for 20-30 minutes or until the ice cream is the consistency of mush; ripen (harden) the ice cream in your freezer
- Best if made a day ahead

In today's world, you would use an electric ice cream maker often sold at kitchen stores.

LIVING IN NEW ENGLAND
CRANSTON, RHODE ISLAND
1970-1973

The movers arrived in 1973 to once again pack up my wooden spoons and all my recipes.

We moved to Rhode Island shortly after a two-year stay in Piscataway, New Jersey. Rhode Island was our very first taste of New England culture.

We learned how to clam dig for Quahogs (very large clams) and we ate tons of fresh lobster and shrimp.

Rhode Island is where we began to make our own bread. I did the mixing and Steve did all the kneading. It was a family fun activity.

BAKED STUFFED SHRIMP
1970

My best friend and neighbor, Mary Chirico, gave me this recipe. I decided to add this recipe in memory of her. She died of breast cancer shortly after we moved from the area.

16 extra-large shrimp about 1½ pounds	2 teaspoons minced garlic
2 cups Ritz crackers, crushed	2 tablespoons Parmesan cheese
½ cup melted unsalted butter or to taste	½ teaspoon salt
4-6 tablespoons melted butter for brushing shrimp and sautéing vegetables	¼ teaspoon pepper
	½ teaspoon paprika
	Dash Worcestershire
1 stalk celery minced	2 tablespoons lemon juice

- Preheat oven to 375°.
- Remove veins and shells from shrimp leaving the last bit of tail on the shrimp.
- Split shrimp almost to center and then flatten cut side up.
- Rinse thoroughly in cold water.
- Brush shrimp with butter.
- Sauté garlic and celery in butter.
- To make the stuffing, combine crumbs, sautéed celery and garlic, salt and pepper, paprika, Worcestershire, lemon juice and cheese.
- Stir in melted butter. Mixture is barely wet. If too dry add a bit of wine or broth.
- Mound stuffing into the center of each shrimp.
- Sprinkle each shrimp with more Parmesan cheese.
- Bake until shrimp changes to a reddish color (12 minutes).
- For a browner top, broil for 1-2 minutes.

Serves: 4-6

You can add some flaked crab to the stuffing for a richer dish.

CLAMS CASINO
1970

Clams casino got its name in 1917 at the Casino at Narragansett Pier in Rhode Island. Apparently a very wealthy women was staying at the casino and asked the maître d' to make her a special appetizer. It is now very popular in the Rhode Island area especially among the Italian population.

24 littleneck clams cleaned
2 tablespoons olive oil
1 tablespoon butter
⅓ cup chopped shallots or onions
¼ cup finely chopped green bell pepper
4 slices bacon cooked until crisp and crumbled

1 garlic clove, minced
¼ teaspoon dried oregano
1 teaspoon fresh parsley chopped
4 tablespoons grated Parmesan cheese
⅓ cup dried breadcrumbs
Dash Tabasco
Paprika

- Preheat oven to 450°
- Cook bacon, crumble and set aside
- Wash clams thoroughly; place on baking sheet
- Put in oven for 1-2 minutes or until the clams open
- Discard any clams that do not open
- Open clams discarding shallow shell
- Add 2 tablespoons oil and 1 tablespoon butter to skillet and sauté onion, green pepper and garlic,
- Cool
- In bowl combine crumbs, bacon, oregano, cheese, sautéed vegetables, Tabasco and mix well
- Place clams on a baking sheet that is lined with a bed of rock salt to stabilize them (optional)
- Place vegetable crumb mixture on top of each clam
- Sprinkle with parsley and paprika
- Drizzle with olive oil
- Bake at 450° for 7–10 minutes

Serves: 6 as an appetizer

STUFFED QUAHOGS
1970

Quahogs are very large clams. Steve and I went digging for these in the shallow waters of the Scarborough Beach area.

- 12 Quahogs steamed in 1 inch of water (reserve liquid)
- 1 clove garlic minced fine
- 1 stalk celery minced fine
- ½ green pepper minced fine
- 1-2 tablespoons butter
- Parsley
- Lemon juice
- ½ cup breadcrumbs
- Salt, pepper and olive oil
- Paprika

- Steam clams until they open; reserve liquid and discard those clams that do not open
- Preheat oven to 375°
- Sauté vegetables in butter
- Chop clams in blender or processor
- Mix together the vegetables, clams, lemon juice, reserved clam broth, bread crumbs, parsley, salt and pepper
- Scrub bottom of the clam shells; spray with PAM
- If stuffing mix is too moist, add more crumbs
- If stuffing is too dry add wine or broth
- Add stuffing to bottom shell and place on cookie sheet
- Sprinkle with olive oil and paprika
- Bake in 375° for 25 minutes

Serves: 12

HOT CRABMEAT
1970

  8 ounces cream cheese
6½ ounces high quality lump crabmeat thoroughly rinsed
  2 tablespoons finely chopped onion
  1 tablespoon milk
 ½ teaspoon creamed horseradish or to taste
 ¼ teaspoon salt, freshly ground pepper
 ⅓ cup toasted slivered almonds

- Preheat oven to 350°
- Combine all ingredients except almonds
- Put into an 8-inch pie plate
- Bake at 350° for 15 minutes
- Sprinkle with toasted nuts, serve with crackers

Serve: 4

APPLE PANCAKE PIE
1970

Margarine or butter	¼ teaspoon cinnamon	½ cup milk
4 tart apples sliced thin	⅛ teaspoon nutmeg	¼ teaspoon salt
10 tablespoons sugar	2 eggs	½ cup stirred flour

- Preheat oven to 450°.
- Melt 6 tablespoons butter in large skillet and sauté apples for 5 minutes.
- Mix 6 tablespoons sugar with cinnamon and nutmeg.
- Sprinkle over the apples, cover and cook on low heat for 10 minutes.
- In a bowl, beat eggs, milk and salt.
- Add flour and beat till smooth.
- In separate heavy 10-11 inch skillet melt 1 tablespoon butter to coat bottom, spray with PAM cooking spray.
- Pour in batter.
- Bake in oven for 15 minutes; prinking with fork when puffy. You will need to do this several times.
- Reduce the oven temperature to 350° and bake 10 minutes more.
- Spoon 2 tablespoons melted butter over the pancake and sprinkle with 2 tablespoons sugar.
- Spoon apple mixture over half of the pancake; then fold.
- Sprinkle with confectioners sugar.
- Serve warm.

Yield: 6

FEATHERY FUDGE CAKE
1970

This picture of our daughter *Mary and me making the traditional Feathery Fudge Cake* was taken September 6, 1971. We were making the cake for Steve's birthday...two days later I was in the hospital with toxemia. Our second daughter, Janet, was born a month later as a tiny preemie weighing 2 ½ pounds.

THE TRADITION CONTINUES
2013

Every summer we retreat to our lake home in Littleton, NC. We are always fortunate to have our granddaughters, Thia and Avery, come to visit. Because *our birthdays are within weeks of each other*, we make the Feathery Fudge Cake together and create a birthday party. The year of this photo we celebrated my 70th, Thia's 10th and Avery's 9th birthday.

FEATHERY FUDGE CAKE
1970

I used this recipe for most of the family birthday cakes. On my granddaughter Thia's fourth birthday I made a hole in the center of the cake and placed a special Barbie doll into the hole. I then rounded the cake to resemble a large skirt. Thia still remembers it with much delight.

- ⅔ cup soft butter or margarine
- 1¾ cups sugar
- 2 eggs
- 2 teaspoons vanilla
- 2½ 1-ounce squares unsweetened chocolate, melted and cooled
- 2½ cups sifted cake flour
- 1¼ teaspoon baking soda
- ½ teaspoon salt
- 1¼ cups ice water

- Preheat oven to 350°.
- Spray two 9-inch round cakes with cooking spray and then line with waxed paper to fit.
- Sift the flour with the baking soda and salt and set aside.
- Cream butter, sugar, eggs and vanilla until fluffy (5 minutes on high speed), scraping bowl occasionally to guide batter into beaters.
- Blend in the chocolate.
- Add the sifted dry ingredients to the creamed mixture alternately with ice water.
- Beat after each addition.
- Distribute the batter evenly between the two prepared cake pans.
- Tap on the counter to remove air bubbles.
- Bake in center of oven for 30-35 minutes (Be sure pans do not touch each other).
- Cake is done when it shrinks slightly from sides of pan and it springs back when pressed lightly with finger and the cake tester comes out clean.
- Cool cake on racks for 5 minutes before removing from pan.
- Remove paper and cool completely. Frost with Chocolate Satin Frosting.

LITTLE MARY'S
CHOCOLATE CHIP COOKIES

1973

When our oldest daughter Mary was about 4 years old she followed me around the kitchen in Cranston, RI with a dishtowel over her shoulder ready to help her mommy. She loved making these cookies. She still loves them to this day. The recipe is from the bag of chocolate chips.

- 2¼ cups flour
- 1 teaspoon baking soda
- ½ teaspoon salt
- 2 sticks butter, softened or margarine
- ¾ cup sugar
- ¾ cup brown sugar, packed
- 1 teaspoon vanilla extract
- 2 eggs
- 12 ounces chocolate chips or white chocolate chips
- 1 cup chopped nuts (optional)

- Preheat oven to 375°
- Sift together flour, baking soda and salt
- Beat butter and sugars until creamy
- Add eggs and beat well
- Gradually add flour mixture, beating well
- Stir in chips and nuts
- Drop by teaspoons full on ungreased cookie sheet
- Bake 8-10 minutes until lightly browned
- Cool completely

Yield: 5 dozen

CHOCOLATE SATIN FROSTING
1970

This frosting is perfect for my feathery fudge cake. It is a fluffy, light-chocolate frosting when whipped by mixer. For a darker and glossier frosting, beat with a wooden spoon instead of the mixer.

- 3½ ounces unsweetened chocolate
- 3 cups sifted confectioners' sugar
- 4½ tablespoons hot water
- 1 egg
- ½ cup soft butter or margarine
- 1½ teaspoons vanilla

- Melt chocolate in microwave
- With electric mixer blend in sugar and water into chocolate
- Beat in egg, then butter and vanilla
- Frosting will be thin at this point, so place bowl in ice water
- Beat until of spreading consistency
- Brush off loose crumbs from cake and place bottom sides together with frosting
- Frosts tops and sides of two 9-inch cake layers

MACARONI AND CHEESE
Mary Chirico 1972

This recipe came from a very dear neighbor in Rhode Island who helped me through some tough times. She is now deceased and whenever I prepare this dish I think of her and her nurturing personality. Over the years I have altered the recipe to include at least three or four different cheeses. This is my granddaughters' favorite supper or lunch.

- 1 pound elbow or penne pasta cooked
- ½ stick unsalted butter
- 4 tablespoons flour
- 1 teaspoon salt
- 1 can evaporated milk
- 1 cup water
- 2-3 cups sharp cheddar cheese or a combination of cheeses of choice

- Preheat oven to 325°
- Grease a 9x13 casserole dish
- Cook pasta and drain, do not rinse

- Melt butter and add flour, cook until well blended for 1-2 minutes
- Stir in evaporated milk, salt and water*
- Bring to boil and add salt and pepper to taste
- Layer macaroni, cheese and sauce until all ingredients are used
- Slice a fresh tomato and overlap down the center of casserole
- Sprinkle top with freshly grated Parmigiano-Reggiano cheese
- Bake 30 minutes covered, then bake uncovered for 15 minutes

* If you prefer a creamier macaroni and cheese add more milk.

Serves: 6

MARY'S SICILIAN PIZZA
Mary Chirico 1972

Providence, RI is a city deeply rooted in the Italian culture. We lived in Cranston, which is part of the Providence metro area. Over 30% of Cranston's residents describe themselves as Italian American. We enjoyed the city's Italian restaurants and markets and often made Mary Chirico's Pizza.

1½ pounds bread dough (I find this in the bakery section of my super market)
1 can peeled tomatoes
Fresh or dried basil
Parmesan cheese
Olive oil

- Grease a 13x9x2 pan with olive oil
- Preheat oven to 375°
- With greased fingers pat the dough in pan making sure to come halfway up the sides of the pan
- Squeeze tomatoes onto top of dough until covered
- Sprinkle with oil and shredded fresh basil
- Sprinkle a goodly amount of Parmesan cheese (you can add Mozzarella cheese)
- Bake for 20 minutes or until done

SNICKERDOODLES
1973

This is my daughter Mary's favorite cookie. She reminded me to include it in this book.

- 1 cup shortening (part margarine or butter)
- 1½ cups sugar
- 2 eggs
- 2¾ cups flour
- 2 teaspoons cream of tartar
- 1 teaspoon baking soda
- ¼ teaspoon salt
- 2 tablespoons sugar
- 2 teaspoons cinnamon

- Heat oven to 400°
- Mix shortening, sugar and eggs thoroughly
- Blend flour, cream of tartar, soda and salt with a wire whisk
- Add the dry ingredients to the shortening mixture and mix well
- Shape dough into 1" balls
- Roll balls into mixture of 2 tablespoons sugar and cinnamon
- Place 2 " apart on ungreased baking sheet
- Bake 8-10 minutes

Yield: 6 dozen

These cookies puff up at first, and then flatten

BLENDER CHOCOLATE FROSTING
1970

- 1 cup sugar
- 4 ounces unsweetened chocolate melted
- 6 ounces can evaporated milk
- Dash salt

- Put sugar into blender and blend at high speed for one minute.
- Add chocolate, milk and salt.
- Blend at high speed for 3 minutes or until thick, using rubber spatula to scrape sides.
- Makes enough to cover tops of an 8-inch cake. Can chill frosted cake for a firmer frosting.

APPLE WALNUT SUPREME CAKE
1973

When the children were very little, my friend Susan and I had tea and sweets while our children played. We took turns going to each other's homes. This is one of Susan's best treats. She baked it in a rectangular pan. I make very large muffins using this recipe and give them away for gifts at Christmas.

- 4 cups coarsely chopped and peeled apples
- 1¾ cups sugar
- 2 eggs
- ½ cup oil
- 2 teaspoons vanilla extract
- 2 cups sifted flour
- 2 teaspoons baking soda
- 1 teaspoon salt
- 2 teaspoons cinnamon
- ½ cup chopped walnuts or to taste

- Preheat oven to 350°
- Grease and flour a 13x9x2 pan
- Combine apples and sugar; set aside
- In a small bowl whisk together the flour, baking soda, salt and cinnamon
- In a large mixing bowl, mix eggs, oil and vanilla
- Beat one minute on medium speed
- Add combined dry ingredients alternately with apple mixture
- Stir in walnuts
- Bake in prepared pan for 45-50 minutes
- Test with toothpick…do not under bake

LEMON GLAZE:

- 1 cup confectioner's sugar
- 1½ tablespoons lemon juice
- ½ teaspoon vanilla
- 1 tablespoon corn syrup

- Blend all ingredients
- Beat and spread over cake

CHERRY CHEESE PIE
1973

This simple pie resembles a cheesecake. My friend Nelda often made this pie when we visited her at their Maine farmhouse. When I began writing this book, I tried the recipe and was unhappy with the crust. Now I make this with my Pate Sucree sweet pastry to improve the quality of the crust. This dessert freezes well.

CRUST:

Pate Sucree (rich sweet pastry)

FILLING:

16	ounces of cream cheese
½	cup powdered sugar
2	tablespoons milk
⅓	cup chopped nuts
½	pint whipping cream (whipped with a bit of sugar)
	Can of cherry or strawberry pie filling

- Cream all together and put on cooled crust
- Cover filling with whipped cream
- Cover with pie filling (can use fresh fruit instead)

Serves: 8

PATE SUCREE

½	cup unsalted butter at room temperature
¼	cup sugar
1	large egg
1½	cups flour
	Pinch of salt
	Egg white, chocolate or warmed fruit jam for sealing crust

- Mix butter until creamy
- Add sugar and beat until fluffy
- Add egg gradually on low
- Add flour and salt
- Mix until it all comes together into a dough

- Put dough onto a piece of plastic wrap, shaping dough into a round about 6-8 inches in diameter
- Wrap and refrigerate for 25 minutes or put in freezer for 10 minutes
- At this point the dough can be stored in the refrigerator for a week or in freezer for up to one month
- Take out of refrigerator and press into your tart pan
- Freeze for 10 minutes
- Place tart pan onto a cookie sheet
- Prick bottom of crust lightly with fork
- Place in 400° oven and bake for 5 minutes
- Lower temperature to 350° and bake for 15 more minutes, or until firm and lightly browned
- Seal bottom and sides of crust with beaten egg white, chocolate or warmed jam to seal
- Place in oven to dry the egg whites just a minute or two
- Cool completely
- Remove from tart pan
- Fill as desired

TINY CHEESE CAKES
1971

A very simple dessert made in a blender or food processor.

16 ounces cream cheese
2 eggs
½ cup sugar
1 teaspoon vanilla (variation 1 tablespoon lime juice plus ½ teaspoon lime zest)
    Cookie mix: Crushed Butter cookies such as Vanilla Wafers mixed with 1 tablespoon sugar and ¼ cup melted butter (variation graham cracker crumbs)
1 (16-ounce) can of Cherry pie filling or fresh fruit of choice

- Preheat oven to 325°.
- Line muffin cups with paper liners or use mini cheesecake pan without liners.
- Beat first 4 ingredients in a blender or food processor (add eggs one at a time).
- Blend the cookie mix and line each tiny muffin cup. Press down with small pestle.
- Top with batter and bake for 15 minutes at 325°.
- Cool on rack, then refrigerate.
- Top with pie filling of your choice or a fresh raspberry or blueberry sprinkled with confectioners sugar.

PUMPKIN WALNUT CAKE
1970

My former sister-in-law, Jackie, gave me this recipe. When we visited Jackie her kitchen often smelled of this wonderful pumpkin cake.

- 3 cups sifted flour
- 2 teaspoons baking powder
- 2 teaspoons baking soda
- 1 teaspoon salt
- 3½ teaspoons cinnamon
- 4 large eggs
- 2 cups sugar
- 1½ cups canola oil
- 1 (16-ounce) can pumpkin (2 cups)
- 1 cup chopped walnuts
- Confectioners sugar for dusting top of cake

- Preheat oven to 350°
- On wax paper, sift together flour, baking powder, baking soda, salt and cinnamon
- In large bowl with electric beater on high beat the eggs
- Add sugar and beat thoroughly
- Add oil
- On low speed add the dry ingredients alternately with the pumpkin; beginning and ending with the dry ingredients
- Beat until smooth and stir in walnuts
- Turn into an ungreased Bundt or tub pan
- Bake at 350° for 1 hour and 10 minutes
- Place cake on wire rack and cool completely before removing from pan
- Sprinkle cake with confectioners sugar

CAPPUCCINO
1971

- 3 cups coffee
- 3 cups half and half
- 4 ounces (½ cup) dark crème de cacao
- 2 ounces (¼ cup) rum
- 2 ounces (¼ cup) brandy

Serves: 6-8

GRAHAM KERR'S
VEAL SCALLOPINE DON QUIXOTE
1970

This recipe is from Naples, Italy taken from the Don Quixote Restaurante. I adapted this recipe from Graham Kerr, a famous TV chef in the 70's. I enjoyed watching him and using his recipes.

4 thinly sliced veal scallopine
Flour for dusting cutlets
3 ounces diced carrots
4 chopped scallions
3 ounces mushrooms

Thinly sliced Italian ham or your choice of ham
Mozzarella cheese shredded or thinly sliced
Parchment paper

- Preheat oven to 500°
- Preheat fry pan
- Add a swirl of olive oil and a dab of unsalted butter
- Sauté the carrots, scallions and mushrooms
- Lightly season with salt and pepper and set aside
- Lightly dust cutlets with flour and just a bit of salt and pepper…remember the cheese and ham are salty
- Add a tablespoon of olive oil and sauté cutlets for about 3 minutes
- Place a cutlet on a piece of parchment paper
- Top with a slice of ham and cheese
- Top off with sauté vegetables
- Fold paper to form a package by crimping the edges
- Repeat for the remainder of packages
- Bake in oven for 5 minutes

Serves: 4

THE ART OF BREAD MAKING
1970-2000

The art of bread making is fun. We began making bread with the hand kneading method in 1970. Steve did all the kneading while I mixed and shaped the loaves. In 1973 Steve bought me a Kitchen Aid standing mixer with a

bread dough attachment. The mixer helped make so many loaves of bread and sweet breads that over time it needed repair. In 1999 I opened a Christmas package containing a bread machine. Now I make my bread with the touch of a button.

FRENCH BREAD
1971

This takes about 4 hours from start to finish, but well worth it. I took advantage of rainy days to make my breads.

- 2 pkgs. Dry yeast dissolved in ½ cup warm water (110°)
- 7–7½ cups sifted flour
- 1 tablespoon salt
- 2 cups lukewarm water
- Corn meal for baking sheets
- 1 egg white and 1 tablespoon water

- Combine salt and 2 cups lukewarm water.
- Beat in 2 cups flour.
- Blend in the softened yeast, then stir in 4 – 4 ½ cups of the flour or enough to make a soft dough.
- Turn out on lightly floured surface.
- Cover and let rest 10 minutes.
- Knead till smooth and elastic (5-8 minutes) working in remaining 1 cup of the flour.
- Place in lightly greased bowl, turning dough once.
- Cover and let rise till double (1½ hours).
- Punch down and let rise till double again (1 hour).
- Punch down, turn out on floured board and divide into 2 portions.
- Cover and let rest 10 minutes.
- Roll each portion into 15x12-inch rectangle.
- Roll tightly, beginning at long side, sealing well.
- Taper ends. Place each loaf diagonally, seam side down, on greased baking sheet that has been sprinkled with corn meal.
- With sharp knife, make slash marks on tops diagonally every 2½ inches about ¼ inch deep.
- Beat 1 egg white just until foamy and add 1 tablespoon water.
- Brush mixture over tops and sides of loaves.
- Cover with damp cloth, but do not let it touch loaves (drape over inverted tall glasses).
- Let double (1½ hours).
- Bake at 375° till light brown, about 20 minutes.
- Brush again with egg mixture.
- Bake about 20 minutes longer.
- Cool on wire racks.

Makes 2 loaves

WHITE BREAD
1970

Starting in 1970 Steve and I made lots of bread. I used this recipe frequently because it makes 6 loaves. I froze some of the loaves for later use.

- 2 cups milk
- ¾ cup sugar
- 8 teaspoons salt
- 1½ sticks butter or margarine (3/4 cup)
- 6 cups warm water (105-115 F)
- 4 packages Fleischman's Active dry Yeast
- 24 cups unsifted flour (about)

- Scald milk; stir in sugar, salt and margarine
- Cool to lukewarm
- Measure warm water into large warm bowl
- Sprinkle in yeast and stir until dissolved
- Add lukewarm milk mixture and 12 cups flour; beat until smooth
- Add enough additional flour to make a stiff dough
- Turn out onto lightly floured board and knead until smooth and elastic about 10-12 minutes
- Place in greased bowl, turning to grease top
- Cover, let rise in a warm place that is free from drafts, until doubled in bulk, about 1 hour
- Punch dough down, cover, let rest 15 minutes
- Divide dough into 6 equal pieces
- Roll each piece to a 14x9- inch rectangle
- Shape into loaves
- Place in 6 greased loaf pans
- Cover and let rise in warm place until doubled in bulk, about 1½ hours
- Bake at 400° for 30 minutes, or until done
- Remove from pans and cool on wire racks

Yield: 6 loaves

Half recipe makes about 4 loaves

MY ITALIAN BREAD
1975

I began making this bread frequently out of pure necessity. I cannot serve spaghetti without freshly baked Italian breads. In the mid 70's and throughout the 80's it was unheard of to find such bread in the supermarkets of the small Southern towns where we lived.

7¼ cups to 7¾ cups flour
2 pkgs. Dry yeast
1 tablespoon salt

Yellow corn meal
1 slightly beaten egg white

- In large bowl, soften yeast in warm (110°) water.
- Stir in 2 cups flour and beat well.
- Add the salt to 4½ cups of flour and mix well.
- Add this salted flour to the flour and yeast mixture mixing well.
- Turn out onto lightly floured board, cover and let rest 10 minutes.
- Knead for 15-20 minutes until smooth and very elastic, kneading in remaining ¾ cups to 1¼ cups flour.
- Place dough in lightly greased bowl, turning once to grease surface.
- Cover and let rise in warm place till double (1½ hours).
- Punch down and let rise again till double about 1 hour.
- Turn out on lightly floured surface.
- Divide in half and form each part into a ball.
- Cover with a kitchen towel and let dough rest for 10 minutes.
- Roll each half of dough into 15x8 rectangles. Beginning at long end, roll up tightly, sealing well.
- Taper ends, place each loaf diagonally, seam side down on a baking sheet that is sprinkled with corn meal (gives bread a crunchy bottom).
- Brush top and sides with egg wash.
- Cover with a damp towel that is not touching the dough and let rise in warm place until double (1-1½ hours).
- Place large shallow pan filled with boiling water on lowest rack of oven. This will make the crust crispier.
- With sharp knife gently make crosswise cuts ½ inch deep down center of loaf.
- Bake in oven at 375° until light brown about 20 minutes; brush again with egg wash.
- Bake another 20 minutes.
- Cool on wire rack.

Makes 2 loaves of bread or 6 rolls

APRICOT DAISY COFFEECAKE
1983

I have made this sweet bread many times in the 80's and 90's. It makes an impressive presentation and adds a nice touch to holiday breakfasts.

- 1 pkg. dry yeast
- ¼ cup water (110°)
- ½ cup scalded milk
- ¼ cup butter
- 2 tablespoons sugar
- 1 teaspoon salt
- 3- 3-½ cups sifted flour (I sift using a wire whisk before measuring)
- 2 beaten eggs

Finish with: confectioner's sugar, 1½ tablespoons milk, vanilla, and apricot jam.

- Soften yeast in warm water
- Combine milk, butter, sugar and salt, cool to lukewarm
- Add 1 cup of the flour and beat well
- Stir in softened yeast and the beaten eggs
- Add enough flour to make a moderately stiff dough
- Turn onto lightly floured surface and knead till smooth and satiny, 8-10 minutes

SHAPE AS FOLLOWS:

- On lightly floured surface or greased baking sheet, roll dough to a 14-inch circle.
- Place a glass in the center of the circle, cut the circle from the edge of the glass into 4 sections. Cut each section in 5 strips (20 in all).
- Take 2 strips that are side by side and crisscross these together; pinch the ends to seal; continue around the circle.
- Remove the glass from the center; coil one of the crisscrossed pairs loosely in a circle and place in the spot where the glass was. This forms the center daisy.
- Bring each of remaining sets up loosely around center coil to form daisies; when finished it will resemble a bouquet of daises (10 in all).
- Let the bouquet of daisies rise in warm place until almost double (about 45 minutes).
- Bake in oven at 375° for 25 minutes or until golden.
- While still warm from the oven, spoon 1 teaspoon of apricot jam into the center of each daisy.
- Drizzle coffeecake with confectioners icing:
    - Confectioner's sugar, 1½ tablespoons milk and ½ teaspoon vanilla
    - Beat until smooth

CRACKED WHEAT BREAD
Bread machine method
1999

After many years of making bread, I received a bread machine for Christmas. I have been making this bread ever since. It is very nutritious and toasts well for breakfast.

- 6 tablespoons cracked wheat
- 1⅛ –1½ cups water (80°)
- 6 tablespoons olive oil
- ¼ cup sugar
- 1½ teaspoons salt
- 2½ cups bread flour
- 1⅓ cups whole-wheat flour
- 4 teaspoons gluten (optional)
- 2½ teaspoons Red Star active dry yeast

- Place cracked wheat and the water in the bread machine, using the least amount of water in the recipe
- Allow to soften for 30 minutes
- Blend all the dry ingredients except the yeast with a wire whisk
- Add the oil to the bread machine pan; then the dry ingredients
- Make an indention in the middle of the dry ingredients and put the yeast into the indentation
- Select Light crust setting, whole wheat cycle, and large size loaf
- Press start
- After the baking cycle ends, remove bread from pan, place on wire rack and allow to cool 1 hour before slicing

Yield: one large loaf

CHEESE BREAD
1975

7-8 cups flour	*(4 cups)
⅓ cup sugar	*(8 teaspoons)
1 tablespoon salt	*(1½ teaspoons)
2 pkgs. Dry yeast	*(1½ teaspoons)
2 cups water	*(1 cup)
⅔ cup milk	*(⅓ cup)
3 cups shredded sharp cheddar cheese	*(1½ cups)

Melted butter for brushing tops of loaves

- Mix 2½ cups flour, sugar, salt and yeast
- Combine water and milk; heat until 120°
- Gradually add the milk to dry ingredients and beat 2 minutes
- Add cheese and ½ cup flour; beat 2 more minutes
- Stir in enough additional flour to make a stiff dough
- Turn out onto lightly floured board
- Knead until elastic 8-10 minutes)
- Place in greased bowl, turning to grease the top
- Cover and let rise for about 1 hour
- **Punch dough down**; turn onto floured board and cover for 15 minutes
- Divide dough in half, roll each half into a 14x9 inch rectangle
- Shape into loaves
- Place loaves into greased bread pans
- Let proof for about 1 hour
- Bake on lowest rack at 375° for about 40 minutes
- Remove from pans and cool on wire racks
- Brush tops with melted butter

Makes 2 loaves

BREAD MACHINE METHOD: * CUT RECIPE IN HALF AND PROCEED *

- Water and milk need only be about 78°
- Put water and milk in bread machine
- Mix together with wire whisk: 4 cups of flour, 1½ teaspoons salt, 1½ cups cheese (cheese must be at room temperature), and 8 teaspoons sugar
- Place dry ingredients in bread pan on top of the liquid
- Make a shallow hole on top of the flour and place 1½ teaspoons yeast in the hole
- Turn bread machine on #6 or dough cycle
- When done; proceed from the PUNCH DOWN and follow directions to the end

Makes 1 loaf

HONEY WHOLE WHEAT BREAD
BREAD MACHINE METHOD
1999

Breads made with 100% whole-wheat flour tend to be very dry, but this recipe makes a very moist and rich bread.

1⅛ cups water 70-80°
3 cups whole wheat four
3/8 cups gluten
¼ cup honey

1¼ teaspoons salt
1½ tablespoons butter
1½ teaspoons active dry yeast

- Pour water into bread pan
- Add the honey and butter to the bread pan
- Whisk together the flour, salt and gluten
- Add to bread pan
- Hollow out the center of the flour and place the yeast in center of hole
- Plug in the machine
- Select the whole wheat mode and 1.5 loaf size (small loaf)
- Start the machine
- When done turn out on rack

Makes one small loaf

ITALIAN BREAD STICKS
1972

1 pkg. active dry yeast
¾ cup water
1 tablespoon sugar
1½ teaspoons salt
2 tablespoons olive oil
2¼-2½ cups sifted flour
1 slightly beaten egg white with 1 tablespoon water

- Dissolve yeast in warm water (110°)
- Stir in sugar, salt, oil
- Add flour to make a soft dough
- Turn dough out on floured board; cover and let rest 10 minutes
- Knead for about 5-8 minutes
- Place dough in greased bowl, turning once to coat
- Cover and let rise for 1½ hours – 2 hours
- **PUNCH DOWN**; cover tightly and refrigerate at least 4 hours or overnight
- Turn out on floured board and divide into 12 equal parts
- Roll each piece with your hands to form a pencil strand
- Smooth each strand as you work
- Place 2 inches apart on a greased baking sheet
- Brush with egg wash
- Let rise uncovered for about 45-60 minutes
- Brush again with egg and sprinkle with coarse salt if desired
- Place large shallow pan on lower rack and fill with boiling water
- Place baking sheet on center rack
- Bake in hot oven 425° for 12-15 minutes

BREAD MACHINE METHOD:

- Mix sugar, salt and flour
- Make sure water is around 78° for best results
- Put water and oil in bottom of bread pan; add flour
- Make a small hole in flour and put yeast into the hole
- Turn bread machine on #6 or dough cycle
- When done; proceed from the **PUNCH DOWN** directions to end

Makes 12-15 sticks

PAN ROLLS
1970

I met my California-born friend, Nelda, while living in Cranston, Rhode Island. On weekends we drove to her restored farmhouse in Paris, Maine. It was a relaxing time for us as we enjoyed the beautiful outdoors and watched our children play in the fields. Nelda made these rolls and served them hot for breakfast with jam and freshly picked raspberries.

1¾ cups warm water	5½-6 cups flour
2 packages dry yeast	1 egg
½ cup sugar	¼ cup butter
1 tablespoon salt	

- Dissolve yeast in 110° water
- Add sugar, salt and half the flour
- Beat for 2 minutes
- Add egg and butter and mix again
- Mix in the rest of the flour with hands or spoon until dough is easy to handle
- Grease a bowl, put dough in bowl and turn so dough is greased on top
- Cover tightly
- Refrigerate at least 2 hours (use dough within 3-5 days) punching down every day and also before using
- Two hours before serving, grease a pan
- Punch down dough
- Shape the dough into 24 balls placed close together in the pan
- Let rise 1½ hours
- Preheat oven to 400°
- When not quite double, sprinkle the rolls with flour
- Bake for 12-15 minutes

Makes two dozen rolls

HOT CROSS BUNS
1971

I made these beautiful buns for many Easters in the 70's and 80's.

- 1 package dry yeast
- ¼ cup water warmed to 110°
- 1 cup milk warmed to 110°
- 6 tablespoons butter melted
- ⅓ cup sugar
- 1 teaspoon salt
- 1 beaten egg

- 3½-4 cups of flour
- ¼ cup wheat germ
- 1 cup raisins
- 2 teaspoons lemon zest
- 2 teaspoons vegetable oil
- 1 egg yolk

ICING:

- 4 tablespoons water
- 1¼ cups confectioner's sugar

- In a large bowl stir together half the flour, the undissolved yeast, the sugar and the salt
- Add the warm liquid ingredients and 4 tablespoons melted butter
- Beat with mixer
- Add the wheat germ, raisins, lemon zest and remaining flour to make a stiff dough
- Scrape down side of bowl and sprinkle the surface of the dough with oil
- Cover and refrigerate overnight
- The next day punch down and shape into a ball
- Cover and let rise for 1½ hours
- Punch down and turn onto floured board and divide the dough into 24 pieces
- Preheat oven to 400°
- Grease three 8-inch baking pans
- Shape each piece into a ball and place about 1 inch apart onto the three greased 8 inch baking pans
- Brush with remaining melted butter
- Bake 20 minutes at 400°
- Remove and cool
- Combine confectioners sugar with 2 tablespoons water
- Use the icing to decorate each bun with a cross

SALLY LUNN BREAD
1983

This recipe comes from the Bake Shop of the Raleigh Tavern in Williamsburg, VA.

- 1 yeast cake or 1 pkg. dry yeast
- 1 cup warm milk (110° for dry yeast, 85° for yeast cake)
- ½ cup butter, softened
- ⅓ cup of sugar
- 3 beaten eggs
- 4 cups flour
- 1½ teaspoons salt

- Put yeast in warm milk (110°) to dissolve
- Cream together butter, sugar and salt
- Add the eggs and mix well
- Sift in 4 cups flour alternately with the milk and yeast
- Stir well and do not knead
- Pour into a well-greased bowl, turning once to grease the top
- Cover and let rise in warm place until doubled (1 hour)
- Punch dough down
- Spoon into a greased and floured 10-inch tube pan
- Cover and let rise until doubled 1 hour
- Bake in 400° oven for about 25-30 minutes, serve with honey butter

GAINESVILLE, GEORGIA
1973-1975

Once again the moving company arrived at our home to pack up my wooden spoons and my recipes.

Steve and I returned to the Peachtree state of Georgia with a family. It became an opportunity to gather some recipes from my Texan neighbor as well as my true Southern friends. Gainesville is 30 minutes from the perimeter of Atlanta. Our favorite restaurants in Atlanta back in the 70's were Pitty Pat's Porch and the Magic Pan Crepe Bistro. The Bistro served many different soups with tiny muffins that I replicated at home.

CORNBREAD STICKS
OR MUFFINS
1973

You can also pour the batter into a greased and preheated cast iron skillet.

- ¾ cup flour
- 3 teaspoons baking powder
- 2 tablespoons sugar
- ¾ teaspoon salt
- ¾ cup yellow or white corn meal
- 1 egg
- 1 cup milk
- ¼ cup melted butter or oil

ALTERNATE VERSION

- 1 cup buttermilk
- 1½ teaspoons baking powder
- 1 teaspoon baking soda

- Preheat oven to 425°.
- Spray 2 cast iron corn stick pans with PAM cooking spray. Can use muffin pans.
- If using cast iron corn stick pans or a cast iron skillet, preheat the pans until hot.
- Sift flour, measure the flour and then resift 4 times with the next 4 ingredients: baking powder, (baking soda with the buttermilk version) sugar, salt, and corn meal.
- Measure milk or buttermilk, add beaten egg and oil, then mix well.
- Pour all at once into the center of the dry ingredients.
- Stir quickly until dry ingredients are just dampened—then stir 3-4 more times.
- Batter should **not** be smooth.
- Spoon quickly into greased **hot** corn stick pans (fill ⅔ full).
- Bake about 18-20 minutes or until brown.
- Serve immediately.

Makes 14 corn sticks and muffins or one 8" cast iron skillet

PEACH COBBLER
1973

My dear friend Suzanne Burris gave me this recipe when we lived in Gainesville, Georgia. Her southern Texas cooking intrigued me.

5-6 fresh peaches, peeled, sliced and sugared; set aside

Melt one stick of margarine or butter in 9x13 Pyrex casserole dish

In small bowl mix together

- 1 cup sugar
- 1 cup flour
- 1 cup milk
- 1 teaspoon vanilla
- ½-¾ teaspoon baking powder

*If using self-rising flour omit the baking powder

- Preheat oven to 350°
- Pour the flour/milk mixture over the top of the melted butter—DO NOT STIR
- Next spread the sugared fruit (about 2 cups) on top of flour/milk mixture
- Bake at 350° for 45 minutes

FRESH PEACH COBBLER
2008

My peach cobbler from 1973 is delicious...made the old Southern way. This cobbler is definitely superior.

FILLING:

- 2½ pounds ripe but firm peaches (6-7)
- ¼ cup sugar
- 1 teaspoon cornstarch
- 1 tablespoon juice from one lemon
- Pinch salt

BISCUIT TOPPING:

- 1 cup flour
- 3 tablespoons plus 1 teaspoon sugar
- ¾ teaspoon baking powder
- ¼ teaspoon baking soda
- ¼ teaspoon salt
- 5 tablespoons cold unsalted butter, cut into cubes
- ⅓ cup whole milk yogurt

- Adjust oven rack to lower middle position and preheat to 425°.
- Spray an 8-inch square pan with PAM cooking spray.
- For the **filling:** peel peaches and cut in half.
- Using a small spoon, scoop out and discard pit. Cut each half into 4 wedges.
- Gently toss the peaches with sugar in a large bowl and let stand for 30 minutes, tossing several times.
- Drain peaches into a colander and set over a large bowl.
- Whisk ¼ cup of the drained peach juice (discard the rest) with cornstarch, lemon juice and salt.
- Toss peach juice mixture with peach slices and transfer to an 8-inch square baking dish.
- Bake until peaches begin to bubble around edges about 10 minutes.
- For the **topping**: while the peaches are baking, put flour, 3 tablespoons sugar, baking soda, baking powder and salt into food processor then pulse a few times to mix.
- Scatter the butter over and pulse until the mixture resembles coarse meal, about ten pulses or so.
- Transfer to medium bowl and add yogurt and toss with rubber spatula until cohesive dough is formed. Do not over mix dough or biscuits will be tough.
- Break dough into 6 roughly shaped mounds.
- After peaches are baked, remove from oven and place dough mounds on top.
- Sprinkle mounds with the 1 teaspoon cinnamon sugar.
- Bake until topping is golden brown and fruit is bubbling (16-18 minutes).
- Cool cobbler on wire rack.

Serves: 6

VARIATION: BLUEBERRY-PEACH COBBLER WITH LEMON CORNMEAL BISCUIT TOPPING:

Follow above recipe using 5-6 peaches and 1 cup fresh blueberries. In biscuit topping substitute 2 T. cornmeal for the flour and add ½ t. grated lemon zest in food processor along with the dry ingredients.

VERMONT BEER CHEESE SOUP
1978

- 3 tablespoons butter
- ½ cup chopped onion
- ½ teasoon minced garlic
- 1 teaspoon Worcestershire Sauce
- 12 ounces beer of choice
- 14 ounces chicken broth or stock
- 4 tablespoons cornstarch
- 1 cup half and half
- 3 cups shredded sharp cheddar cheese
- Salt if needed

- Sauté butter, onion, garlic and Worcestershire sauce
- Add beer and boil for 3 minutes to remove alcohol
- Make a slurry with cornstarch and the broth
- Add slurry to the beer mixture and boil again
- Blend well with an immersion blender
- Slowly add the half and half and cheese
- Cook slowly until all cheese is fully melted and soup is thick

SHERRIED ROCKY ROAD PUDDING
1975

Children love chocolate pudding. My daughters loved this simple pudding recipe. They loved all desserts, but I would try to concentrate on making desserts with a milk base to add to their nutrition value.

- 1 package chocolate pudding
- 1½ cups milk
- ¼ cup sherry (or less) Optional
- 1 cup marshmallow pieces
- ½ cup chopped walnuts
- ½ cup heavy cream whipped

- Combine pudding mix with milk and sherry
- Cook stirring until thickened
- Stir in marshmallow pieces, nuts and whipped cream
- Spoon into dessert glasses
- Chill
- Garnish with more whipped cream and chocolate chips

Serves: 6

SUZANNE'S
CHEESE ENCHILADAS
1973

My Texas friend, Suzanne Burris, shared this recipe with me. It became a family favorite and my first experience preparing Southwestern food.

- 1 package of corn tortillas
- 16 ounces shredded sharp cheddar cheese
- 1 large onion chopped
- 3 tablespoons butter or oil
- 3 tablespoons flour
- 2 tablespoons chili powder or as desired
- 1 clove minced garlic
- 1 (8-ounce) can tomato sauce
- ¾ cup water
- ½ cup milk
- ½ teaspoon salt

- Preheat oven to 350°.
- Spray one 9x13" oblong Pyrex dish with PAM cooking spray.
- In a saucepan melt 3 tablespoons butter or oil.
- Add 3 tablespoons flour and mix well (roux).
- Add 2 tablespoons chili powder, garlic, tomato sauce, water, milk and salt.
- Cook over medium heat stirring constantly until thick. If it is too thick, thin with more water.
- Lower the heat and cook for 15 minutes. Set aside.
- Grate 16 ounces cheddar cheese.
- Chop 1 large onion.
- Heat oil and quickly fry the tortillas one at a time (until lightly crisp).
- Dip the tortilla into the sauce and place in a 13x9 baking dish.
- Put small amount of cheese and onion in the middle of the tortilla and roll up tightly.
- Place tortilla on bottom of dish, seam side down.
- Continue dipping, filling and rolling all of the tortillas making sure they are placed close together in the pan but not on top of each other.
- Spoon the remaining sauce and cheese over the tortillas.
- Cover with foil and bake for 25 minutes at 350°.

Serve with crispy tortilla chips and a salad.

Serves: 4

SUZANNE'S
CHOCOLATE CAKE
1973

This cake is very moist.

- 1 stick butter or margarine melted
- 4 tablespoons cocoa
- ½ cup vegetable or canola oil
- 1 cup water
- ½ cup buttermilk
- 1 teaspoon vanilla

- 2 cups sugar
- 2 cups flour
- 1 teaspoon soda
- 1 teaspoon salt
- 2 eggs

- Preheat oven to 350° for metal pans or 325° for glass pans
- Grease pan with PAM, line with waxed paper, spray paper with PAM
- Mix together the butter, cocoa, oil, water, buttermilk and vanilla
- In another bowl whisk together the sugar, flour, soda, and salt
- Pour the wet mixture over the dry mixture and mix well with beater
- Add the eggs
- Pour into either a 9x13x2 inch pan or two 8-inch round pans
- Bake for 30-35 minutes
- Cool upside down on racks
- When cool remove pan and peel off paper

CHOCOLATE FROSTING

- 1 stick butter or margarine
- 6 tablespoons milk
- 6 tablespoons cocoa

- 1 box powdered sugar
- 1 teaspoon vanilla

- Heat the butter, cocoa and milk until bubbly
- Remove from the heat and add the sugar and vanilla
- Mix well and frost cake

RUM BALLS
1975

Christmas is a very special time at our home. It is a time for extensive baking and preparing food gifts for neighbors and work friends. Every year Steve and I prepared crocks of cheese for friends and neighbors, and I prepared a huge tray of assorted Italian cookies for his office. These rum balls were always a hit among his fellow workers.

1 cup crushed vanilla wafers *
1 cup confectioners' sugar
1½ cups chopped pecans
2 tablespoons cocoa

2 tablespoons light corn syrup
¼ cup dark rum or bourbon
¼ cup fine granulated sugar

- Combine wafer crumbs with sugar
- Add pecans and cocoa
- Add corn syrup and liquor
- Mix well
- Shape into one-inch balls
- Roll half in granulated sugar and remainder in ½ cup finely chopped nuts

* one box of vanilla wafers yields 3 times the recipe

Yield: 2 dozen

MOCHA TRUFFLES
1975

These chocolate truffles are presented each Christmas beside my assorted cookie tray.

12 ounces (2 cups) semisweet chocolate (use a high quality chocolate)
½ cup coffee-flavored liqueur (Kahlua or Tia Maria)
4 large egg yolks, at room temperature
½ cup unsweetened cocoa powder
½ cup finely chopped nuts (optional)

- Melt chocolate in the microwave then stir until it is completely melted
- In a 2-cup glass measuring cup, heat the coffee-flavored liqueur in the microwave on high power for 1-2 minutes until it comes to a simmer
- Remove the container from the microwave
- In large bowl, using a hand-held electric mixer on medium-high speed, beat the yolks for 2 minutes, until the mixture forms a thick yellow ribbon
- Continue to beat the yolks while very slowly adding the hot liqueur
- At low speed, beat in the melted chocolate and continue mixing for 30 seconds until smooth
- Cover the surface with plastic wrap and refrigerate for 1½ hours, or until firm
- Place the cocoa in a shallow bowl (you can use finely chopped nuts for a variety)
- Using a melon baller or teaspoon, scoop the truffle mixture and roll it into irregularly-shaped 1-inch balls
- Roll each truffle in the cocoa or in the nuts or a combination of both
- Store in an airtight container in the refrigerator for up to 2 weeks

Yield: 3 ½ dozen

BROCCOLI SOUP
1974

While shopping at Lenox Square in Atlanta I frequently had lunch with friends at the Magic Pan Bistro. My favorite lunch order was one of their wonderful homemade soups that were served with an assortment of miniature muffins.

4 tablespoons butter	3 tablespoons flour
4 cups chopped fresh broccoli	Salt and pepper
4 cups chicken stock	½ cup cream
1 large onion, quartered	Lemon slices for garnish
1 garlic clove, halved	

- Melt butter and add broccoli, onion, salt and pepper
- Sauté for about 6 minutes
- Add flour and cook another minute
- Add stock and bring to a boil
- Simmer uncovered for about 15 minutes or until broccoli is soft
- Pour in cream
- Puree mixture until smooth in food processor or hand held immersion blender
- Return to pan and add the seasonings
- Heat through
- Serve with homemade croutons or bran raisin muffins

Variation: add 1¼ cups medium sharp cheddar cheese

CROUTONS:

Day old French bread cubed	Salt and pepper
Olive oil	¼ teaspoon pepper flakes

- Preheat oven to 400°
- Toss all together in bowl
- Spread on cookie sheet
- Bake for 15 minutes

ICED CUCUMBER SOUP
1977

4 seedless, burpless cucumbers
2 shallots
7 cups chicken stock
¼ cup butter

2 tablespoons flour
Salt and pepper
Few drops of green coloring

LIAISON

3 egg yolks
½ cup heavy cream

GARNISH

¼ cup cream
1 tablespoon mint or chives

- Peel cucumbers and cut into ½-inch slices
- Combine cucumbers, onions and chicken stock
- Simmer 15-20 minutes or until soft
- Puree the mixture with an immersion blender or food processor
- In pan melt butter, stir in flour while whisking until bubbly
- Season and simmer 2-3 minutes
- Mix egg yolks and cream in bowl
- Add a little hot soup to this liaison (yolks and cream) and stir back gently into the soup until the mixture thickens slightly, but DO NOT BOIL
- Color soup with green food coloring to your liking and chill covered with plastic wrap touching the soup to prevent a skin from forming
- Whip the cream until it holds a soft shape
- Serve the soup in chilled bowls and gently stir in a spoonful of the whipped cream
- Garnish with mint or chives
- Can also be served hot

Serves: 4-6

BROCCOLI CASSEROLE
1973

I have several broccoli casseroles. This one has a bit of a twist in taste with the crumbled blue cheese.

- 2 tablespoons butter
- 2 tablespoons flour
- 3 ounces softened cream cheese
- ¼ cup crumbled blue cheese
- ½ teaspoon salt
- 1 cup milk or sour cream
- 2 (10-ounce) packages frozen chopped broccoli, cooked and drained
- ⅓ cup rich round crackers, crushed (I use cheddar cheese goldfish crackers)

- Preheat oven to 350°
- Grease a 1 quart casserole dish
- In a saucepan, melt butter
- Blend in flour and cheeses
- Add milk or sour cream and cook stirring until mixture boils
- Stir in broccoli
- Put into prepared casserole
- Top with cracker crumbs
- Bake for 30 minutes

Serves: 8

BROCCOLI SUPREME CASSEROLE
1974

This vegetable casserole has a stuffing mix that makes it a rich side dish.

- 1 10-ounce package frozen chopped broccoli
- 1 can cream of chicken soup
- 1 tablespoon flour or as needed
- ½ cup sour cream
- ¼ cup grated carrots
- 1 tablespoon grated onion
- ¼ teaspoon salt
- Pinch of fresh pepper
- ¾ cup herb-seasoned stuffing mix
- 2 tablespoons melted butter

- Preheat oven to 350°
- Grease a 2-quart casserole dish
- Cook broccoli
- Blend together the soup and the flour
- Add sour cream, carrot, onion, salt and pepper
- Stir in cooked broccoli
- Turn into a 2-quart casserole
- Combine stuffing mix with butter
- Sprinkle around edge of dish
- Bake 30-35 minutes

Serves: 6

NIEMAN-MARCUS
$250 CHOCOLATE CHIP COOKIES
1978

A wonderful bistro located at Niemen Marcus in Lenox Square Atlanta served these wonderful cookies. The urban legend that has survived for over 50 years is that the recipe was sold to a customer for $250. In 2001 I found the recipe online supposedly submitted by the customer who purchased it back in the 70's.

2 cups butter	1 teaspoon salt
4 cups flour	1 8-ounce Hershey bar (grated)
2 teaspoons baking soda	4 eggs
2 cups sugar	2 teaspoons baking powder
5 cups blended oatmeal	2 teaspoons vanilla
24 ounces chocolate chips	3 cups chopped nuts
2 cups brown sugar	

- Preheat oven to 375°
- Measure oatmeal and blend in a blender to a fine powder
- Cream butter and both sugars (white and brown)
- Add eggs and vanilla
- Mix together in a small bowl the flour, oatmeal, salt, baking powder and baking soda
- Mix the dry ingredients into the wet ingredient mixture
- Add chocolate chips, Hershey bar and nuts
- Roll into balls and place two inches apart on a cookie sheet
- Bake 10 minutes

Makes 112 cookies

This recipe can be cut in half

BLUEBERRY MUFFINS
1975

This is an old recipe that my daughters loved growing up. Today my granddaughter Avery is the biggest fan of these muffins. I make her a special batch every time she visits.

These muffins were also part of my centerpiece for my Rocky Mount coffees back in the 80's.

3 cups all-purpose flour	1 cup milk	1 teaspoon vanilla extract
1¼ cups sugar	2 cups fresh blueberries	½-1 teaspoon lemon zest
4 teaspoons baking powder	½ cup oil	
1 teaspoon salt	2 eggs	

- Preheat oven to 375°.
- Whisk together the flour, sugar, baking powder and salt in a bowl.
- In another bowl mix the milk, oil, vanilla and eggs.
- Make a well in the center of the dry ingredients and pour the liquid mixture into the well.
- Stir until blended. Do not over mix.
- Fold in blueberries.
- Spoon batter into well-greased muffin tins or paper lined muffin tins.
- Bake at 375° for 30 minutes or until toothpick inserted comes out clean.

Yield: 2 dozen

DOUBLE CHOCOLATE CHIP MUFFINS
2012

It is important to satisfy grandchildren. **I came up with this recipe for Thia** *who does not enjoy the blueberry breakfast muffins that her sister loves.*

- 2 eggs
- ½ cup oil
- 1 cup milk
- 1 teaspoon vanilla
- 1¾ cup flour
- ½ cup sugar
- ¼ cup cocoa
- 1 tablespoon baking powder
- ½ teaspoon salt
- ½ cup semi-sweet chocolate chips
- Extra chocolate chips for top

- Preheat oven to 400°
- Mix eggs, oil, milk and vanilla in small bowl
- Mix flour, sugar, cocoa, baking powder, salt and chocolate chips
- Combine wet ingredients with dry and fold together gently until just mixed
- Spoon into prepared cupcake tins and sprinkle with extra chocolate chips
- Bake for 20 minutes, remove and cool on rack

Yield: 18 muffins

YOGURT BLUEBERRY MUFFINS
2014

I baked this version of blueberry muffins for little Avery and she absolutely loved them. This recipe may take the place of the 1975 muffins as a favorite. It is very moist and the blueberries on top add a nice presentation.

- 3 cups minus 2 tablespoons flour
- 1 teaspoon baking soda
- 2 teaspoons baking powder
- ¼ teaspoon salt
- 1 cup sugar
- ½ cup vegetable oil
- 1 egg
- lemon zest
- 1 cup plain unflavored yogurt (I only had blueberry yogurt and the muffins came out wonderful and were actually blue)
- 2 cups fresh blueberries (reserve ½ cup for top of muffins)
- 1 teaspoon vanilla extract
- Raw sugar for sprinkling on top of muffins

- Preheat oven to 375°
- Line muffin pans with paper cups or spray with PAM
- Sift or whisk flour, baking soda, baking powder and salt and set aside
- Whisk together sugar, oil, vanilla, egg and yogurt in a bowl
- Add the dry ingredients and stir just until blended…do not over stir
- Add the blueberries and stir about 3 times to blend
- Spoon mixture into prepared muffin pans
- Sprinkle remaining berries on top and press down a bit
- Sprinkle raw sugar over the top
- Bake for 20-25 minutes
- Place muffins on cooling rack and cool completely
- Serve warm or freeze for a later time

Yield: 18 muffins

ROCKY MOUNT, NC
THE LEAN YEARS
1975 – 1980

In 1980 my wooden spoons went North to a tiny town in eastern North Carolina.

Moving to North Carolina turned out to be the area where we raised our children and lived for just over 20 years. My cooking experiences grew tremendously. I learned quickly the art of making casseroles so that I could inexpensively feed

our little family. It was the era of the crock-pot meals. Many of our family suppers were created in the crock-pot before I took off for work in the morning. Now, of course, the old-fashioned crock-pot has turned into the sophisticated slow cooker, but the process is the same and enjoyed by many working moms.

In 1977 I started a gourmet group. We ladies sought out recipes and developed very classy menus.

In the mid 80's through the late 90's I organized many ladies coffees and dinner parties.

BAKED ARTICHOKE SPREAD
1976

I acquired this recipe from my neighbor Mary Frances in Rocky Mount, NC.

- ¾ cup mayonnaise
- ¾ cup grated Parmesan cheese
- ½ teaspoon garlic powder (optional)
- 1 (14-ounce) can artichoke hearts, drained
- ¼ cup Parmesan cheese for final topping

- Preheat oven to 350°
- Place the above ingredients in the food processor and puree
- Put into a greased small casserole dish
- Sprinkle with additional Parmesan cheese
- Bake for 15 minutes
- Spread on toasted crostini or crackers

You can broil for a few minutes at the end if the top is not browned

HOT CHICKEN SALAD
1975

- 2 cups cubed cooked chicken
- 2 cups thinly sliced celery
- 2 cups croutons
- 1 cup mayonnaise
- ½ cup slivered almonds, toasted
- 2 tablespoons fresh lemon juice
- 2 teaspoons instant minced onion or mince one small shallot
- ½ teaspoon salt
- ½ cup shredded cheddar or Swiss cheese

- Preheat oven to 450°
- Prepare six 1-cup baking dishes with PAM spray
- Mix all ingredients except 1 cup of the croutons and the cheese
- Spoon into six 1-cup baking dishes
- Sprinkle with remaining croutons and the cheese
- Bake 10-15 minutes or until bubbly

Yield: 4-6

You can use fewer croutons. I cut the croutons into tiny bits. Adding some milk or sour cream gives it a creamier texture.

HAM AND SCALLOPED POTATOES
SAUCE METHOD
1975

I have two methods for making this casserole dish. My daughters loved both the sauce and the layered method. When I used the cream of mushroom soup instead of the homemade sauce they noticed no difference.

2 pounds potatoes (about 6 medium)
3 tablespoons butter
3 tablespoons flour
Salt and pepper
2½ cups milk

¼ cup finely chopped onion or onion slices
1 tablespoon butter
1½ cups cubed cooked ham or ½ pound sliced cooked ham
Cheddar cheese

- Heat oven to 375°
- Peel and wash potatoes
- Cut potatoes into thin slices to measure about 4 cups or use sliced parboiled potatoes in produce section of your grocery store
- Melt 3 tablespoons butter and blend in flour and seasonings
- Cook over low heat; stirring until mixture is smooth and bubbly
- Remove from heat and stir in milk **
- Heat to boiling, stirring constantly and boil for 1 minute
- In greased 2-quart casserole, arrange potatoes in 2 layers, topping each with half the onion, ⅓ the sauce, half the ham
- Top with remaining potatoes and sauce
- Dot with 1 tablespoon butter
- Cover and bake for 45 minutes
- Uncover and bake 15-30 minutes longer or until potatoes are tender
- Let stand 5-10 minutes before serving

**If desired you can sprinkle cheese over top for last 10 minutes or include the cheese in the sauce.

VARIATION:

Mix ¾ cup milk with 1 can cream of mushroom or cream of potato soup. Alternate as above.

Serves: 6

HAM AND SCALLOPED POTATOES
LAYERED METHOD
1975

I have always used this method to save time. For a quicker method I use a can of cream of mushroom soup for a sauce.

2	pounds potatoes (about 6 medium)
3	tablespoons butter
3	tablespoons flour
	Salt and pepper
2½	cups milk
¼	cup finely chopped onion or onion slices
1	tablespoon butter
1½	cups cubed cooked ham or ½ pound sliced cooked ham
	Cheddar cheese

- Use same ingredients as ham and scalloped potatoes sauce method
- In greased 2-quart casserole, arrange potatoes in 4 layers, sprinkling each of the first 3 layers with some of the flour, sliced onion, ham, salt and pepper and 1 tablespoon butter
- Heat milk just to scalding
- Pour over potatoes almost to cover potato
- Cover and bake 45 minutes
- Uncover and bake 15 – 30 minutes longer
- Let stand 5-10 minutes before serving

VARIATION:

- Mix ¾ cup milk with 1 can cream of mushroom or cream of potato soup. Alternate potatoes and this mixture

Serves: 4-6

TACO CASSEROLE
1981

My friend, Pat Slock, gave me this recipe back in the 80's. My kids loved it.

1 envelope taco seasoning mix
1 pound ground beef
1½ cup crushed Dorito chips
1 (16-ounce) can diced tomatoes
½-1 cup shredded cheddar cheese

- Preheat oven to 350°
- Brown the meat and drain
- Add tomatoes and mix
- Put into a casserole dish
- Sprinkle with chips and cheese
- Bake for 15 minutes

Serves: 4

Serve with shredded lettuce and diced fresh tomatoes.

SPANISH PORK CHOPS
1975

4 pork chops seasoned with salt and pepper
1 tablespoon oil plus 1 tablespoon butter
1 box of Beef Rice a Roni
2½ cups boiling water to make the broth from the broth packet in the box
4 cups (one 15-ounce can) stewed tomatoes

- Brown the chops in the oil and butter then remove from the skillet
- Add the beef Rice a Roni to the oil and butter and brown
- Make a broth with the water and broth packet
- Add the tomatoes and stir
- Return the chops to the skillet and cover
- Simmer for 35-45 minutes

STUFFED GREEN PEPPERS
1979

6 large green peppers
1 tablespoon butter and 1 tablespoon oil
1 pound ground beef or ½ pound beef and ½ pound ground pork
½ cup chopped onion
1 teaspoon salt
1 clove garlic minced
½ teaspoon dried oregano
½ teaspoon dried basil or 1 teaspoon fresh basil
1 teaspoon salt
Pepper to taste
1 teaspoon Worcestershire sauce
½ cup uncooked rice
1 cup water or chicken broth
1 (15-ounce) can tomato sauce or two 8 ounces cans
1 cup shredded cheese of your choice

- Heat oven to 350°.
- Place the rice and water or broth in a pot.
- Bring to boil, lower heat and cook 20 minutes.
- Cut thin slice from stem end of each pepper.
- Remove all seeds and membranes, wash inside and outside.
- Steam peppers in water for 5 minutes and drain.
- Arrange peppers in a baking dish facing upward (slice bottom a bit if they will not sit upright).
- In skillet add oil and butter and sauté ground beef, onion, and garlic until onion is tender. Drain off fat.
- Stir in rice, salt, pepper, Worcestershire sauce and one cup of the tomato sauce.
- Lightly stuff each pepper.
- Mix the remaining 8 ounces of tomato sauce with the oregano and basil and pour over peppers.
- Bake 45-50 minutes.
- Sprinkle with cheese and bake 10 minutes longer.

Yield: 6 servings

SHRIMP AND ARTICHOKE HEARTS
CASSEROLE
1980

6½ tablespoons butter divided
4½ tablespoons flour
¾ cup milk
¾ cup heavy cream
½ teaspoon salt
Freshly ground pepper to taste
1 (10-ounce) can artichoke hearts, drained
1 pound shrimp cleaned and cooked. Can leave tails on for better presentation
4 ounces mushrooms, sliced
¼ cup dry sherry
1 tablespoon Worcestershire sauce
¼ cup Parmesan cheese or to taste
Paprika

- Preheat oven to 375°
- Grease a shallow baking dish
- In saucepan melt 4½ tablespoons butter
- Whisk in flour until blended
- Gradually beat in milk and cream
- Cook and stir until thickened and smooth
- Season with salt and pepper and set aside
- In greased shallow baking dish, arrange artichoke hearts around the outer edge of the pan
- Arrange shrimp in the middle of the artichoke ring
- In small skillet sauté mushrooms in remaining 2 tablespoons butter for about 6 minutes
- Spoon over artichoke hearts and shrimps
- Add sherry and Worcestershire to cream sauce then pour over mushrooms
- Sprinkle with cheese and paprika
- Bake for 20 minutes or until bubbly

Serves 4

Serve with mashed potatoes or pan fried potatoes and salad.

CHICKEN DIVAN
1982

I make this with chicken breasts or leftover sliced turkey. If I use the leftover turkey meat, I make one casserole of the divan and one casserole of turkey tetrazzini and freeze one of the casseroles for a later time.

- ¼ cup butter
- ¼ cup flour
- 1½ cups chicken broth
- 2 tablespoons sherry
- ⅛ teaspoon nutmeg (pinch)
- ½ cup whipping cream, whipped
- ½ cup grated Parmesan cheese
- 1½ pounds fresh broccoli spears, cooked and drained
- 5 large slices cooked chicken breast or turkey
- ½ cup grated Parmesan cheese for topping

- Set broiler to 550°
- Melt butter in saucepan, blend in flour and cook until smooth and bubbly
- Remove from heat and stir in chicken broth
- Heat to boiling, stirring constantly
- Boil and stir for one minute more and remove from heat
- Stir in sherry and nutmeg
- Gently fold in whipped cream and ½ cup of cheese
- Place hot broccoli in ungreased baking dish
- Top with turkey slices
- Pour sauce over meat
- Sprinkle with remaining ½ cup cheese
- Broil 3-5 inches from heat until cheese is brown

Serves: 5

Serve with a fresh garden salad.

TURKEY TETRAZZINI
1982

TOPPING:

- 4 slices of hearty white bread, torn into pieces
- 2 tablespoons melted butter

Process in food processor and set aside.

CASSEROLE:

- 1 pound fettuccine or spaghetti (cooked al dente with 1 tablespoon salt in the water; drain and toss with 1 tablespoon olive oil; set aside
- Salt and pepper to taste
- 5 tablespoons butter
- 20 ounces fresh white mushrooms, sliced
- 2 onions finely chopped
- 4 garlic cloves minced
- 1 tablespoon minced fresh thyme
- ⅛ teaspoon cayenne pepper (optional)
- ¼ cup flour
- 2 cups chicken broth
- 2 cups half and half
- 2 ounces Parmesan cheese grated (1 cup)
- 4 cups cooked turkey meat cut into ½ inch pieces
- 1½ cups frozen baby peas

- Preheat oven to 400°
- Grease a 13x9 inch baking dish
- Cook and prepare the pasta as stated above and set aside
- In the same pot that you boiled the pasta, add butter and melt
- Add mushrooms and 1 teaspoon salt, cook until browned 7-10 minutes
- Add onions and cook another 4-5 minutes
- Stir in garlic, thyme, and cayenne (30 seconds)
- Add flour and cook for a minute
- Slowly whisk in broth and the half and half
- Bring to a simmer and cook whisking often until thickened
- Take off the heat and whisk in Parmesan cheese
- Season with salt and pepper to taste
- Transfer your cooked pasta to colander and rinse with hot tap water
- Mix together pasta, turkey, peas and sauce
- Pour into casserole dish and sprinkle with topping
- Bake for about 40-45 minutes or until the topping has browned

Serves: 6-8

CHICKEN POT PIE
1978

This is a comfort food that is popular during the cold wintery months. You can poach chicken breasts or sauté seasoned chicken tenders. When store-bought rotisserie chicken became popular, I took advantage of this short cut.

	Olive oil and butter
2-3	carrots cut into ½ inch pieces
2	stalks celery cut into ½ inch pieces
1	medium onion chopped
½	cup flour
4	cups hot chicken stock
¼	cup heavy cream
	Salt and pepper to taste
	Fresh herbs, rosemary or thyme and some parsley
1	store bought rotisserie chicken; shredded or poached chicken breasts cubed
	Cubed red potatoes
1	box frozen baby peas
1	bay leaf
1	box frozen puff pastry, thawed

- Preheat oven to 350°
- Sauté carrots, celery and onion in oil and butter until soft
- Add flour and cook a bit
- Add hot stock and stir thoroughly
- Add heavy cream, salt and pepper
- Add herbs, bay leaf, and potatoes
- Cook until about to bubble
- Add chicken and peas
- Cook until hot and bubbly and potatoes are cooked
- Adjust seasoning and remove bay leaf
- Place puff pastry on floured board (or cornmeal pastry below)
- Cut rounds to accommodate size of casserole tops
- Spoon chicken mixture into small crocks or large casserole dish
- Place puff pastry rounds on top
- Sprinkle with Parmesan cheese and bake at 350° for 20 minutes

POACHED CHICKEN BREAST:

- Cover breasts with water or broth
- Boil, lower heat, simmer 10 minutes
- Turn off heat let stand 20 minutes
- Slice, shred or cube

CORNMEAL – CHIVE PASTRY VARIATION FOR TOP:

1¾	cups flour with ½ teaspoon salt
⅔	cups yellow cornmeal
3	tablespoons chives minced
½	cup iced cold water
1¼	sticks cold butter (½ cup)

Prepare the cornmeal pastry as you do with other pastries.

DOUBLE CRUSTED
CHICKEN POT PIE
1980

CRUST:

- 3 cups flour
- 1 cup diced cold shortening
- ½ teaspoon salt
- 1 beaten egg
- 5 tablespoons iced cold water
- 1 tablespoon white vinegar

- Mix egg, water and vinegar together
- Put flour into food processor
- Add shortening and pulse until mixture resembles cornmeal
- Add half liquid and pulse
- Add enough of the remaining liquid until dough stays together when pinched, but is not wet
- Form into two balls; larger for bottom and smaller for top
- Form into disks
- Roll out or refrigerate until ready to use

POT PIE:

SEE RECIPE FOR CHICKEN POT PIE

- Preheat oven to 400°
- Roll out pastry dough and put into deep dish
- Add cooled chicken filling
- Roll out top crust
- Make a few slits on top crust
- Brush with egg wash
- Bake for about 40 minutes

CREAMY BAKED CHICKEN BREASTS
With French Rice
1976

CHICKEN BREASTS

- 4 whole boneless and skinless chicken breasts
- 8 (4x4-inch) slices of Swiss cheese
- 1 (10-ounce) can cream of chicken soup, undiluted or use homemade béchamel sauce made with chicken broth
- ¼ cup dry white wine (I use dry white vermouth)
- 1 cup herb-seasoned stuffing mix, crushed
- ¼ cup margarine, melted

- Preheat oven to 350°
- Arrange chicken in a lightly greased 13x9x2 inch baking dish
- Top with cheese slices
- Combine soup and wine, stirring well
- Spoon sauce evenly over chicken and sprinkle with stuffing mix
- Drizzle butter over crumbs
- Bake at 350° for 45-55 minutes

Yield: 8

FRENCH RICE

- 1 (10-ounce) can onion soup, undiluted
- ½ cup margarine melted
- 1 (4½-ounce) jar sliced mushrooms
- 1 (8-ounce) can sliced water chestnuts
- 1 cup uncooked regular rice.

- Combine soup and butter and stir well
- Drain mushrooms and water chestnuts, reserving the liquids
- Add enough water to the reserved liquids to equal 1⅓ cups
- Add mushrooms, water chestnuts, liquid, and rice to soup mixture, stir well
- Pour into a lightly greased 10x6x2 in. baking dish
- Cover and bake at 350° for 1 hour

Yield: 6

These oven dishes work very well together. Fifteen minutes after you put the rice in the oven you can put the chicken in, and they will come out together. Serve with vegetable or salad.

CHICKEN AND VEGETABLES
WITH SUPREME SAUCE
1971

This was one of our family's favorite casseroles in the 70's. I made the recipe and divided it into two casseroles. I popped one in the freezer for later and baked one for dinner.

- 6 large boneless, skinless chicken breasts, cooked
- 1 (16-ounce) can whole small carrots, drained or 1 pound fresh carrots steamed
- 1 (15½-ounce) can pearl onions
- 2 (9-ounce) packages of frozen artichoke hearts, cooked and halved or vegetable of choice
- 3 tablespoons butter or margarine
- ¼ cup flour
- ¾ teaspoon salt
- 2½ cups milk
- ½ cup mayonnaise
- ¼ cup dry sherry
- 1 cup (4 ounces) shredded cheddar cheese

- Preheat oven to 350°
- Cut cooked chicken into chunks
- Arrange chicken and vegetables in 13x9x2-inch baking dish and set aside
- In sauce pan, melt butter; blend in flour and salt and cook for a minute
- Add milk all at once
- Cook, stirring constantly, until the mixture thickens and bubbles
- Cook for 2 minutes more
- Remove from heat
- Stir in mayonnaise and sherry
- Pour sauce over vegetables
- Bake covered in 350° oven for 25 minutes
- Uncover and sprinkle with cheese
- Return to oven and bake uncovered 3-5 minutes or until the cheese melts
- Served with fresh salad and crisp fresh bread

Yield: 8 servings

CORNED BEEF AND CABBAGE
1975

In the 70's corned-beef was not as expensive as it is today. I bought a brisket and served the family a wonderful Irish supper. Leftover corned beef made wonderful sandwiches on rye bread or hash.

3-4 pounds lean corned-beef brisket	2 bay leaves
2 onions, sliced	6 small to medium potatoes, pared
2 cloves garlic, minced	6 small carrots, pared
6 whole cloves	6 cabbage wedges (1 head)

- Barely cover the beef with hot water.
- Add the onions and seasonings.
- Cover and simmer for about 1 hour per pound of meat or until tender.
- Remove the meat from the liquid.
- Add potatoes, and carrots.
- Cover and bring to a boil and cook 10 minutes.
- Add the cabbage and cook another 20 minutes.
- Slice brisket and serve with vegetables.
- If you would like a glaze over the meat, top the meat with mustard, brown sugar and ground cloves. Then bake for 15 minutes to form a glaze on top of the meat.

Yield: 6

BEEF STEW
1965

Today I make my stew a bit heartier and richer since 1965. I add red wine and a richer beef stock.

2 pounds stew meat, cut into 1-cubes and dried with paper towel
½ cup flour or as needed to coat all the beef cubes
1 teaspoon salt
¼ teaspoon pepper
2 tablespoons oil or as needed
3 cups hot beef consommé or rich beef stock
1 cup red wine (for a richer stock)
4 carrots cut into 1-in pieces
   Optional fresh string beans cut into 2-in pieces
1 cup sliced celery
1 large onion, diced
2 small cloves garlic, minced
1 teaspoon salt or as needed
1 tablespoon Worcestershire sauce
4 fresh thyme stalks minced or ½ teaspoon dried thyme
½ teaspoon dried marjoram or fresh rosemary and parsley
1 bay leaf
3 peeled medium potatoes cut into 1-inch cubes
8 ounces quartered mushrooms
   Small bag of frozen peas or as desired

- Mix flour with 1 teaspoon salt and the pepper
- Coat meat with seasoned flour
- Preheat pan and add oil
- Brown meat thoroughly in batches
- Remove the browned meat and set aside
- Sauté the onions, thyme, and garlic for a few minutes
- Add wine and deglaze the pan thoroughly
- Add consommé or beef stock and Worcestershire sauce
- Add the browned beef cubes
- Simmer uncovered 15 minutes to help thicken the stew
- At this point simmer the beef covered on the stove for 1-2 hours
- Stir in remaining vegetable ingredients and add a pinch of sugar
- Simmer uncovered for 30 minutes until vegetables are tender
- Last minute you can add frozen peas
- Stir into stew, heat to boiling, stirring constantly
- Boil and stir for 1 minute

- Remove bay leaf
- If needed thicken stew by whisking ½ cup beef stock and 2 tablespoons flour until blended
- Let stand 15 minutes before serving

If using a crock-pot, use less liquid. Cook on High for 30 minutes, then on Low for 6 hours. Thicken stew at end and simmer uncovered for 15 minutes.

Yield: 6

SLOW COOKER
BEEF STEW

Gallon size baggie	4 large potatoes unpeeled and cut into chunks
½ teaspoon salt	2 cups boiling water
3 pounds stew meat	1 envelope onion soup mix
Oil for browning meat	3 tablespoons butter
1 cup baby carrots	3 onions sliced
1 tablespoon dried parsley or 3 tablespoons freshly chopped parsley	¼ cup red wine
1 teaspoon black pepper	2 tablespoons flour
	¼ cup warm water

- Put meat, flour and salt in baggie; shake
- Brown meat in skillet with oil
- Put meat into cooker
- Add the carrots, parsley, black pepper, chopped potatoes to cooker
- Dissolve the onion soup mix in boiling water and add to cooker
- Melt the butter and sauté the onions until soft then add to cooker
- Pour wine in skillet and deglaze pan then add to the cooker
- Cover the cooker and cook on High for 30 minutes
- Lower to Low and cook for 6 hours
- Just before the cooking time is done
- Mix the flour and warm water
- Stir into stew and cook 15 minutes uncovered

Serves: 6

SLOW COOKER
BEEF POT ROAST
1980

- 1 5-pound bone-in beef chuck pot roast, or bone out tied
- 1 tablespoon flour
- 2 tablespoons vegetable oil
- 8 ounces sliced mushrooms
- 1 medium onion, chopped
- 2 garlic cloves, minced
- 1 tablespoon butter
- 1½ tablespoons flour
- 1 tablespoon tomato paste
- 2½ cups chicken broth
- 4 medium carrots cut into chunks on the diagonal
- 2 stalks celery, cut into chunks on the diagonal
- Fresh rosemary
- Fresh thyme

- Wipe roast dry with paper towel
- Season both sides of roast generously with salt and pepper, sprinkle flour over the top and sides until well coated, pat flour into roast
- Heat oil and sear roast on all sides until well browned
- Chop all vegetables and put the carrots and celery on bottom of slow cooker
- When roast is well browned put on top of the carrots and celery and add rosemary and thyme
- Add butter to skillet and add mushrooms; cook a few minutes
- Stir in onion and sauté; add garlic and sauté one minute more
- Stir in flour and cook for a minute; then add the tomato paste; cook another minute
- Slowly add the chicken stock and return to a simmer
- Pour the onion mushroom mixture over the roast
- Cover and cook on high for 6 hours
- Skim off fat and season with salt and pepper
- Make gravy with juices
    - Blend the flour and melted butter to make a roux
    - Add the juices and cook until thickened

Serves: 6

SHRIMP CREOLE
1971

During the lean years I used inexpensive canned shrimp or small frozen cooked shrimp. Now I use frozen or fresh jumbo or large shrimp.

- ¼ cup vegetable oil
- 2 cups chopped onions
- 1 cup chopped green bell pepper
- 1 cup chopped celery
- 4 cups peeled, seeded and chopped plum tomatoes or 1 large can crush tomatoes
- 1 tablespoon chopped garlic
- 1½ teaspoons salt or to taste
- ¼-½ teaspoon cayenne pepper or to taste
- Dash Worcestershire sauce
- Dash hot sauce
- 1 cup water
- 2 bay leaves
- 2 pounds large shrimp, peeled and deveined
- 2 tablespoons flour mixed with ¼ cup water
- Emeril's Creole Seasoning adds a bit more spice (optional)
- 6 cups cooked white or brown rice

- Wash and prepare shrimp
- Sprinkle shrimp with Creole seasonings if desired
- In a large sauté pan, heat oil
- Add the onions and sauté 2-3 minutes
- Stir in the peppers and celery and sauté for 2 minutes or until starting to wilt
- Season the vegetables with salt, cayenne, Worcestershire and hot sauce
- Stir in the tomatoes and garlic
- Sauté for 2 more minutes
- Stir in the water and bay leaves and bring to a boil
- Reduce heat and simmer for 20 minutes
- Add shrimp and cook for 2-3 more minutes
- Stir in flour mixture and simmer for 2 minutes or until thickens
- Check the seasonings
- Serve over rice

Yield: 6 servings

BROCCOLI AND RICE CASSEROLE
1975

This casserole is good as a vegetable dish or as a main course. I add 2-3 cups chopped or shredded cooked chicken when I make it as a main dish. I have also substituted very small shell pasta cooked instead of rice.

- 1 large package frozen chopped broccoli cooked and drained or fresh broccoli florets cooked and chopped
- 2 cups cooked rice (brown rice optional)
- 1 can cream of mushroom soup
- ½ cup cheddar cheese grated
- ¼ cup mayonnaise
- ¼-½ cup milk
- ½ teaspoon lemon juice
- ¼ stick butter
- ½ cup onion
- About ¾ teaspoon salt
- Freshly ground pepper
- Cheese for topping
- Crumbled potato chips

- Preheat oven to 350°
- Grease a casserole dish
- Cook rice and broccoli
- Melt butter and sauté onion until soft
- Mix mayo and milk with mushroom soup
- Combine all ingredients together
- Add salt and pepper to taste
- Stir until well mixed
- (Can add cooked chicken as an option here)
- Put mixture into greased casserole dish
- Sprinkle additional cheese on top
- Sprinkle potato chips on top
- Bake for 30 minutes

Serves: 6

SHEPHERD'S PIE
1979

Although this pie is traditionally made with ground lamb I used ground round beef for a more frugal version.

- 4 small potatoes
- ¼ cup half and half
- 4 tablespoons butter
- ¾ teaspoon salt
- Ground white pepper
- 1 egg yolk

FILLING:

- 2 tablespoons oil
- 1 onion chopped
- 2 carrots diced
- 2 cloves garlic, minced
- 1½ pounds ground lamb or beef
- 1 teaspoon salt
- Freshly ground pepper
- 2 tablespoons flour
- 2 teaspoons tomato paste
- 1 cup chicken broth
- 1 teaspoon Worcestershire sauce
- 2 teaspoons finely chopped rosemary leaves
- 1 teaspoon minced fresh thyme
- ½ cup frozen corn
- ½ cup frozen peas

- Preheat oven to 400°.
- Peel potatoes and cut into chunks.
- Add water and salt to potatoes, bring to a boil, cover, and simmer for 10-15 minutes or until tender.
- Mash the potatoes.
- Microwave milk and butter for about 30 seconds and then add to the mashed potatoes.
- Cool for a few minutes and then add egg yolk to potatoes and mix well.
- In large preheated skillet add oil. Sauté onions and carrots for a few minutes.
- Add garlic, stir and sauté a few seconds.
- Add meat, salt and pepper and cook until browned.
- Sprinkle the flour over the meat and toss.
- Add tomato paste, Worcestershire sauce and herbs, stir.
- Bring to boil and simmer covered for 12 minutes.
- Add the corn and peas and spread into a 7x11 baking dish.
- Top with the potatoes making sure to bring the potatoes to the edges of the casserole.
- Bake on a cooking sheet for 25 minutes.
- Cool for 15 minutes before serving.

Serves: 6

STUFFED ROUND STEAK
1977

- 4 slices bacon, diced
- 1 onion chopped
- 1½ cups toasted bread cubes
- 2 tablespoons minced parsley
- ½ teaspoon celery salt
- ¼ teaspoon sage or 1 teaspoon chopped fresh sage
- 2-2½ pounds round steak thinly sliced
- ½ teaspoon salt, freshly ground pepper
- 1 cup beef stock
- 1 (8-ounce) can tomato sauce

STUFFING:

- Sauté bacon with the onion.
- Remove bacon and onion from pan and place into small bowl.
- In the bowl, add bread cubes, parsley, celery salt and sage to the bacon and onion.

STEAK:

- Set aside while you prepare the steak.
- Cut steak into 4 portions making sure it is cut thin. If not thin, pound with mallet.
- Sprinkle steak with salt and pepper.
- Spread each portion with stuffing and roll up.
- Hold together with toothpicks.
- Place in large skillet.
- Pour beef stock over all.
- Cover and simmer 1 hour.
- Pour in tomato sauce.
- Replace the cover and simmer 45 minutes.
- If the gravy is too thin, remove the cover for a few minutes.

Serves: 4

Serve with fluffy potato casserole.

FLUFFY POTATO CASSEROLE

2 cups mashed potatoes
2 eggs
Salt and pepper

2 tablespoons chopped fresh chives
8 ounces softened cream cheese
1 can fried onion rings

- Beat all together on high for 3 minutes
- Pour into greased casserole dish
- Top with onions
- Bake at 325° for 30 minutes

SWISS STEAK
1975

I used an electric skillet to make many of my braised dishes in the 70's. This was one of the family favorites.

2 pounds round steak about 1 inch thick
¼ cup flour
1 teaspoon salt
Freshly ground pepper

1 onion chopped
1 can diced tomatoes
1 green pepper chopped

- Cut the steak into serving pieces
- Mix flour, salt and pepper
- Dust steak pieces with flour mixture
- Pound the flour into the steak with mallet
- Heat skillet, add oil and brown steak pieces
- Add tomatoes, cover skillet and cook 1½ hours
- Add chopped green pepper
- Cover and cook another 15 minutes
- Serve with your favorite mashed potatoes or rice

Serves: 6

CHICKEN MARENGO
1977

2½ pounds whole chicken cut up into pieces
¼ cup oil
½ cup chopped onion
1 clove garlic, minced
¼ teaspoon marjoram, crushed
1 teaspoon salt and some freshly ground pepper

½ cup dry white wine or chicken broth
1 (3-ounce) can mushrooms or sliced fresh mushrooms
2 tomatoes, peeled, seeded and cut into quarters or chopped

- Brown chicken slowly in oil
- Add onion, garlic and marjoram
- Cook until onion is soft, season with salt and pepper
- Add wine or broth and the liquid drained from the can of mushrooms
- Scrape bottom of pan to loosen browned bits
- Cover and cook over low heat until chicken is tender (about 35 minutes)
- Skim off fat then add mushrooms and tomatoes
- Cook another 5 minutes
- Garnish with roughly chopped fresh parsley

PORK CUTLETS
WITH ORANGES
1980

1¼ pound pork cutlets
Flour for dusting
1 egg beaten with 2 tablespoons milk
½ cup of bread crumbs
3 tablespoons butter

Juice of one orange
Zest of one orange
1 orange peeled and sliced
Salt and pepper to taste
Fresh or dried thyme

- Coat cutlets with flour
- Dip into egg mixture
- Coat with the bread crumbs
- Heat butter with a bit of oil in skillet
- Brown cutlets on one side, turn, cover, and cook for 5 minutes
- Uncover and sauté a few minutes more on each side
- Remove to hot platter
- Add orange juice to skillet to deglaze the pan
- Add the orange zest and orange slices
- Add seasonings
- Heat all and pour juices over the cutlets

Serves: 4

Serve with Chantilly potatoes and minted peas.

RECIPES FOR SPECIAL MASHED POTATOES

CHANTILLY POTATOES

- 3 pounds Yukon Gold potatoes, peeled and cut into cubes
- 1 teaspoon salt
- ¼ teaspoon white pepper
- 1¼ cup heavy cream chilled and whipped
- ¾ cup Parmesan cheese
- ¾ cup shredded Swiss cheese

- Preheat oven to 400°
- Grease an oblong casserole dish
- Prepare mashed potatoes adding the salt and pepper
- Whip heavy cream until stiff peaks form
- Fold in about ⅔ of the whipped cream into the mashed potatoes
- Fold all cheeses except ¼ cup of each cheese for top
- Spread potato mixture in prepared pan
- Spread remaining cream then sprinkle with remaining cheeses *
- Run under the broiler for 2-3 minutes until golden brown
- Let rest for 5 minutes before serving

* To make ahead refrigerate and bake later at 400° for 20 minutes

Serves: 4-6

MASHED POTATOES BAKED
WITH THREE CHEESES

- 4 large potatoes (2½ pounds)
- 4½ ounces Brie cheese (rind removed, ½-inch dices)
- 5½ ounces Goat cheese crumbled
- ¾ cup Parmesan cheese
- ¼ cup milk
- Kosher salt and ground white pepper
- 2 tablespoons fresh Italian parsley or fresh-snipped chives

- Preheat oven to 350°
- Grease a casserole dish
- Cook potatoes in boiling water, drain and turn into a bowl
- Dry the cooking pot and wipe dry
- Return the potatoes to the dried pot
- Add ⅔ of Brie, ⅔ of goat cheese and ⅔ of Parmesan cheese to potatoes
- Mash and add ¼ cup milk and salt and white pepper

- Add more milk 1 tablespoon at a time then transfer to greased casserole dish
- Sprinkle with remaining cheeses and bake for 20 minutes
- Sprinkle with parsley or chives

Good with salmon, chicken or lamb chops.

CREAMY POTATO BAKE
1980

3 cups mashed potatoes
8 ounces sour cream
5-6 slices bacon, cooked and crumbled
3 small green onions, chopped
1 cup sharp shredded cheddar cheese

- Preheat oven to 325°
- Lightly grease 10x6x2 baking dish
- Evenly spread the potatoes into the prepared dish
- Top with sour cream
- Sprinkle with bacon and green onions
- Top with cheese
- Bake for 30 minutes
- Serve hot

Serves: 6

FLUFFY POTATO CASSEROLE

2 cups mashed potatoes
2 eggs
Salt and freshly ground pepper
2 tablespoons chopped chives
8 ounces cream cheese softened
1 can fried onion rings for topping

- Preheat oven to 325°
- Beat all together on high for 3 minutes
- Pour into greased baking dish
- Top with onions
- Bake 325° for 30-35 minutes

TWICE-BAKED POTATOES
1980

- 2 large russet potatoes
- 4 tablespoons butter
- ¼ cup milk
- ½ cup sour cream
- ¾ cup shredded cheddar, divided
- ¼ teaspoon salt
- Freshly ground pepper
- Paprika (for garnish)
- 1-2 scallions chopped fine (for garnish)
- 4 slices bacon, cooked and drained (for garnish)

- Preheat oven to 375°.
- Scrub, pierce and bake potatoes for about 60-90 minutes.
- Fry the bacon, drain, and put aside.
- Let potatoes cool for about 10 minutes.
- Using a oven mitt, cut potatoes lengthwise.
- Scoop out most of the potato into a bowl. Leave enough potato in the skin for support, sprinkle some salt into the shells.
- In a large bowl mix with a hand mixer all the ingredients except ¼ cup cheese and the chopped green onion. If mixture is not creamy, add more milk.
- Adjust seasonings as needed.
- Spoon potato mixture into potato shells.
- Top with remaining ¼ cup of cheese and the chopped onions.
- Sprinkle with paprika.
- Bake the potatoes for another 15-25 minutes.
- Form the bacon into curls and secure with toothpicks.
- Top each potato with a bacon curl.

TO FREEZE:

- Place potatoes on sheet and freeze. Wrap each potato with plastic wrap and foil freeze for up to 2 weeks.
- To prepare, thaw potatoes then heat the potatoes without wrap and foil for 30 minutes at 375°.
- Fry bacon, make curls and place atop each potato.

Serves: 4

SAUTÉED MUSHROOMS
1975

- 1 tablespoon vegetable oil
- 1½ pounds white mushrooms, cleaned, stems removed and quartered
- 1 tablespoon unsalted butter
- 1 medium shallot, minced
- 1 tablespoon minced fresh thyme
- ¼ cup dry marsala wine
- Salt and freshly ground pepper

- Heat oil over medium-high heat
- Add mushrooms and cook, stirring occasionally, until mushrooms release liquid about 5 minutes
- Increase heat to high and cook, stirring until liquid has completely evaporated about 8 minutes longer
- Add butter, reduce heat to medium and continue to cook, stirring once every minute, until mushrooms are dark brown, about 8 minutes longer
- Add shallot and thyme and cook until softened, about 3 minutes *
- Add wine and cook until liquid has evaporated about 2 minutes
- Season

Serves 4

SAUTÉED MUSHROOMS
WITH GARLIC, PARMESAN AND BREAD CRUMBS

- Prepare fresh bread crumbs by taking 2 slices bread pulsed in a food processor and tossing with 2 tablespoons melted butter.
    - * When making mushrooms follow above recipe through adding shallots, thyme and wine and instead use garlic and stir for about 30 seconds.
- Season with salt and pepper and transfer to bowl.
- Toss the hot mushrooms with ½ cup freshly grated Parmesan cheese. Toss with bread crumbs and 2 tablespoons minced fresh parsley.

CHICKEN BREASTS SUPREME
1982

- 6 whole chicken breasts boned and skinned
- ¼ cup butter
- ¼ cup flour
- ¼ cup chicken broth
- 2½ t salt
- 1 teaspoon paprika
- Chopped parsley
- 2 teaspoons cornstarch
- 1½ cups half and half
- ¼ cup sherry
- 1 teaspoon lemon juice
- 1 teaspoon lemon zest
- ½ cup grated Swiss cheese

- Melt butter
- Flour the breasts and brown lightly on both sides in butter
- Add ¼ cup water or chicken broth and simmer for 30 minutes
- Remove to hot platter and keep warm
- Mix cornstarch with ¼ cup half and half
- Stir into the drippings, cook slowly while gradually stirring in remaining cream
- Add sherry, lemon zest and juice
- Continue cooking until the sauce thickens
- Pour over chicken
- Sprinkle with cheese and dust with paprika
- Melt cheese in the oven
- Garnish with parsley

Serves: 6

CHOW MEIN
OR CHOP SUEY
1975

What better dish to cook for a family of four inexpensively than Chinese food. Our family loved frequenting a restaurant called the Canton Station in Rocky Mount, NC. I had the pleasure of attending a cooking demonstration in the kitchen of this restaurant. It was a very fun experience and I quickly learned how to make wonderful Chinese dishes at home using canned Chinese vegetables.

- 1 pound lean pork or chicken diced
- 2 tablespoons canola oil
- 2 tablespoons soy sauce
- ¼ teaspoon salt
- 1 cup beef stock
- 1 cup chopped onions
- 2 cups thinly sliced celery
- 1 can Chinese vegetables, drained. Rinse under cold water to crisp
- 1 tablespoon cornstarch
- ¼ teaspoon ground ginger or 1 teaspoon grated fresh ginger
- 1 tablespoon molasses
- ¼ cup water

- Brown meat in oil
- Add soy sauce, salt and stock
- Cover and cook until meat is tender
- Add onions, celery, Chinese vegetables
- Cook 10 minutes
- Blend cornstarch, ginger, molasses and water
- Add and stir until thickened
- Serve over Chow Mein noodles and sprinkle with soy sauce

ORIENTAL SKILLET CHICKEN
1975

1 whole chicken breast skinned, boned, and cut into chunks
Salt and pepper
¼ cup flour
¼ cup oil
¼ cup green pepper strips
¼ cup chopped green onions
1 garlic clove minced

1 tablespoon cornstarch
2 tablespoons soy sauce
1 can Chow Mein vegetables, drained and run under cold water to crisp
1 package (6-ounce) frozen pea pods, thawed

- Coat chicken with flour, salt and pepper
- In Wok or large skillet, heat oil
- Add chicken and stir-fry over high heat 2-3 minutes
- Push meat to one side and add green pepper, onions and garlic
- Sauté until onions are soft
- Combine cornstarch with chicken broth and soy sauce
- Add to wok and cook stirring constantly, until mixture thickens
- Add Chow Mein vegetables and pea pods
- Heat through
- Serve immediately over Chow Mein noodles or hot rice

Serves: 6

SHRIMP CANTONESE
WITH RICE
1976

3 cups cooked rice
12 ounces peeled deveined raw shrimp, halved lengthwise
2 tablespoons butter
2 cups diagonally sliced celery
2 cups sliced onions

4 cups fresh spinach leaves
1 can Chinese vegetables drained and run under cold water
¼ teaspoon soy sauce
1¼ cups chicken broth
2 tablespoons cornstarch

- While rice is cooking, sauté shrimp in butter for 1 minute or until they turn pink
- Add celery and onions, cook stirring for 2 minutes
- Add spinach and Chinese vegetables
- Cover and cook 1 minute
- Blend soy sauce, chicken broth and cornstarch
- Stir into shrimp vegetable mixture, season to taste
- Continue stirring until sauce is clear and thickened, serve over beds of white or brown rice

Serves: 6

PATRICIA'S
BAKED BEANS
1975

After years of soaking beans and baking them for 7 hours, I decided to use this easy recipe. I have been making this easy version for over 30 years.

- 4 slices bacon
- ½ cup chopped onion
- 2 (1-pound) cans pork and beans—I use the vegetarian style or original style
- 2 tablespoons brown sugar or to taste
- 1 tablespoon Worcestershire sauce
- 1 teaspoon mustard or dry mustard
- ¼ cup of your favorite barbeque sauce or to taste
- 2 tablespoons ketchup

- Spray a casserole dish with cooking spray (PAM)
- Preheat oven to 325°
- Cook bacon until crisp reserving bacon drippings
- Crumble bacon
- Cook onion in reserved drippings until tender but not brown
- Add onions with the bacon and the remaining ingredients
- Mix well and turn into prepared casserole dish
- Bake uncovered for 2 hours

Serves 6

CHARITY BALL SALAD
Women's Guild Rocky Mount, NC
1975

2 (9 ounce) packages frozen cut green beans
1 (14-ounce) can drained artichoke hearts, cut in half
1 (7-ounce) can pitted black olives, drained and sliced
1 (8-ounce) can button mushrooms, drained
1 (4-ounce) can sliced pimento, drained
1 small red onion, sliced and separated into rings

MARINADE:

1 cup vinegar
1 cup oil
1 onion, diced
1½ teaspoons seasoned salt
¾ teaspoon pepper
1 teaspoon garlic salt
1 teaspoon oregano
2 tablespoons sugar

- Cook beans until slightly underdone and drain thoroughly
- Mix marinade ingredients and bring to a boil and cool
- Add artichokes, mushrooms, pimento, olives and onion rings to the beans
- Pour cooled sauce over all the vegetables, refrigerate overnight

CRABMEAT BALL
1980

1 package (4-ounce) good quality crabmeat
1 or 2 packages (8 ounces each) cream cheese
2 teaspoons chopped chives
Pinch of garlic salt
¼ teaspoon salt
½ cup chopped pecans

- If crab is frozen, thaw. If crab is from fish department or canned, rinse thoroughly
- Blend softened cream cheese, chives, garlic and salt
- Fold in crabmeat
- Shape into a ball and wrap with plastic wrap
- Refrigerate until firm
- Place pecans* on a sheet of waxed paper
- Place ball on top of pecans and roll until the crab ball is covered with pecans
- Refrigerate, serve with crackers

*Can substitute fresh parsley for pecans

SPINACH QUICHE
1982

1 pastry crust
1½ cups shredded Swiss cheese (I use Gruyere)
¼ cup Parmesan or Romano cheese, grated
Olive oil for sautéing
Chopped cooked spinach
¼ cup chopped onion

3-4 eggs
1 cup heavy cream
½ cup skim milk
½ teaspoon salt
¼ teaspoon white pepper
Dash cayenne
1 egg white, beaten

- Preheat oven to 400°.
- Prepare pie crust.
- Prick bottom of crust with a fork; freeze for 20 minutes.
- Place parchment or foil on bottom of crust and add weights (dried beans or metal beans purchased in a kitchen shop).
- Bake crust with beans at 400° for about 6-8 minutes.
- Remove the beans and paper and bake another 3-4 minutes.
- Lower oven to 375°.
- Brush crust with beaten egg white and cool.
- Sauté spinach and onion in a bit of olive oil.
- Put spinach, onion, and cheese on crust. Pour liquid ingredients over.
- Bake at 375° for about 35 minutes on bottom rack of oven.

Variation: Use ham or crisp bacon and cheese with dash of sugar

PASTRY CRUST:

2¼ cup unbleached flour
¾ teaspoon salt

¾ cup cold vegetable shortening
6-7 tablespoons iced cold water

FOOD PROCESSOR METHOD

- Process flour and salt.
- Add shortening and pulse 15 times or until it looks like bread crumbs.
- Add 4 tablespoons water and pulse 5 times.
- Add 2 tablespoons water and pulse 3 more times.
- Add more water 1 teaspoon at a time if needed.
- Dough should be damp enough to mass together.
- Can use right away or refrigerate up to 2 days.
- If refrigerated, bring to room temperature before rolling out.

FUDGE PIE
1976

1½ sticks of butter or margarine
3 squares unsweetened chocolate
3 eggs
1½ cups sugar
¾ cup flour
1 teaspoon vanilla
Dash salt

- Preheat oven to 350°
- Grease a 9-inch pie pan
- Melt together over low heat the butter and unsweetened chocolate
- Beat eggs and add flour and sugar
- Mix well
- Add chocolate and butter and mix
- Add vanilla and salt, mix well
- Pour into greased pie pan and bake at 350° for about 18 minutes
- Should be soft in the center when done
- Serve with vanilla ice cream or coffee rum cream on top

For brownies, add chopped pecans and bake in square cake pan. Cook about 20 minutes. Freezes well.

COFFEE RUM CREAM

1 pint coffee ice cream softened
4 teaspoons rum

- Combine rum and ice cream
- Garnish with chocolate curls

DERBY PIE
1976

Rich and delicious!

- 1 single pastry crust unbaked
- 2 eggs, slightly beaten
- 1 stick melted butter, cooled
- 1 cup sugar
- 1 teaspoon vanilla
- ½ cup flour
- 1 cup chopped pecans
- 1 (6-ounce) package chocolate chips
- One unbaked pie shell

- Preheat oven to 375°
- Prepare pastry crust for single pie
- Mix all ingredients together and pour into unbaked pie shell
- Bake 30 minutes at 375°
- Serve at room temperature or warm with whipped cream or vanilla ice cream

STRAWBERRY PIE
1980

- 1 pastry crust for single pie
- ¼ cup strawberry Jell-O
- ¼ cup cornstarch
- ½ cup sugar
- 1 cup water

- Preheat oven to 400°
- Prepare pie pastry, prick bottom of crust
- Bake on bottom rack 15 minutes, prick again and bake 10 more minutes
- Cool pie crust and set aside
- In saucepan boil together the Jell-O, cornstarch, sugar and water
- Add 1 pint sugared or unsugared strawberries
- Pour into baked pie shell
- Chill

Can use peach Jell-O and fresh peaches.

HOMEMADE GRANOLA
1975

Parenting young children is always a struggle when you are introducing nutrition. I made many attempts to make homemade snacks and this granola recipe became a mainstay in our home. Of course I liked it more than the kids, but I persisted.

4 cups old-fashioned oats	½ teaspoon cinnamon
½ chopped pecans	1 teaspoon vanilla
½ cup chopped walnuts	¼ cup honey
½ cup brown sugar	¼ cup canola oil
Salt	1 cup raisins

- Preheat oven to 300°
- In a bowl mix the oats, nuts, brown sugar, salt and cinnamon
- In saucepan warm the oil and honey; add vanilla
- Pour liquid over the oat mixture
- Stir gently
- Spread onto a 15x10 baking pan
- Bake 40 minutes stirring every 10 minutes or so
- Transfer to a rack to cool
- Stir in raisins
- Seal in airtight container or baggie
- Will keep up to a week or freeze for up to 3 months

HOMEMADE SNACK MIX
1975

As a young mom I made many bags of this mix. I mixed and matched the cereals. We all loved the flavor it provided.

- 3 cups rice Chex
- 2 cups cheerios
- 3 cups corn Chex
- 3 cups wheat Chex
- 1 cup mixed nuts
- 1 cup pretzels of choice

- 6 tablespoons melted butter
- 2 tablespoons Worcestershire sauce
- 1½ teaspoons seasoned salt
- ¾ teaspoon garlic powder
- ½ teaspoon onion powder

- Preheat oven to 250°
- In large bowl mix cereals, nuts, pretzels and set aside
- In microwaveable dish melt butter
- Add seasonings to butter
- Toss butter mixture and cereals
- Spread on baking sheet
- Bake 1 hour stirring every 15 minutes
- Cool on paper towels
- Store in airtight container

DELICIOUS BUNDT CAKE
1975

My sister, Bev Murphy, and I made this recipe during one of her visits to our home in Rocky Mount, NC.

- ½ cup butter
- ½ cup shortening
- 2 cups sugar
- 4 eggs, room temperature
- 1 teaspoon lemon extract
- ½ teaspoon almond extract
- 2 cups sifted flour
- 1 tablespoon baking powder
- 1 cup milk, room temperature

- Preheat oven to 325°
- Grease a 3 quart Bundt pan or a 10-inch tube pan
- Beat butter and shortening
- Gradually add sugar until fluffy
- Add flavorings
- Add eggs one at a time beating after each
- Sift together the flour and baking powder
- Alternate milk and flour starting with flour and ending with flour
- Mix well
- Pour into greased pan
- Bake for 1 hour and 10 minutes or until the cake tester comes out clean
- Invert onto wire rack and cool completely
- Sift confectioners sugar over top

Set oven at 300° if using Teflon coated pan.

ALMOND POUND CAKE

1982

- 1 cup butter or margarine (I used unsalted butter)
- 3 cups sugar
- 5 eggs
- 1 teaspoon vanilla extract or vanilla paste
- 1 teaspoon almond extract
- 3 cups cake flour
- 7/8 cup ginger ale

- Preheat oven to 275°
- Grease and flour Bundt Pan and set aside
- In large bowl, beat butter and sugar until light and fluffy
- Beat in eggs, one at a time
- Blend in extracts
- Gradually beat in flour, alternating with ginger ale, until well blended
- Pour into Bundt pan
- Bake at 275° for 1 hour and 45 minutes or until toothpick inserted comes out clean
- Cool 25 minutes in pan
- Remove from pan and cool completely
- Drizzle chocolate ice cream topping over cooled cake
- Top with sliced almonds, garnish with strawberries

ZUCCHINI WALNUT BREAD
1980

My youngest sister Bev shared this recipe with me.

- 1 cup chopped walnuts
- 4 eggs
- 1 cup oil
- 3½ cups flour
- 2 cups sugar
- 1½ teaspoon salt
- 1 teaspoon cinnamon
- ¾ teaspoon baking powder
- 2 cups grated zucchini (I use the grating disk on my food processor)
- 1 cups raisins
- 1 teaspoon vanilla

- Preheat oven to 350°
- Grease and flour two 9x5-inch bread pans or one Bundt pan
- Beat eggs and then gradually beat in sugar
- Add oil and vanilla
- In small bowl, combine all the dry ingredients and whisk
- Add dry ingredients to egg, sugar, oil and vanilla mixture alternately with the grated zucchini
- Stir in raisins and walnuts
- Turn into prepared pans
- Bake for 55 minutes and cool on rack

CHEESE STRAWS
1980

- 8 ounces New York extra sharp cheddar cheese
- 1 stick butter (do not use margarine) at room temperature
- 1 teaspoon salt
- 1 teaspoon baking powder
- ¼ teaspoon cayenne pepper or to taste
- 1½ cups all-purpose flour

- Preheat the oven to 375°
- Grate cheese and place in a large mixing bowl
- Line a cookie sheet with parchment paper
- Cream the butter and cheese well
- Add dry ingredients and mix on low speed until smooth
- Shape the dough into a cylinder, wrap in glad wrap and refrigerate
- When ready to bake, allow the dough to come to room temperature
- Pipe through a cookie press 4-6 inch ribbons one inch apart onto the prepared baking sheet
- Bake for 13 minutes, watching closely so that straws do not burn
- They should be barely brown around the edges
- Cut into pieces while warm
- Place in airtight tins (will keep for 3 weeks)
- Can also freeze in airtight container for no longer than 3 months

MINI CHEESE BALLS
1982

- 2 cups shredded firm cheese of choice, I use extra sharp cheddar
- 8 ounces cream cheese
- 1 teaspoon dry mustard
- 1 teaspoon Worcestershire sauce
- ¼ teaspoon cayenne pepper
- ¼ cup toasted white or black sesame seeds
- Finely chopped nuts

- Mix all ingredients well
- Shape into tiny balls
- Roll balls in nuts or sesame seeds
- Refrigerate
- Bring to room temperature before serving
- Put a pretzel stick into each ball for presentation

CHOCOLATE CRINKLES
1982

½ cup oil
4 ounces unsweetened chocolate melted
2 cups granulated sugar
4 eggs
2 teaspoons vanilla
2 cups flour
2 teaspoons baking powder
½ teaspoon salt
1 cup confectioners' sugar

- Preheat oven to 350°
- Mix oil, melted chocolate and granulated sugar
- Blend in one egg at a time until well mixed
- Add vanilla
- Whisk together the flour, baking powder and salt in small bowl
- Stir flour, baking powder and salt into oil mixture
- Chill several hours or overnight
- Drop teaspoonful's of dough into confectioners sugar
- Roll in the sugar and shape into balls
- Place about 2 inches apart on a greased baking sheet
- Bake 10-12 minutes, do not over bake

Yield: 6 dozen

RAISIN BRAN MUFFINS
1977

This recipe is developed as a low calorie muffin. Use regular sugar, whole eggs and regular Bisquick if you do not want a low calorie muffin.

- 1 (15-ounce box) raisin bran cereal
- 3 cups flour
- 2 cups reduced-fat baking mix (Bisquick)
- 3 cups sugar or half sugar and half Splenda
- 1 tablespoon baking soda
- 1 cup egg substitute or 4 regular eggs beaten
- 1 quart buttermilk
- ½ cup canola oil
- Vegetable cooking spray
- (Optional) flax seed and walnuts and extra raisins

- Preheat oven to 400° if you plan to bake immediately
- Combine first 5 ingredients in a large bowl
- Make a well in the center of the mixture and add the egg, milk and oil
- Stir just enough to moisten
- Cover tightly and store in the refrigerator until ready to bake, up to three weeks
- When ready to bake, lightly spray muffin tins with cooking spray or use paper liners
- Fill each muffin cup ⅔ full
- Bake 400° for 15-20 minutes

Yield: 48 muffins

HUMMUS
1979

- 4 cups (about 2½ cans) garbanzo beans, drained
- ½ cup tahini (sesame paste available in grocery stores)
- ⅓ cup warm water
- ⅓ cup high quality olive oil
- Juice of 2 lemons
- 4 cloves garlic, minced or to taste
- ½ teaspoon ground cumin
- Freshly ground black pepper to taste
- 1½ teaspoons salt

- Drain beans and rinse
- Combine beans, tahini, water, olive oil and juice of one lemon a food processor with steel blade
- Process until smooth and creamy, scraping down sides with spatula
- Add garlic, salt, cumin, and pepper
- Process again until very smooth
- Taste and correct seasonings with more lemon juice to taste
- Refrigerate until ready to use

Yield: 1 quart

Serve with hot pita bread or homemade pita chips. Good accompaniment with a cold lunch or appetizer plate.

PITA CHIPS

These crispy chips work well with any kind of dip. I serve them with my hummus and my beer cheese dip. They are easy to make and come out much like homemade croutons.

- Cut pita bread rounds in half and then cut into wedges
- Toss with olive oil, salt and pepper
- Lightly sprinkle with dried Italian herbs (optional but adds a nice flavor)
- Bake at 400° for 5-6 minutes, turn and bake other side for another 5-6 minutes

BEER CHEESE DIP
1970

- Put 8 ounces softened cream cheese and ½ cup beer into food processor or blender
- Process for 20 seconds
- Add ¼ cup beer, 8 ounces diced extra sharp cheddar cheese, and 1 clove garlic
- Blend 20 more seconds or until smooth
- Chill

Makes 3 cups

CHEESE BALL
WRAPPED IN NUTS
1978

For many years I prepared these recipes and then gave them to our neighbors and friends as Christmas gifts.

½	pound (8-ounce) high quality sharp cheddar cheese grated
8	ounces cream cheese
2	tablespoons butter
1	cup finely chopped nuts
	Dash Tabasco
2-3	tablespoons rum

- Cream cheeses and butter
- Add nuts, Tabasco sauce
- Blend in the rum until desired consistency
- Put on waxed paper and form into a ball by pulling paper around cheese
- Refrigerate until firm
- Place nuts on a sheet of waxed paper and roll cheese ball in nuts until covered completely
- Wrap and refrigerate until ready to serve
- Bring to room temperature and serve with crackers
- Can also be packed into cheese crocks
- Can be frozen

Yield: 2½ jars or one large ball

CHEESE SPREAD
1970

- 16 ounces cream cheese
- 16 ounces good quality sharp cheddar cheese
- ½ cup butter
- ¼ cup dry vermouth
- ¼ cup dry sherry
- ½ teaspoon Worcestershire sauce
- 2-3 drops pepper sauce (Tabasco)
- ¼ teaspoon seasoned salt
- ¼ teaspoon celery salt
- ¼ teaspoon oregano, rosemary or dill

- Blend all together
- Chill and allow to season
- Pack into jars

Yield: 4 cups or 3 jars

SPINACH BALLS
1980

My sister, Bev, gave me this recipe. She often makes this today and brings it when she visits us.

- 1 small bag herb seasoning bread stuffing
- Pinch of fresh pepper
- 2 packages frozen chopped spinach, well drained
- 6 eggs
- ¾ cup melted butter
- ½ cup Parmesan cheese
- ½ teaspoon garlic salt or grated fresh garlic
- ½ teaspoon thyme

- Preheat oven to 400°
- Mix all ingredients and roll into one inch balls
- Place on cookie sheet
- Bake 8-10 minutes

Yield: 60 balls

MILE HIGH ICE CREAM PIE
1980

One baked 9-inch piecrust cooled
- 1 pint vanilla bean ice cream softened
- 1 pint chocolate ice cream softened
- 4 egg whites
- ½ teaspoon vanilla
- ¼ teaspoon cream of tartar
- ½ cup sugar

- Layer vanilla ice cream in shell
- Layer chocolate ice cream in shell
- Beat whites with vanilla and cream of tartar until soft peaks form
- Gradually add sugar, beating until stiff and glossy and all sugar is dissolved
- Spread meringue over ice cream sealing to edges of pastry
- Broil 30 seconds to one minute to brown
- Freeze pie several hours or overnight
- To serve take out of freezer 15 minutes early
- Slice into wedges and drizzle with chocolate sauce

CHOCOLATE SAUCE

- 4 ounces unsweetened chocolate
- ¾ cup water
- 1 cup sugar
- Dash salt
- 6 tablespoons butter
- 1 teaspoon vanilla

- Heat chocolate and water together stirring constantly until all is smooth and melted
- Add sugar and salt
- Simmer until slightly thickened about 5 minutes
- Remove mixture from heat
- Blend in butter and vanilla
- Serve warm over pie

Serves: 8

CHOCOLATE PECAN BARS
1981

CRUST

1½ cups flour
½ teaspoon cinnamon
¼ teaspoon baking powder
½ cup firmly packed light brown sugar
¾ cup (1½ sticks) butter softened

CHOCOLATE FILLING

3 eggs
½ cup firmly packed light brown sugar
1 cup dark corn syrup
¼ cup flour
2 squares semisweet chocolate, melted and cooled
1 teaspoon vanilla
¼ teaspoon salt
1½ cups coarsely chopped pecans

- Preheat oven to 350°.
- Grease a 13x9x2-inch baking pan.
- Sift the 1½ cups flour, cinnamon and baking powder into a large bowl.
- Stir in the ½ cup light brown sugar.
- Cut in butter with a pastry blender or food processor until mixture is crumbly.
- Pat into prepared baking pan.
- Bake in oven for 10 minutes. Remove to wire rack. Leave oven on.
- Beat eggs, ½ cup brown sugar, syrup, ¼ cup flour, chocolate, vanilla and salt in a large bowl.
- With an electric mixer, mix until blended.
- Pour over the baked crust layer in the baking pan.
- Sprinkle with nuts.
- Return to oven and bake 30 minutes longer.
- Cool on wire rack.
- Cut into bars.

LEMON MERINGUE BARS
1981

- 1 package of piecrust mix
- ¼ cup sugar
- 4 eggs at room temperature
- 1 cup sugar
- 1½ teaspoons grated lemon rind
- ¼ cup lemon juice
- 1 tablespoon flour
- 2 egg whites, at room temperature
- ⅛ teaspoon cream of tartar
- 3 tablespoons sugar

- Preheat oven to 350°
- Grease a 13x9x2-inch baking pan
- Blend with a pastry blender or food processor the piecrust mix, the ¼ cup sugar and one of the eggs
- Pat dough evenly into prepared baking pan
- Bake for 10 minutes
- Remove to wire rack leaving the oven on
- Beat the remaining three eggs and the 1 cup sugar until light and fluffy
- Beat in the lemon rind and the juice and flour
- Pour mixture over the pie crust
- Return to oven and bake for 15 minutes
- Beat the egg whites with the cream of tartar with electric mixer until frothy
- Beat in remaining 3 tablespoons of sugar, 1 Tablespoon at a time, until the meringue forms stiff peaks
- Remove the pan from the oven
- Raise the oven to 450°
- Spread the meringue mixture over the lemon mixture
- Return to the oven and bake 5 minutes more until the peaks are golden brown
- Cool on wire rack
- Cut with a wet knife

Yield: 32 bar cookies

EGG ROYAL CASSEROLE

1981

My friend, Pat Slock, gave me this recipe during our Gourmet Group days. The guys made a huge brunch buffet once a year as part of our Gourmet Group. This recipe was one of our favorites along with the Grits Soufflé recipe.

- 3 slices bread crumbled into pieces
- ½ pound sharp cheddar cheese shredded
- 4 beaten eggs
- 2½ cups milk
- 1 teaspoon salt
- 1 teaspoon dry mustard
- 4-5 tablespoons chives chopped
- 6-8 slices cooked bacon crumbled

- Put bread and cheese into greased 13x9x2 inch rectangular casserole.
- Mix eggs, milk, salt, dry mustard and chives
- Pour over bread and cheese
- Cover and refrigerate overnight
- Preheat oven to 350°
- Prepare a pan larger than your 13x9 casserole with hot water
- Sprinkle crumbled bacon on top of the casserole
- Bake uncovered in a pan of hot water at 350° oven for about 50 minutes or until knife comes out clean
- Cut into squares and serve warm

Serves: 4-6

CRANBERRY JELL-O SALAD
1978

Steve's aunt, Pauline Buicko, gave me this recipe one Thanksgiving while we were visiting her in Maryland. It is a wonderful accompaniment to a turkey dinner. Aunt Pauline was always a role model for both Steve and me. She was a very strong-minded woman of the Great Generation.

- 1 large package of raspberry or lemon Jell-O
- 1 (16-ounce) can whole cranberries
- ½ cup chopped celery
- ½ cup chopped pecans
- 1 teaspoon fresh lemon juice
- 1 (8-ounce) can crushed pineapple (optional)
- 1 cup hot water to dissolve the Jell-O
- ½ cup cold water

- Dissolve the Jell-O in hot water
- Add cold water and lemon juice
- Let sit in refrigerator until almost congealed
- Add remaining ingredients
- Turn into a square dish
- Return to refrigerator until completely set
- Cut into squares

Serves: 6-8

OVERNIGHT SALAD
1980

My friend, Judy Drones, made this salad every time we got together for a shared supper. This turned out to be Steve's favorite salad. I make it every summer for him during our time at our lake house in North Carolina.

1 head of iceberg lettuce shredded	½ teaspoon salt
1 cup chopped celery	Shredded Swiss or cheddar cheese or a combination of each
1 red onion sliced into rings	Parmesan cheese
1 box frozen petite peas (unthawed)	Crumbled bacon bits
1 cup mayo, can use more if desired	
2 tablespoons sugar	

- Shred the lettuce and line a **deep** bowl with the lettuce (I use a very large rectangular Tupperware container
- Begin to make layers:
    - Celery
    - Onion
    - Peas
    - Salt
    - Mayo
    - Sugar
    - Shredded cheese
    - Parmesan cheese
    - And finally top with bacon

Refrigerate at least 24 hours. Toss completely before serving

Serves 4-6

BROCCOLI SALAD
1968

1 package fresh broccoli florets
1 small red onion, chopped
8 slices bacon browned and crumbled
½ cup raisins or Craisins
1 cup salted sunflower seeds (optional)
½ cup shredded carrots

DRESSING:

1 cup mayonnaise
2 tablespoons white vinegar
¼-½ cup sugar to suit your taste

- Combine the broccoli florets, onion, bacon, raisins, nuts and carrots
- Toss with the dressing no more than 1 hour before serving

If desired, add pecans.

GARDEN MACARONI SALAD
1978

I have added the vegetables to Barney's classic macaroni salad.

¾ cup mayonnaise
1 teaspoon salt
8 ounces elbow macaroni cooked
1 cup diced seedless cucumber
1 cup diced celery
¼ cup diced green pepper
¼ cup diced radishes
2 tablespoons sliced or chopped onion
2 tomatoes seeded and diced

- Mix first 3 ingredients
- Add remaining
- Cover and chill

Serves: 8

RICE AND VEGETABLE SALAD

1999

This salad can be a side salad or a main salad by adding chicken.

- 4 cups hot cooked rice (I use Basmati rice)
- 1 cups vinaigrette (recipe follows)
- 1 small Bermuda onion diced
- 3 scallions finely sliced
- ½ red pepper, cut into thin julienne
- ½ green pepper cut into thin julienne
- ½ cup dried cranberries, currants or raisins
- 1 shallot minced
- ½ package (5 ounces) frozen peas, thawed and blanched for 3 minutes
- 4 tablespoons pitted black olives minced
- Handful of purple seedless grapes sliced in half
- Toasted pine nuts or pecans
- 2 tablespoons roughly chopped Italian parsley
- ¼ cup chopped fresh dill
- Salt and freshly ground pepper to taste
- Can add diced cooked chicken breasts for a heartier salad

- Cook rice and place in mixing bowl
- Pour about
- Transfer rice to a mixing bowl and pour ½ cup of the vinaigrette, toss and cool
- Add the remaining ingredients to the rice and toss thoroughly
- Taste; correct seasoning and add more dressing if needed
- Serve at room temperature or cover and refrigerate for up to 4 hours
- If refrigerated, return to room temperature before serving

Yield: 4-6 servings

VINAIGRETTE

- 2 tablespoons Dijon mustard
- 8 tablespoons Red wine vinegar
- 2 teaspoons sugar
- 1 teaspoon salt
- ½ teaspoon black pepper
- Minced parsley or fresh chives
- 1 cup olive oil

- Measure mustard into bowl; whisk in vinegar, sugar, salt, pepper and herbs
- Continue to whisk while slowly adding the olive oil
- Adjust seasonings to taste
- Cover until ready to use
- Whisk again before using

Yield: 2 cups

GOURMET CHICKEN SALAD

2006

Chicken salad is a lunch mainstay in our house. I often make it with leftover chicken, but when I serve it as a main course I use this recipe to jazz up plain old chicken salad.

- 4 boneless chicken breasts cooked
- 1 cup sliced green seedless grapes
- 2 tablespoons minced fresh parsley
- ¼ teaspoon fresh dill minced
- 1 cup finely diced celery
- ¼ cup finely chopped scallions
- ½ cup toasted pecan halves or walnuts
- ½ cup half and half
- 1 cup mayonnaise
- Salt and fresh black pepper to taste

- Cook chicken breasts in water or chicken broth
- Drain and cool
- Cut into bite size pieces
- Mix with remaining ingredients and adjust seasoning with salt and pepper
- Chill well before serving

Presentation: arrange on a bed of green leaf lettuce or curly endive leaves and garnish with small cluster of green grapes.

COOKING/POACHING CHICKEN BREASTS IN BROTH

- Place breasts in broth, add herbs
- Bring to a simmer
- Simmer gently for 10 minutes
- Turn off heat and let sit in hot broth for another 20-25 minutes

ROCKY MOUNT, NC
THE GOURMET YEARS
1982-1990

"Refine the palate while building friendships" was a tiny motto that I wrote in calligraphy to highlight the menu on individual place cards for our dinner tables. We were four couples who loved to cook and dine together.

The ladies got together about 2 weeks prior to our scheduled dinners. A nice wine was served, and then we began to mull over tons of recipes and cookbooks to develop our menus.

For each dinner, the hostess prepared the entrée and the rest of the ladies shared the remaining menu items. The cost, to include all the wines, was divided by four. After the dinner, I was in charge of typing the menus and recipes for distribution. We each then created our own gourmet book for future use.

SEA LEGS DIABLE

1988

I make this often when at our lake home. I accompany this appetizer with toasted crostini's.

- 8 ounces imitation crab
- ¼ cup olive oil
- 1 clove garlic minced
- 1 onion chopped
- ½ green pepper chopped
- 4 medium tomatoes, skinned, seeds removed, and chopped
- 2 tablespoons fresh parsley
- 1 teaspoon dried oregano or 1 tablespoon fresh oregano chopped
- Dash Tabasco sauce
- Cayenne pepper to taste
- ¼ cup red wine

- Sauté garlic, onion and pepper in olive oil
- Add tomatoes, parsley, oregano, Tabasco, cayenne, and wine
- Bring to a boil
- Add crab
- Simmer 12-15 minutes
- Serve on toast, in patty shells, or with toasted crostini

TOASTED CROSTINI

- Slice several diagonally slices of ciabatta bread
- Preheat grill and toast crostini
- Brush with olive oil

Serves: 4 appetizers

SALMON SPREAD
IN FISH MOLD
GOURMET GROUP ROCKY MOUNT, NC
1983

- 2 (15-ounce) cans red salmon or poached salon
- 16 ounces cream cheese, softened
- 2 tablespoons lemon juice
- 1 tablespoon plus 1 teaspoon grated onion
- 2 teaspoons celery seeds
- 2 teaspoons prepared horseradish
- ½ teaspoon salt
- Coarsely ground black pepper to taste
- 1 cup finely toasted almond slivers for fish scales
- Spanish olives sliced for eyes
- Pimento strips
- Fresh parsley

- Drain salmon; remove skin and bones
- Flake salmon with a fork
- Combine next 7 ingredients and mix well
- Gently stir in salmon
- Spoon mixture into a well-oiled 5-cup fish mold
- Chill several hours or overnight
- Unfold onto serving platter and gently arrange almond slivers to resemble fish scales
- Add Spanish olive slices (with pimento center) as the eyes
- Place pimento strips on tail of fish
- Fresh parsley for garnish
- Serve with assorted crackers

Yield: 14-16 servings

MUSHROOMS STUFFED
WITH SPINACH & ANCHOVIES
1983

- 1 pound large mushrooms
- 1 pound fresh spinach chopped or 1 box frozen chopped spinach, thawed and squeezed dry
- 2 tablespoons anchovy paste
- ½ teaspoon chopped garlic
- ½ cup heavy cream
- 3 tablespoons melted butter
- ¼ cup grated Parmesan cheese
- Olive oil

- Preheat oven to 400°.
- Remove stems from mushrooms chop and reserve.
- Melt 1 tablespoon butter in saucepan and add the flour to make a roux. Stir with a wire whisk.
- When blended, add the milk stirring rapidly, add salt and pepper.
- In another pan, heat 2 Tablespoons butter and add the scallions and mushrooms stems.
- Cook 4 minutes.
- Add crab meat, stir to blend and add the cognac.
- Add the white sauce and salt and pepper to taste.
- Blend; add egg yolk and Tabasco.
- Place the mushroom caps, hollow side down, in a buttered baking dish.
- Brush with half the melted butter and bake for 10 minutes and cool.
- Stuff each with the crab mixture.
- Arrange in baking dish and sprinkle with cheese.
- Bake 20 minutes.

Yield: 6

CHAMPIGNONS FARCIS
STUFFED MUSHROOMS
1980

The following stuffing will stuff 12 large mushrooms.

- 3 slices bacon
- 12 mushrooms
- One onion finely chopped
- ¼ cup finely chopped green pepper
- 1 cup soft stale breadcrumbs
- 2 tablespoons chopped fresh parsley
- ½ teaspoon salt
- A bit of chicken stock to moisten
- Salt and pepper to taste
- Dry white wine or chicken stock
- Parmesan cheese grated

- Preheat oven to 325°
- Remove mushroom stems and chop
- Cook the bacon until crisp; crumble and remove from skillet
- Remove bacon fat from skillet leaving about 2 tablespoons
- Cook chopped onion, green pepper and mushroom stems in skillet
- Cook until tender
- Add bread crumbs, crumbled bacon, parsley, salt and a little chicken stock to moisten
- Season with salt and pepper
- Stuff mushroom caps, sprinkle with cheese
- Place in shallow baking pan with small amount of water or wine to ½ inch deep
- Bake for 25 minutes

Allow two large mushrooms per serving for vegetable side. Use smaller mushrooms as an appetizer before dinner.

Serves: 6

MUSHROOMS STUFFED
WITH CRAB MEAT
1983

- 1 pound large mushrooms
- 3 tablespoons butter
- 1 tablespoon flour
- ½ cup milk
- Salt and freshly ground pepper to taste
- ½ cup finely chopped scallions
- ⅓ pound crab meat, use lump crab
- 1 tablespoon cognac
- 1 egg yolk
- Tabasco to taste
- 3 tablespoons melted butter
- ¼ cup grated Parmesan cheese

- Preheat oven to 400°.
- Remove stems from mushrooms chop and reserve.
- Melt 1 tablespoon butter in saucepan and add the flour to make a roux. Stir with a wire whisk.
- When blended, add the milk stirring rapidly, add salt and pepper.
- In another pan, heat 2 tablespoons butter and add the scallions and mushrooms stems.
- Cook 4 minutes.
- Add crab meat, stir to blend and add the cognac.
- Add the white sauce and salt and pepper to taste.
- Blend; add egg yolk and Tabasco.
- Place the mushroom caps, hollow side down, in a buttered baking dish.
- Brush with half the melted butter and bake for 10 minutes; cool.
- Stuff each with the crab mixture.
- Arrange in baking dish and sprinkle with cheese.
- Bake 20 minutes.

Yield: 6

MONTRACHET & SUN-DRIED TOMATO MOLD
1987

My sister, Marie Bauer, shared this recipe from one of her gourmet group dinners. I make it frequently and have shared it with my daughters.

- 1 package sun-dried tomatoes (softened in water and chopped)
- 1 (3½-ounce) jar pesto or homemade pesto
- 8 ounces goat cheese, softened
- 8 ounces cream cheese, softened
- ½ cup toasted pine nuts

- Preheat oven to 400°
- Toast pine nuts for (4-5 minutes) until golden brown
- In a medium size bowl, mix the goat cheese and the cream cheese until the mixture is smooth and creamy
- Line a small loaf pan or a small bowl with plastic wrap so that the wrap hangs over the sides of the pan or bowl
- Spread ⅓ of the goat cheese mixture in bottom of pan
- Spread ½ of the pesto very gently over the cheese mixture
- Top with ½ of the sun-dried tomatoes
- Sprinkle with ½ of the pine nuts
- Top with another ⅓ cheese mixture, spreading gently with a spatula
- Top with the other half of the pesto
- Sprinkle with remaining half of the sun-dried tomatoes and pine nuts
- Spread the last layer of the cheese mixture
- Fold the plastic wrap over the top of the cheese and press slightly to compact the mold
- Refrigerate at least 2-3 hours until the cheese is firm

TO SERVE:

- Lift mold out gently using the overhang of plastic wrap to lift
- Invert onto a plate and gently remove the plastic wrap
- Serve with crackers or bread rounds

Can be frozen.

HOT CRAB RANGOON DIP
1981

This recipe is another version to my hot crabmeat of the 70's. We served this dip in a chafing dish with crispy crackers.

- 8 ounces cream cheese softened
- ¼ cup sour cream
- 2 green onions chopped
- ¾ teaspoon Worcestershire sauce
- 1 tablespoon powdered sugar
- ¼ teaspoon garlic powder
- ¼ teaspoon lemon juice
- 8 ounces jumbo crabmeat thoroughly rinsed

- Preheat oven to 350°
- Soften cheese, add remainder of ingredients
- Bake at 350° for 30 minutes, serve hot

Serves: 4-6

POTATO SKINS
1981

- Preheat oven to 400°
- Hollow out baked potato
- Cut the skins into long strips
- Butter thoroughly
- Sprinkle with salt and fresh pepper
- Bake 375-400° until crisp
- Top with cheese, return to oven until cheese is melted

MARINATED VEGETABLES
1981

- ¼ cup lemon juice
- ½ cup vinegar
- ¼ cup water
- 2 tablespoons chopped shallot
- ⅛ teaspoon pepper
- 1-2 tablespoons minced garlic
- 1 tablespoon freshly chopped parsley
- ½ teaspoon salt
- ½ teaspoon sugar
- ⅛ teaspoon oregano

Cook any variety of vegetables and add to the above marinade.

QUICHE DE LANGOUSTE
GOURMET GROUP
1982

We served this beautiful quiche as our appetizer or first course. Our second course was a cucumber soup followed by Duck A L'Orange and Potatoes Anna.

2	lobsters cooked or 3-4 lobster tails cooked
	Pastry for one crust 9-inch pie unbaked
2	tablespoons chopped onion
¼	cup butter
¼	cup brandy
	Salt and pepper to taste
1–1¼	cups heavy cream
4	eggs
	Dash of ground nutmeg

- Preheat oven to 400°
- Roll out pastry and line a 9-inch pie pan
- Chill pastry shell
- Place a piece of foil over pastry and fill with dry beans to weight down the pastry
- Bake in oven for 10 minutes
- Remove foil and beans
- Reduce oven temperature to 375°
- Remove lobster meat from shells and cut into convenient pieces
- Sauté onion in butter until tender
- Add lobster and heat through
- Add brandy and season to taste with salt and pepper
- Arrange lobster and onion in pastry lined pie pan
- Beat eggs and remaining cream together and season with salt
- Pour over lobster, dust top with a little nutmeg
- Bake in the 375° oven for 35 minutes or until firm
- Serve at once

Yield: 6 appetizers or 4 lunch entrees

COQUILLES ST-JACQUES
1980

This French dish of scallops poached in white wine was popular in the 50's. It found its way to our table in the 80's.

¼ cup minced onions
1 tablespoon butter
3 shallots, minced
1 small clove garlic, minced
6 ounces mushrooms chopped
6 large sea scallops quartered, about 1½ pounds
   Salt and pepper to taste
   Flour for coating scallops
1 tablespoon olive oil and 2 tablespoons butter for sautéing scallops
½ cup dry vermouth plus 3 tablespoons water (can also use dry white wine without water)
1 bay leaf
¼ teaspoon minced thyme
½ cup grated Swiss or Parmesan cheese or combination of both

- Lightly grease 6 scallops shells with cooking spray
- Cook onions until soft then add mushrooms and cook until there is no liquid
- Add the garlic and shallots
- Cook and set aside
- Pat the scallops with paper towels and sprinkle with salt and pepper
- Dredge in flour then sauté in oil and butter for about 2 minutes
- Add the wine, water, herbs and the cooked onion/shallot/mushroom mixture
- Cover and simmer for 5 minutes
- Remove the scallops
- Rapidly boil down the liquid uncovered until it is thickened, correcting seasonings
- Discard the bay leaf
- Add the scallops to the sauce
- Spoon the scallop mixture into prepared shells
- Sprinkle with cheese
- Dot with butter
- At this point you can refrigerate until ready to broil
- Put scallops shells under broiler for 4-5 minutes to heat through and brown the cheese

Serves: 6

DUCK A L'ORANGE
1982

  5 -pound duck, cleaned wing tips and fat removed
     Zest of 2 oranges
     Juice of two oranges or about 2 cups
½ cup sugar
1½ cups chicken stock
¼ - ½ cup orange liqueur
     Arrowroot for thickening sauce

- Preheat oven to 450°
- Prick the skin of the duck to allow fat to escape
- Pat dry the duck, sprinkle with a bit of salt and pepper
- Put duck in roasting pan with rack, add water to bottom of pan
- Bake for about 30 minutes just to brown the duck
- Reduce oven to 300° and continue roasting for about 1 hour
- While duck is roasting put orange juice, zest and sugar in saucepot
- Heat and reduce to half and set aside
- Add hot chicken stock to reduced orange mixture and simmer for about 10-15 minutes
- Add arrowroot to thicken
- Remove duck from pan, let rest for about 15 minutes
- Remove all fat drippings from roasting pan and deglaze pan with orange liqueur
- Cook until reduced to about a few tablespoons
- Add orange sauce to roasting pan, mix well
- Carve duck and serve with sauce

Serves: 4

BRANDIED SHRIMP PROVENCALE
1981

This dish can be served as an entrée over risotto or as an appetizer with toasted crostini.

- 4 tablespoons butter
- 1 tablespoon chopped onion
- 1 clove garlic minced
- 4 raw shrimp
- 2 ounces brandy
- 1 cup peeled, seeded and cubed fresh tomatoes
- 1 tablespoon chopped fresh parsley
- Salt and pepper

- Preheat skillet, then add the butter
- Add onion and garlic and shrimp
- Stir rapidly for 2 minutes
- Pour in brandy and ignite
- Shake pan fast
- Add tomatoes and parsley
- Season to taste with salt and pepper

Yield: 4

SOMERSET POTTED CHEDDAR
WITH WALNUTS
1983

- 16 ounces high quality sharp cheddar cheese grated
- 1½ sticks unsalted butter, room temperature
- 2 tablespoons dry sherry
- ½ teaspoon Worcestershire sauce
- Salt and fresh pepper
- 4 ounces (1 cup) coarsely chopped walnuts

- Combine cheese and butter in electric mixer, blend well
- Mix in sherry, Worcestershire, salt and pepper
- Add walnuts
- Pack into cheese crocks
- Let stand at room temperature one hour before serving

MUSHROOM SPREAD
1981

We served this warm spread on baked pita chips or crisp crackers.

- 4 slices bacon
- 8 ounces fresh mushrooms chopped
- 1 medium onion finely chopped
- 1 clove garlic, minced
- 2 tablespoons flour
- ¼ teaspoon salt
- Freshly ground pepper
- 8 ounces cream cheese cubed
- 2 teaspoons Worcestershire sauce
- 1 teaspoon soy sauce
- ½ cup sour cream

- In skillet, cook bacon until crisp; drain reserving 2 tablespoons drippings
- Crumble bacon and set aside
- Cook mushrooms, onion and garlic in bacon drippings until tender
- Cook until most of the liquid has evaporated
- Stir in flour, salt and pepper
- Add the cream cheese, Worcestershire sauce and soy sauce
- Heat and stir until cheese is melted
- Stir in sour cream and bacon
- Heat through, DO NOT BOIL
- Serve warm with toasted bread rounds or crackers

MARINATED MUSHROOMS
1981

- ¼ cup lemon juice
- ½ cup vinegar
- ¼ cup water
- 2 tablespoons chopped onion
- 1-2 teaspoons minced garlic
- 1 tablespoon fresh parsley chopped
- ½ teaspoon salt
- ½ teaspoon sugar
- ⅛ teaspoon oregano
- ⅛ teaspoon pepper
- ⅓ cup olive oil

- Wash fresh mushrooms or use canned mushrooms
- Pour marinade over mushrooms
- Marinate in refrigerator for 3 days

CHEESY NUT BALL
1978

This is by far our favorite cheese ball or cheese crock recipe. The blue cheese gives it a wonderful flavor. I usually serve this with cranberry/nut crackers found in Fresh Market stores. My friend, Mary Hoofnagel, shared this recipe with me. It is another cheese recipe that I pack into jars and gave to friends during the holidays.

- 8 ounces cream cheese
- 8 ounces sharp cheddar cheese grated
- ½ cup crumbled blue cheese
- 2 teaspoons grated onion or dash of onion powder
- ½ cup finely chopped salted peanuts, finely chopped toasted walnuts or finely chopped pecans (my preference is pecans)

- Grate the cheddar cheese
- Add cheddar, cream cheese, and blue cheese to food processor
- Add onion or onion powder
- Process until smooth
- Moisten hands, then shape into a ball
- Wrap in waxed paper and refrigerate until firm
- Place ball on a piece of waxed paper sprinkled with the nuts.
- Roll ball until it is covered with nuts
- Chill, serve with crackers
- Bring to room temperature before serving
- You can also pack this into cheese crocks and add the nuts into the mixture

Yield: one large cheese ball or 2 ½ 8-ounce jars

HOT CRAB DIP
1981

- 8 ounces cream cheese
- 3 tablespoons mayonnaise
- 1 teaspoon Dijon mustard
- 2 tablespoons dry white wine
- 7 ounces crabmeat, lump

- Mix together and warm in a chafing dish
- Serve in chafing dish with crackers

Yield: 2 cups

HOT TACO DIP
1987

- 1 (32-ounce) can of refried beans
- 1 package taco seasoning mix
- 1 large tomato seeded and chopped
- 2 cups sour cream
- 2 cups guacamole
- ½ cup chopped green onions
- 1 (4-ounce) can chopped green chilies
- 1 cup sliced black olives
- 1-2 cups sharp cheddar cheese

- Spread refried beans in the bottom of a 9x12 pan
- Sprinkle the seasoning packet over the beans
- Layer the tomatoes, the sour cream, and the guacamole
- Sprinkle the green onions and green chilies
- Sprinkle top with olives
- Top with the cheese
- Serve hot or cold

Serves: 10

BARBECUED CHICKEN WINGS
GOURMET GROUP APPETIZER
1977

- 35-40 whole chicken wings
- 1 bottle Chinese BBQ sauce or sauce of choice
- 3 tablespoons honey

- Cut up wings
- Mix sauce and honey
- Toss wings in sauce
- Refrigerate overnight
- Preheat oven to 350°
- Bake 45 minutes turning 2-3 times

PORK OR BEEF RIBLETS
1977

Pork or beef riblets
⅓ cup soy sauce
½ cup salad oil
½ cup wine vinegar
½ cup lemon juice
1 tablespoon grated fresh ginger
¼ teaspoon freshly ground pepper
2 cloves crushed garlic

- Mix all together
- Add small pork or beef riblets
- Marinate 3-4 hours
- Bake in 350° oven 45 minutes or until done

MINCED OYSTER APPETIZER
GOURMET GROUP
1980

1 cup finely chopped celery
1 tablespoon melted butter
1 pint oysters rinsed and drained finely chopped
1 cup toasted breadcrumbs
2 beaten eggs
1 tablespoon fresh lemon juice
1 teaspoon grated onion
½ teaspoon salt
Fresh pepper to taste
Parmesan cheese for top

- Preheat oven to 350°
- Grease a 1-quart casserole dish or four 1 cup ramekin or oyster shells
- Sauté celery in butter until tender
- Stir in oysters and breadcrumbs, eggs, lemon juice and seasonings
- Cook until heated through
- Spoon into prepared dishes
- Sprinkle with more toasted crumbs and cheese
- Bake for 30 minutes

CRAB PROFITEROLES
1981

PUFF SHELLS:

½ cup water
4 tablespoons butter
¼ teaspoon salt

½ cup flour
2 eggs

- Preheat oven to 425°
- Lightly grease a cookie sheet
- Boil water, butter and salt
- Add flour all at once
- Stir until mixture forms a ball and leaves the sides of the pan
- Remove from heat
- Add eggs one at a time beating after each addition
- Beat until satiny
- Drop by teaspoons onto cookie sheet
- Bake 18 minutes
- Lower heat to 375° and bake 10 minutes longer
- 5 minutes before done, pierce each puff with sharp knife to let steam escape
- When cool, cut tops off for stuffing and set aside while you make the filling

FILLING:

14 ounces crabmeat, use lump crabmeat
½ cup mayonnaise

3 teaspoons Worcestershire sauce
1½ teaspoons minced onion

- Mix mayonnaise, Worcestershire and onion
- Fold in crab
- Cut tops off puffs
- Stuff profiteroles with filling

PALATE CLEANSERS
GOURMET GROUP
1977

We served a fresh palate cleanser just before we served the main entrée. These very small scoops of flavored fresh sorbet are laced with Vodka or Champagne and served in small wine glasses with tiny spoons. The purpose is to cleanse the palate after soup and/or appetizer before savoring the main entrée. Today I cut corners and buy high quality sorbet and serve with a splash of Vodka or Champagne.

CHAMPAGNE SORBET
March 1982

- 1 cup whipping cream
- ¾ cup sugar
- 1½ cups champagne
- 1 (10-ounce) package of frozen strawberries thawed
- 2 egg whites
- ¼ teaspoon cream of tartar
- Few drops red food coloring

- Combine cream and ½ cup sugar
- Cook and stir over medium heat until sugar dissolves; cool
- Stir in champagne and undrained berries
- Pour into an 8x8x2 square pan, cover and freeze
- Beat whites and cream of tartar
- Slowly add remaining sugar, beating until stiff
- Break up frozen berry mix and turn into chilled bowl
- Beat smooth with beater
- Fold in whipped egg whites
- Tint with coloring, cover and freeze

PINEAPPLE SORBET
February 1982

2 (20-ounce) cans pineapple rings
Champagne

- Arrange pineapple rings on cookie sheet and freeze
- Cut into pieces, transfer to food processor and puree until smooth and creamy
- Scoop 20 one-inch balls onto cookie sheet and freeze
- Arrange 2 scoops of sorbet in a small wine glass
- Pour 3-4 tablespoons champagne over each

CAULIFLOWER SOUP
1981

2 tablespoons butter
½ cup minced onion
1 medium cauliflower about 4 cups cut into ½ inch pieces
1½ cups chicken stock
1 cup whipping cream or to taste
Salt, pepper and nutmeg
1-2 tablespoons sherry, madeira or dry white wine
Butter for enrichment

- Melt butter and add onion
- Cover and cook 10 minutes
- Add cauliflower; cover and cook 5 minutes, stirring halfway through cooking time
- Pour in enough stock barely to cover ingredients
- Cover pan partially and bring to boil
- Let boil until cauliflower is tender, about 10 minutes
- Puree in food processor or use immersion blender
- Thin the soup with the cream
- Season
- Stir in the wine
- Enrich with butter while hot
- Serve hot

Yield: 4

FRENCH ONION SOUP

1982

This is Steve's favorite soup.

- ½ cup unsalted butter
- 4 onions, sliced
- 2 garlic cloves, chopped
- 2 bay leaves
- 2 fresh thyme sprigs
- Kosher salt and freshly ground black pepper
- 1 cup red wine
- 3 tablespoons flour
- 2 quarts rich beef stock
- 1 baguette, sliced
- ½ pound grated Gruyere
- Salt and freshly ground pepper to taste

- Melt the butter in a large pot over medium heat.
- Add the onions, garlic, thyme, bay leaves, salt and pepper and cook until the onions are very soft and caramelized, about 25 minutes
- Add the wine, bring to a boil, reduce the heat and simmer until the wine has evaporated and the onions are dry, about 5 minutes
- Discard the bay leaves and thyme sprigs
- Dust the onions with the flour and stir
- Lower the heat to medium low so the flour doesn't burn, and cook for 10 minutes to cook out the raw flour taste
- Add the beef stock, bring the soup back to a simmer, and cook for 10 minutes
- Season with salt and pepper
- Ladle the soup into bowls, top each with 2 slices of bread and top with cheese
- Put the bowls into the oven to toast the bread and melt the cheese, or broil

Yield: 4-6

CRAB LOUIS SALAD
1982

This is a classic. It is an ideal salad for a light luncheon or you can put the crab mixed with the dressing into avocado halves for an attractive alternative.

- 12 ounces lump crabmeat
- 4 tomatoes quartered
- 4 hard-cooked eggs, quartered
- Ripe or green olives
- 4 cups bite-size pieces salad greens, chilled

- Rinse and drain crabmeat, remove cartilage, chill
- Prepare the Louis Dressing (recipe below)
- Arrange crab, tomatoes, eggs, olives on greens
- Pour dressing over salad
- OR mix crab with Louis dressing and scoop into avocado halves

Yield: 4 servings

LOUIS DRESSING:

- ¾ cup chili sauce
- ½ cup mayonnaise
- 1 teaspoon instant minced onion or diced shallots
- ½ teaspoon sugar
- ¼ teaspoon Worcestershire sauce
- Salt to taste

- Mix all ingredients. Chill for 30 minutes

Yield: 1cup dressing

BASIC CAESAR SALAD
WITH VARIATIONS
GOURMET GROUP
May 1980

I ordered this salad at high-end restaurants and was impressed how they prepared it at a side table for our viewing.

- 1 clove garlic
- ½ cup olive oil
- ½ head romaine lettuce cut into pieces
- ½ bunch curly endive, optional
- 1 cup good quality croutons
- 1 (2-ounce) can anchovy fillets (I often use anchovy paste)
- 1 coddled egg
- ½ cup grated Parmesan cheese
- ¼ cup lemon juice
- 1 teaspoon Worcestershire sauce
- ½ teaspoon fresh pepper
- ½ teaspoon salt

- Wash lettuce and cut into pieces, set aside.
- Mash the garlic in the bottom of a wooden salad bowl.
- Add the oil, let stand to flavor the oil.
- Coddle the egg by placing it into 3 cups of boiling water. Let it stand in the water for 1 minute, remove and let cool.
- Add the cooled egg, Worcestershire sauce, lemon juice, fresh pepper and salt into wooden bowl and whisk until well blended.
- Add the anchovies and mash thoroughly, whisk dressing again.
- Add the lettuce into the salad bowl.
- Add croutons and cheese.
- Toss all together.
- Pour over salad and toss lightly.

Serves: 4-6

VARIATIONS:
- Add chopped cooked chicken breast.
- Add 1 pound of cooked shrimp and 3-4 cut tomatoes.

SPINACH SOUFFLE
GOURMET GROUP
1977

This is truly a wonderful vegetable dish and well worth the extra time. You will receive lots of compliments.

- 1 ounce grated Swiss cheese
- 2 ounces grated Parmesan cheese
- 2 (10-ounce) pkgs. frozen chopped spinach cooked
- 1 tablespoon chopped onion
- ½ cup parsley
- 5 large egg yolks
- ¼ cup flour
- 1 teaspoon salt
- ½ teaspoon nutmeg
- ½ teaspoon freshly grated pepper
- 1 cup heated milk
- 5 large egg whites at room temperature
- Pinch of salt
- ½ teaspoon cream of tartar

- Preheat oven to 375°.
- Grease a 6-cup soufflé mold and sprinkle with 1 tablespoon Swiss cheese and 1 tablespoon Parmesan cheese.
- Cook spinach (I cook the spinach in the microwave).
- Add to spinach chopped onion, parsley, egg yolks, flour, salt, nutmeg and pepper in food processor or blender.
- Blend, with the motor running, pour in 1 cup heated milk.
- Pour into pan and cook until thickened.
- Remove from heat and cool.
- At this point you can stop and refrigerate the mixture and finish the next day. You must reheat the mixture before continuing if you do continue later.
- Beat the egg whites with salt until foamy.
- Add the cream of tartar and beat until just very soft peaks form...do not overbeat or the soufflé will be dry.
- Fold some whites into the spinach mix until entirely combined.
- Fold in the remaining cheeses and egg whites.
- Put into dish.
- Bake 35-40 minutes or until lightly browned.

Serves: 6-8

BROCCOLI PUFF
GOURMET GROUP
1977

2 (10-ounce) packages chopped broccoli, or fresh broccoli cooked and chopped
3 eggs separated at room temperature
1 tablespoon flour
   Pinch nutmeg
1 cup mayonnaise
1 tablespoon butter softened
¼ teaspoon salt
¼ teaspoon freshly ground pepper
¼ cup plus 1 tablespoon grated Parmesan cheese

- Preheat oven to 350°
- Cook broccoli and drain well
- Beat egg yolks, add flour and mix well
- Stir in nutmeg, mayonnaise, butter, salt, pepper, and cheese
- Add broccoli, mixing lightly
- Beat egg whites (at room temperature) until stiff but not dry
- Gently fold into broccoli mixture
- Pour into lightly greased 9-inch square baking dish
- Sprinkle top with additional Parmesan cheese
- Bake 350° for 30 minutes
- Cut into squares to serve

Yield: 6-8 servings

PARLIAMENT POTATOES
1985

My sister Marie shared this recipe with me. It was a hit at her gourmet group as well as mine.

- 4 medium baking potatoes, peeled
- ½ cup melted butter
- 1½ tablespoons olive oil
- 1 small clove garlic minced or grated
- Salt and pepper to taste
- 3 ounces Parmesan cheese, freshly grated

- Preheat oven to 375°
- Thinly slice each potato ¾ of the way through crosswise carefully leaving the bottom of the potato whole
- Combine the butter, oil and garlic in small shallow bowl
- Roll potatoes in the butter mixture
- Place the potatoes in a large shallow roasting pan
- Pour the remaining butter mixture over the potatoes
- Season with salt and pepper
- Bake potatoes, basting frequently, until done and golden brown
- Bake about 1½ hours
- Sprinkle potatoes with Parmesan cheese just before serving

The potatoes can be baked earlier in the day and reheated just before serving. Use one potato per serving.

Serves: 4

CHATEAU POTATOES

- 8 tablespoons butter
- 2 pounds potatoes cut into ovals, large chucks, or sliced
- 1 tablespoon minced fresh parsley
- ¾ teaspoon salt and freshly ground pepper

- Melt the butter in a large ovenproof skillet over medium-high heat
- Sauté the potatoes in the butter for 5 minutes
- Place the skillet into a 400° oven and roast the potatoes, stirring often, for 20 minutes
- Remove the skillet from the oven and sprinkle the chopped parsley, salt, and pepper

Serves: 4-6

POTATO CHEESE CUPS
1980

This recipe serves two people.

- 1 medium potato grated or use Simply Shredded Potatoes found in the egg section of your supermarket
- ½ cup grated Gruyere cheese
- 2 tablespoons minced onion
- ¼ teaspoon chervil or fresh parsley minced with a pinch of fines herbs
- Salt and freshly ground pepper
- Butter
- Paprika
- 2 thick slices of tomato

- Position oven rack in center
- Preheat oven to 350°
- Peel and coarsely grate potato into small bowl of water
- Drain and squeeze dry
- Combine potatoes with cheese, onion, chervil, salt and pepper
- If you are using the store bought shredded potatoes just combine them with the cheese, onion, chervil and salt/pepper
- Generously coat inside of two 6-ounce ramekin dishes with butter and PAM spray
- Sprinkle ramekins with paprika
- Divide potato mixture between the cups, pressing down
- Bake for about 40 minutes until edges are brown and crisp and center is no longer moist
- Remove from oven and cool slightly
- Loosen potato with knife and invert each onto a thick tomato slice

POMMES ANNA
1977

2 pounds potatoes, peeled and cut into ⅛ inch thick slices
Unsalted Butter melted, preferably clarified*
Salt and freshly ground pepper to taste

- Preheat oven to 425°
- Cut a circle of parchment paper to fit the bottom of a round shallow baking dish with a cover or a 10-inch pie plate and cover with buttered aluminum foil
- Butter pan generously, put paper in bottom and then butter paper
- Arrange a layer of overlapping slices of potato in the pan starting in the middle and making circles to the edge
- Pour 1 tablespoon melted butter over the layer
- Sprinkle with salt and pepper
- Continue adding more layers of potatoes, buttering and seasoning each layer
- There should be 3-4 layers
- Pour another 1 tablespoon butter on top
- Bake on the bottom shelf of oven for 50 minutes or until fork tender
- Drain off the butter
- Carefully turn potatoes upside down on a round plate and peel off paper
- The potatoes should be well browned on the bottom; if not, run under the broiler until golden brown

Serves: 6

*Clarified butter has a much higher smoke point than regular butter. To make clarified butter, melt the butter and then spoon off the top foam. Allow the rest to settle until the milk solids fall to the bottom. Pour off only the yellow butter on top and throw away the milk solids found on the bottom. You should be left with a bright yellow substance that will keep very well in the refrigerator. I have found clarified butter in Fresh Market stores.

ZELDA'S FETTUCCINI
GOURMET GROUP
1978

- 2 cups sour cream (use nonfat sour cream for a lower calorie option)
- ¾ cup Parmesan cheese
- ¼ cup dry vermouth
- 1 tablespoon flour
- 1 tablespoon fresh lemon juice
- 2 garlic cloves, minced
- ½ teaspoon dried oregano crushed
- ½ teaspoon dried basil, crushed
- ½ teaspoon dried marjoram, crushed
- Salt/pepper
- ½ cup unsalted butter
- ¾ pound Spinach fettuccini

- Combine first 10 ingredients in medium bowl and blend well
- Melt butter and stir in the blended ingredients
- Simmer 20 min
- Combine with the noodles and toss
- Serve immediately

Serves: 6*

*1 ½ TIMES THE RECIPE SERVES 8

- 3 c. sour cream
- 1¼ cups Parmesan cheese
- ⅓ cup vermouth
- 2 tablespoons flour
- 1½ tablespoons lemon juice
- 3 garlic cloves, minced
- Just a bit more of the spices
- ¾ cup unsalted butter
- 1–1½ pounds fettuccini

This sauce can also be used over broccoli or cauliflower.

ARTHUR'S
STUFFED FILET MIGNON
GOURMET GROUP
1982

We used this recipe in our Rocky Mount gourmet group. Absolutely delicious.

- 2 tablespoons unsalted butter
- 4 (6-ounce) beef filets
- ½ pound crabmeat
- 3 shallots, minced
- 1 tablespoon chives
- 8 medium mushrooms sliced and sautéed
- 2 cups rich beef stock
- 1 cup Madera wine

- Preheat oven to 450°
- Sauté shallots in butter
- Add crab and chives
- Butterfly filets and flatten
- Stuff with crab mixture and close
- Preheat a good stainless or cast iron skillet until hot
- Sear filets on both sides about 3 minutes per side until well browned
- Put in 450° oven until done (4 minutes for rare, 6 minutes for medium)
- Add beef stock to skillet and scrap pan to deglaze
- Add the cooked mushrooms and wine, salt and pepper
- Reduce to ½ (can be thickened with roux if desired)
- Put filets on plate and top with mushroom sauce

Wild rice is a nice accompaniment

Wine Pairing: Cabernet Sauvignon, Pinot Noir, Bordeaux, and Merlot

Serves: 4

STEAK DIANE
1984

- 4 filet mignons cut into medallions
- (Variation) 4 (8-ounce) sirloin steaks about 1" thick
- Salt and freshly ground pepper
- Butter
- Minced shallots
- 1 teaspoon grated garlic
- 1 cup sliced mushroom caps
- ¼ cup brandy or cognac
- 2 teaspoons Dijon mustard
- ¼ cup cream
- 2 teaspoons Worcestershire sauce
- Garnish: parsley and/or chopped green onion tops
- ¼ cup beef stock

- Quickly brown medallions in butter on one side and turn
- Reduce heat
- Add shallots and garlic and shake pan
- Add mushrooms quickly sauté
- Move meat to a hot platter
- Add warm brandy
- Ignite sauce by pulling pan away from heat and tilting pan to catch gas flame
- Shake pan to blend until flame goes out
- Add mustard, cream, Worcestershire sauce and stock
- Return meat to pan to coat with the sauce
- Serve with onions and parsley
- Serve with a baked potato or wild rice

If using sirloin steak cook steak for about 4-5 minutes on second side.

Wine Pairing: Cabernet Sauvignon, Chianti Classico

Serves: 4

BEEF WELLINGTON
WITH PERIGUEUX SAUCE
GOURMET GROUP
1979

In place of the Perigueux sauce you can also use my brown sauce for steak found in the sauce section of the book. A good portion of the prep time can be done the day before.

- 2 tablespoons unsalted butter and 2 tablespoons of olive oil
- 1¼ pounds mushrooms, very finely chopped
- 5 shallots, very finely chopped
- 3 tablespoons minced parsley
- 1 sprig of fresh thyme, finely chopped
- 2-3 cloves of garlic, minced
- 1½ cups rich beef stock
- 1 tablespoon arrowroot or cornstarch
- ⅓ cup madeira wine
- Salt and fresh pepper
- 1 pound frozen puff pastry
- 1 whole beef filet mignon about 3 pounds trimmed of fat and silk removed
- 1 (5-ounce) can pate or ½ cup homemade chicken liver pate
- 1 egg beaten mixed with a bit of water or cream

- Cook the mushrooms and shallots in butter and oil until all moisture is cooked away, add the parsley, thyme and salt and pepper to taste.
- Cool the mixture and cover and refrigerate if you are doing the prep the day before.
- Make the Perigueux sauce by heating the beef stock with 1¼ tablespoons butter, adding the cornstarch or arrowroot dissolved in ⅓ cup madeira wine.
- Stir over low heat until thick. Season with salt and pepper and store in the refrigerator.
- Take the mushroom mixture and meat from the refrigerator and bring to room temperature.
- Thaw the puff pastry and lightly flour a wooden board to roll pastry.
- Preheat the oven to 400°.
- Season the beef with salt and pepper and rub with olive oil.
- Sear the meat on top of the stove turning often to be sure it is browned on all sides. Moisten with madeira as you turn meat. Deglaze the pan with some madeira wine and add to the Perigueux sauce.
- Cool meat on a plate.
- Add the pate to the mushroom mixture and add 1 teaspoon Perigueux sauce.
- Roll out the puff pastry into a rectangle 14x9.
- Spread the mushroom mixture over the pastry.
- Place the meat in center of pastry and fold he pastry over the meat and seal the seam and ends with water.
- Beat the egg with a bit of water or cream.

- Place, seam-side down, on a cookie sheet and brush the top and sides with the beaten egg.
- Prick thoroughly with a fork in a crisscross design.
- Bake in a preheated oven for about 30-45 minutes or until pastry is browned and meat registers 125. Let rest a few minutes before slicing.

Thinly slice and serve with the sauce.

Serve: 8-10

Wine Pairing: Malbec, Cabernet Sauvignon, Shiraz, Merlot

CRUSTLESS SPINACH QUICHE
1981

1 tablespoon olive oil
1 large onion, chopped
1 (10-ounce) package frozen spinach thawed and squeezed to remove as much moisture as possible
5 eggs
¾ pound Gruyere cheese, grated
Salt and pepper to taste

- Preheat oven to 350°
- Grease a 9-inch pie plate, sprinkle with Parmesan cheese
- Heat oil in skillet; add onion and sauté until wilted
- Add spinach, cook until moisture is evaporated
- Cool
- Beat eggs in bowl, add cheese
- Stir into onion-spinach mixture and season to taste
- Turn into pie plate spreading evenly

BOEUF BOURGUIGNON
1973

To make the rich sauce, which is the key to the flavor of this dish, it is important not to rush the initial searing of the meat.

- ½ pound bacon diced
- 1 tablespoon olive oil
- 3 pounds lean-stewing beef cut into 2-inch cubes
- 1 teaspoon salt
- ¼ teaspoon fresh pepper coarsely ground
- 2 tablespoons flour
- 2 medium onions coarsely chopped
- 1 medium carrot cut into pieces
- 2 garlic cloves, minced
- 1 tablespoon tomato paste
- 2-3 cups beef bouillon, use a high concentrated type such as: Superior Touch Better than Bouillon or beef stock found in the soup section at your market
- 1 bottle red Burgundy wine, medium priced (about 3 cups)
- Cracked peppercorns
- ½ teaspoon thyme
- 1 bouquet garni *
- 1 pound mushrooms, quartered
- 4 tablespoons butter
- 15-24 pearl onions peeled; soak them first in warm water for 15 minutes to pop off the peel or use canned or frozen pearl onions

*Bouquet garni consists of a number of fresh herbs and sometimes spices tied together. I use stalks of parsley including the stems, fresh thyme, a bay leaf, and maybe some fresh oregano). I simply tie with string and pop it into the pot.

- Preheat oven to 400°.
- Heat olive oil in your Dutch oven and cook bacon until crisp. Using a slotted spoon transfer to paper towels.
- Pat the beef with paper towels and season with the salt and pepper.
- Brown meat in the bacon fat, the meat must be dark brown. Brown the beef in about 4 manageable batches. Make sure beef pieces do not touch during the browning process. Set aside batches in a bowl while you continue to brown the meats.
- Sauté the onion and the carrot.
- Return meat and bacon to pot with the vegetables and toss with ½ teaspoon salt, freshly ground pepper and the flour, and toss.
- Put pot into oven uncovered for 4 minutes to brown the flour.
- Lower oven to 325°.

- Slowly add the wine and the bouillon just to cover the meat. Deglaze the pan by using a wooden spoon until there are no more browned bits. This is the true flavor of the dish and is very important.
- Add the tomato paste, bouquet garni, garlic and pepper.
- Bring liquid to a boil.
- Cover the pot and place in lower third of the oven and cook for about 2-3 hours or until the beef is very tender.
- Prepare the mushrooms and onion.
- Heat 1½ tablespoons butter with 1½ tablespoons oil to pan.
- Add the peeled onions and cook another 10 minutes.
- Add ½ cup beef stock, salt, pepper, bay leaf, and fresh thyme, cover and simmer for 40 minutes then set onions aside.
- In a skillet add butter and cook mushrooms.
- When meat is very tender, remove from oven and pour through a chinois or sieve over a saucepot. Remove bouquet of garni, carrot, beef, and bacon.
- Pour sauce through a defatter and simmer until it begins to thicken.
- Wash out the pot and return the beef and bacon to the pot, add the mushrooms and onions.
- Pour the defatted sauce over the meat, onions, and mushrooms.
- Simmer covered for 2-5 minutes.
- Season to taste; Serve with boiled or mashed potatoes or buttered noodles.

This dish can be made ahead of time and refrigerated. To reheat, simmer over heat for about 20 minutes.

Wine Pairing: Pinot Noir, Red Burgundy, Merlot, Chateau neuf de pape

Serves: 6

ELEGANT SALAD
1982

- 1 head romaine torn into pieces
- 1 tomato chopped
- 1 (14-ounce) can artichoke hearts rinsed, drained and halved)
- 1 head Bibb torn into pieces
- 1 (14-ounce) can hearts of palm rinsed, drained and sliced

LEMON MUSTARD DRESSING

This is a great dressing for just about any salad.

- 6 tablespoons oil
- 2½ tablespoons fresh lemon juice
- 1 teaspoon sugar
- 1 teaspoon salt
- ½ teaspoon freshly ground pepper
- ½ teaspoon Dijon mustard
- 1 small clove garlic, minced

Put into jar and shake well...serve over salad.

CHICKEN MARBELLA

1980

My boss's wife was a caterer and shared this wonderful chicken dish with me. This dish is served at room temperature. It makes a wonderful party or picnic dish.

- 4 chickens quartered (2½ pounds each) works best with dark chicken meat
- ½ head garlic cloves finely minced
- 2-4 tablespoons dried oregano
- Salt and pepper to taste
- ½ cup red wine vinegar
- ½ cup olive oil
- 1 cup pitted prunes
- ½ cup pitted Spanish green olives
- 1 small jar capers with a bit of juice
- 6 bay leaves
- 1 cup brown sugar
- 1 cup white wine
- ¼ cup finely chopped Italian parsley

- In a large bowl combine chicken quarters, garlic, oregano, pepper, salt, vinegar, olive oil, prunes, olives, capers and juice and bay leaves
- Cover and let marinate in refrigerator overnight
- Preheat oven to 350°
- Arrange chicken in a single layer in one or two large shallow baking pans and spoon marinade over it evenly
- Sprinkle chicken pieces with brown sugar and pour white wine around them
- Bake for 50 minutes to 1 hour, basting frequently with pan juices
- Chicken is done when thigh pieces, pricked with a fork at their thickest, yield clear yellow (rather than pink) juice
- With a slotted spoon transfer chicken, prunes, olives and capers to a serving platter
- Moisten with a few spoonful's of pan juices and sprinkle generously with parsley
- Pass remaining pan juices in a sauceboat
- If chicken has been covered and refrigerated, allow it to return to room temperature before serving
- Spoon some of the reserved juice over chicken

Serves: 10-12

Wine Pairing: Pinot Noir, Chardonnay

BREAST OF CHICKEN PERIGOURDINE
WITH BROCCOLI AND PARSLEY POTATOES
1982

I often chose this dish to serve when Steve's boss came for dinner or for special guests.

3 boned whole chicken breasts with skin attached	1 cup chicken broth
3 tablespoons butter	½ cup white wine

SAUCE:

3 tablespoons butter	Salt and pepper to taste
¼ cup flour	Broccoli spears cooked
1 cup light cream	Parsley new potatoes sautéed in butter

- Preheat oven to 375°
- Season chicken with salt and pepper
- Brown chicken breasts in 3 tablespoons butter
- Place in 9x9 inch baking dish, add chicken broth
- Bake in oven for 45-50 minutes or until tender
- Prepare broccoli and potatoes, keep warm
- When chicken is done place on oven-proof platter, keep warm
- Melt butter and blend in flour, cook for a minute or so
- Stir in the reserved broth and cream
- Cook and stir sauce until the mixture thickens and boils
- Season to taste with salt and pepper
- Arrange hot broccoli and potatoes around the chicken on the chicken platter
- Sprinkle chicken with paprika for color
- Pour some of the sauce over all and pass the remainder

Serves: 4

Wine Pairing: Anjou or Chardonnay

ROCK CORNISH GAME HENS
WITH GRAPES
Jockey Restaurant in Madrid, Spain
1982

When we serve this dish Steve grills the hens. We split the hens and save the backs to create the fond (browned bits) for the sauce.

- 2 Cornish hens, salt, pepper
- 3 half slices bacon
- 2 slices bread cut into triangles and sautéed in 2 tablespoons butter until golden on both sides. Drain on absorbent paper.

- Preheat oven to 350°
- Sprinkle hens with salt and pepper
- Arrange in a well-buttered shallow roasting pan
- Cover each with bacon half
- Roast for 50 minutes, basting several times with juices in pan
- Prepare bread slices
- Remove hens cut in half
- Arrange each half on a triangle of fried bread on a hot serving platter
- Keep warm while preparing sauce

SAUCE

- Put roasting pan over direct heat
- To liquid and fond (browned bits) in pan add ½ cup cream and deglaze the pan with a wooden spoon
    - If you choose to grill the hens, you use the backs of the hens and brown them in a skillet for several minutes to create the fond (browned bits) needed to flavor the sauce
- Boil until sauce is reduced to a creamy consistency
- In a small pan heat 1 tablespoon butter
- Add 2 finely chopped scallions
- Sauté for 2 minutes
- Add 1 can (8-ounce) Light seedless grapes or one cup regular grapes halved
- Add ½ cup port wine
- Heat and ignite, stir until the flame burns out
- Strain the cream gravy from the roasting pan into the wine and grape sauce
- Correct seasonings with salt and cayenne pepper
- Add 1 tablespoon fresh lemon juice
- Pour the sauce over hens and serve

Serves: 2-4
Wine Pairing: Pinot Noir, Chenin Blanc

STUFFED SOLE
WITH SAUCE NEWBURG
1982

There is no fish whose name has more meanings than "sole." Whether it is shipped directly from its natural habitat of the English Channel or found within the waters of various areas in America, it is a flat fish with a mild flavor. I use flounder for this recipe.

- 1¼ cups finely minced celery
- 1¼ cups finely minced onion
- 1 green pepper finely minced
- 10 tablespoons unsalted butter
- 2-3 teaspoons sweet paprika or 2 teaspoons Old Bay Seasoning
- Salt and freshly ground pepper
- ½ pound raw shrimp (about 12), shelled and deveined and finely chopped
- 1½ cups fresh breadcrumbs
- 16 small sole or flounder fillets (2 pounds)
- Newburg sauce

- Preheat oven to 450°.
- Spray a baking sheet with cooking spray.
- Combine the celery, onion, and green pepper.
- Melt 6 tablespoons butter and add vegetables. Sprinkle with 1 teaspoon paprika salt, and pepper to taste, cook, stirring about 5 minutes.
- Add chopped shrimp to vegetables, cook 30 seconds, stirring, remove from heat.
- Add breadcrumbs and blend, cool. Add a bit of stock to bind if necessary.
- Place 8 flounder fillets on flat surface and sprinkle lightly with salt and pepper.
- Spoon equal amounts of filling on each filet and pat the filling to shape it to the fillets.
- Cover each with another fillet.
- Spray a baking dish, arrange the fish in dish and brush with 4 tablespoons melted butter.
- Sprinkle remaining paprika, bake 15 minutes.
- Serve with sauce and lemon wedges.

NEWBURG SAUCE:

- 3 egg yolks plus ¼ cup cream
- ¼ cup dry sherry, splash of cognac

- Melt butter; add flour, stir with wire whisk.
- Add paprika, 1¾ cups cream, cook stirring constantly until well blended, salt and pepper.

- Beat yolks lightly and add the remaining ¼ cup cream to yolk, stir, add yolk mix to sauce stirring rapidly, remove from heat, continue stirring DO NOT BOIL, add sherry and cognac, stir. Serve over fish.

Serves: 8

Wine Pairing: Fume Blanc

SEAFOOD RAMEKINS
Gourmet Club 1980

This dish proved to be one of the best entrees for our little Gourmet Group. My family enjoyed this dish so much that it became our traditional Christmas Eve favorite. I prepare this dish every Christmas Eve to this day. Some years I add a bit of chopped lobster meat to the seafood mix.

7 tablespoons butter
½ cup raw shrimp cut up
½ cup fresh crabmeat
½ cup raw scallops cut up
1 tablespoon chopped onion
2 tablespoons sherry
½ teaspoon salt
¼ teaspoon black pepper

3 tablespoons flour
1½ cups of milk or half and half for a richer dish
½ cup of breadcrumbs
¼ cup of grated Parmesan cheese
Box of phyllo sheets
Puff pastry sheets (optional)

- Preheat oven to 400°.
- Grease ramekins or large scallop shells.
- Heat 4 tablespoons butter. Add seafood and onion. Cook for 4 minutes, sprinkle with sherry, salt and pepper, put in warm plate and set aside.
- Heat milk in microwave.
- Melt remaining butter and add flour to make a roux. Cook for about 1 minute, then add milk all at once and cook until thickened.
- Add seafood to sauce.
- Spoon into ramekins or shell dishes lined with phyllo. Top with 2-3 pieces of phyllo dough (see directions on phyllo dough box for preparation) OR cut a round the size of your ramekin out of puff pastry dough (also in frozen food section). Sprinkle top of dough with breadcrumbs mixed with Parmesan cheese.
- Bake 12-15 minutes or brown under broiler.

Serves: 6

Wine Pairings: Chablis, White Boudreaux or Sauvignon Blanc

SEAFOOD STRUDEL
Gourmet Group 1979

For the crust you can use a puff pastry, but this recipe uses Greek phyllo.

SAUCE

- 2 tablespoons unsalted butter
- 2 tablespoons flour
- ½ teaspoon Dijon mustard
- Salt, cayenne pepper
- ¾ cup milk plus 2 tablespoons heavy cream
- 1 cup breadcrumbs
- ¼ cup grated Parmesan cheese
- ¼ teaspoon dry mustard

FILLING

- 1 pound cleaned, shelled cooked crab, shrimp, lobster or halibut or a combination of all, cut seafood into bite-size pieces
- ½ cup grated high quality Swiss cheese
- 2 hard-cooked eggs, chopped
- ¾ cup sour cream
- ¼ cup chopped parsley
- ¼ cup diced shallots
- 2 tablespoons chopped chives
- 1 large clove garlic minced
- ¾ cup (1½ sticks) unsalted butter
- 2 tablespoons chopped parsley for garnishing
- 2 tablespoons grated Parmesan cheese
- Minced parsley

- Melt 2 tablespoons butter and stir in 2 T. flour to make a roux. Cook gently until bubbly.
- Remove from heat and add mustard, pinch of salt and a pinch of cayenne pepper.
- Slowly stir in milk and heavy cream, cook on medium stirring constantly until bubbly and thick.
- Taste for seasonings and adjust if necessary, cover and chill sauce until very thick and firm (2 hours).
- Preheat oven to 375°, spray a large baking sheet with cooking spray.
- Combine breadcrumbs, Parmesan cheese and dry mustard in small bowl.
- Spray or brush melted butter on several sheets of phyllo. While you are working with the phyllo, keep a damp cloth on sheets not being used while you prepare each layer.
- Layer seafood evenly onto the short end of your layered stack of phyllo.
- Sprinkle seafood with Swiss cheese and chopped egg.
- Dot with sour cream, sprinkle with parsley, shallots, chives and garlic.
- Dot with chilled sauce.
- Roll up as a strudel. Roll 3 times, then fold ends in and finish rolling.

- Bake for 12 minutes seam side down.
- Remove from oven and brush with more butter.
- Slice diagonally with a serrated knife into 1½ inch slices.
- Push slices together to reshape a loaf.
- Add parsley to remaining butter and brush again.
- Repeat brushing 3 more times during baking, reserving a little butter to brush on just before serving.
- Bake 35-40 minutes longer until crisp and golden brown.
- Warm large serving platter.
- Remove strudel from oven and brush with parsley butter.
- Cool 10 minutes and transfer to warmed platter.
- Dust with Parmesan cheese and minced parsley.
- Garnish with crab or lobster claws if desired.

Serves: 6-8
Wine Pairing: Chardonnay

SHRIMP DU JOUR
1975

This recipe comes from the famous Philadelphia's Bookbinder Restaurant. I serve it in individual gratin dishes.

5 pounds shrimp shelled and dried (about 80 good size shrimp)
4 tablespoons unsalted butter
  Dry breadcrumbs
  Parmesan cheese to sprinkle on top
2 teaspoons Worcestershire sauce
1 clove of garlic minced or grated
¼ cup chopped parsley
¼ cup chopped chives, salt and pepper to taste
1 stick melted butter for top or less

- Heat 4 tablespoons butter and quickly cook the shrimp until they turn pink. About 2-3 minutes
- Add Worcestershire sauce, garlic, chopped parsley, chopped chives, salt and pepper
- Mix together and place in single layer in buttered baking dish or individual dishes
- Sprinkle with dry bread crumbs and Parmesan cheese
- Pour 1 stick of melted butter over top or to taste
- Put under broiler until brown

Serves: 6
Wine Pairing: Sauvignon Blanc

FLANK STEAK
WITH BRANDY CREAM SAUCE
1982

This is an excellent dish to serve your guests. I serve it with my Potato cheese cups and a simple spinach salad with Pine nuts. Brandy Ice is a wonderful ending to this meal.

- 2 pounds flank steak
- 4 tablespoons butter room temperature
- 2 tablespoons Dijon mustard
- 1½ teaspoons Worcestershire sauce
- ¾ teaspoon curry powder
- ¼ teaspoon crushed mustard seed or dry mustard
- 1 garlic clove, crushed
- Salt and fresh pepper
- ¼ cup sherry or madeira wine
- ¼ cup white wine vinegar (sherry vinegar is best)
- ½ pound fresh mushrooms, sliced
- 1 shallot, minced
- ¾ cup sour cream
- 3 tablespoons brandy
- Fresh parsley roughly chopped

- The night before or early in the morning, put the steak in a shallow dish.
- Combine 2 tablespoons butter, mustard, Worcestershire, curry, mustard seed, garlic, salt and pepper and mix to a paste.
- Spread mixture evenly over the top of the steak.
- Pour sherry and vinegar over meat.
- Cover loosely and refrigerate at least 8 hours or let stand at room temperature for 2 hours.
- Meat must be at room temperature before cooking.
- Preheat broiler or grill.
- Place meat on rack and broil or place on preheated grill 3-4 minutes on first side; turn and cook another 3-4 minutes on second side for MEDIUM RARE. For RARE cook about 2-3 minutes per side.
- While steak is cooking, melt remaining butter in skillet.
- Add mushrooms and shallot and sauté until soft; set aside.
- Transfer meat to platter and keep warm.
- Take the juices from the broiler pan or some rich beef stock and put over heat; gradually stir in sour cream and brandy, blending well.
- Continue simmering gently about 4 minutes stirring constantly.
- Blend in mushroom/shallot mixture and heat, remove from heat.
- Cut steak diagonally against the grain into very thin slices.
- Spoon sauce over steak slices and sprinkle with parsley.

Serves: 4-6

Wine Pairing: Pinot Noir

SPINACH SALAD

1980

We served this salad at one of our gourmet dinners. It is a very tasty salad but bacon drippings are not exactly healthy. Today I use 1 Tablespoon of the bacon grease and 3 Tablespoons of canola oil. You can purchase the Beau Monde seasoning salt at the grocery store or simply use salt and pepper.

- 1 garlic clove
- 1 cup sliced fresh mushrooms
- 12 strips of bacon cooked and crumbled (reserve 4 tablespoons for dressing)
- 2 cans of mandarin oranges or fresh orange sections
- 2 tablespoons tarragon vinegar
- Fresh spinach washed
- Beau Monde seasoning salt or salt and pepper to taste
- Croutons
- Red onion slices

- Rub wooden bowl with garlic clove
- Drain juice from oranges and boil juice until reduced

DRESSING

- Combine the reduced orange juice, bacon drippings and vinegar
- Bring to just a warm temperature
- Pour over spinach
- Toss with oranges, mushrooms and bacon
- Season to taste and top with croutons and red onion slices

BRANDY ICE
1974

One half-gallon vanilla bean ice cream
⅓ cup Cointreau
⅓ cup Kuala
⅓ cup Apricot Brandy

- Mix all together in a mixer
- Freeze immediately
- Will keep indefinitely

CHOCOLATE MOUSSE GALLIANO
GOURMET GROUP
1980

  6 eggs (separated) room temperature
½ cup sugar
¼ cup Liquor Galliano, Kahlua or Frangelico
¼ cup strong black coffee
13 ounces semi-sweet chocolate
  3 ounces butter
  1 tablespoon sugar
1½ cups heavy cream whipped
Toasted slivered almonds, whipped cream and chocolate shavings for garnish

- Beat together the egg yolks and ½ cup sugar until light and fluffy
- Beat in ¼ cup Galliano and beat for a full 5 minutes
- Melt chocolate over hot water or in microwave
- Blend in butter
- Add to egg yolk mixture stirring
- Whip egg whites to soft peaks and beat in 1 tablespoon sugar until stiff peaks form
- Fold the egg whites into the chocolate mixture
- Fold whipped cream into mousse
- Chill in serving dishes
- Garnish with whipped cream, chocolate shavings and toasted slivered almonds

Serves: 6-8

BANANAS FOSTER
1983

This recipe came from the chef at Brennan's in New Orleans.

¼ cup butter
4 bananas cut lengthwise
¼ cup brown sugar
¼ cup banana liqueur

Cinnamon
½ cup white rum
Toasted slivered almonds

- Melt butter in frying pan or chafing dish
- Stir in brown sugar until melted
- Add banana
- Sauté lightly until hot
- Sprinkle with cinnamon
- Pour warmed liqueur and rum over bananas
- Tilt pan to flame and Ignite
- Pour over bananas and baste
- Serve over vanilla bean ice cream
- Sprinkle with almonds

Serves: 4

RUM COFFEE ICE CREAM
1975

I recommend preparing this cream just before serving to resemble a nicely chilled Devonshire cream.

2 pints coffee ice cream, slightly softened
8 teaspoons dark Jamaica rum
Bittersweet chocolate curls
Crumbled English toffee or espresso powder for garnish

- Combine ice cream and rum in food processor
- Add rum and mix until smooth
- Divide between 4 dessert dishes or wine glasses
- Garnish with chocolate curls

It can also be prepared ahead and frozen if you prefer a firmer ice cream consistency

Serves: 4

CHOCOLATE MOUSSE PIE
Gourmet Group 1985

The chocolate cookie crumb crust enriches this easy to make but dramatic dessert. It can be prepared ahead and frozen. Thaw overnight in the refrigerator.

CRUST:

- 3 cups chocolate wafer crumbs
- ½ cup butter melted

FILLING:

- 16 ounces semisweet chocolate
- 2 eggs
- 4 egg yolks
- 2 cups whipping cream
- 6 tablespoons powdered sugar
- 4 egg whites, room temperature

CHOCOLATE LEAVES:

- 8 ounces semisweet chocolate
- 1 tablespoon vegetable shortening
- Camellia or other waxy leaves; washed thoroughly
- 2 cups whipping cream
- Powdered sugar to taste

FOR CRUST:

- Combine crumbs and butter
- Press on bottom and sides of a 10-inch spring form pan
- Refrigerate 30 minutes or chill in freezer

FOR FILLING:

- Soften chocolate in top of double boiler or in microwave, let cool
- Add whole eggs and mix well
- Add yolks and mix until blended
- Whip cream with powdered sugar until soft peaks form
- Beat egg whites until stiff but not dry
- Stir a little of the whipped cream and egg whites into the chocolate mixture to lighten
- Fold in the remaining cream and whites until completely incorporated
- Turn into crust and chill at least 6 hours, preferably overnight

FOR LEAVES:

- Melt chocolate and shortening in microwave
- Using spoon generously coat the UNDERSIDE of leaves, chill or freeze until firm

ASSEMBLE:

- Whip remaining 2 cups cream with sugar to taste until quite stiff
- Loosen crust on all side using sharp knife, remove pie from the spring form pan
- Spread all but ½ cup cream over top of pie
- Pipe remaining cream into rosettes in center of pie
- Separate chocolate from leaves starting at stem end of leaf
- Arrange in overlapping pattern around rosettes

Serves: 10-12

ELODIE'S
CHOCOLATE CAKE
1987

This flourless cake recipe came from my sister Marie's gourmet group in the late 1980's. I made it frequently. It is a wonderful cake by itself topped with fresh raspberries or used as a base topped with ice cream and toppings. I make it for my friends as personal birthday cakes.

- 10 ounces Bittersweet or semisweet chocolate chopped. I use Lindt chocolate with 50-60% cacao
- 1 cup (2 sticks) unsalted butter cut into small pieces
- 5 large eggs
- 1¼ cups sugar
- 5 tablespoons flour
- 1½ teaspoons baking powder

- Preheat oven to 325°
- Butter and flour a 10-inch spring form pan
- Stir chocolate and butter in a saucepan over low heat until melted and smooth (can use microwave)
- Beat eggs and sugar until smooth and thickened
- Mix flour and baking powder together and whisk
- Stir flour and baking powder over eggs and fold in
- Fold in chocolate mixture
- Pour into pan
- Bake 20 minutes
- Cover pan with foil and bake until tester inserted into the center comes out with moist crumbs still attached…about 30 more minutes
- Uncover pan and cool in the pan on a rack (cake will fall as it cools)
- Can be made 1 day ahead
- Cover and let stand at room temperature
- Cut around sides to loosen
- Release pan sides
- Sift powdered sugar over cake and cut into wedges

I usually cut this cake into fourths and freeze, then serve it in dessert dishes with fudge sauce and fresh whipped cream, garnish with fresh raspberries.

JANICE CHOATE'S
ICE CREAM PIE
1982

CRUST

- 24 single soda crackers, crushed in food processor
- 3 egg whites beaten
- 1 cup sugar
- ½ teaspoon baking powder
- 1 teaspoon vanilla
- ½ cup chopped pecans

2 pints vanilla bean ice cream or flavor of choice

TOPPING:

- 3 egg whites
- ½ teaspoon vanilla
- ¼ teaspoon cream of tartar
- ⅓-½ cup sugar

- Preheat oven to 350°
- Grease a pie plate with cooking spray
- Combine crust ingredients and pat into the greased pie plate
- Bake at 350° for 30 minutes
- Cool slightly then put into freezer until very cold
- When cold, remove from freezer and pile on vanilla ice cream
- For meringue topping, beat 3 egg whites with sugar to make a meringue
- Brown meringue under broiler
- Put back into the freezer until ready to serve
- Let stand 10 minutes then slice and serve with chocolate sauce

Serves: 6-8

SAUCE:

In saucepan add:
- 1 stick butter
- 4 ounces dark chocolate (high quality chocolate such as Lindt)
- 1 cup sugar
- 1 large can evaporated milk
- 1 teaspoon vanilla

- Whisk carefully and bring to boil
- Simmer until desired consistency

MISSISSIPPI MUD PIE
1990

Our daughter Janet always loved this pie. She tells me she makes it for her husband's birthday dessert.

CRUST:

21	cream-filled Oreo cookies (7½ ounces), broken in pieces
¼	cup butter or margarine, melted

FILLING:

2	pints coffee ice cream, slightly softened

CHOCOLATE GLAZE:

1½	tablespoons water
2	tablespoons light corn syrup
1½	tablespoons butter or margarine, cut into small pieces
1	ounce unsweetened chocolate, chopped fine
1	ounce semisweet chocolate, chopped fine

- To prevent crust from sticking to the pie plate press 12-inch square of foil firmly into a 9-inch pie plate, using a folded towel or a potholder to attach the foil. Fold the edges of foil tight over the pie plate rim. Set aside.
- In food processor or blender whirl the cookies to make about.
- 1¾ cups of fine crumbs. Mix well with the butter and turn the mixture into the pie plate. Distribute evening and loosely over the sides, being careful that the top edge is not too thin.
- Press firmly on the bottom. (Crust must be very firm with no loose crumbs.) Now FREEZE for several hours or overnight or until very firm.
- Gently peel away the foil (it will peel easily in one piece) by supporting the bottom of the crust with one hand and peeling a bit at a time with the other hand, rotating the crust gently. Support the bottom of crust with small spatula or knife; ease the crust back into the pie plate very gently so it will not crack.
- Turn the ice cream into the crust and spread, mounding in the middle. Return to the freezer until very firm.
- While the pie is freezing prepare the glaze:
    - In small saucepan over moderate heat bring water, syrup and butter to boil, stirring occasionally
    - Add the chocolate, remove from heat. Stir with small whisk until the chocolate is melted and the mixture is smooth
    - Pour glaze over the frozen pie to cover completely. Return pie to freezer for a few hours or more
    - When the glaze is firm, wrap the pie airtight with plastic wrap
- Serve as is or garnish with rum flavored whipped cream and toasted almonds

Serves: 10

CHOCOLATE CHARLOTTE RUSSE
1980

I made this dessert often when my families came to visit. It serves enough to last a weekend of guests.

- 4 ounces unsweetened chocolate, high grade
- ¾ cup sugar
- ⅓ cup milk
- 6 eggs separated and at room temperature
- 1½ cups unsalted butter
- 1½ cups confectioners' sugar
- Pinch salt
- 1½ teaspoons vanilla
- 3 dozen ladyfingers split
- 1 cup heavy cream whipped
- Shaved chocolate

- Melt chocolate in microwave and cool
- Mix sugar, milk and egg yolks in saucepan
- Add the cooled chocolate and cook until smooth and thickened, stirring constantly, cool and set aside
- Cream butter well
- Add ¾ cup confectioners' sugar and cream thoroughly
- Add cooled chocolate mixture and beat well
- In a separate bowl beat egg whites with salt until just stiff
- Gradually beat in remaining ¾ cup confectioners' sugar
- Fold into chocolate mixture
- Add vanilla
- Line bottom and sides of a deep 9-in spring form pan with split ladyfingers
- Put one third of mixture, then more ladyfingers, one third mixture, a layer of ladyfingers, keep layering and end with ladyfingers on top
- Chill overnight
- Remove to a cake plate
- Garnish with whipped cream and shaved chocolate

Serves: 12

ZUPPA INGLESE
1991

Italian English soup cake. This is the dessert I made to top off many of my neighborhood Italian dinner parties. It always reminded me of our wedding cake. Back in 1965 our wedding cake came from a famous Utica, NY Italian bakery.

CAKE:

- 4 egg yolks
- 1¼ cups sugar
- 1 teaspoon vanilla
- ½ teaspoon lemon peel
- 4 egg whites
- ½ teaspoon cream of tartar
- 1 cup flour and ¼ teaspoon salt whisked together

- Grease and flour two 8" round cake pans.
- Preheat oven to 350°.
- Beat yolks 5 minutes or until thick and lemon colored.
- Very gradually add sugar, vanilla and lemon peel. Beat 5 more minutes.
- Beat egg whites together until stiff peaks form, but not too dry.
- Stir small amount of beaten egg whites into yolks. FOLD yolk mixture into remaining whites.
- Sift ¼ of the flour mix at a time over the egg mixture and FOLD in.
- Spread batter into prepared cake pans.
- Bake 350° for 20 minutes.
- Invert and **cool in pans** completely.

CREAM:

- 2 cups half and half
- 6 large egg yolks
- ½ cup sugar
- Pinch salt
- ¼ cup flour
- 4 tablespoons cold butter, cut into pieces
- 1½ t vanilla extract

- Heat the half and half in saucepan until just simmering.
- Whisk yolks, sugar and salt in bowl until smooth.
- Add flour to yolk mixture and whisk.
- Remove half and half from heat and whisking constantly slowly add ½ cup to the yolk mixture to temper.

- Whisking constantly, return tempered yolk mixture to remaining half and half in saucepan.
- Return to heat and cook, whisking constantly until the mixture thickens slightly about 1 minute.
- Reduce heat and continue to simmer whisking constantly for another 8 minutes.
- Increase heat and cook whisking constantly until the pudding bubbles and bursts on the surface (1-2 minutes).
- Remove from heat and whisk in butter and vanilla.
- Place a sheet of saran wrap or greased waxed paper over the filling to keep a "skin" from forming making sure the wrap touches all of the filling.
- Refrigerate for at least 2 hours or up to 24 hours before assembling cake.

ASSEMBLY

- Split each cake layer in half.
- Place cut side up on plate.
- Mix ¼ cup rum and ¼ cup fruit brandy.
- Sprinkle first layer of cake with 2 tablespoons liquor mixture.
- Top with cream.
- Repeat with next layers.
- Top with final cake layer.
- Chill 5-6 hours. Whip fresh cream and frost the entire cake. Garnish with shaved chocolate.

LEMON CHARLOTTE
1980

- 1 family size package of lemon Jell-O
- 3 cups water
- Juice of two lemons
- 4 eggs separated and at room temperature
- ½ cup sugar
- ¼ teaspoon salt
- Grated rind from one lemon
- 1 cup heavy cream whipped
- 18 unfilled ladyfingers split

- Line the bottom and sides of an 8 or 9-inch spring form pan with ladyfingers
- Make the lemon Jell-O with 1 cup hot water and 2 cups cold water
- Chill until just beginning to jell
- Beat egg yolks until smooth, add sugar and lemon rind and blend
- Add lemon juice
- Whip cream until stiff
- Beat egg whites until soft peaks form
- Fold whipped cream and egg whites into lemon Jell-O mixture
- Pour into pan
- Chill for 3 hours or overnight
- Carefully remove sides of spring form pan
- Garnish with lemon cartwheel slices and fresh mint leaves

Yield: 12

ROCKY MOUNT, NC
DINNER PARTIES AND COFFEES
1990-1999

I took a trip to Charleston, SC and my daughter Mary and I found a *wooden stirring stick* to add to my wooden spoon collection. I was thrilled and began to use it to stir pasta, puddings and many sauces. With this new implement in hand I began to have many dinner parties.

There is no pleasure greater than the reward one receives from having a dinner party. It brought back great memories of dad's restaurant when the customers enjoyed the food and the service. Our colonial home in Rocky Mount was small but large enough to have a dinner party for 16-18 neighbors and friends. I set up tables for 4-6 in each of the downstairs rooms. The buffet was located in the dining room. I spent hours creating my hand calligraphy menus and table arrangements not to mention preparing the food. It was an exhausting experience, but one I treasure.

Of all my dinner parties the one I enjoyed the most was my Italian party. I made all kinds of Italian foods and topped it off with my Zuppa Ingelese or my Tiramisu.

In the Southern town of Rocky Mount coffees were a very popular event. A coffee is a morning gathering of friends to enjoy sweets and coffee while building friendships. I invited 20-30 ladies and served coffee punch, fresh juices and an assortment of freshly baked coffee cakes and egg casseroles.

COFFEE PUNCH
1990

Excellent for warm summer and early fall days.

½ gallon instant coffee or dark roasted brewed coffee
1 gallon vanilla ice cream
1 small container cool whip (whipped cream)
1 bottle ginger ale

- Make coffee and chill overnight
- Pour chilled coffee into a punch bowl
- Place ice cream in the punch bowl 30 minutes before serving
- 15 minutes before serving add the cool whip and ginger ale
- Mix all together

Yield: 12-15 (half recipe)
Yield: 25-30 (full recipe)

ENGLISH MUFFIN LOAVES
1979

This bread resembles an English muffin in texture. It is an excellent bread for breakfast or afternoon tea.

2 packages dry yeast
6 cups unsifted flour
1 tablespoon sugar

2 teaspoons salt
2 cups milk
¼ teaspoon baking soda

½ cup water
Cornmeal

- Preheat oven to 400°
- Grease and sprinkle cornmeal in two 8x4-inch loaf pans
- Combine 3 cups flour, yeast, sugar, salt and soda
- Heat liquids until very warm (120-130°)
- Add to dry mixture; beat well
- Stir in the remainder of flour to make a stiff batter
- Spoon mixture into pans and then sprinkle tops with cornmeal
- Cover, let rise in warm place for 45 minutes
- Bake for 25 minutes
- Remove from pans immediately, cool on wire rack

Yield: 2 loaves

CHEESY GRITS SOUFFLE
1977

1½ cups uncooked grits
½ cup butter
3 cups (3/4 pound) shredded sharp Cheddar cheese
3 eggs beaten
1 tablespoon Worcestershire sauce or to taste
2 teaspoons paprika, divided

- Preheat oven to 325°
- Lightly grease a 2-quart casserole dish
- Cook grits according to package directions
- Add butter and cheese; stir until melted
- Add Worcestershire sauce and 1 teaspoon paprika, mixing well
- Add a small amount of the hot grits to the eggs, stirring well, stir egg mixture into remaining grits
- Pour grits into a lightly greased 2-quart baking dish, sprinkle with 1 teaspoon paprika
- Cover and refrigerate overnight
- Remove from refrigerator 15 minutes before baking
- Bake, uncovered at 325° for 1 hour

Serves: 8

BREAKFAST BACON ROLLUPS
1979

12 slices white bread
    Cream cheese softened
12 slices bacon

- Preheat oven to 375-400°
- Cut crusts off bread slices
- Spread each slice with softened cream cheese
- Roll each slice of bread into a tube
- Wrap a piece of bacon around each tube
- Bake in oven for 20 minutes turning after 7 minutes
- Serve immediately
- If used the next day, reheat under broiler

MOCK SOUFFLE EGG CASSEROLE
1980

My favorite.

- 1 pound bulk pork sausage cooked and scrambled (I use ½ pound hot and ½ pound mild sausage)
- 8 beaten eggs
- 1 cup shredded sharp cheddar cheese
- 2 cups milk
- 1 teaspoon salt
- 1 teaspoon dry mustard
- Dash Tabasco and Worcestershire sauce
- 3-5 slices white bread cubed

- Preheat oven to 350°
- Grease a 13x9x2 rectangular pan
- Mix together the eggs, milk and seasonings
- Layer sausage on bottom, then bread cubes
- Pour egg mixture over top
- Sprinkle with cheese
- Assemble the casserole the day before and **refrigerated overnight**
- The next day bake in 350° oven for 40-45 minutes
- Cut into squares and serve warm
- Good served with fresh fruit and English muffins

Yield: 8

EGG CASSEROLE
WITH CANADIAN BACON
1978

- 8 eggs beaten
- ½ cup sour cream
- 1 cup shredded cheddar cheese
- ¾ teaspoon salt
- 2 tablespoons minced onion
- Canadian bacon

- Preheat oven to 350°
- Grease a 13x9x2 baking pan
- Put bacon, ham or whatever meat you choose on the bottom of a greased oblong casserole dish
- Mix eggs, sour cream, cheese, salt, onion and pour over bacon
- Put one more layer of bacon on top (like a sandwich)
- Dot with 2 tablespoons butter on top
- Bake 350° for 20 minutes

MY SECRETARY'S DELICIOUS
CHOCOLATE CAKE
1990

During the 80's and 90's I worked for North Carolina Wesleyan College. I had a wonderful creative staff as is indicative of my secretary's cake.

6 eggs at room temperature
1 cup flour (self-rising)
1 teaspoon vanilla
1 cup sugar

1 can Hershey chocolate syrup
1 stick butter
1 cup chopped nuts

- Preheat oven to 350°
- Grease a 13x9 inch pan
- Cream sugar and butter
- Add eggs one at a time until lemon color
- Add chocolate syrup
- Add flour and vanilla
- Bake at 350° for 30-35 minutes
- Frost with frosting
- Sprinkle with nuts

FROSTING

12 ounces semi-sweet chocolate morsels
1 cup sugar
½ cup milk

1 teaspoon vanilla
1 cup nuts

- Combine the chocolate, sugar and milk in a saucepot
- Melt all together
- Add 1 teaspoon vanilla
- Bring to a boil and cook until it comes to a soft ball temperature
- Whip with a wooden spoon and add 1 cup of chopped nuts

BROWN SUGAR POUND CAKE
1982

I found this recipe the Christmas of 1982 and made it a Christmas tradition. Sometimes I make very large cupcakes or small loaf cakes. I freeze these treasures and give as hostess gifts throughout the year.

- 1 cup butter softened
- ½ cup shortening
- 1 (16-ounce) box light brown sugar
- ½ cup sugar
- 5 large eggs
- ½ teaspoon baking powder
- 3 cups flour
- 1 cup milk
- 2 tablespoons vanilla extract
- 1 cup chopped pecans
- Cream cheese frosting

- Preheat oven to 350°
- Grease and flour a 10-inch Bundt or tube pan
- Cream butter and shortening
- Gradually add sugar beating until light and fluffy
- Add eggs, one at a time, beating well after each addition
- Combine baking powder and flour
- Add to creamed mixture alternately with milk, beginning and ending with flour
- Beat well after each addition of milk and flour
- Stir in vanilla and pecans
- Pour batter into tube pan
- Bake for 1 hour and 10 minutes
- Cool in the pan for 10 minutes
- Invert onto wire rack and cool completely
- Frost with cream cheese frosting

CREAM CHEESE FROSTING

- ½ cup butter or margarine, softened
- 1 8-ounce package of cream cheese softened
- 2 teaspoons vanilla
- 1 (16-ounce) box powdered sugar

- Combine all ingredients
- Mix until smooth

Yield: one 10-inch cake serves 16

PECAN TOPPED COFFEE CAKE
1982

My sister Marie gave me this recipe. I use a Bundt cake pan for this cake.

- ⅔ cup butter
- 1 cup sugar
- ½ cup brown sugar
- 2 eggs
- 1 teaspoon vanilla
- 2 cups flour
- 1 teaspoon baking powder
- 1 teaspoon baking soda
- ½ teaspoon salt
- 1 teaspoon cinnamon
- 1 cup buttermilk

TOPPING:

- 1 cup chopped pecans
- ½ cup brown sugar
- ½ teaspoon cinnamon

- Preheat oven to 350°
- Grease and flour a 13x9x2 inch pan
- In small bowl combine flour, baking powder, soda, salt and cinnamon, whisk together until well blended
- Cream butter, gradually add 1 cup sugar and ½ cup brown sugar, beat well
- Add eggs, one at a time; beating well after each egg addition
- Stir in vanilla
- Add dry ingredients to creamed mixture alternately with buttermilk, beginning and ending with the flour mixture
- Pour batter into prepared pan
- Combine pecans, brown sugar and cinnamon, stir well
- Sprinkle over batter
- Bake 35 minutes or until wooden pick inserted comes out clean

QUICHE-LORRAINE SQUARES
1985

These tiny quiche squares make wonderful appetizers or breakfast items. I always displayed a plate of these tasty quiches at my coffees.

- 1 package piecrust mix or 2 refrigerated piecrust sheets
- 1 egg white, slightly beaten
- 1 pound bacon fried crisp and crumbled
- 3 cups good quality Swiss chees
- 6 eggs
- 4 cups light cream
- 1½ teaspoons salt
- ¼ teaspoon nutmeg
- ¼ teaspoon pepper
- Dash cayenne

- Preheat oven to 375°
- Prepare piecrust
- On lightly floured surface, roll out pastry to an 18x15 rectangle
- Use rolled-out pastry to line a jelly-roll pan
- Brush bottom and sides of pastry with egg white
- Refrigerate
- Prepare bacon and sprinkle evenly over bottom of pie shell
- Sprinkle cheese over the bacon
- In large bowl beat eggs, cream, salt, nutmeg, pepper and cayenne with wire whisk or electric mixer
- Pour over prepared shell
- Bake 35-40 minutes, or until golden and center is firm when gently pressed with fingertip
- Let cool on wire rack for 10 minutes
- Cut quiche into squares about 1½ inches
- Cool completely
- Remove from pan
- Serve
- To freeze: arrange squares on foil-lined cookie sheet
- Freezer, then wrap and freeze until ready to use
- To serve: unwrap; bake on cookie sheet (still frozen) at 400° oven for about 10 minutes; serve at once

Makes 54 squares

BUTTER PECAN TURTLE COOKIES
1985

CRUST:

2 cups flour
1 cup brown sugar
½ cup butter

- Preheat oven to 350°
- Combine flour, brown sugar and butter
- Pat into an ungreased 13x9x2 pan
- Sprinkle pecans over the unbaked crust
- Prepare the caramel layer

CARAMEL LAYER:

⅔ cup butter
½ cup of brown sugar
1 cup pecan halves
1 cup milk chocolate chips

- Combine the sugar and butter.
- Cook over medium heat stirring constantly until the entire surface of the mixture begins to boil
- Boil for ½-1 minute. Stir constantly.

- Pour the caramel mixture over the pecans and the crust
- Bake for 18-22 minutes or until caramel layer is bubbly and the crust is golden brown
- Remove immediately
- Sprinkle with chocolate chips
- Allow the chips to melt slightly 2-3 minutes
- Slightly swirl chips as they melt—leave some whole for a marbled effect
- Cool completely
- Cut into bars

Yield: 3-4 dozen bars

CHEESE KRISPIES
1979

- 2 sticks butter
- 2 cups flour (sift before measuring)
- 2 cups grated sharp cheddar cheese
- 1 teaspoon salt, more if you use unsalted butter
- 2 cups Rice Krispies
- Dash Tabasco
- 1 cup chopped pecans
- ½ teaspoon Cayenne pepper or to taste

- Preheat oven to 400°
- Mix margarine, cheese and Tabasco
- Add flour and mix
- Add Rice Krispies, pecans and mix
- Shape into small balls and press with a fork dipped in flour
- Place a pecan half on each wafer before baking (optional)
- Bake on ungreased cookie sheet for 10-12 minutes

BACON-WRAPPED APPETIZERS

Using a sharp knife cut partially cooked bacon slices in half crosswise and again crosswise for a length needed to wrap around the following variations of appetizers:

Drained and dried pineapple cubes

Drained and dried pimento olives

Pitted prunes, soaked in sherry and stuffed with a walnut, almond or piece of crystallized ginger

Pitted dates stuffed with a piece of Asiago cheese, blue cheese, or whole almond

Pitted dates wrapped in Prosciutto

Fresh scallops

- Preheat oven to 350-375°
- Secure the bacon with a toothpick
- Arrange on baking sheet seam side down and bake for about 20-25 minutes
- Turn to crisp both sides
- Cool and serve

CHOCOLATE CHIP CAKE
1983

CAKE:

- ¾ cup sugar
- ½ cup butter, 1 stick
- 2 cups flour
- 8 ounces sour cream
- 2 eggs
- 1 teaspoon baking soda
- 1 teaspoon baking powder
- 1 teaspoon vanilla
- ½ cup chocolate chips

TOPPING:

- ½ cup brown sugar
- ½ cup flour
- ¼ cup butter
- ½ cup chocolate chips
- 2 teaspoons cocoa powder
- ½ cup chopped walnuts

- Preheat oven to 325°
- Grease a tube or Bundt pan
- On high speed, mix sugar and butter in a mixer until fluffy
- On low speed, beat in 2 cups flour and next 5 ingredients
- Increase to medium speed and beat for 2 minutes
- Stir in ½ cup chocolate chips
- Spoon batter into pan
- Using a pastry blender or food processor, combine the brown sugar, cocoa, ½ cup flour and ¼ cup butter for topping
- Stir in walnuts and chocolate chips
- Crumble topping mix over the batter in the tube pan
- Bake 1 hour and 15 minutes or until the cake pulls away from sides or toothpick comes out clean when inserted in middle
- Cool cake IN THE PAN on a wire rack
- Loosen cake with spatula
- Remove and slice

MAGIC COOKIE BARS
1980

1½ cups graham crackers crumbs
3 tablespoons sugar
½ cup melted butter
1 cup chocolate chips

1⅓ cups flaked coconut
1 cup coarsely chopped walnuts
1 can sweetened condensed milk

- Preheat oven to 350°
- Combine graham cracker crumbs, sugar and butter baking sheet
- Mix thoroughly and press out with back of spoon into a 13x9x2 baking sheet
- Scatter chocolate chips over the crust
- Spread the coconut evenly
- Sprinkle walnuts over coconut
- Pour milk over walnuts
- Bake for 25 minutes or until lightly browned around edges
- Cool and chill
- Cut into bars

Yield: 54 bars

CRANBERRY-ORANGE BREAD
1985

I made this bread every Christmas to give to friends and neighbors. It was a hit at my neighborhood coffees.

2 cups flour
¾ cup sugar
1½ teaspoons baking powder
1 teaspoon salt
½ teaspoon soda
1 cup coarsely cut fresh cranberries

½ cup chopped walnuts
1 tablespoon grated orange peel
1 beaten egg
¾ cup orange juice
2 tablespoons vegetable oil

- Preheat oven to 350°
- Grease a 9x5 loaf pan, set aside
- Sift dry ingredients together
- Stir in cranberries, nuts and grated orange peel
- Combine egg, orange juice and salad oil
- Add to dry ingredients, stirring just until moistened
- Bake in loaf pan at 350° for 50 minutes or until done
- Cool in pan on wire rack for 15 minutes, then remove from pan and cool

JEWISH COFFEE CAKE
1968

Steve's cousin, Betts Weber, gave me this recipe during a time we stayed with her for a three-week period of time. We were in the process of moving from Ft. Benning Georgia to New Jersey. Our little town house was not ready so Betts helped us out. It was a very special time in our lives. I made this cake for many of my coffees.

- ½ pound butter (2 sticks)
- 2 cups sugar
- 3 cups flour
- 2 teaspoons baking soda
- 3 teaspoons baking powder
- 1 pint sour cream (2 cups)
- 2 teaspoons vanilla
- 4 eggs

TOPPING:

- 1 cup sugar
- 1-2 teaspoons cinnamon depending on taste
- ¾ cup chopped walnuts

- Preheat oven to 350°
- Grease and flour a 13x9-inch baking pan
- Make topping and set aside
- Cream together the butter and sugar
- Mix in the sour cream, baking soda and eggs one at a time
- Sift the flour and baking powder in small bowl
- Add flour mixture to other mixture
- Add vanilla
- Stir ¾ of topping mixture into batter
- Pour batter into pan
- Sprinkle remaining ¼ topping mixture on top
- Bake in prepared pan for 55 minutes or until toothpick comes out clean
- Cool in pan on a wire rack
- Cut into squares and serve

CREAM CHEESE BRAIDS
1980

This cheese braid is delicious with coffee. I sliced the braids and served at my neighborhood coffee events.

- 8 ounces sour cream scalded
- ½ cup sugar
- ½ cup butter, melted
- 1 teaspoon salt
- 2 pkgs. dry yeast
- ½ cup warm water (105-115°)
- 2 beaten eggs
- 4 cups flour

- Combine scalded sour cream, sugar, butter and salt, mix well, let cool to lukewarm
- Dissolve yeast in warm water in a large mixing bowl, stir in sour cream mixture and eggs
- Gradually stir in flour (dough will be soft)
- Cover tightly and chill overnight
- Prepare filling
- Divide dough into 4 equal portions
- Turn each portion out onto a heavily floured surface and knead 4-5 times
- Roll each into a 12x8 rectangle
- Spread ¼ of the filling over each rectangle, leaving a ½-inch margin around edges
- Carefully roll up jellyroll fashion, beginning at long side
- Firmly pinch edge and seal the ends
- Carefully place rolls, seam side down on greased baking sheets
- Make 6 equally spaced x-shaped cuts across the top of each loaf
- Cover and let rise in warm place (85°) for 1 hour or until doubled
- Preheat oven to 375°
- Bake 10-20 minutes
- Spread loaves with glaze and serve while warm

FILLING:

- 16 ounces softened cream cheese
- ¾ cup sugar
- 1 beaten egg
- Pinch of salt
- 2 teaspoons vanilla

- Combine all ingredients, process in food processor until blended

GLAZE:

Mix well
- 2 cups sifted powdered sugar
- ¼ t milk
- 2 teaspoons vanilla

BLENDER CHOCOLATE MOUSSE
1985

⅓ cup **hot** coffee
1 (6oz) package semisweet chocolate morsels
4 eggs, separated (make sure eggs are at room temperature)
2 tablespoons crème de cacao
Whipped cream
Sliced toasted almonds

- Combine coffee and chocolate morsels in container of electric blender, process until smooth
- Add egg yolks and coffee liqueur, process 1 minute
- In a separate bowl, beat egg whites (at room temperature) until stiff peaks form
- Gently fold the chocolate mixture into the beaten egg whites until thoroughly mixed
- Spoon into stemmed glasses chill until set
- Top with whipped cream and shaved almond slices

Yield: 6-8

FRESH STRAWBERRY MOUSSE

1 pint strawberries
1 (3-ounce) package strawberry-flavored Jell-O
⅓ cup sugar
2 cups whipping cream

- Mash strawberries; drain, reserving juice. Set pulp aside
- Add enough water to the juice to make 1½ cups liquid
- Bring juice mixture to a boil and add Jell-O, stirring until dissolved
- Chill Jell-O mixture until consistency of unbeaten egg whites
- Combine the strawberry pulp and sugar, stirring well
- Stir into the chilled Jell-O mixture
- Pour whipping cream into a chilled bowl, and beat until soft peaks form
- Fold whipped cream into Jell-O mixture
- Pour into stemmed glasses and chill until thoroughly set

MY TYPICAL ITALIAN
DINNER PARTY
1990

This menu reflects one of my Italian Dinner Parties. We invited 16-18 neighbors and tennis friends. One month in advance I made my breads and lasagna. The freezer was my friend. You can find these recipes throughout this book.

Caponata with Vodka

Toasted Crostini

Assorted Italian olives

Assorted Italian cheeses

Zelda's Fettuccini

Baked Lasagna

Italian Sausage and Peppers

Cheese Stuffed Shells

Chicken Saltimbocca

Italian Salad with Homemade Dressing

Homemade Italian Bread

Italian Bread Sticks

Zuppa Inglese

Or

Tiramisu

PATRICIA'S
ITALIAN SALAD DRESSING
1965

  ¾ cup high-grade virgin olive oil
  ¼ cup red wine vinegar or ⅛ cup wine vinegar and ⅛ cup balsamic vinegar
  1 teaspoon salt
½-1 teaspoon Dijon mustard
    Pinch of sugar
    Fresh basil chopped
    Fresh oregano chopped
    Fresh parsley chopped
    Freshly ground pepper
    Pinch of cayenne pepper OR two shakes of Emeril's original seasoning
    Half clove of garlic (optional)

- Put garlic into a jar
- Mix Dijon mustard and vinegars in a small bowl and whisk
- Add herbs and seasonings
- Slowly whisk oil into vinegar mixture
- Place all ingredients in a jar and shake well

Dried herbs can be used, be sure to crush before using to bring out the flavor.

CAPONATA
WITH VODKA
1975

Caponata means compost or end of the garden season. Italians pretty much add whatever is left in their gardens to this dish.

1 (2-pound) eggplant cubed (skin on)	2 tablespoons sugar
½ cup olive oil	3 tablespoons raisins
1 large onion, thinly sliced	¼ cup toasted pine nuts
3 tablespoons tomato paste	1 cup seeded tomatoes
4 stalks celery, thinly sliced	¼ cup vodka
8 cloves garlic, peeled and sliced	½ cup red wine vinegar
½ cup capers, rinsed	½ cup pitted black olives
Fresh basil chopped	½ cup pitted green olives

- Prepare eggplant by putting into a colander with sea salt.
- Place colander over a dish and put a weight directly over the eggplant. This allows the eggplant to drain.
- Let eggplant stand for 1 hour then rinse and dry.
- Preheat a large skillet.
- Heat oil and cook onion, celery, and garlic stirring until onion is transparent.
- Remove vegetables and add more oil if necessary and cook the eggplant cubes, stirring until lightly browned.
- Return onion mix to pan along with all ingredients except the olives and the vinegar.
- Cover and cook mixture stirring until vegetables are very tender, about 30 minutes.
- Add the olives and capers to pot halfway through the cooking.
- Add the vinegar the last 5 minutes.
- Garnish with fresh Italian parsley.

Pack in glass jars and refrigerate until ready to serve. Will keep for 2 weeks. Can also be frozen.

Serve: As part of an antipasto selection: bread, salami and cheese OR with garlic bread as a first course.

VEAL OR CHICKEN SALTIMBOCCA
Pronounced: sal tim bocca
1999

Saltimbocca translates to "hopping in the mouth." These tiny pockets of thin veal or chicken are well seasoned with sage and a wine reduction.

- 4 veal or chicken scaloppine
- 4 large sage leaves plus 2 more for deglazing the pan
- 4 large slices prosciutto plus one slice cut into pieces
- Flour
- Salt and pepper
- 4 tablespoons olive oil
- 2 tablespoons butter
- 4 shallots, thinly sliced
- ½ pound oyster or shitake mushrooms, sliced
- 1 cup dry white wine or marsala
- ½ cup chicken stock
- 2 tablespoons butter

- Lightly pound the scaloppine to ¼-inch thick
- Place some flour in a shallow bowl and season with salt and pepper
- Season the scaloppine with salt and pepper and lay one sage leaf on each scaloppine
- Lay 1 slice of prosciutto over each and fold in half like a book
- Secure the two sides with a toothpick and dredge the whole piece in flour
- In a 14-in sauté pan heat oil and 2 tablespoons butter
- Add the scallopine and sauté until golden brown on both sides
- Remove the toothpicks and set aside
- Add shallots and mushrooms and cook until sweated, about 5 minutes
- Add prosciutto pieces and sage, quickly sauté
- Add wine and chicken stock to deglaze the pan
- Add scaloppini back into pan and cook over high heat until liquid is reduced to a sauce consistency
- Swirl in 2 tablespoons butter and serve

Serves: 4

Serve with a Merlot or a Sangiovese red Italian wine.
A suggested side dish for this Italian meal is **sautéed greens**.

- 2 pounds of escarole
- 2 cloves garlic
- Half of a lemon juiced

- Cook escarole, drain and dry
- Sauté escarole in 2 tablespoons olive oil with minced garlic
- Continue to sauté until tender (5 minutes)
- Season with salt, pepper and lemon juice

TIRAMISU
1998

- 5 eggs, separated
- 6 tablespoons sugar
- 1 -pound (16-ounce) mascarpone (this is Italian cream cheese)
- ¼ cup heavy cream, whipped
- 6 tablespoons coffee flavored liqueur
- ¾ cup espresso or strong coffee
- 3 tablespoons rum or brandy
- 30 ladyfingers or Italian Amore (Italian cookies)
- 2 ounces semi-sweet chocolate, grated
- 2 tablespoons cocoa powder

- Beat egg yolks and sugar until they are pale and form a ribbon.
- Mix the Mascarpone and cream so that it will be light enough to fold into the egg mixture.
- Stir them together and add the liqueur.
- Whip two of the egg whites until stiff peaks form; then fold into mixture.
- Combine the espresso coffee and rum.
- Brush the ladyfingers with the mixture. Make certain that your cookies are soaked enough with the coffee. If you brush it on be certain to sprinkle any remaining mixture over the cookies. Instead of brushing you can dip them briefly.
- Line the bottom of a bowl or a glass rectangular dish with half of the cookies and cover with **half** the Mascarpone mixture.
- Sprinkle with **half** the grated chocolate.
- Put remaining Mascarpone mixture over top and refrigerate for six hours or overnight.
- Spoon into individual dishes and sprinkle with cocoa and remaining chocolate.

Makes 8-10 servings. Recipe can be cut in half and put into individual large glass goblets.

1 ½ RECIPE FOR 12 SERVINGS:

- 7 ½ eggs
- 9 tablespoons sugar
- 24 ounces Mascarpone
- 3 ounces heavy cream whipped
- 9 tablespoons coffee liqueur
- 9 ounces coffee
- 4½ tablespoons rum
- 45 ladyfingers
- 3 ounces grated chocolate

COCKTAIL PARTIES
1990's

Typically our cocktail parties centered on a huge punch bowl surrounded by a variety of appetizers and hors d'oeuvres. We used one of the three punches listed below. It was a popular and inexpensive way to entertain friends in the 90's.

Southern Punch

Champagne Punch

Planters Punch

Barbecued Chicken wings

Crabmeat Ball

Somerset Potted Cheddar and Walnuts

Hummus with Pita Chips

Sausage Balls

Salmon Spread in Fish Mold

Quiche Lorraine Squares

Assorted Cheese Platter

Cheese Krispies

Dessert Table

Charlotte Russe

Tiny Cheese Cakes

Assorted Fruits

SOUTHERN PUNCH
1990

A good punch can provide an inexpensive cocktail party. Nothing measures up to it in flavor or elegance. This punch is a bit strong so plan on just enough for the number of guests.

1 quart Southern Comfort	1½ cups fresh lemon or lime juice
3½ quarts 7UP or Sprite chilled	Dash of bitters (optional)
5 cups cranberry juice cocktail	Ice ring

- Chill all ingredients, then pour into a large punch bowl
- Add 7 Up or Sprite just before serving
- Add an ice ring
- Decorate with slices of oranges and lemons

1 Quart yields 40 five-ounce cups
Yield: 12-15 people

CHAMPAGNE PUNCH

Juice of two lemons	1 bottle sauterne
Juice of two oranges	¼ cup pineapple juice
4 ounces brandy or rum	1 bottle champagne

- Place all ingredients into punch bowl with an ice ring
- Add champagne last

Yield: 13-1 5 five- ounce cups

PLANTERS PUNCH

This is a "knock out" punch that will surely get you intoxicated if overdone. We made this punch and brought it to picnics. I do not recommend drinking too many or use less rum.

1 bottle rum 4/5 quart	6 ounces grenadine
12 dashes Angostura Bitters	18 ounces orange juice
12 teaspoons sugar	18 ounces grapefruit juice
12 teaspoons fresh lime juice	

- Mix all together in punch bowl and garnish with fresh fruit and an ice ring

NORTHERN CHICAGO
1999-2003

By the time the moving van came to collect and pack up all of my kitchenware, I had a very large collection of various wooden spoons and was ready for the big city of Chicago.

Our move from North Carolina to the Northern area of Chicago was a big one for both my husband and me. It was the first time we had the opportunity to live close to a large city. *I was like a child in a candy shop*. There were so many opportunities opened to us. Steve found a cooking school in the near city area and decided to send me to the school for one week. It turned out to be a hands-on cooking class directed by two crazy restaurant chefs. Both chefs were employed in Chicago French restaurants and started a small cooking school in the Chicago suburbs. I learned many cooking tips in addition to great recipes.

You will notice a difference in the verbiage of these Chicago school recipes. I quickly learned that highly skilled chefs pretty much go by a feel rather than a step–by-step method of cooking.

I also included in this section many other recipes collected and prepared while living in the Chicago area.

PATE SUCREE
CHICAGO COOKING SCHOOL
2001

This is a sweet pastry used in making fruit or cream tarts. It is a rich and sweet pastry with a crisp cookie-like texture. Once you make this pastry, it can be stored in the refrigerator for several days. You can also freeze it for a month.

½ cup unsalted butter at room temperature
¼ cup sugar
1 large egg
1½ cups flour
Pinch of salt
Egg white, melted chocolate, or warmed fruit jam for sealing bottom of crust

- Mix butter until creamy
- Add sugar and beat until fluffy
- Add egg gradually on low
- Add flour and salt
- Mix until it all comes together into a dough
- Put dough onto a piece of plastic wrap, shaping dough into a round about 6-8 inches in diameter
- Wrap and refrigerate for 25 minutes or put in freezer for 10 minutes
- At this point the dough can be stored in the refrigerator for a week or in freezer for up to one month
- Take out of refrigerator and press into your tart pan
- Freeze for 10 minutes
- Place tart pan onto a cookie sheet
- Prick bottom of crust lightly with fork
- Place in 400° oven and bake for 5 minutes
- Lower temperature to 350° and bake for 15 more minutes, or until firm and lightly browned
- Seal bottom and sides of crust with beaten egg white, melted chocolate or warmed jam to seal
- Place in oven to dry the egg whites just a minute or two
- Cool completely
- Remove from tart pan
- Fill as desired

LEEKS AU GRATIN
CHICAGO COOKING SCHOOL
2001

3 leeks (white part) carefully washed
Swiss Cheese
Lemon juice

Salt and pepper
Dash of sugar
Basic Béchamel sauce

- Prepare Béchamel sauce
- Cook leeks in water with lemon juice, salt, pepper, a dash of sugar and butter until tender
- Squeeze leeks to remove water
- Cut leeks in half lengthwise
- Sauté in butter
- Grease a gratin dish
- Place leeks in dish,
- Cover with Béchamel sauce
- Sprinkle with Swiss cheese and dots of butter
- Broil

If made ahead and the au gratin is coming from the refrigerator, bake at 425° instead of broiling.

BASIC BECHAMEL SAUCE

2 tablespoons unsalted butter
2 tablespoons flour
1¼ cups whole milk
½ cup heavy cream

¼ teaspoon salt
Freshly ground pepper
4-5 scrapes of fresh nutmeg

- In saucepan, melt butter and add flour to make a roux
- Whisk to blend and cook, whisking for about 1 minutes
- Take pan off heat and pour in ¼ cup of the milk, whisk to form a smooth paste, then whisk in the remaining milk and the cream
- Return to heat and bring to a simmer, whisking frequently
- Simmer giving the sauce an occasional whisk until smooth and glossy and no taste of the flour remains (8-10 minutes)
- Add salt, pepper and nutmeg

LIGHT AND DARK ROUX
(ROUX BLOND ET ROUX BRUN)
2001

LIGHT ROUX

4 tablespoons (2½ ounces) unsalted butter
5 tablespoons flour

- Melt butter in saucepan. Add flour and stir constantly until the roux starts foaming and whitens…no color
- Remove from heat, allow to cool and store until needed
- Use to thicken stock, milk or any liquid

DARK ROUX

- Same as light roux but cook the mixture until it becomes brown

Chef's comments: When using roux to thicken a sauce, either stir **hot** liquid into **cold** roux or **cold** liquid in **hot** roux. Continue stirring until the liquid boils to avoid lumps

Roux can be cooked in a large quantity in moderate oven 250° for 1½ hours rather than over low heat.

GRATIN DAUPHINOIS
CHICAGO COOKING SCHOOL
2001

5 potatoes (about 1 pound) sliced thin. Do not rinse potatoes after you slice them.
2 minced garlic cloves
1½ cups whole milk (do not use half and half)
1 cup cream
Salt and pepper

- Preheat oven to 325°
- Put salt (heavy salt because the potatoes will not be salted), pepper and garlic on the bottom of baking dish or pan
- Pour 1 cup cream and about 1½ cups whole milk in pan and boil
- Put in thinly sliced potatoes and stir after each entry of potatoes
- Bake till done (35-45 minutes)
- Let set up before serving
    * The liquid should cover the potatoes by at least ⅛ inch in order to produce a moist gratin

Yield: 4

BASIC CHICKEN STOCK
CHICAGO COOKING SCHOOL
2001

Every morning we three students would begin the day by making our stocks. Before class the chefs stopped at the nearby markets and bought bruised vegetables for the stocks. I was always amazed at how they would use whatever was available to make stock. While I was learning to make a basic stock, I was introduced to the chinois.

4 pound chicken (neck, wing tips, carcasses or legs and thighs)	Bouquet garni (green leaves of the leeks, fresh thyme, bay leaves and stalks from parsley)
2-3 carrots washed but unpeeled	Whole peppercorns
1 large onion cut in half	Coarse salt
3-4 garlic cloves cut in half and unpeeled	White pepper
2 leeks (washed thoroughly)	3-4 quarts of water
2-3 celery stalks	

- Cut chicken into small pieces
- Place in stock pot, cover with cold water
- Add just a handful of the salt
- Add vegetables and bouquet garni; bring to a boil
- Skim the foam off the top constantly
- When foam is completely gone add the peppercorns
- Simmer uncovered for 3 hours adding water if necessary to compensate for the reduction
- Pass through a *chinois,* do not press the solids
- Let cool in separate containers

VEAL STOCK:

- Replace chicken with veal bones and simmer for 4-5 hours

PORK STOCK:

- Brown pork neck bones in oil in a 400° oven until browned
- Sauté 6 cloves garlic (smashed and unpeeled and cut in half), carrots, celery, and onion
- Add browned bones
- Deglaze the roasting pan with water, add to stock pot and cover with 2-3 cups water plus the deglazed water
- Add some cooked tomato paste and salt
- Add bouquet of garni (add fresh rosemary to bouquet)
- Add peppercorns
- Cook 3-4 hours, skim foam frequently

SAUTEED BASS
WITH HERB BUTTER
CHICAGO COOKING SCHOOL
2001

2 filet of bass 1½ pounds
1 tablespoon unsalted butter or olive oil

Fresh parsley
Artichoke bottoms sliced thin

GARNISH:

1 teaspoon fresh chervil
1 teaspoon fresh tarragon
1 teaspoon fresh chives

1 tablespoon diced tomatoes (seeded and skinned)

BEURRE BLANC –BUTTER SAUCE:

1 tablespoon chopped shallots
1½ ounces (3 tablespoons) white wine
⅔ ounce (2 tablespoons) white wine vinegar
1½ ounces (3 tablespoons) heavy cream
7 ounces (6½ tablespoons) cold unsalted butter cut into tiny pieces
Salt and pepper to taste
Cayenne pepper (optional)

- Rinse and dry the two filets of bass
- Roughly chop the herbs and prepare the tomato; set aside
- Put the shallots, white wine and vinegar into a saucepan
- Bring to boil and reduce to syrupy consistency
- Add the cream, bring back to boil and whisk in the butter a few pieces at a time
- Season to taste
- Pass through a fine chinois
- Keep at a warm temperature
- Cook the fish; sauté in oil or butter for 2-3 minutes each side (can also braise the fish in white wine in 425° oven for 3-4 minutes
- Reheat the beurre blanc sauce
- Add fresh herbs and diced tomatoes
- If sauce is too bland, flavor with fresh lemon juice
- To serve, place each filet in middle of plate, spoon the herb butter sauce around the filet, decorate with fresh parsley and artichoke bottoms slices thin

Serves: 4

ROAST CHICKEN
CHICAGO COOKING SCHOOL
2001

1 whole chicken (about 4 pounds) thoroughly washed and dried both inside and outside
Oil and butter
Lemons
Fresh herbs (thyme, parsley, tarragon, basil, marjoram, oregano)
White wine
Chicken stock
Butter

- Preheat oven to 400°
- Truss chicken (tie legs together, tuck wings under body
- Rub with butter or olive oil and sprinkle with salt
- Stuff cavity with herbs, salt, pepper and cut lemons
- Start roasting chicken on its side and brown
- Then turn to other side, rotating every 20 minutes for even browning
- Cut string around the legs half way through the cooking
- Baste frequently
- Roast about 1 hour to 1 hour 15 minutes or internal temperature of 160
- Take out of oven and let stand for about 15 minutes with a tent of foil over the chicken
- Make Au Gus while chicken is resting
- Deglaze the roasting pan with wine
- Add chicken stock
- Reduce to a nice sauce consistency then strain
- Add a bit of butter

CREPE SUZETTE
CHICAGO COOKING SCHOOL
2001

6 tablespoons flour
Pinch of salt
3 whole eggs

½ quart milk
2 tablespoons unsalted butter

- In bowl mix flour and salt with fork, make a "well" in the middle of the flour
- Break the eggs, one at a time into the "well"
- Slowly mix the batter adding milk a little at a time
- Let batter stand for 2-3 hours before making the crepes
- In small frying pan melt butter until it turns light brown
- Add this butter to the batter and gently whisk to blend
- Heat a crepe pan and ladle scoop of batter onto pan
- Roll the batter quickly around pan to make an even, thin coat
- When edges begin to turn dull and light brown, turn the crepe over with a large spatula
- Repeat until batter is used up

FILLING:

6 oranges juiced
Zest of the oranges
6 tablespoons sugar

6 tablespoons softened unsalted butter
3-4 tablespoons Grand Marnier

- Peel and zest oranges
- In skillet add sugar to pan to make the caramel
- When it starts to liquefy and take a bit of color, take off the heat
- Add the orange juice to stop the cooking
- Briefly place the pan back on low heat and add the butter
- Heat just long enough to melt the butter
- Fold crepes in half and add to the sauce
- Once the crepes are covered in the sauce add the Grand Marnier
- Heat on low flame just long enough to heat the alcohol
- Take off heat and flambé
- Once the flame dies down, add butter and heat just long enough to melt the butter
- Fold the crepes in half again and place on dessert plates
- Spoon sauce over them and garnish with a sprinkling of the orange zest and powdered sugar

Serves: 6

SOUFFLE GRAND MARNIER
CHICAGO COOKING SCHOOL
2001

This recipe makes two light soufflés 4 inches in diameter.

3 large eggs separated, room temperature
2 tablespoons Grand Marnier
   Zest of one orange
4 tablespoons sugar
   Powdered sugar to top the soufflés
½ teaspoon cream anglaise (optional)

- Preheat the oven to 450°
- Combine egg yolks, Grand Marnier, zest and ½ of the sugar in a mixing bowl
- In another bowl beat the egg whites until foamy
- Add the remaining sugar to the egg whites and continue beating until soft peaks form, do not overbeat or the soufflé will be dry
- Fold the whites into the egg yolk mixture
- Butter and sprinkle sugar on two soufflé ramekins approximately 4 inches in diameter
- Fill with batter
- Level off the top and clean the rim
- Bake for 15-18 minutes

CREAM ANGLAISE

½ liter of whole milk
5 egg yolks
9 tablespoons sugar

1 teaspoon vanilla bean cut in half and scraped
Grand Marnier to taste

- Bring milk to a boil
- Add vanilla bean; mix egg yolks and sugar
- Pour milk on top of the egg yolk mixture
- Cook on medium until the cream is thick enough to coat a wooden spatula
- Pass through a fine mesh sieve; cool off quickly
- When cream is cold, add the Grand Marnier
- With a spoon make a tiny well in the top of each soufflé and pour in a small amount of Cream Anglaise
- Sprinkle powdered sugar on top of the soufflés and serve immediately

CRÈME BRULÉE
CHICAGO COOKING SCHOOL
2001

2 cups heavy cream
½ vanilla bean, split
3 eggs

½ cup sugar
2 tablespoons sugar in the raw (natural cane sugar)

- Preheat oven to 250°
- In saucepan heat cream and vanilla bean until just boiling
- Remove from heat, and remove the bean scraping the seeds back into the cream
- In bowl whisk together eggs and sugar
- Slowly whisk 1 cup hot cream into egg mixture until the sugar has dissolved
- Slowly whisk in remaining cream
- Evenly divide into six 6-ounce cups
- Place cups in baking pan
- Pour in enough hot water to come halfway up sides of cups
- Bake 1 hour and 15 min or until custard is set
- Remove from baking pan; let cool
- Cover with plastic wrap and refrigerate until ready to use
- Heat broiler
- Sprinkle raw sugar over custard
- Broil 2 inches from heat until sugar melts and bubbles, or use a kitchen torch
- Serve warm

Yield: 6

BUTTERNUT SQUASH SOUP
1999

I made soups frequently in Chicago because 90% of the time the weather was so cold we just craved hot soups.

- 2-3 pound butternut squash, peeled and seeded
- 2 tablespoons unsalted butter
- 1 medium onion or leek
- ½ cup chopped peeled apples
- 4-6 cups chicken stock depending how thick you want your soup
- Nutmeg to taste
- Pinch of cayenne pepper
- Pinch of cumin
- 2 teaspoons salt
- White pepper
- ¼ cup heavy cream
- Crème fraiche
- Toasted walnuts or hazelnuts

- Cut squash into 1-inch chunks
- In large pot melt butter
- Add onion or leek and cook about 8 minutes
- Add squash, apples and stock
- Bring to a simmer and cook until squash is tender (15-20 minutes)
- With immersion blender puree soup until smooth
- Stir in seasonings
- Stir in cream and some unsalted butter
- Serve in bowls; top with crème fraiche and sprinkle with nuts

Serves 6

CHILLED ASPARAGUS SOUP
WITH TIMBALE OF CAVIAR, CRAB AND AVOCADO
1999

- 2 tablespoons butter
- 2 small Leeks (white & pale green parts only), halved lengthwise and thoroughly washed
- 1½ pounds asparagus, ends trimmed, spears coarsely chopped
- 4 cups chicken stock or canned low-salt chicken broth
- 3 cups chopped spinach leaves (about 3½ ounces)

TIMBALES

- 6 tablespoons flaked fresh crabmeat
- 2 tablespoons fresh lemon juice
- 1 tablespoon minced shallot
- ¾ cup diced peeled pitted avocado

- Melt butter in heavy large saucepan over medium heat. Add leeks and sauté until soft, about 5 minutes.
- Add asparagus and stock.
- Bring to boil. Reduce heat to medium, cover and simmer until asparagus is tender, about 8 minutes.
- Add spinach, cover and simmer until wilted, about 4 minutes.
- Working in batches, puree soup in blender until smooth. Transfer soup to large bowl; season to taste with salt and pepper. Can use an immersion blender.
- Cool, then cover and chill until cold, at least 2 hours or up to one day.
- Mix crabmeat, 1 tablespoon lemon juice and shallot in small bowl. Season to taste with salt and pepper.
- Mix avocado and remaining 1 tablespoon lemon juice in another small bowl, mash coarsely. Season to taste with salt and pepper.
- Place timbale cutter (tomato paste can or very small biscuit cutter) in center of a soup bowl. Spoon in 1 tablespoon avocado mix; smooth top.
- Spoon in 1 tablespoon crab mixture; press lightly to compact.
- Spoon in 1 tablespoon avocado mixture.
- Top with 1 teaspoon caviar.
- Carefully lift off the cutter or can. Repeat in remaining soup bowls with remaining timbale ingredients.
- Ladle soup around each timbale.
- Serve immediately.

Yield: 6

SUPER QUICK MINESTRONE
2003

1 cup tubetti pasta
Extra virgin olive oil
6 cups chicken stock
¼ pound pancetta, cut into pieces (can use bacon)
6 garlic cloves, minced
2 cups finely chopped onions
1 cup diced celery
1 cup diced carrots
1 tablespoon finely chopped rosemary or thyme leaves
1 (14-ounce) can cannellini beans, drained and rinsed
1 (14-ounce) can diced tomatoes
4 cups diced zucchini
2 cups diced peeled russet potatoes (1 large Potato)
1 cup freshly grated Parmesan cheese
Salt and pepper to taste

- Bring a pot of salted water to boil
- Add pasta and cook to al dente
- Drain pasta and toss with a bit of oil to prevent sticking and set aside
- Warm the chicken stock
- In another saucepan heat ¼ cup oil
- Add pancetta and cook until it begins to brown (3-4 minutes)
- Add garlic and cook about 1 minute
- Lower heat and add onions, celery and carrots
- Cook until soft (about 8-10 minutes)
- Add the chopped herbs
- Raise the heat to high and add the beans, tomatoes, zucchini and potatoes
- Add the stock and bring to a boil
- Lower heat and cook until the potatoes are tender
- Skim foam off the soup
- Season with salt and pepper
- Add the pasta
- Serve warm with cheese and olive oil passed at the table

Tip: Add the cooked pasta just before serving. If it sits in the soup too long, it develops a flabby texture. Tubetti (little hollow tubes) are the classic pasta for minestrone, but you can substitute another small shape of pasta.

Serves: 8-10

AVOCADO AND SHRIMP SALAD
2003

3 tablespoons olive oil
2 tablespoons white wine vinegar (preferably French)
1 teaspoon Dijon mustard
1 pound fresh shrimp, cooked, shelled, deveined and cubed
1 cup mayonnaise
2 tablespoons chili sauce or ketchup
1 large garlic clove, crushed
   Hot pepper sauce
   Salt and freshly ground pepper
   One large ripe avocado
   Juice of ½ lemon
2 tablespoons finely minced fresh dill
2 tablespoons dill sprigs, lemon wedges and avocado slices (garnish)

- Whisk together first 3 ingredients until well blended. Add to shrimp, toss thoroughly, cover and marinate for 2 hours.
- Meanwhile, whisk mayonnaise, chili sauce, garlic, hot pepper sauce, salt and pepper until smooth, set aside.
- Peel, seed and cube avocado.
- Sprinkle with lemon juice and set aside.
- Drain shrimp. Add cubed avocado, dill and chives and toss. Fold in enough mayonnaise mixture to coat lightly.
- Taste and adjust seasonings.
- Cover and chill until serving time.
- Divide salad among chilled plates and garnish with dill sprigs, lemon wedges and avocado slices.
- Serve immediately.

Serves: 4

LIVER PATE
MARY CERJAN
2003

Our daughter Mary shared this wonderful Pate recipe with me during one of our Thanksgivings in her Chicago condo.

14	tablespoons unsalted butter, room temperature
1	pound chanterelle or stemmed shitake mushrooms, brushed clean, thinly sliced
4	whole green onions, chopped
4	green onions (white part only) chopped
1½	pounds chicken livers, trimmed
½	cup dry white wine (vermouth is good)
2½	teaspoons salt
1	teaspoon dry mustard
½	teaspoon ground nutmeg
¼	teaspoon ground cloves
1	8-ounce package cream cheese, cut into pieces, room temperature
¼	cup Cognac or Brandy
	Baguette slices

- Melt 2 tablespoons butter and add mushrooms
- Sauté until tender and beginning to brown and all juices have evaporated (15 minutes)
- Melt 4 tablespoons butter in another skillet
- Add all green onions and sauté 2 minutes
- Add livers, stir to coat, cover, cook until no longer pink; stirring often (10 min)
- Add wine and next 4 ingredients, simmer uncovered for 1 minute
- Using slotted spoon, transfer livers to processor
- Puree 30 seconds
- Gradually add wine mixture from skillet, puree until smooth
- Add cream cheese, cognac, ½ cup butter and all but ⅓ cup mushrooms
- Puree until fully blended
- Transfer pate to serving dish
- Arrange reserved ⅓ cup mushrooms atop pate
- Cover and chill at least 1 day and up to 2 days
- Place dish with pate in center of platter, surround with toasted baguette slices

Serves 12

TAPENADE
WITH SUN-DRIED TOMATOES
1996

This olive paste can be used as a pizza topping, as a flavor pickup for purchased pasta sauces and as a spread for crostini slices.

¼ cup olive oil
2 cups sliced onions
½ cup drained oil-packed sun-dried tomatoes, chopped
½ cup chopped pitted brine-cured black olives such as Kalamata

- Heat oil over low heat
- Add onions and sauté until dark brown, occasionally scraping up browned bits about 30 minutes
- Transfer onions to processor
- Add tomatoes and olives
- Using pulse, process until chunky paste forms (do not puree)
- Season with pepper and cool

Can be made one week ahead: cover and chill. Bring to room temperature before using

Yield: 1 cup

SPICY SWEET POTATOES
2000

2 sweet potatoes
1 tablespoon olive oil or to taste
½ teaspoon salt
⅛ teaspoon freshly ground pepper
⅛ teaspoon cayenne or to taste
⅛ teaspoon ground allspice

- Preheat oven to 500°
- Pell potatoes and halve lengthwise, then cut each half lengthwise into 4 wedges
- Transfer to a shallow baking pan and toss with oil to coat
- Combine salt and spices and sprinkle over potatoes, toss
- Roast potatoes in lower third of oven, turning over half-way through roasting until tender and browned
- About 15-20 minutes

Serves: 4

BRIE CHEESE
IN PUFF PASTRY
2000

- 10 ounces wheel of Brie cheese
- 3 tablespoons apricot preserves
- ¼ cup chopped pecans or shaved almonds
- ½ package frozen puff pastry, thawed
- 1 egg white, beaten

- Preheat oven to 375°
- Lightly grease a cookie sheet or line with parchment for faster cleanup
- Slice one wheel of cheese in half (length-wise) to make two circles
- Spread apricot preserves on the cut side half of one circle
- Sprinkle with nuts
- Make sandwich out of the two halves so that the preserves are in the center of both halves
- Wrap the entire wheel of cheese with one sheet of puffed pastry and pull up edges to make a bow
- Brush with egg white
- Place the Brie package onto the cooking sheet
- Bake for 30 -40minutes
- Let stand for 10-15 minutes before cutting (very important step)

Serves: 6

MEXICAN CHEESECAKE
COURTESY OF ANN MILAM
2001

My very special friend, Ann Milam, wrote this recipe in her cookbook. I was so inspired with her book that I decided to write this book. With her permission I am sharing this recipe with you. I have served this to entertain a crowd on our dock on Lake Gaston.

- 16 ounces cream cheese softened
- 2 cups shredded sharp cheddar cheese
- 2 cups sour cream, divided
- 1½ packages taco seasoning mix
- 3 eggs, room temperature
- 1 (4-ounce) can green chilies drained and chopped
- ⅔ cup salsa

- Preheat oven to 350°
- Combine cheeses and beat until fluffy
- Stir in 1 cup sour cream and taco seasoning
- Beat in eggs, one at a time, mixing well after each addition
- Fold in chilies
- Pour into 9-in cheesecake pan
- Bake 35-40 minutes or until center is firm
- Remove from oven and cool 10 minutes
- Spoon remaining 1 cup sour cream over cheesecake
- Bake 5 minutes longer
- Cool completely
- Cover and refrigerate several hours
- Before serving, remove sides of pan and top with salsa
- Serve with plain taco chips

Serves: 10

OVEN-DRIED TOMATO AND EGGPLANT TIMBALES
WITH PESTO
DEAN AND DELUCA
1999

While living in the Chicago area, I often visited my sister Marie in Atlanta. She took me to the Dean and DeLuca café for lunch and bought me their cookbook. This recipe is from that book. The tomatoes are so sweet and the timbales make a very impressive appetizer.

DRIED TOMATOES:

4 ripe tomatoes
Olive oil for brushing tomatoes
Salt and pepper to taste

- Preheat oven to 150
- Cut tomatoes in half crosswise, place on baking sheet cut sides up
- Brush with oil, salt and pepper
- Bake for 20 hours or when tomatoes are about half their original size yet still moist

You can also sprinkle with salt, pepper, and olive oil and roast for 15 minutes at 400°, reduce oven to 300° and roast another 1-2 hours or until half their size.

TIMBALES:

1 small eggplant (6 ounces)
Extra virgin olive oil
3 tablespoons freshly made pesto, salt to taste
4 small ramekins that hold 2½ ounces of liquid

- Puncture eggplant all over, place in 400° oven, cook until quite soft (30 minutes) remove and cool.
- Smear each ramekin with oil; place a tomato half, into ramekin skin side down, top with a teaspoon of pesto, top with ½ -inch slice of eggplant. Salt the eggplant.
- Top with a teaspoon of pesto and then the other half of tomato, cut side down.
- Serve immediately, or let sit at room temperature for several hours to allow the flavors to mingle.
- To serve, run a small knife around and under the vegetables to prepare for unmolding; turn upside down; serve on small plate, drizzle with a little olive oil.

Serves: 4 appetizers

PASTA SALAD
1999

There is nothing better than a nice pasta salad to accompany a summer meal. I make this frequently in the summer months.

- 1 pound tri-colored pasta swirls
- 2 cups cooked broccoli flowerets or 1 bag of frozen broccoli, cauliflower, carrots (cooked)
- ½ cup sliced black olives
- 1 can cut up artichokes, drained and rinsed
- 2 tomatoes seeded and chopped or grape tomatoes cut in half
- 1 (16-ounce) bottle of Italian dressing. I use the Paul Newman brand or my homemade Italian dressing
- ½ cup Parmesan cheese

- Cook the pasta until al dente
- Drain well and rinse with cold water
- Cook the vegetables and drain well
- Combine the pasta, vegetables and salad dressing
- Toss thoroughly
- Add cheese and toss again
- Chill for at least 1 hour (tastes better if made a day or two ahead)

Serves: 10

CARROT LOAF (TERRINE)
2001

This recipe was adapted from Wolfgang Puck. As anything he creates it has a lengthy prep time, but is well worth the effort. It can be reheated for another day's vegetable.

Prep time: 45 minutes

- 2 pounds carrots, peeled and cut into ¼ inch slices or 2 bags of shredded carrots found in the produce section of grocery store
- 5 ounces unsalted butter
- ¼ pound mushrooms, sliced
- ½ pound spinach, cleaned
- 5 eggs
- 4 ounces grated Swiss cheese, I use Gruyere
- 1 teaspoon salt
- Freshly ground pepper to taste

- Preheat the oven to 400°
- Trace the **bottom** of an 8x4x2 loaf pan onto parchment paper and cut to fit the bottom of the pan
- Turn pan upside down and trace the **top** of the pan onto parchment paper
- Butter the pan and the **bottom** parchment paper with 1 ounce of the butter or spray with a cooking spray
- Sauté the carrots slowly in 2 ounces of butter until tender
- Chop the carrots coarsely and reserve in a large mixing bowl
- Over high heat sauté the mushrooms in 1 ounce butter for 2 minutes
- Chop the mushrooms coarsely and add them to the carrots
- Sauté the spinach in 1 ounce butter
- Chop coarsely and reserve in a separate bowl and cool
- Once the spinach is cooled, beat one egg and mix with the spinach
- Beat together the remaining 4 eggs and the cheese in a separate bowl
- Combine this egg/cheese mixture thoroughly with the carrots and mushrooms
- Add the salt and pepper, taste and correct seasonings if necessary
- Fill the pan with half the carrot/mushroom mixture, cover with the spinach
- Top with the remaining carrot/mushroom mixture
- Top with the **top** piece of buttered parchment paper
- Place the prepared carrot loaf in a bain-marie (large shallow pan with 1–2 inches of hot water)
- Bake for 1 hour and 15 minutes or until a knife inserted into the center comes out clean (if water evaporates, add more)
- Invert onto a warm serving platter and remove the parchment paper
- Slice and serve immediately

Serves: 8

BAKED ZITI

2003

Marinara Sauce (recipe follows)
1 pound ziti
1½ pounds ricotta cheese
1 egg
½ teaspoon salt
½ teaspoon garlic powder or fresh garlic minced
Pepper to taste
1 pound mozzarella cheese cut into small cubes
4 ounces (2 cups) sharp provolone cheese shredded

- Preheat oven to 350°
- Grease baking dish
- Bring a large pot of salted water to a boil
- Cook the ziti thoroughly according to package directions and drain well and set aside
- In the same pot, blend ricotta with the egg, ½ teaspoon salt, garlic and pepper
- Stir in the drained ziti, mozzarella cubes and half the marinara sauce
- Spread into a 9x13-inch pan
- Cover with the remaining marinara and sprinkle with the provolone
- Bake until bubbly hot and lightly browned on top (30-40 minutes)
- Serve with a salad and garlic bread

Dish can be assembled and then frozen until ready to bake.

Serves: 12

MARINARA SAUCE

1 tablespoon olive oil
1 onion diced
½ teaspoon salt and freshly ground pepper to taste
2-4 cloves garlic finely chopped
1 tablespoon dried oregano or 1 teaspoon dried and 2 tablespoons chopped fresh oregano
¼ teaspoon crushed red pepper
Small bunch fresh basil
⅓ cup white or red wine
1 (28-ounce) can crushed tomatoes
1 (28-ounce) can whole tomatoes diced
½ teaspoon sugar (optional)

- Heat oil in large saucepan and add onions salt and pepper
- Cook until onions are translucent

- Add garlic, when onions start to brown, add oregano, red pepper, basil and salt and pepper to taste
- Cook over medium heat, stirring occasionally, until onions caramelize
- Add the wine and turn up the heat to medium-high
- Cook stirring until most of the liquid is gone
- Add the tomatoes and bring to a boil
- Reduce heat to low; cover and simmer 20-30 minutes stirring occasionally

PENNE PASTA
WITH FIVE CHEESES
2001

I adapted this recipe from Ina Garten.

½-1 teaspoon sea salt
2 cups heavy cream
1 cup crushed tomatoes in thick tomato puree
½ cup freshly grated Pecorino Romano (1½ ounces)
½ cup shredded imported Italian fontina (1½ ounces)
¼ cup Gorgonzola (1½ ounces)
2 tablespoons ricotta cheese
¼ pound fresh mozzarella, sliced
6 fresh basil leaves, chopped
1 pound penne pasta
4 tablespoons (½ stick) unsalted butter

- Preheat oven to 500°
- Bring salted water to boil
- Combine all the ingredients except the pasta and butter in a large bowl
- Mix well
- Cook pasta in the boiling water for about 4 minutes
- Drain well in a colander
- Add to the ingredients in the mixing bowl, tossing to combine
- Divide the pasta among 6 ceramic gratin dishes (1½ to 2 cup capacity)
- Dot with the butter
- Bake until bubbly and brown on top 7-10 minutes

Serves: 6-8

BASIC RISOTTO
1999

4-5 cups canned low-salt chicken broth
1-2 tablespoons butter, and 2 tablespoons extra-virgin olive oil
  1 large onion finely chopped
  1 small celery stalk finely chopped
  2 large garlic cloves, minced
  8 ounces dry white vermouth or dry white wine
1½ cups to 2 cups risotto (Arborio) rice
    Sea salt and freshly ground pepper
  5 tablespoons butter
  4 ounces freshly grated Parmesan cheese
    Additional grated Parmesan cheese

- Bring broth to simmer in saucepan.
- Cover broth and keep hot over low heat.
- Put olive oil and butter into a separate pan.
- Add onions, garlic and celery.
- Cook very slowly for about 15 minutes.
- Add the rice and turn up the heat.
- The rice will now begin to lightly fry, keep stirring.
- After a minute it will look slightly translucent. You will see a white dot in the center of each grain.
- Add the vermouth or wine and keep stirring until the liquid is absorbed.
- Add one ladleful of hot broth, a good pinch of salt, and some freshly ground pepper, turn the heat down at this point so the rice does not cook too quickly.
- Keep adding a ladleful of stock, stirring, allowing each ladleful to be absorbed before adding the next ladleful of stock. This process will take about 15 minutes.
- Taste the rice to check if it is cooked. If not, keep adding stock until the rice is soft but with a slight bite.
- If you run out of stock before the rice is done, add some boiling water.
- Remove from the heat and add the butter and Parmesan cheese. Stir well.
- Place a lid on the pan and allow it to sit for 2 minutes, as this is when it becomes creamy.
- Serve immediately.

Yield: 6 first-course or 4 main-course servings

You can prepare the risotto ahead up to about ¾ done and leave. When guests are 10 minutes from eating, reheat the risotto and the stock and continue to add a ladleful of broth at a time until the risotto is soft. Finish with the butter and cheese. Allow it to sit for 2 minutes covered.

RISOTTO AND BEANS
MARY CERJAN
1997

This is the first recipe my daughter shared with me. It is always a delight when your children share in the love of cooking.

¼	cup extra-virgin olive oil
3	strips of bacon, chopped
6	fresh sage leaves, chopped
3	cups chicken or vegetable stock
2	cups Arborio rice
14	ounces cannelloni beans, drained and rinsed
	Freshly ground black pepper
	Shaved Parmesan cheese

RICE MIXTURE:

- Add olive oil, bacon and half the sage to a saucepan
- Fry over medium heat until bacon is almost cooked
- Add rice and stir for a few minutes until the rice is well coated with the oil
- Pour boiling stock into pan with rice, return to boil and cover
- Reduce heat to low and simmer 20 minutes

BEAN MIXTURE:

- In another fry pan add oil, 2 strips of bacon, and 3 leaves of sage, fry for a few minutes
- Add beans and simmer over very low heat
- When rice is done, uncover rice and stir
- If stock is not fully absorbed, cover and cook for a few more minutes
- Spoon into plates then pile bean mixture on top of risotto
- Grind black pepper over all and add shavings of Parmesan cheese

VARIATIONS:

    Porcini mushrooms added to the rice
    Sautéed onion and 2 chopped tomatoes with a few basil leaves with the rice
    Sauté 8 ounces chicken filet (cut into small pieces) with a chopped onion
    A handful of chopped sun dried tomatoes with the uncooked rice

Serves: 4

VEAL PICCATA
ANGEL HAIR PARMIGIANA-REGGIANO
1987

- ½ cup flour
- ½ teaspoon salt
- ½ teaspoon freshly ground pepper
- 2 pounds veal cutlets (Scallopine) pounded to ¼-inch thick (can use chicken cutlets)
- 5 tablespoons unsalted butter
- 2 tablespoons extra virgin olive oil
- ½-1 cup dry white wine (dry vermouth or sauvignon blanc) heated
- 1 cup chicken stock or canned chicken broth
- 2-3 tablespoons fresh lemon juice
- 2 tablespoons minced shallots
- 3 tablespoons capers drained and rinsed
- 2 tablespoons flat leaf parsley, chopped
- 1 clove minced garlic
- ½ pound fresh mushroom sliced and sautéed in butter (optional)

- If using mushroom, sauté in butter and set aside
- Combine flour, salt and pepper in shallow bowl
- Lightly season both sides of scallopine with salt and pepper
- One at a time lightly dredge each Scallopini in the seasoned flour
- Heat 2 tablespoons oil and 1 tablespoon butter in a large skillet
- Add the veal in batches and cook until golden and just cooked (1-2 minutes)
- Place in warm dish while you make the sauce
- Add the wine to the juices remaining in the pan and bring to a boil scraping bottom of pan with a wooden spoon
- Reduce the wine by half, add butter, sautéed mushrooms, garlic, and shallots
- Add the chicken stock, lemon juice, capers and return to a boil, stirring until the mixture is thickened (4 minutes)
- Stir in remaining 2-4 tablespoons butter and 1 tablespoon parsley
- Return all of the scallopine to the pan and cook until heated

PASTA:

- ½ pound angel hair
- 2 tablespoons extra virgin olive oil or as needed
- ½ teaspoon salt
- ¼ teaspoon pepper
- 3 tablespoons fresh flat leaf parsley chopped
- 2 teaspoons fresh basil chopped
- 2 tablespoons freshly grated Parmigiano-Reggiano or to taste
- Pasta water as needed

- Cook pasta until just al dente (4 minutes)
- Drain and return to pot
- Add oil, salt, pepper, parsley, basil and cheese
- Toss, cover to keep warm

Cooked, chilled broccoli dressed with olive oil, lemon juice and pine nuts makes a good side dish for this veal dish

Serves: 6

Wine Paring: Chardonnay, Alsace Pinot Blanc, light pinot noir

VEAL MARSALA
2003

- 8 veal cutlets (about 3 ounces each) can also use chicken cutlets pounded thin
- Salt and freshly ground black pepper
- 2-3 tablespoons extra-virgin olive oil
- 2-4 tablespoons unsalted butter
- 1 large shallot, finely chopped
- 2-4 garlic cloves, smashed
- 2 ounces assorted mushrooms, sliced
- ½ cup sweet marsala wine
- ¾ cup low-salt chicken broth
- Leaves from 1 fresh rosemary sprig finely minced

- Pound cutlets thin.
- Dredge cutlets in flour.
- Sprinkle the veal with salt and pepper.
- Melt 1 tablespoon of butter and 1 tablespoon of oil in a heavy large skillet over medium-high heat.
- Add 4 veal cutlets and cook until golden brown, about 1½ minutes per side.
- Transfer the veal to a plate.
- Add another tablespoon of butter and oil, if necessary. Repeat with the remaining 4 cutlets.
- Set the cutlets aside.
- Add 1 tablespoon of oil to the skillet.
- Add the shallot and garlic.
- Sauté until fragrant, about 30 seconds.
- Add a tablespoon of the olive oil, if necessary and add the mushrooms and sauté until tender and the juices evaporate, about 3 minutes.
- Season with salt and add the marsala wine.
- Simmer until the marsala reduces by half, about 4 minutes.
- Add the broth and the rosemary leaves.
- Simmer until reduced by half about 4 minutes.
- Return the veal to the skillet.
- Pour in all of the pan juices and cook until heated through, turning to coat, about 1 minute.
- Stir the remaining 1 tablespoon of butter into the sauce.
- Season with salt and pepper to taste.
- Using tongs, transfer the veal to plates.
- Spoon the sauce over the veal and serve.
- Garnish with cherry tomatoes and parsley.
- Can be made 24 hours in advance. To reheat, cover with foil and bake 350° for 30 minutes.

Serves: 4

Wine pairing: Chardonnay or Merlot
Fettuccini Alfredo goes well with this dish

FRESH SEAFOOD PASTA
2000

2 tablespoons olive oil
1 cup minced shallots
2 teaspoons chopped garlic
  Salt, pepper
2 cups chopped tomatoes, peeled and seeded
1 pound fresh mussels, scrubbed
1 pound rock shrimp, peeled
2 cups dry white wine
1 pound lump crabmeat,
½ cup chopped green onions, green part only
1 pound penne pasta, cooked until tender
4 ounces freshly grated Parmigiano-Reggiano cheese
¼ cup Chiffonade fresh basil
  White truffle oil

- Cook pasta in boiling salted until tender
- Add oil to a large sauté pan
- When oil is hot add the shallots and garlic, salt and pepper
- Sauté for 1 minute
- Add tomatoes and sauté for 1 minute
- Add the mussels and shrimp; season with salt and pepper, sauté 2 minutes
- Add wine, bring to a simmer and cover, cook until the clamshells open, 4-6 minutes (discard any shells that do not open)
- Add crab and green onion
- Season with salt and pepper; sauté for 1 minute
- Add pasta, toss and continue cooking until the pasta is heated through
- Toss the pasta with the seafood, cheese and basil
- Spoon into serving dishes
- Garnish with a drizzle of truffle oil

Yield: 4-6

LAMB
WITH PINE NUTS, SPINACH AND SUN-DRIED TOMATOES
1999

This lamb recipe comes from the Astor Restaurant & Bar on Rundle Street in Adelaide, South Australia. Fourteen years later I visited Australia and quickly learned that lamb is the country food.

½	cup chopped spinach leaves
½	cup pine nuts
½	cup chopped drained oil-packed sun-dried tomatoes
2	pounds boneless lamb loin roast
1½	tablespoons olive oil
½	cup finely chopped shallots
1½	cups beef stock
1½	cups chicken stock
1	fresh rosemary sprig
1	teaspoon balsamic vinegar

- Quickly sauté spinach in skillet just until wilted, pat dry
- In a small bowl, combine spinach, pine nuts and sun-dried tomatoes
- Butterfly lamb by cutting horizontally almost in half
- Open lamb roast as a book
- Sprinkle with salt and freshly ground pepper
- Spoon half spinach mixture down center, fold long side over filling to enclose
- Secure with toothpicks (lamb can be prepared 8 hours ahead/cover and refrigerate)
- Heat 1½ tablespoons olive oil in heavy skillet
- Sprinkle lamb with salt and pepper, place in pan and cook to desired doneness turning frequently (about 15 minutes) for medium rare
- Transfer to plate and tent with foil
- Add shallots to skillet, stir 1 minute
- Add beef and chicken stock, rosemary and vinegar
- Boil until reduced to ¾ cup (15 minutes)
- Strain sauce
- Cut lamb in half crosswise, then cut each piece in half crosswise on diagonal
- Spoon sauce onto plates
- Place lamb pieces atop sauce in center of each plate, overlapping lamb slightly

Serves: 4

PORK CHOPS
WITH TOMATO, SHITAKE MUSHROOMS AND MARSALA
1999

Four 5- to 6-ounce boneless center-cut pork loin chops
    Flour
2 eggs, beaten
4 cups dry seasoned breadcrumbs
3 tablespoons olive oil
4 tablespoons butter
2 tablespoons minced garlic
8 ounces shitake mushrooms, stems removed, caps sliced
¾ cup marsala wine
¾ cup chicken broth
1 large tomato, seeded, chopped
¼ cup chopped fresh basil

- Place chops between sheets of waxed paper and pound to ½ inch
- Sprinkle pork chops with salt and pepper
- Dip into flour, then beaten eggs, then into breadcrumbs, coating completely
- Heat oil over medium-high heat
- Add chops; sauté until just cooked through, about 4 minutes per side
- Transfer chops to serving platter, tent with foil
- Pour off oil and wipe out skillet
- In same skillet, melt butter and add garlic; sauté for 1 minute
- Add mushrooms, cook 2 minutes
- Add marsala, broth and tomato
- Boil until thick, about 6 minutes
- Stir in basil and season
- Serve chops with sauce

Serves: 4

OVEN-ROASTED LEG OF LAMB

2002

1 (6-9) pound leg of lamb, marinated for 24 hours

MARINADE:

- 4 cloves garlic cut into slivers
- ½ cup olive oil
- ½ cup lemon juice
- 1 tablespoon fresh oregano leaves
- 1 teaspoon salt
- 2 teaspoons fresh rosemary, chopped fine
- Fresh black pepper

GRAVY:

- 2 tablespoons olive oil
- 3 shallots, finely chopped
- 1 cup red wine
- ½ cup chicken stock
- 2 tablespoons flour mixed with 2 tablespoons unsalted butter

- With sharp knife cut many slits in the skin of the lamb
- Insert the garlic into the slits
- In bowl combine the oil, lemon juice, oregano, salt, rosemary and pepper
- Brush the lamb with this mixture
- Place the lamb in a roasting pan
- Cover and refrigerate for 24 hours
- Uncover the lamb and bring to room temperature
- Preheat oven to 325°
- Roast lamb for 1 hour
- Drain off the fat and pour about ½ cup hot water into the pan
- Continue roasting allowing 20 minutes per pound or 140-170° internal temperatures: 140°=rare, 160°=medium, 170°=well done
- Remove lamb from oven, lightly cover for 20 minutes
- Skim the fat from the juices and strain
- To prepare the gravy, heat oil in skillet, add sauté shallots, add wine and reduce by half
- Add the strained pan juices and chicken stock and simmer
- Whisk in the half of the butter and flour mixture
- Simmer until thickened, taste and adjust seasonings
- Serve this gravy over the lamb

Serves: 8-10

Serve with Asparagus Salad with Lemon Herb Dressing.
Wine Pairing: Pinot Noir: Ropiteau Bourgogne 2009 or Luc Pirlet 2010

RACK OF LAMB
2002

- 2 racks of lamb "Frenched"
- 2 tablespoons minced fresh rosemary leaves
- 3 cloves of garlic, minced
- ½ cup Dijon mustard
- 1 tablespoon balsamic vinegar
- 2 teaspoons salt

- In food processor process the salt, rosemary and garlic until very minced
- Add the vinegar and the mustard and process another minute or so
- Coat the lamb racks and let stand on kitchen counter for 1 hour
- Preheat oven to 450° or prepare a hot grill
- Roast for 20 minutes for rare, 25 minutes for medium-rare
- Remove and cover with foil
- Let the lamb sit for 15 minutes
- Cut into ribs and serve

A RECOMMENDED SIDE DISH:
   Roasted potatoes and vegetables
   Grilled or roasted asparagus dusted with Parmesan cheese

Wine pairing: Pinot Noir

MICROWAVE SPAGHETTI SQUASH

- 1 spaghetti squash
- ½ cup Parmesan cheese
- Salt and pepper to taste
- 3 tablespoons butter

- Wash squash and dry
- Pierce deeply in several places
- Place in microwave on high
- Cook 4-5 minutes
- Rotate and cook another 4-5 minutes until outside is soft
- Let cool
- Cut in half, remove seeds
- Scoop out the squash, add butter, salt, pepper and cheese

RASPBERRY-TOPPED
CHOCOLATE TARTS
WITH PECAN CRUST
1999

The first time I made this wonderful dessert was for Steve's boss in Northern Chicago and I made these tarts often in Costa Rica for guests. Sometimes I fill the baked crusts with ice cream, stuff with lots of ice cream and top with meringue. I bake these mini Baked Alaskas and serve for birthday cakes for my family.

- 2 cups pecans, toasted
- 6 tablespoons (packed) light brown sugar
- ¼ teaspoon cinnamon
- ¼ cup (1/2 stick) unsalted butter, melted
- ¾ cup whipping cream
- 6 ounces bittersweet or semisweet (not unsweetened) chocolate
  - * Use a good product such as Lindt
- 2½ pints fresh raspberries
- ¼ cup seedless raspberry jam
- 4-inch tart pans

- Preheat oven to 325°
- Finely grind pecans, sugar and cinnamon in a food processor
- Add butter and process until moist clumps form (this is your crust for your tart pans)
- Press onto bottom and up sides of four 4-inch diameter tart pans with removable bottoms
- Bake crusts until golden brown and firm to the touch about 30 minutes
- Transfer to rack and cool completely
- Bring cream to simmer in saucepan
- Remove from heat
- Add chocolate; stir until melted and smooth
- Pour mixture into crusts, dividing equally
- Chill until set about 1 hour
- Can be made 1 day ahead, cover each tart and chill
- Arrange raspberries over tops of tarts
- Stir jam in saucepan over low heat until melted or use microwave
- Brush melted jam over raspberries

Serves: 4

WARM CHOCOLATE PUDDING CAKES
1999

1½ ounces high grade unsweetened chocolate, finely chopped
½ ounce high-grade semi-sweet chocolate finely chopped
1 teaspoon unsalted butter softened (to butter the ramekins)
3 tablespoons unsalted butter softened
3 tablespoons sugar
1 large egg
3 tablespoons flour
¼ teaspoon baking powder
¼ teaspoon ancho powder (optional)
½ tablespoon unsweetened cocoa powder

TOPPING

Whipped cream for garnish
Cocoa powder for garnish

- Lightly butter 2 ramekins with 1 teaspoon butter set aside
- In top of double boiler or microwave place semi-sweet and unsweetened chocolate until melted
- Remove from heat and stir in 3 tablespoons butter and sugar until smooth,
- Add eggs, flour, baking powder and cocoa
- With electric mixer, beat at med-high speed until pale and very thick about 5 minutes
- Place mix in ramekins; filling about half-full
- Cover with plastic wrap and freeze for at least 3 hours
- When ready to serve, preheat oven to 375°
- Place ramekins on the middle shelf in the oven and bake until edges are set but centers are still shiny, about 10-11 minutes
- Invert pudding cakes onto plates and serve immediately
- Garnish with whipped cream and dust with cocoa powder

Serves: 2

Desserts can be served directly from ramekins. This recipe can be doubled or tripled to suit your needs.

CHOCOLATE SOUFFLES
2000

These little soufflés can be prepared ahead.

10 ounces bittersweet or semisweet chocolate chopped; use the best quality chocolate you can purchase, do not use unsweetened chocolate
10 tablespoons unsalted butter (1¼ sticks)
1 cup sugar
4 large eggs
4 large egg yolks
Pinch of salt
½ cup flour

- Butter and flour TEN ¾-cup ramekins
- Melt chocolate and butter in medium bowl set over simmering water or in microwave
- Cool chocolate to lukewarm
- Using an electric mixer on high speed, beat sugar, eggs, yolks and salt in large bowl until batter falls in heavy ribbons when beaters are lifted (about 6 minutes)
- Sift flour over mixture and fold in
- Gradually fold in lukewarm chocolate mixture
- Divide mixture among ramekins
- At this point the soufflés can be prepared ahead
- Cover soufflés individually with plastic and refrigerate up to 1 day or freeze up to 1 week
- Preheat oven to 400°
- Place ramekins on baking sheet
- Bake until puffed and beginning to crack on top (centers will still be soft)
- Bake about 18 minutes (19 minutes if frozen)

Serves: 10

BANANA BREAD
WITH CHOCOLATE CHIPS AND WALNUTS
2000

- 1½ cups flour
- 1 teaspoon baking soda
- 1 teaspoon baking powder
- ¼ teaspoon salt
- ¾ cup semisweet chocolate chips
- ¾ cup walnuts, toasted, chopped
- ½ cup (1 stick) unsalted butter, room temperature
- 1 cup sugar
- 2 large eggs
- 1 cup mashed ripe bananas
- 2 tablespoons fresh lemon juice
- 1½ teaspoons vanilla extract

- Preheat oven 350°
- Grease and flour a 9x5x2-inch metal loaf pan
- Whisk first 4 ingredients in medium bowl to blend
- Combine chocolate chips and walnuts in small bowl, add 1 tablespoon flour mixture and toss to coat
- Beat butter in large bowl until fluffy
- Gradually add sugar, beating until well blended
- Beat in eggs one at a time
- Beat in mashed bananas, lemon juice and vanilla extract
- Beat in flour mixture
- Spoon ⅓ of batter into prepared pan
- Sprinkle with half of nut mixture
- Spoon ⅓ of batter over
- Sprinkle with remaining nut mixture
- Cover with remaining batter over the nut mixture
- Run knife through batter in zigzag pattern
- Bake bread until tester inserted into center comes out clean, about 1 hour and 5 minutes
- Turn out onto rack and cool

Yield: one 9-inch loaf

MILK CHOCOLATE CHEESECAKE
2001

This recipe is adapted from Emeril. I have changed the crust.

CRUST:

- 4 cups thin chocolate wafers crumbs
- ¼-½ cup melted unsalted butter or as needed

FILLING:

- 3 pounds softened cream cheese
- 2 cups sugar
- 6 eggs
- 1 cup heavy cream
- ½ cup flour
- ½ teaspoon salt
- 1 teaspoon vanilla
- 1 cup melted milk chocolate

SAUCE:

- 2 cups fresh raspberries
- Juice of one lemon
- ¼ cup Grand Marnier

- Preheat oven to 350°
- Combine crumbs and butter. Mix and press into a 12-inch spring form pan. Press high up sides to accommodate the huge amount of batter.
- In food processor, with the metal blade, mix the cream cheese until smooth
- Add sugar, and then add the eggs one at a time to thoroughly incorporate into the cheese mixture.
- Add the heavy cream.
- Add the flour, salt and vanilla and blend until smooth.
- In a steady stream, pour in the melted chocolate.
- Pour into the prepared pan.
- Place a cookie sheet under the cake pan…butter tends to spill out
- Bake for 1 hour 15 minutes or until the cake is set.
- Remove from oven and with a knife loosen the sides from the pan. This will prevent the cake from splitting down the center.
- Completely cool the cake before cutting.

TOPPING: PRESENTATION

Top with fresh whipped cream in a pastry bag with star tip, fresh mint sprigs, chocolate curls, powdered sugar in shaker, cocoa powder in shaker.

Place a piece of the cake on a plate. Spoon the raspberries over the top. Garnish with whipped cream, chocolate curls, mint, powdered sugar and cocoa powder.

Yield: 12-14 servings with a full recipe.
6-8 servings with half recipe in a 9-inch spring form pan.

MIXED BERRIES
WITH ROMANOFF SAUCE
2005

½ cup sour cream
3-4 tablespoons brown sugar
2 tablespoons Grand Marnier or Brandy

½ cup heavy cream
3 tablespoons sugar
Fresh mixed berries

- Mix sour cream, brown sugar and liquor
- Whip the cream until it just begins to thicken
- Add sugar and whip until thick
- Fold the sour cream mixture into the cream mixture
- Serve over berries, top with shaved chocolate

Serves: 4

PIE PASTRY
FOOD PROCESSOR METHOD
2002

Makes enough for a two-crust 9-inch pie or one 10-inch quiche.

- 2 cups flour
- 1 teaspoon salt
- ¾ cup chilled shortening
- 4-8 tablespoons iced cold water

IN FOOD PROCESSOR:

- Add flour, salt, shortening
- Rapid pulse 15 times
- Add 4 tablespoons water and pulse 5 times
- Add 2 tablespoons water and pulse 3 times
- Dough should be just damp enough to mass together (can add more water one teaspoon at a time)
- Chill and roll out
- You can also use a pastry blender instead of the food processor

For quiche blind bake for 5-7 minutes with weights.
For pudding pies prick bottom before and after blind baking.

PIE PASTRY
RICH CRUST

- 1½ cups plus 2 tablespoons flour
- 1 tablespoon sugar
- ½ teaspoon salt
- 1 stick cold butter
- 2 tablespoons shortening
- 3 tablespoons ice water

- Put into processor and press 10 pulses
- Add 1 tablespoon water pulse 3 times
- Add 1 tablespoon water pulse 3 times
- Add 1 tablespoon water pulse 3 times
- Dough should mass together (can add more water if needed)
- Gather into a ball and chill for 30 minutes before rolling out

Makes a single crust. Double recipe for double crust or single deep dish crust.

PIE CRUST
FOOL PROOF DOUGH

2½ cups unbleached flour, plus extra for work surface
1 teaspoon salt
2 tablespoons sugar
12 tablespoons cold unsalted butter, cut into ¼-in pieces
½ cup cold vegetable shortening cut into 4 pieces
¼ cup cold vodka
¼ cup cold water

- Process 1½ cups flour, the salt and sugar in food processor, pulse about 1 second
- Add butter and shortening and process until dough just starts to collect in uneven clumps, about 15 seconds
- Scrape bowl with rubber spatula and redistribute dough evenly around blade
- Add remaining 1 cup flour and pulse until mixture is evenly distributed and mass of dough has been broken up (4-6 pulses)
- Empty mixture into a bowl
- Sprinkle vodka and water over mixture
- With rubber spatula, use folding motion to mix, pressing down on dough until dough is slightly tacky and sticks together
- Divide dough into 2 even balls, and flatten each into 4-6 inch disks
- Wrap each in plastic wrap and refrigerate at least 45 minutes or up to 2 days
- Remove from refrigerator, let rest 10 minutes, roll out

BEST PECAN PIE
BY MEL
2001

I never seem to be satisfied repeating the same recipe so I made this exceptional pie one Thanksgiving in lieu of my Not So Sweet Pecan Pie of the 1960's. It is truly delicious!

¾ cup chopped pecans
3 tablespoons bourbon
¼ cup melted butter
1 cup sugar
3 eggs

¾ cup maple syrup
1 teaspoon vanilla
¼ teaspoon salt
¾ cup chocolate chips
9 -inch prepared piecrust

- Preheat oven to 375°
- Soak pecans in the bourbon; set aside
- Beat melted butter, sugar and eggs until fluffy
- Blend in syrup, vanilla, and salt
- Stir in chocolate chips until evenly distributed
- Pour mixture into piecrust
- Sprinkle bourbon-soaked pecans over top of filling
- Bake for 45-55 minutes
- Check at 45 minutes, it may brown quickly

APPLE CRUMBLE PIE
WITH ALMONDS
2001

This pie is delicious. Serve it with ice cream or whipped cream.

STREUSEL TOPPING:

- 1 cup flour
- ½ cup sugar
- ¼ teaspoon salt
- 6 tablespoons unsalted butter, chilled

FILLING AND PASTRY

- Basic pie pastry for a 9-inch deep-dish pie shell
- ⅓ cup sugar
- 2 tablespoons flour
- ½ teaspoon cinnamon
- ¼ teaspoon nutmeg
- 7 large tart apples, peeled, cored and thinly sliced
- ½ cup golden raisins
- 1 tablespoon fresh lemon juice
- Slivered or sliced almonds

- Preheat oven to 450°
- To make the topping combine the flour, sugar and salt in a mixing bowl and stir together
- Cut the butter into tablespoon-sized pieces and add them to the flour mixture
- With your fingertips, two knives, a pastry blender, or a processor work the ingredients together until you have a mixture of fine, irregular crumbs, set aside
- Roll out the pastry and line a 9-inch pie pan
- Combine the sugar, flour, cinnamon and nutmeg
- Add the apples, raisins and lemon juice and toss
- Pile the fruit into the pastry-lined pan and spread the streusel mixture evenly over the top
- Bake for 20 minutes
- Reduce the oven to 350°
- Bake until the crust is browned and the apples are tender when pierced with a knife (35-40 minutes more)
- Sprinkle slivered or sliced almonds over pie for last 10 minutes

CHOCOLATE POTS de CRÈME
2000

This is a very tasty dessert that is so easy to make. I serve it with shaved Lindt intense orange chocolate and a few fresh raspberries.

- 9 ounces high grade semisweet chocolate, chopped
- 1½ cups whole milk
- 1½ cups heavy cream
- 6 large egg yolks
- 8 tablespoons sugar (add an extra tablespoon if using bittersweet chocolate)
- ¼ teaspoon salt
- 1 tablespoon confectioners' sugar

- Put chocolate into blender
- In a saucepan whisk together the milk, 1 cup of the cream, the egg yolks, the sugar and the salt
- Over medium heat, cook, stirring constantly with a spatula just until it is thick enough to coat the spatula and almost to a boil (5-6 minutes)
- Quickly pour the milk mixture over the chocolate in the blender
- Blend until combined and very smooth (scrape sides often)
- Pour chocolate mixture into ramekins
- Refrigerate for about 2 hours or until it is set
- Whip the remaining ½ cup of the heavy cream with the confectioners' sugar and beat until soft peaks form
- Top pots with whipped cream and shaved chocolate

Serves: 6-8 depending on the size of the ramekins

FRANGIPANE FRUIT TART
2000

Frangipane is a filling flavored with ground almonds used in pies, tarts and cakes. I use it on top of a baked Sucre crust and topped with fruit, baked and then topped with melted fruit preserves laced with brandy.

It is varied in substance. The more flour used and it becomes a firm tart crust. When eggs and milk are added, it becomes a creamy filling for dessert crepes.

- 6 tablespoons softened butter
- ½ cup sugar
- ¾ cup sliced almonds ground to a fine meal
- 2 teaspoons flour
- 1 teaspoon almond extract
- 1 egg and 1 egg white

- Grind the nuts in a food processor, add the sugar, butter, flour, eggs and extract
- Process until creamy
- Pipe onto a baked Sucre, top with sliced fruit, bake at 375° for 45-50 minutes
- Glaze with fruit preserves combined with a bit of water and liquor

EL SABOR DE COSTA RICA
THE TASTE OF COSTA RICA
2001-2004

I never in my wildest dreams thought I would move my wooden spoons overseas again.

In 2001 we moved to Santa Anna, Costa Rica. During the three years that we lived in this village, we had the privilege of housing a Costa Rican "Tico" girl named Magaly.

Magaly was our live-in housekeeper. Although she wanted very much to cook all of our meals, I could not forgo cooking. Our compromise was for her to prepare lunch and dinner three days a week. The remaining days, she helped me prep and we cooked together.

Translating her recipes was a challenge for me, but worth the effort. The signature dish of the country is Arroz con pollo (chicken and rice). I hope you will enjoy the Central American cuisine as much as we did back in 2001.

Other than typical "Tico" recipes I have also included some of the dishes I made for our staff cocktail parties and ladies brunches as well as recipes I served on a daily basis. Television in Costa Rica consisted of CNN and the Cooking Channel. Yes, I spent many hours watching the American Cooking Channel.

ARROZ CON POLLO
CHICKEN WITH RICE
2001

Magaly made this every week. I often would sit out on the open terrace overlooking the mountains enjoying this dish for my lunch.

- 1½ cups rice
- 1 boneless chicken breast
- 3 cups chicken stock
- 2 cloves garlic, minced
- Salt and pepper to taste
- Fresh oregano minced
- Fresh thyme minced
- 1 teaspoon paprika
- 1 red pepper minced
- Stalk of celery, minced
- Cilantro, minced
- 1 carrot, minced
- 1 chopped onion
- Corn
- Small can of peas

- Cook the rice in the chicken stock until done
- Season the chicken with salt and pepper
- Brown the chicken in vegetable oil, remove and set aside (can also braise in chicken broth)
- Sauté the onion and garlic; add paprika, salt, and pepper, cook until onion is transparent
- Add the minced cilantro; thyme, oregano, carrots, celery, and red pepper
- Cook 15 minutes more
- Shred the chicken
- Add the peas and the chicken
- Add all to rice
- Serve

Serves 6

BLACK BEAN SOUP
2001

Black beans signify what the Costa Ricans are all about. They love their beans and this soup is served throughout the country in homes and restaurants as one of the favorites.

BEAN PREPARATION:

- 5 cups water, plus extra as needed
- 2½ cups dried black beans, picked over and rinsed
- 4 ounces ham steak (optional, but adds a good flavor)
- 2 bay leaves
- ⅛ teaspoon baking soda
- 1 teaspoon salt

- Place water, beans, ham, bay leaves and soda in large pot with lid
- Bring to boil, stir in salt and reduce heat to low, cover and simmer until beans are tender 1¼ - 1½ hours
- Remove bay leaves and ham steak, set aside

SOUP PREPARATION:

- 3 tablespoons oil
- 1 large onion, finely chopped
- 1 large carrot, finely chopped
- 3 celery stalks, minced
- ½ teaspoon salt
- 5 cloves garlic minced
- Dash of red pepper flakes
- 2 teaspoons cumin
- 6 cups chicken stock
- 2 tablespoons cornstarch
- 2 tablespoons water
- 2 tablespoons lime juice

- Heat oil, add onions, carrot, and celery, salt. Cook until vegetables are soft (12-15 minutes).
- Reduce heat, add garlic, pepper flakes and cumin, cook about 3 minutes.
- Stir in beans with all the cooking liquid and the chicken stock, bring to boil.
- Reduce heat and simmer uncovered for 30 minutes.
- Ladle 1½ cups beans and 2 cups liquid into food processor, process until smooth, return to pot. If you like a more pureed soup; add more beans and liquid to the processor.
- Stir together cornstarch and water, gradually stir half of cornstarch mix into soup.
- Bring to boil stirring to fully thicken. If soup is too thin, stir in remaining cornstarch mixture.
- Take soup off the heat and stir in lime juice, serve immediately.

Will hold in refrigerator for 4 days. If too thick when reheating, add additional stock.

Serves: 6

GALLO PINTO
RICE AND BEANS
2001

Translated gallo pinto means rice and beans. It is the mainstay of the country. Costa Ricans eat this every day for breakfast with scrambled eggs and sausage. The black bean is the most popular bean in the country.

- 3 cups white rice cooked, add a bit of oil and salt
- 2 cups uncooked black beans soaked overnight, then add enough water to cover the beans; add 3 cloves garlic, pinch of salt, and 2 bay leaves, cook for 2-3 hours or until tender but still firm
- 1 medium red pepper diced
- 1 onion diced
- 2 tablespoons olive oil
- 3 bay leaves
- Salt, pepper, cumin, and salsa Lizano (hot sauce)
- Half a bunch of fresh cilantro, roughly chopped
- Pinch of red pepper flakes

- Cook beans
- Cook the rice
- Over medium heat combine oil, pepper and onion and cook until golden brown
- Add the cooked beans including all the water the beans cooked in
- Bring to a boil, lower to simmer
- Add all other spices (except the cilantro) and stir constantly until most of the water has evaporated
- While beans are still moist, add the white rice and blend all together
- Just before serving, mix in the chopped cilantro

Tip: It takes a long time to cook the beans. Magaly made extra beans and we froze half. Of course, you can use canned beans, but the taste is not the same.

HERB CRUSTED BEEF TENDERLOIN

2002

Steve and I entertained his staff at our beautiful house for many cocktail parties. This was one of my favorite buffet items. I sliced the beef tenderloin diagonally and served it on the buffet table with fresh rolls and assorted mustards and horseradish. This recipe is adapted from Emeril Lagasse. I have made alterations to the original recipe to suit our taste.

3 tablespoons vegetable oil	Thyme, finely chopped
One (4-pound) beef tenderloin trimmed	Salt and pepper for seasoning
½ cup spicy whole-grained mustard	Wine or beef stock for deglazing
4 cloves garlic, minced	Horseradish cream
Rosemary, finely chopped	

- Preheat oven to 425°
- Heat oil in large heavy duty skillet
- Season meat on all sides with salt and pepper
- Brown on all sides turning beef
- Transfer beef to a platter; rub the mustard and garlic all over the beef using a spatula
- Place meat in roasting pan and cook for about 20-25 minutes: internal temperature 125= medium rare, 120=rare
- Remove from oven and let beef rest tented in foil for 15 minutes
- Slice and serve
- Deglaze the skillet with wine or beef broth and make a pan sauce or serve with horseradish cream

Serves: 8-10 can also be served at room temperature

POTATO FRITTATA
1980

I made this dish whenever Magaly and I were dining alone during the many times Steve had dinner meetings. This can also serve as a side to accompany meats.

- 2 tablespoons vegetable or olive oil
- 2 pounds potatoes (about 6 med.) sliced
- 1 large onion, chopped
- 5 eggs
- 2-4 tablespoons grated Parmesan cheese
- 1 teaspoon salt
- ¼ teaspoon pepper

- Heat 1 tablespoon of oil in large **non-stick** skillet
- Add potatoes and onion and cook over medium-low heat
- Turn occasionally and cook until tender and browned
- Meanwhile, beat eggs, cheese, salt and pepper
- Add remaining oil to skillet and pour in egg mix over the potatoes
- Lower heat
- Cook gently pushing in sides of egg mixture as it sets with a spatula
- When mixture is set, raise heat to high and brown underside
- Invert frittata onto platter
- Slide frittata back into skillet and brown the underside
- Invert onto plate and serve

Serves: 4 as a side dish
Serves: 2 as an entree

ROASTED ASPARAGUS
2004

2 pounds fresh asparagus
   Extra-virgin olive oil
   Kosher salt, plus extra for sprinkling
   Freshly ground black pepper
   Lemon zest

- Preheat oven to 400°
- Break off the tough end of one asparagus spear, determine the length and cut the remainder to that length
- Place on a baking sheet
- Drizzle with oil, then toss to coat
- Spread the asparagus in a single layer and sprinkle liberally with salt and pepper
- Sprinkle with lemon zest
- Roast for 25 minutes or until tender but still crisp

CARAMELIZED ONIONS
2002

I serve these onions with roast beef sandwiches, steaks or include them with my brown rice pilaf.

4 tablespoons unsalted butter
1 pound yellow onions, peeled and very thinly sliced

- Melt butter in large sauté pan
- Add the onions and lower heat to medium-low
- Cook slowly, stirring occasionally, until golden brown and caramelized
- This takes 30-40 minutes

SWEET AND SOUR PORK
2002

Fresh pineapple is the signature fruit in Costa Rica. Every week I bought a fresh pineapple from the Super Mercado and Magaly would core and cut it for us. One day I decided to make her this pork dish and use her fresh pineapple. It was a real challenge explaining how I wanted the vegetables for this recipe prepared, but together we prepared this dish using fresh pork tenderloin. It turned out to be one of her favorite dishes. I adapted this recipe from my favorite chef, Emeril. Once I learned about Emeril's seasoning, I began making batches for my kitchen and use it as a general spice on many foods.

- ½ cup fresh pineapple juice
- ½ cup ketchup
- ½ cup light brown sugar
- ¼ cup water
- ¼ cup cider vinegar
- 4 teaspoons soy sauce
- 2 teaspoons red pepper flakes
- 1 teaspoon sesame oil
- 3 tablespoons vegetable oil
- 2 tablespoons minced fresh ginger
- 2 teaspoons minced garlic
- 1 tablespoon cornstarch
- 2 tablespoons sherry
- 2 tablespoons vegetable oil
- 1 pound lean pork, cubed
- 2 teaspoons Emeril Lagasse Essence, spice (found in spice isle)
- 1 green pepper, cut into strips
- ½ medium onion, thinly sliced
- 2½ cups fresh cubed pineapple
- Steamed basmati rice or steamed brown rice
- Toasted slivered almonds

- Toast the almonds in oven.
- Combine the juice, ketchup, brown sugar, vinegar, water, soy sauce, pepper flakes and sesame oil.
- Heat 1 tablespoon oil and add the ginger and garlic, cook for 15 seconds.
- Add the pineapple juice mixture and bring to a boil.
- Reduce heat and simmer for about 3 minutes.
- In small bowl dissolve the cornstarch in the sherry. Add to the simmering sauce and whisk. Simmer for about 3 minutes to thicken. Remove from heat.
- Season the pork with the *Essence* spice. Heat 1 tablespoon oil in heavy skillet and add the pork. Brown on all sides, set aside onto a warm platter.
- In same skillet on high heat add 1 tablespoon oil. Add the pepper and onions and cook 2 minutes.
- Reduce heat and add the sauce, bring to a boil, add the pineapple and the pork.
- Slowly cook until the pork is warm, adjust seasonings and serve over rice.
- Sprinkle with slivered almonds.

Serves: 4

BAKED STUFFED LOBSTERS
2002

Lobster and "Corvina" (sea bass) are two of the most popular seafood items in Costa Rica. The Costa Rican lobster does not have claws and has a milder flavor than our Maine American lobster. The stuffing used in this recipe can also be used to stuff shrimp. I adapted this recipe from Emeril Lagasse.

- 4 lobster (1½ pounds each) or 4 lobster tails boiled and meat removed
- 2 cups crushed Ritz crackers or butter crackers
- 1 tablespoon unsalted butter for sautéing vegetables
- 1 stick unsalted butter, melted
- ¼ cup finely chopped celery
- ¼ cup finely chopped green pepper
- 1 teaspoon minced garlic
- 1 tablespoon minced parsley
- 1 tablespoon fresh lemon juice
- ¼ teaspoon Worcestershire sauce
- ½ teaspoon paprika
- 1 teaspoon Emeril's *Essence* spice
- ½ teaspoon salt, freshly ground pepper

- Preheat oven to 375°.
- Fill large stockpot with salted water and bring to boil.
- Plunge lobsters into water head first and cook 6-7 minutes.
- Drain and put into a bowl filled with iced water, cool.
- Place lobsters on their backs and cut each down the middle from the head to the tail using heavy scissors. Press the lobster open so it will lie flat.
- Lift out the roe and green tomalley.
- Discard stomach sac from back of the head and the spongy gray tissue.
- Remove the meat from the tail and leave the claws intact.
- Coarsely chop the meat and set aside, place the shells on a baking sheet.
- In skillet, melt the 1 tablespoon butter and add the shallots, celery, green pepper and cook for 2-4 minutes.
- Add the garlic and cook a minute, add the chopped lobster meat and cook another couple of minutes, remove from the heat.
- In bowl, combine the lobster meat, (roe and tomalley if desired), sautéed vegetables, cracker crumbs, parsley, lemon juice, *Essence* and salt.
- Stir and add enough melted butter to make a paste-like consistency.
- Fill the cavity of each lobster and bake for about 15 minutes.
- Turn broiler on and broil until golden brown 2-3 more minutes.
- Garnish with lemon wedges.

Serves: 4

PELICANO CORVINA
PLAYA HERRADURA
2001

One of our favorite restaurants near Jaco is a tiny open-air restaurant called El Pelicano. The restaurant is approximately 25 yards from the Pacific's waters. Their signature dish is Corvina, sea bass, cooked in foil.

4	Corvina (bass) fillets
	Red pepper cut into very thin strips
	Cheddar cheese
	White wine
	Butter
	Seeded and peeled fresh tomato cut into tiny bits
	Celery finely minced
1	teaspoon finely minced garlic or to taste

- Preheat oven to 350°
- Rinse fish fillets and pat dry
- Cut four pieces of aluminum foil; brush with oil or spray with PAM
- Place one fillet on each piece of foil
- Sprinkle with red pepper, tomato, celery and garlic
- Top with cheese, butter bits and wine
- Seal up each package tightly
- Bake for about 20 minutes

FISH FILLETS A LA LUIS
Pescado de Luis
2003

Family and friends visited us frequently during our stay in Costa Rica. Our chauffeur, Arturo, was always happy when we had visitors because he loved to plan day trips to tour the country. It was his opportunity to show off his native country and learn English at the same time.

Since we always returned home late and weary, Magaly had dinner prepared for us. She became proficient at setting an attractive table with flowers and welcomed us home with tantalizing cooking aromas.

This recipe came out of a cookbook I bought for her. The book was written in two languages, Spanish and English, so we regularly shared the book when we cooked together.

1 pound fish fillets
1 medium onion cut into cubes
1 red pepper cut into thin strips
2 cloves of garlic minced
3 tablespoons pitted olives, sliced
1 large ripe tomato, peeled, seeded and chopped
1 tablespoon ketchup
1 cup dry white wine
Olive oil

- Season the fish with salt and pepper
- In skillet heat oil and sauté the fish fillets until only lightly browned and not completely cooked
- Heat 2 tablespoons of olive oil and add the onion, peppers and garlic, sauté until soft
- Add the tomato and sauté one more minute
- Add the wine, ½ cup water and the tomato ketchup
- Let the sauce boil
- Check seasoning
- Add the sauce to the fish, cover, and cook covered until fish is completely cooked
- Serve with white rice or brown rice or a pilaf

Serves: 4

ASPARAGUS SALAD
WITH LEMON HERB DRESSING
2002

- 1 pound asparagus, stems snapped and asparagus peeled near snapped end
- Juice and zest of one lemon, 3 tablespoons juice
- ½ cup olive oil
- 1 teaspoon each chopped mint, dill and parsley
- 2 teaspoons Dijon mustard
- 2 teaspoons honey
- 1 clove garlic minced or grated
- 1 tablespoon chopped chives
- Salt and pepper
- Salad greens

- Boil one large pot of salted water
- Cook spears until tender but not mushy (3-5 minutes)
- Drain and shock spears in ice water to cool quickly
- Drain and pat dry
- To make ahead, blanch the asparagus and refrigerate in a large baggie for 24 hours (be sure the asparagus is well dried)
- In a small bowl whisk together remaining ingredients until emulsified
- The vinaigrette can be refrigerated for up to 3 days
- Line the salad plates with torn lettuce greens, top with asparagus, add a slice of fresh tomato for color and a tiny slice of Brie cheese
- Right before serving drizzle with lemon dressing
- Sprinkle chives over salad

Serves: 4-6

LIME GOAT CHEESE
CHEESECAKE

2003

Lemons in Costa Rica are green. I used the green lemons as limes and found this tasty dessert that worked well with the country's green lemon.

CRUST:

- 2 tablespoons pistachios (finely chopped)
- ½ cup graham cracker crumbs
- 3 tablespoons melted butter
- Press into muffin cups

CHEESECAKE:

- 11 ounces cream cheese
- 4 ounces goat cheese
- ⅓ cup honey
- 2 eggs
- ½ teaspoon grated lime zest
- 1 tablespoon lime juice

GARNISH:

Fresh raspberries

- Preheat oven to 300°
- Make crust and press into 4-ounce ramekins
- For cheesecake combine all ingredients and pour into ramekins
- Place ramekins in pan of hot water (water should be about half way up the ramekins)
- Bake at 300° for 20-25 minutes or until slightly firm in the center
- Let stand in the hot water bath for 10 more minutes
- Put individual ramekins on a rack and cool completely
- Run knife around cups to remove cake
- Invert onto individual dessert plates
- Serve with fresh raspberries and a sprig of fresh mint

FLAN
VANILLA CUSTARD WITH CARAMEL SAUCE
2001

Every restaurant, café or roadside eatery throughout the country has flan as a dessert option. It is a Spanish classic.

2 cups whipping cream	3 large eggs
¾ cup whole milk	2 large egg yolks
Vanilla bean split	6-8 ramekins or baking dish
1 cup sugar	

For the caramelized sugar coating use ½ cup sugar

- Preheat oven to 325°. Position rack in center of oven.
- Heat 4-5 cups of water to use in the water bath.
- Place square, round, or rectangular standard baking dish, into a larger baking dish to accommodate the water bath.
- Spread the ½ cup sugar evening in the bottom of a heavy saucepan.
- Place on medium heat and keep the sugar moving with the back of a wooden spoon. It takes several minutes (about 10 minutes) for the sugar to melt.
- WITHOUT STIRRING watch the sugar carefully until it turns a brown caramel color.
- When brown in color remove immediately from heat and quickly pour liquid into the baking dish, set aside.
- Whisk the eggs and egg yolks and the 1 cup of sugar until foamy.
- In a saucepan combine the milk, whipping cream and vanilla.
- Scald the milk and cream, remove the vanilla bean and scrap out the seeds into the milk mixture, let cool.
- Pour the cooled milk over the egg mixture and whisk until well blended.
- Pour the mixture through a fine sieve into the baking dish.
- Carefully pour enough hot water into the larger baking pan to come halfway up the sides of the smaller baking dish.
- Bake uncovered for about 50 minutes. At 45 minutes, test for doneness with a knife. If it comes out clean, the flan is done.
- Carefully remove from the oven and place on cooling rack, cool completely.
- Refrigerate at least 2 hours.
- To serve, place a plate over the baking dish and turn upside down.
- Tap top of the dish and the flan should fall onto the plate with the syrup running over the flan.

PARADISE IN FLORIDA
2004 to present

Retiring with my wooden spoons was an exciting adventure. In 2004 we moved to Sarasota, Florida.

Retiring among a diverse set of friends from many countries and cultures I have learned much about international and cultural cooking. With the onset of the Internet and TV's famous chefs I find I am still learning about the taste of fine food and my love to experiment with different recipes.

BAKED OLIVES
2000

2 cups assorted olives
Orange zest cut into thin strips
Sprig of rosemary minced

¼ cup olive oil
¼ teaspoon chili flakes

- Toss all together
- Bake at 400° for 10 minutes

OLIVE NUT SPREAD
2001

My friend, Ann Milam, shared this recipe with me. She often serves this wonderful spread with cocktails while we sit and enjoy a beautiful Lake Gaston view.

8 ounces cream cheese
½ cup mayonnaise
½ cup chopped pecans

1 cup chopped green olives with pimento
1 or 2 tablespoons olive juice
Dash of pepper

- Soften the cream cheese
- Add mayonnaise
- Blend well
- Stir in pecans and olives
- Add olive juice and pepper
- Stir well
- Refrigerate
- Serve on crackers

LOUIS DRESSING

Great with Crab Louis Salad or sandwich spread.

- ¾ cup chili sauce
- ½ cup mayonnaise
- 1 teaspoon instant minced onion or diced shallots
- ½ teaspoon sugar
- ¼ teaspoon Worcestershire sauce
- Salt to taste

    - Mix all ingredients.
    - Chill for 30 minutes

Yield: 1 cup dressing

SHRIMP, OLIVE,
AND TOMATO SALAD
2005

This makes a colorful display to serve with drinks before dinner. I serve this salad on a large platter with three separate bowls: marinated artichokes, assorted baked olives, and this shrimp, olive and tomato salad. A tiny cup filled with bread sticks completes the arrangement.

- 16 cooked peeled large shrimp with tails left intact
- 16 pitted Kalamata olives
- 1 cup diced seeded tomatoes (about 3)
- 2 tablespoons chopped fresh Italian parsley
- 2 tablespoons extra virgin olive oil
- 1 tablespoon finely grated lemon peel firmly packed
- 1 tablespoon fresh lemon juice

    - Combine all ingredients in medium bowl and toss to blend. Season to taste with salt and pepper
    - Can be made up to 4 hours ahead, cover and refrigerate

Serves: 4-6

ASPARAGUS
WRAPPED IN CRISP PROSCIUTTO
2012

Makes a delicious appetizer or served as a vegetable.

Olive oil
Fresh asparagus spears, washed and trimmed and dried
Prosciutto
Parmesan cheese

- Preheat oven to 450°
- Line a baking sheet with aluminum foil, and coat with olive oil
- Wrap one slice of prosciutto around each asparagus spear, starting at the bottom and spiraling up to the tip
- Place the wrapped spears on the baking sheet
- Bake for 5 minutes; remove baking sheet and shake the pan back and forth to roll the spears over
- Return to the oven for another 5-10 minutes or until the asparagus is tender and the prosciutto is crisp
- Sprinkle with cheese
- Serve immediately

I serve 3 spears per appetizer before serving dinner. Goes well with a spaghetti dinner.

FRENCH LENTIL SOUP
2011

3 tablespoons olive oil	4 cups vegetable stock
2 cups chopped onions	1 cup chopped carrots
1 cup chopped celery	1½ cups lentils, rinsed and drained
2 garlic cloves, minced	1 (14-ounce) can of diced tomatoes

- Heat oil and add onions, celery, carrots and garlic, sauté for about 12 minutes
- Add 4 cups stock, the lentils and the tomatoes with the juice from the tomatoes and bring to a boil
- Reduce the heat, cover and simmer until the lentils are tender (35 minutes)
- Transfer about 2 cups of the soup to the food processor and puree until smooth
- Return the puree to the soup pot, thin the soup with more stock if needed
- Season with salt and pepper

Serves: 6

CARAMELIZED ONION AND ROQUEFORT TART

2007

- 2 tablespoons unsalted butter
- 3 cups thinly sliced yellow onions (2 large onions)
- ¼ cup dry white wine (vermouth)
- 1 tablespoon chopped fresh thyme
- ½ teaspoon salt
- ¼ teaspoon ground black pepper
- ⅓ cup toasted chopped walnuts
- 4 ounces chopped prosciutto
- 2 sheets prepared puff pastry, thawed
- 1 large egg, beaten
- 4 ounces blue cheese crumbled
- 3 cups assorted baby greens, tossed with extra virgin olive oil

- Preheat oven to 400°
- Grease a large baking sheet or line with parchment and set aside
- In large skillet, melt butter
- Add the onions and sauté until caramelized, 12-15 minutes stirring occasionally
- Add the wine and cook until dry 2 more minutes
- Add the thyme, salt and pepper, stir well and remove from the heat
- Add the walnuts and prosciutto and stir well
- Let cool
- On a floured surface, roll out each of the pastry sheets to about 12 x 12 inches
- Cut each into an 11-inch round
- Place one round on the prepared baking sheet
- Brush a ½ inch border of egg wash around the outside of the round
- Spread the onion mixture evenly across the round
- Top with the blue cheese
- Top with the remaining pastry round
- Press down on the edges of the pastry to close
- Crimp edges with a fork to seal
- Paint the top pastry with egg wash and cut small slits in the center to vent
- Bake until golden and puffed, 20-25 minutes
- Remove from the oven and cut into 4-8 wedges
- Place wedges on lettuce and serve

Yields: 4–8 appetizers

CROSTINI
2008

    Ciabatta, cut diagonally into ½ inch slices
1 large clove garlic, peeled and cut in half
    Extra virgin olive oil

- Grill slices of bread. While still hot, rub gently with garlic and drizzle with oil. Finish with your favorite toppings

TOPPINGS:

Squashed cannelloni beans with garlic   *Adapted from Jamie Oliver*

- Mince a sprig of rosemary very fine. Using a mortar and pestle pound with salt and then add a couple of swirls of olive oil to make an infused olive oil.
- Sauté 2 sliced cloves of garlic in a little olive oil until lightly golden.
- Add 1¾ cups of drained and rinsed cannelloni beans and continue to simmer gently for 7 minutes.
- Season with salt and pepper. Add a red wine vinegar to taste about ¼ cup.
- Mash them using the back of a fork until you have a coarse puree.
- Spread onto your hot crostini and spoon the rosemary oil over the top.

Tomatoes and olives   *Adapted from Jamie Oliver*

- 20 ripe cherry tomatoes of various colors cut into little pieces.
- Remove pits and chop ½ cup Italian black or green olives.
- Toss in a bowl with the tomatoes along with 2-3 tablespoons of extra virgin olive oil and a swig of balsamic vinegar.
- Season carefully with salt and pepper and a dash of red cayenne pepper.
- Some olives are salty so go easy on the salt.
- Spoon over each crostini and sprinkle with Chiffonade basil leaves.

Tomato and Basil

- Chop 3 small plum tomatoes that have been halved and seeded.
- Chiffonade (roll up and slice thinly) basil leaves.
- Combine tomatoes with basil, add a drizzle of extra-virgin olive oil and salt to taste.
- Toss.

Mushroom artichoke heart:

- Sauté in olive oil, fresh mushrooms sliced, clove garlic minced, fresh rosemary minced and chopped artichoke hearts.
- Place on crostini and top with chopped seeded tomatoes and feta cheese.
- Broil.

PROSCIUTTO WRAPPED SCALLOPS
2006

One of my favorite celebrity chefs is Giada De Laurentiis. I find most of her recipes lite and fresh. I adapted this recipe from one her TV shows.

- ¼ cup chopped sun-dried tomatoes
- 2 tablespoons chopped fresh basil leaves
- 2 tablespoons chopped pitted black olives (about 10)
- ¼ cup extra-virgin olive oil
- 12 medium scallops
- ¼ teaspoon salt
- Freshly ground black pepper to taste
- 12 thin slices prosciutto
- 2 cups mixed lettuce leaves, arugula, baby kale, mixed baby greens
- 1½ tablespoons balsamic vinegar
- 1 tablespoon extra-virgin olive oil

- Preheat oven to 350°
- In a food processor, add the tomatoes, basil, olives and olive oil process until finely chopped
- Season both sides of the scallops with salt and pepper
- Rub each scallop with tomato mixture
- Fold each slice of prosciutto in half lengthwise, then wrap each scallop in 1 slice of prosciutto
- Place wrapped scallops in a buttered baking dish seam side down
- Bake until scallops are cooked through, about 15 minutes
- In a medium bowl, toss the mixed greens with the vinegar and olive oil
- Season the arugula with salt and pepper
- Place the greens on individual dishes
- Top with the scallops and serve immediately

Serves 4

SPINACH-CHEESE SWIRLS
2012

1 sheet of puff pastry
1 egg
1 tablespoon water
½ cup shredded Muenster or Jack cheese
¼ grated Parmesan cheese
1 green onion, chopped
⅛ teaspoon garlic powder
1 (10-ounce) package frozen chopped spinach, thawed and squeezed dry

- Thaw pastry sheet at room temperature (about 40 minutes)
- Preheat oven to 400°
- Lightly grease 2 baking sheets or line with parchment paper
- Stir egg and water together in small bowl
- In a medium bowl stir together the cheese, Parmesan cheese, onion, and garlic powder
- Unfold pastry sheet onto floured board
- Brush with egg mixture
- Top with cheese mixture and spinach
- Starting at short side closed to you; roll up like a jelly roll
- Cut into 20 (1/2-inch) slices
- Places slices cut-side down on baking sheets
- Brush with egg mixture
- Bake 15 minutes or until golden brown
- Serve warm or at room temperature

VARIATIONS:

SAVORY:

4 ounces cream cheese,
3 tablespoons pesto
¼ cup finely chopped walnuts

SWEET:

Cinnamon, nuts and sugar

- Brush with melted butter before baking

CREAM CHEESE, PESTO AND SUNDRIED TOMATOES
IN PUFF PASTRY
2012

My very dear English friend, Jan Wallace, shared this special appetizer with me. It is worth sharing with you.

- 1 Pillsbury original croissant package
- Cream cheese softened
- Pesto
- Sundried tomatoes (julienned strips in oil)
- Egg yolk beaten with 1 tablespoon water for brushing pastry
- Poppy seed

- Preheat oven to 350°
- Roll out the dough
- Squeeze together the dotted lines on the pastry and spread with cream cheese thickly over one half
- Top with pesto and sundried tomatoes
- Fold pastry over and squeeze ends together
- Brush with egg yolk
- Sprinkle poppy seeds on top
- Bake for 20 minutes or until it is well browned
- Cut into tiny squares

ARIZONA GRANOLA
COMPLIMENTS OF THE ENCHANTMENT RESORT SEDONA, ARIZONA
2014

- 20 ounces oats
- 12 ounces sliced almonds
- 1¼ cups honey
- ½ cup vegetable oil
- 1 tablespoon cinnamon
- 6 ounces sunflower seeds
- 6 ounces pumpkin seeds
- ¼ cup brown sugar
- ½ teaspoon vanilla extract
- 4 ounces hazelnuts
- 4½ ounces sesame seeds
- ½ teaspoon almond extract
- ½ teaspoon orange extract

- Preheat oven to 300°
- Mix all dry ingredients in large bowl
- Bring all the liquid ingredients to a boil
- Mix liquid with dry ingredients and mix for 2-3 minutes with large wooden spoon until well combined
- Spread on sheet pan and bake until brown

OATMEAL AND WHEAT
BLUEBERRY PANCAKES
2012

I am always looking for a new pancake to add to my breakfast recipe collection. It has lots of good protein from the oats and a bit of sweetness from the berries as well as the brown sugar.

½ cup whole-wheat flour
½ cup all-purpose flour
2 tablespoons brown sugar
2 tablespoons baking powder
¾ teaspoon salt

1½ cups quick cooking oats
2 cups milk
3 eggs beaten
¼ cup olive oil
½ cup blueberries

- Preheat a lightly oiled griddle over medium heat.
- In large bowl, mix all the dry ingredients except the oats.
- In small bowl, mix oats and milk. Whisk in the eggs and olive oil.
- Pour into the flour mixture all at once.
- Continue mixing until smooth.
- Gently fold in blueberries, pour batter ¼ cup at time onto griddle.

HEARTY PANCAKES
2007

A pancake low in saturated fat, high in iron, calcium and fiber.

1 cup whole-wheat flour
¼ cup all-purpose flour
2 tablespoons sugar
1 teaspoon baking soda
1 teaspoon baking powder
½ teaspoon salt

1½ cups low fat milk or vanilla soymilk
¼ cup canola oil
1 egg
½ cup golden raisins
½ cup coarsely chopped walnuts
¼ cup low calorie maple syrup

- Combine flours, baking soda, baking powder, salt, and sugar, whisk to blend.
- Combine milk, egg and oil in another bowl.
- Add milk mixture to flour mixture, stirring until well combined.
- Let batter stand for 5 minutes.
- Heat griddle and coat with cooking spray.

Yield: 6 servings (2 pancakes and 2 teaspoons syrup per person)

BREAKFAST FRITTATA

2001

- 1 tablespoon unsalted butter
- 1 tablespoon olive oil
- PAM spray
- 2 medium potatoes peeled and sliced thinly or use grocery refrigerated sliced potatoes
- ½ cup onion sliced
- Salt and fresh pepper to taste
- 4 eggs beaten
- Chopped parsley, basil, chives, tarragon or whatever herb and assortment of herbs you prefer
- ¼ cup half and half
- ¼-½ cup freshly grated Parmesan cheese
- ¼ cup coarsely chopped ham
- ¼ cup shredded cheddar cheese or cheese of your choice

- Preheat oven to 350°
- Boil potatoes for about 5 minutes or use grocery refrigerated potatoes from package
- Heat a large nonstick skillet and spray generously with PAM
- Whisk the eggs, cream, Parmesan cheese, herbs in a medium bowl to blend
- Melt butter and add oil
- Add onion and cook slowly until soft
- Stir in eggs, cream, potatoes, ham, Parmesan cheese, salt and pepper
- Cook over medium-low heat until the egg mixture is almost set but the top is still loose, about 5 minutes
- Sprinkle cheddar cheese on top
- Place in preheated oven until cheese is melted and eggs are completely firm about 10 minutes
- Using a rubber spatula, loosen the frittata from the skillet and slide onto a cutting board or round platter
- Cut into wedges

VARIATIONS:

- 8 ounces asparagus, trimmed and cut on bias with deli ham cut into cubes and 3 ounces of gruyere cheese
- One leek, white part only sliced thin, 4 ounces goat cheese, 3 ounces prosciutto, ¼ chopped fresh basil

Serves: 4

LOBSTER BISQUE
2003

This recipe takes time but it is well worth the effort.

- 1 large lobster tail (14 ounces) or 2 medium weighing 7 ounces each
- 3 ounces butter
- 1 large onion
- 1 large carrot
- 1 celery stalk
- 1 cup dry white wine
- ¼ cup cognac
- Fresh parsley
- Dried thyme
- 2 bay leaves
- 1 tablespoon tomato paste
- 2 tomatoes chopped (can use canned)
- 34 ounces freshly made fish stock OR use Super Touch Better than Bouillon Lobster or you can use boxed fish stock. You can find either of these in the soup section
- 3-4 tablespoons cornstarch depending on thickness you desire
- ½ cup sour cream or whipping cream
- Fresh oregano and paprika
- Salt and freshly ground pepper

- Peel and slice carrot
- Peel and mince onion
- Cut celery into pieces
- Cut the lobster shell with scissors and take the flesh out, cube the lobster flesh and reserve it in the refrigerator
- Heat butter, add onion, carrot and celery and cook for 20 minutes on medium low, vegetables must soften but not brown
- Heat and flame the cognac and pour it on the vegetables, shake until flame goes out
- Add the white wine and the lobster shell
- Boil this mixture until it reduces to half
- Add parsley, thyme, bay leaves, tomatoes and tomato paste
- Add the fish stock
- Simmer for 45 minutes and mix often
- Take the shell out and blend the remaining mixture with an emersion hand blender to get a very thin soup
- Pour the soup into a clean saucepan
- Mix the cornstarch with the cream and incorporate it into the soup
- Heat on medium for 5 minutes
- Add the lobster flesh and adjust seasoning
- Gently cook for 10 minutes which will cook the lobster flesh
- Blend again, top with oregano leaves and a bit of paprika if desired

Serves: 4-6

SALAD VINAIGRETTES

The magic formula for salad dressings is 3-1. It is a good starting point. You can then move in both directions to your taste. The best way to taste your dressing is to dip a piece of lettuce into the vinaigrette. You may add juices as a nice component. Juices are usually used to complement and enhance the vinegar, rather than replacing it altogether; although a simple dressing of olive oil and lemon juice drizzled over a fresh summer salad is hard to beat.

> TIP: Vinaigrettes have temporary emulsion that means you have to continue to shake or whisk to keep the oil and vinegar from separating.

FRENCH VINAIGRETTE:

- 2 tablespoons Champagne or White Wine vinegar
- 2 tablespoons Dijon mustard
- Salt and fresh pepper to taste
- 6 tablespoons extra-virgin olive oil

  - Whisk together vinegar, mustard, salt and freshly ground pepper
  - Add oil in a slow steady stream, whisking constantly
  - Toss with fresh fall greens, add blue cheese, toasted walnuts and dried cherries

OIL AND LEMON SALAD DRESSING:

Great on salad Nicoise or any salad. Toss a combination of Romaine and Bibb with

- ½-1 tablespoon lemon zest
- ¼ teaspoon salt, pinch of pepper and 1 teaspoon sugar
- ½ tablespoon Dijon mustard
- 2 tablespoons fresh lemon juice
- 4 tablespoons extra virgin olive oil

  - Whisk together lemon juice, mustard, salt, sugar and pepper
  - Add oil in slow steady stream, whisking constantly

RED WINE VINEGAR DRESSING

works well with tart lettuces: 2 tablespoons red wine vinegar with 6 tablespoons olive oil plus seasonings

WHITE WINE VINEGAR DRESSING: works well with mild lettuces:

2 tablespoons white wine vinegar
6 tablespoons olive oil, plus seasonings

CHICKEN SALADS: use walnut or hazelnut oil, tarragon vinegar or lemon juice

SUMMER SALADS:

- Chicken breasts, sliced
- Tomatoes, eggs, olives, water crest
- Red wine vinegar dressing
- Stuffed avocado with crabmeat, sliced tomatoes, scoop of potato salad, curled carrots, and marinated asparagus
- Shrimp, eggs, lemon, olives, and tomatoes

BASIC BALSAMIC VINAIGRETTE:

¾ cup extra virgin olive oil
¼ cup balsamic vinegar, salt and pepper, fresh herbs
½ teaspoon Dijon mustard

CLASSIC VINAIGRETTE

2 tablespoons red-wine vinegar
½ teaspoon Dijon mustard
½ teaspoon salt
⅛ teaspoon freshly ground black pepper
⅓ cup oil

- In a small bowl, whisk together the vinegar, mustard, salt and pepper.
- Add the oil slowly while whisking.

CREAMY CAESAR SALAD
WITH SPICY CROUTONS
2006

DRESSING:

- 1 clove garlic halved
- ½ cup nonfat mayonnaise
- 2 tablespoons red wine vinegar
- 2 teaspoons Dijon mustard
- 2 teaspoons white wine Worcestershire sauce
- 1 teaspoon anchovy paste
- ¼ teaspoon pepper

- Drop the garlic halves through the opening in blender lid with blender or food processor on, process until minced
- Add mayonnaise and next 5 ingredients (mayo through pepper), process until well blended
- Cover and chill at least 1 hour

CROUTONS:

- 2 teaspoons olive oil
- ¾ teaspoon Cajun seasoning
- 1 garlic clove, minced
- Sourdough bread cubes

- Preheat oven to 400°
- Combine oil, Cajun seasoning and minced garlic in a medium microwave-safe bowl
- Microwave at high for 20 seconds
- Add bread cubes and toss gently to coat
- Spread bread cubes in a single layer on a baking sheet
- Bake at 400° for 15 minutes or until golden brown

PREPARING THE SALAD:

- 18 cups torn romaine lettuce
- ⅓ cup grated fresh Parmesan cheese

- Place lettuce in a large bowl
- Add dressing and toss gently to coat
- Sprinkle with Parmesan cheese and top with croutons

Serves: 6

ROASTED BEET SALAD
2013

Adapted from Ina Garten (Barefoot Contessa). I have added and changed a few ingredients to make the salad more interesting.

- 4 large or 8 medium beets scrubbed, tops removed
- ¼-½ cup balsamic vinegar depending on your taste
- ½ cup extra virgin olive oil
- 2 teaspoons Dijon mustard
- ½ teaspoon salt and freshly ground pepper
- 4 ounces arugula
- ⅓ cup roasted almonds, walnuts or pistachios
- 2 cups fresh peaches sliced, sliced pears or fresh orange segments
- 4-6 ounces soft goat cheese

- Preheat oven to 400°
- Wrap beets in foil and put on sheet pan
- Roast for 50 minutes to 1 hour
- Insert a sharp knife in center to see if they are tender
- Unwrap and set aside for 10 minutes
- Peel with small knife over the foil or a sheet of parchment paper (prevents staining your cutting board)
- Whisk together vinegar, oil, mustard, ½ teaspoon salt and fresh pepper, set aside
- While beets are warm cut in half and then in half into 4-6 wedges and place in bowl
- As you are cutting the beets, toss them with half the vinaigrette (warm beets absorb more vinaigrette) taste for seasonings
- Place the greens or arugula in separate bowl with enough vinaigrette to moisten
- Put greens on serving platter and arrange the beets, almonds, goat cheese and fruit on top
- Drizzle with more vinaigrette
- Sprinkle with salt and pepper if needed
- Serve warm or at room temperature

Serves: 6

TOMATO OMBRE
ON GRILLED RUSTIC BREAD
2013

My friend, Jackie, and I prepared a charity dinner for 12. We used this recipe for one of the appetizers. It is very fresh and makes a beautiful presentation.

1 large ciabatta loaf
2 garlic cloves split half crosswise
3 pounds ripe tomatoes, red, orange and green
½ cup high quality extra virgin olive oil
1½ teaspoons sea salt
Freshly ground pepper

- Trim the top off the loaf of the ciabatta to make it flat
- Slice to create two loaves
- Grill until charred (1-2 minutes)
- Rub both sides with garlic
- Place cut side up on platter
- Cut the tomatoes into thin slices
- Collect the tomato juices, drizzle onto the bread with the oil, salt and pepper
- Shingle the tomato slices covering the entire surface of the bread
- Sprinkle salt and pepper over tomatoes
- Cut into wedges and serve

ROASTED TOMATO AND RICOTTA CROSTINI

3 tablespoons good quality extra virgin olive oil
2 pints grape tomatoes
Salt and freshly ground pepper
2 cups ricotta cheese
Balsamic vinegar

- Preheat oven to 300°
- Take a rimmed baking sheet and drizzle oil over the pan
- Place tomatoes, salt and pepper
- Bake until the tomatoes are soft (about 1 hour)
- Refrigerate roasted tomatoes up to 3 days
- Divide the cheese among crostini
- Top with tomatoes
- Drizzle with olive oil, salt and pepper
- Serve

WINTER GREENS SALAD
WITH GOAT CHEESE
2008

This refreshing salad combines three members of the chicory family, which has a pleasantly bitter taste. Oranges add sweetness, while goat cheese lends a creamy texture.

CHAMPAGNE VINAIGRETTE:

- 1 tablespoon champagne or white wine vinegar
- Zest of ½ of an orange
- 1 tablespoon fresh orange juice
- 1 teaspoon Dijon mustard
- ¼ cup olive oil or infused orange olive oil
- Salt and fresh pepper to taste

SALAD:

- 8 ounces log of goat cheese
- 1 cup finely chopped toasted pecans
- 1 head frisee
- ½ head radicchio thinly sliced
- 4 Belgian endive thinly sliced
- 4 oranges, peeled and segmented

- Preheat oven to 350°
- Make the vinaigrette and whisk together until emulsified
- Set aside
- Cut the goat cheese into 1-oz rounds
- Using fingers carefully reshape any uneven rounds
- Roll the goat cheese rounds in the pecans, pressing lightly
- Transfer to baking sheet
- Bake till warm 5-7 minutes
- Combine the frisee, radicchio and endive
- Add the vinaigrette and toss to coat greens
- Divide among 8 salad bowls or salad plates
- Transfer 1 goat cheese round to each salad
- Garnish with orange segments

Serves: 8

CRISP
APPLE AND ORANGE SALAD
2011

1 Granny Smith apple peeled and thinly sliced
1 red apple peeled and thinly sliced
2 large oranges peeled and segmented

⅓ cup toasted almonds or pecans
   Mixed greens Bibb lettuce, Red and Green Leaf Lettuces
   Oil and lemon dressing

- Tear greens into bowl
- Add apples and oranges
- Toss with dressing
- Sprinkle with nuts and serve

OIL AND LEMON SALAD DRESSING:

Great on salad Nicoise or on any salad

¾ cup extra virgin olive oil
¼ cup white wine vinegar
3 tablespoons lemon juice

2 tablespoons orange juice
¼ teaspoon lemon zest
   Pinch of sugar

- Zest lemon
- In small bowl whisk together the mustard, juices, zest, vinegar and sugar
- Slowly whisk in oil

ORANGE VINAIGRETTE WITH CANDIED WALNUTS:

WALNUTS:

- Toast walnuts
- Add 3 tablespoons syrup to walnuts, cook and cool

DRESSING:

½ cup orange juice concentrate
¼ cup balsamic vinegar
½ cup olive oil (blood orange infused olive oil is best)
   Salt and pepper to taste

- Blend thoroughly and toss with salad greens, orange sections and blue cheese

WATERCRESS SALAD
WITH DRIED FRUIT AND ALMONDS
2007

- 2 teaspoons red wine vinegar
- 3 tablespoons extra virgin olive oil
- Kosher salt and freshly ground pepper
- 2 bunches watercress, hand torn
- 1 cup toasted slivered almonds
- ¼ cup dried cranberries

- Make a quick vinaigrette by whisking together the vinegar, oil, salt and pepper
- Pour vinaigrette over the watercress and toss to coat
- Garnish with toasted slivered almonds and cranberries

Serves: 4

ROASTED SQUASH
2012

Acorn, butternut, kabocha or delicate squash
Olive oil
Fresh sea salt and pepper

- Preheat oven to 425°
- Wash squash thoroughly
- Cut in half and remove seeds
- Slice into 1-inch wedges
- Toss squash with 1 tablespoon oil on baking sheet, season with salt and pepper
- Roast squash, turning occasionally until golden and tender 35-40 minutes

If using acorn, kabocha or delicate squash you do not need to peel because the skin will soften during roasting and is edible.

GREEN BEAN SALAD
WITH SHITAKE MUSHROOMS
2005

We served this salad at one of our Warwick Gardens neighborhood progressive dinners.

- 1½ pounds green beans
- 1 tablespoon olive oil
- ⅓ pound shitake mushrooms, stems removed and caps sliced
- ½ tablespoon chopped fresh thyme or ⅛ teaspoon dried
- 1 shallot minced
- Classic vinaigrette (see below)
- ½ teaspoon salt
- 8 radicchio leaves

- In large pot of boiling salted water cook beans until tender (10 minutes)
- Drain, rinse with cold water and drain thoroughly
- Pat dry with paper towels
- In fry pan, heat oil over medium heat
- Add mushrooms and thyme and cook, stirring occasionally until mushrooms are brown (5 minutes)
- Add shallot and cook until soft (2 Minutes)
- Transfer to a large container
- Toss the green beans, mushrooms and vinaigrette with ½ teaspoon salt
- Put one radicchio leaf on each plate and arrange the salad on the leaves

CLASSIC VINAIGRETTE

- 2 tablespoons red-wine vinegar
- ½ teaspoon Dijon mustard
- ½ teaspoon salt
- ⅛ teaspoon freshly ground black pepper
- ⅓ cup oil

- In a small bowl, whisk together the vinegar, mustard, salt and pepper
- Add the oil slowly while whisking

Serves: 6-8

LEEK AND POTATO GRATIN
WITH CREAM
2007

- 18 ounces white part of the leek
- 2 tablespoons butter
- 18 ounces, firm, waxy potatoes peeled and thinly sliced (can use package of sliced potatoes found in the egg section of your grocery store)
- 1 cup heavy cream
- Salt and pepper
- White cheddar cheese shredded
- Minced fresh rosemary

- Preheat oven to 400°
- Grease a gratin pan or casserole dish
- Melt butter with 4 tablespoons of water in a saucepan, add leeks, salt and pepper
- Cover and cook for 10 minutes
- Layer potatoes, leeks, rosemary, cheese, cream, salt and pepper
- Continue layers
- Cover with foil for first 15 minutes
- Take foil off and bake another 20-30 minutes

Serves: 4-6

EASY CAULIFLOWER GRATIN
2013

- 1 head of cauliflower, chopped
- 1 (15-ounce) jar Alfredo sauce
- ½ cup panko breadcrumbs

- Preheat oven to 400°
- Chop cauliflower
- Combine cauliflower and Alfredo sauce in baking dish
- Top with bread crumbs
- Bake for 30-35 minutes or until bubbly and cauliflower is tender

ROASTED SWEET POTATOES
AND WHITE POTATOES

1 cup diced sweet potatoes
1 cup diced white potatoes
½ cup olive oil
Salt and pepper

- Preheat oven to 350°
- Lightly coat both potatoes in oil
- Season
- Place in roasting pan
- Roast until tender, about 45 minutes

GREEN BEANS
WITH ALMONDS
1999

2 pounds French haricots verts or string beans
½ cup slivered almonds, toasted
1-2 tablespoons unsalted butter
1-2 tablespoons olive oil
Shallots, minced or sliced
Freshly ground pepper
Coarse salt
Chopped Italian parsley

- Bring a pot of salted water to a full boil
- Add beans and cook until tender (about 5 minutes)
- Drain and rinse with cold water
- Pat dry with paper towels
- In large skillet toast the almonds and transfer to a plate
- Melt the butter with the oil, add the shallots and sauté for about 4 minutes
- Increase the heat and add the beans, salt and pepper
- Shake pan frequently and add the almonds

I cook the beans the day before and refrigerate until ready to use.

Serves: 8

MINT STUFFED MUSHROOMS
2012

- ½ cup grated Romano cheese
- ½ cup Italian breadcrumbs
- 2 cloves of garlic, minced
- 1 tablespoon fresh mint minced or a combination of basil and mint
- Salt
- Fresh ground pepper
- 2 tablespoons Italian parsley minced
- ⅓ cup olive oil
- Large white mushrooms, stemmed

- Preheat oven to 400°
- Stir together crumbs, cheese, garlic, parsley, mint, salt and pepper
- Add about 2 tablespoons olive oil
- Grease a baking sheet with oil or PAM cooking spray
- Stuff each mushroom and place on baking sheet
- Drizzle with the remaining olive oil
- Bake for about 25 minutes

SAUTEED ITALIAN SPINACH
AND CANNELLINI BEANS
2000

- 3 tablespoons olive oil
- 2 large garlic cloves sliced
- 1 (15-ounce) can cannelloni beans, rinsed and drained
- 2 large bags of fresh washed spinach
- 1 tablespoon lemon zest
- Coarse sea salt
- Freshly ground pepper

- Heal oil
- Add garlic and cook for about 1 minute till lightly browned
- Stir in beans and cook just one minute
- Add spinach
- Cook turning until just wilted about 2-3 minutes
- Remove from the heat and add the salt, pepper and lemon zest
- Turn into a heated dish and drizzle with olive oil
- Sprinkle Romano cheese atop

OVEN ROASTED VEGETABLES

2 medium zucchini
2 small slender eggplants
2 shallots
2 cloves minced garlic

1 sprig of fresh rosemary finely chopped
Salt and pepper
3 tablespoons olive oil

- Preheat oven to 400°
- Slice zucchini and eggplant into half inch rounds and place in a bowl
- Peel and finely slice shallots and add to the bowl along with the garlic, rosemary, salt and pepper and olive oil
- Mix lightly and pour contents onto a lightly oiled sheet pan
- Roast vegetables on the highest shelf of oven for 30-40 minutes until vegetables are roasted and tinged brown at the edges
- Serve hot or at room temperature

GRILLED GARDEN VEGETABLES
2006

8 cups of vegetables, cut into ¼ inch slices or sticks. Use an assortment of the following:

Peeled eggplant
Blanched, peeled carrot
Zucchini

Endive
Yellow, red and green bell pepper
Asparagus

4 plum tomatoes, quartered lengthwise
8 green onions, roots removed
½ cup olive oil
2 tablespoons chopped fresh thyme
2 teaspoons chopped fresh rosemary
2 teaspoons chopped fresh sage
2 teaspoons chopped fresh oregano
2 teaspoons salt and freshly ground pepper
Freshly grated Parmigiano-Reggiano cheese for sprinkling

- Preheat the grill to medium-hot.
- On a lightly oiled grilling tray, arrange the vegetables in a single layer
- Whisk together olive oil, herbs, salt and pepper
- Drizzle mixture over the vegetables or toss the vegetables with the mixture
- Grill for 5-8 minutes, or until the vegetables are nearly tender
- Serve hot or at room temperature, sprinkled with Parmigiano-Reggiano cheese

PIEDMONT ROASTED PEPPERS
2008

A recipe I treasure from my English friend Jackie. Jackie is probably one of the best cooks I have ever known. This recipe is an upgrade from the way my mom roasted her red peppers over the gas burner.

4 large red peppers
4 medium tomatoes or small plum tomatoes
   Anchovy paste, or 1 can anchovy fillets drained
2 cloves garlic
   Olive oil
   Freshly ground pepper

- Preheat oven to 350°
- Cut peppers in half, including the stems, remove seeds and pith
- Lightly oil a shallow roasting pan, rub the peppers with oil and place the halves in the pan cut side up
- Skin and deseed the tomatoes (pour boiling water over tomatoes, leave for 1 minute, drain and then slip the skins off)
- Cut the tomatoes into quarters and divide amongst the pepper halves
- Peel and chop the garlic cloves and add to the anchovy paste or anchovies
- Sprinkle 1 tablespoon olive oil over the contents of each pepper half
- Season with black pepper (no salt because of the salt flavor of the anchovies)
- Roast in oven on upper shelf for 50 minutes to 1 hour

Can be served at room temperature as a side dish or served hot from the oven with good crusty bread to soak up all the juices as an appetizer

Serves: 8 as a side dish
Serves: 4 as an appetizer

BAKED ZUCCHINI
2014

2 medium zucchini
Olive oil for brushing
Garlic minced or salt
Small tomatoes sliced
Mozzarella cheese and Parmesan cheese shredded
Fresh basil chopped

- Preheat oven to 375°
- Slice zucchini in half and cut a tiny slice off bottom
- Brush with oil
- Sprinkle garlic, tomatoes, cheeses and basil on top
- Bake for 20-30 minutes

GREEN BEAN BUNDLES
2007

1 pound fresh whole green beans
Olive oil
Salt and pepper
Strips of bacon cut in half lengthwise

- Preheat oven to 375°
- Blanch green beans for 3 minutes
- Toss lightly with oil, salt and pepper
- Bundle about 5-8 beans and wrap a piece of bacon around the bundle
- Make a knot
- Place on a roasting sheet and roast for 15-20 minutes until bacon is cooked

Serves: 6-8

TOMATO VEGETABLE CASSEROLE
JANET CERJAN
2009

Our daughter, Janet, shared this recipe with me. It is a staple recipe that never fails.

- 1 medium potato, peeled and cut into ½-inch pieces
- 1 medium yam, peeled and cut into ½- inch pieces
- 1 red bell pepper, seeded and cut into ½-inch pieces
- 2 carrots cut into ½-inch pieces
- 5 tablespoons olive oil
- 1 red onion, thinly sliced into rings
- 1 large zucchini, cut crosswise into ¼-in pieces
- Salt and pepper to taste
- 2 large ripe tomatoes cut crosswise into ¼-in thick pieces
- ½ cup grated Parmesan
- 2 tablespoons dried Italian-style breadcrumbs
- Fresh basil sprigs, for garnish

- Preheat oven to 400°
- Toss potato, yam, pepper, carrots and the olive oil in a 13x9x3-in baking dish
- Toss with hands to coat vegetables with the oil
- Sprinkle with salt and pepper and toss again
- Spread vegetables evenly over the bottom of the pan
- Arrange the onion slices over the vegetables
- Arrange the zucchini over the onion
- Drizzle with 2 tablespoons olive oil
- Sprinkle with salt and pepper
- Arrange tomato slices over the zucchini
- Stir the Parmesan and bread crumbs in small bowl
- Sprinkle crumbs over vegetables
- Drizzle with more olive oil (1 tablespoon)
- Bake uncovered until the vegetables are tender and topping is golden brown about 40 minutes
- Garnish with basil

Yield: 6 servings

VEGETARIAN CHILI
2014

Over time people move away from traditional cooking to a focus on vegetable diets. I use this recipe for times when I need a strict vegetarian dish.

- 2 tablespoons oil
- 1½ cups red peppers diced
- 2 cloves garlic minced
- 1½ cups diced onions
- 1 zucchini diced
- 2 cups fresh corn cut off the cob
- 1 pound cremini mushrooms cubed
- 4 large tomatoes, peeled, seeded and chopped
- ⅛ teaspoon cayenne pepper
- 2 tablespoons chili powder
- 1 tablespoon cumin
- 1¼ teaspoons salt
- Freshly ground pepper
- 3 cups black beans rinsed and drained1
- 1 large (15-ounce) can tomato sauce
- 1 cup chicken or vegetable stock

- Heat oil and add the red pepper, garlic and onion until soft
- Add the mushrooms, corn and zucchini and cook until soft
- Add the seasonings and tomatoes
- Add the beans, tomato sauce and stock
- Bring to a boil then reduce heat and simmer for 20 minutes
- Adjust seasonings to taste
- Serve in bowls

Serves: 6

BRUSSELS SPROUTS
WITH PANCETTA
2012

This vegetable dish makes a nice pairing with a Standing Rib Roast.

	Fresh Brussels sprouts, trimmed
	Olive oil
	Pancetta or bacon, chopped
	Salt and fresh pepper
¾	cup chicken stock
1-2	cloves garlic, minced

- In pot boil water with added salt
- Cook the spouts for just 3-4 minutes
- Sauté the pancetta or bacon until crisp
- Gently sauté garlic just until golden
- Add the sprouts and sauté
- Season with salt and pepper
- Add the broth and cook on simmer until chicken stock is reduced

Serves: 4

CHICKEN FLORENTINE

2007

Adapted from Paula Deen. I altered her recipe to include low-fat sour cream and low-fat mayonnaise.

- 2 (10-ounce) pkgs. frozen chopped spinach or a large bag of fresh spinach
- 6 chicken breast halves (about 4 pounds), cooked, boned and shredded
- 2 (10¾-ounce) cans condensed cream of mushroom soup
- 1 cup low-fat mayo
- 1 cup low-fat sour cream
- 2 cups grated sharp cheddar cheese
- 2 tablespoons fresh lemon juice
- 1 teaspoon curry powder
- Salt and freshly ground black pepper to taste
- ½ cup dry white wine
- ½ cup freshly grated Parmesan cheese
- ½ cup soft breadcrumbs
- 2 tablespoons butter

This recipe makes enough for 6-8 servings. You can make two casseroles: one for supper and one for the freezer or cut the recipe in half.

- Preheat oven to 350°.
- Spray a 11x9 inch casserole dish with PAM cooking spray.
- Remove the outer wrappers from the boxes of spinach. Open one end of each box and microwave for 2 minutes, until thawed. Drain, squeeze and put into a large bowl.
- If you use fresh spinach, quickly sauté in a dry skillet until wilted and then chop and squeeze dry.
- Add the shredded chicken to the spinach.
- In a medium bowl, combine soup, mayo, sour cream, cheddar, lemon juice, curry powder, salt, pepper and wine. Whisk together to make a sauce.
- Pour over the spinach and chicken.
- Mix well with spatula.
- Place the mixture into an prepared casserole dish sprayed with cooking spray.
- Pat down evenly and smooth with spatula.
- Combine the Parmesan and bread crumbs and sprinkle over the top.
- Dot with butter.
- Bake uncovered at 350° for about 30 minutes until bubbly. Convection oven about 20 minutes.
- If you freeze a casserole, wrap uncooked casserole with plastic wrap, then wrap in foil. Place in a freezer bag and seal. Allow to thaw 24 hours in refrigerator. When ready to bake, remove the plastic wrap and foil and bake.

RIGATONI
WITH SQUASH AND SHRIMP
2010

- 6 tablespoons olive oil
- 1 pound butternut squash, peeled and cut into 1-inch cubes
- 2 cloves garlic, grated
- 2 teaspoons salt
- ¾ teaspoon freshly ground pepper
- 1 cup vegetable stock
- 1 pound rigatoni
- 1 pound shrimp, peeled and deveined
- ¾-1 cup milk
- ½ cup chopped fresh basil
- ¼ cup Parmesan cheese grated

- Clean the shrimp and toss with 1 teaspoon salt and ½ teaspoon pepper, set aside
- Warm 3 tablespoons oil in preheated heavy skillet
- Add squash, garlic and 1 teaspoon salt and ¼ teaspoon pepper
- Sauté until the squash is golden and tender (5-7 minutes)
- Transfer the squash mixture to a blender or food processor and puree
- Bring pot of salted water to a boil and add the pasta, cook until al dente, then drain
- While pasta is cooking, warm the last 3 tablespoons oil
- Add shrimp to pan and sauté just until pink (about 3 minutes)
- In large pot over low heat combine the cooked and drained pasta, pureed squash mixture and ¾ cup milk, stir to combine
- Add the remaining ¼ cup milk if sauce needs to be thinned*
- Add the cooked shrimp, basil and cheese
- Stir until warm and serve
- * If sauce is still too thick you can continue to thin with milk

Serves: 4-6
Wine pairing: Chardonnay

PASTA
WITH TRUFFLE SAUCE
2012

This is an elegant dish taken from Chef Kurt's kitchen on the Seabourn Cruise line. He gave us this recipe on our Baltic cruise. I buy homemade pasta from my favorite Italian Market to save time.

PASTA:

- 3 cups flour
- 2 teaspoons salt
- 18 egg yolks
- 3 eggs
- 1 tablespoon olive oil
- ½ tablespoon milk

- Sift flour and salt in an electric mixer fitted with the hook attachment.
- Add the yolks, eggs, oil and milk
- Work for about 20 minutes
- Wrap in plastic wrap and rest for at least 2 hours before rolling out
- Run through roller of pasta machine; run through fettuccini side of machine to make the noodles for this dish

TRUFLE SAUCE:

- 2 tablespoons butter
- 2 tablespoons fresh button mushrooms, chopped
- 2 tablespoons shallots grated
- 1 teaspoon peppercorns crushed
- 2 bay leaves
- 1 cup white wine (Pinot Grigio)
- 1 cup heavy cream
- ½ cup madeira wine
- 4 tablespoons finely chopped truffles
- Salt and pepper to taste
- 2 cups chicken stock

- Melt the butter, add mushrooms, shallots, peppercorns and bay leaves
- Reduce over high heat for about 2 minutes
- Add cream, bring the mixture to a boil, then reduce by one-third and make it a smooth consistency, adjust the seasoning
- In another sauté pan, add wine to 3 tablespoons of truffles, reduce over high heat for 2-3 minutes
- Strain the cream sauce into the truffles and wine, and then reduce it to a smooth consistency
- Boil the noodles quickly, put pasta in pan with sauce
- Toss well until all is heated through

PASTA
WITH VODKA SAUCE
"Chicken riggies or sausage riggies"
2009

- ½ pound small rigatoni pasta
- 2 tablespoons olive oil
- ½ pound Italian sausage mild or hot or chicken breasts cut into bite size pieces (If you use hot sausage omit red pepper flakes)*
- 1 cup onions chopped
- 1 teaspoon salt
- Pinch crushed red pepper flakes*
- 4 teaspoons minced garlic
- 1 cup crushed tomatoes
- 6 tablespoons vodka
- 4 tablespoons heavy cream
- 3 tablespoons Chiffonade of fresh basil leaves

Freshly grated Parmigiano-Reggiano cheese

- Preheat large skillet and add oil. Add sausage or chicken and cook until browned and almost cooked, drain off some of the sausage fat
- Add onions, salt, red pepper and cook until onions are golden (5 minutes)
- Add garlic, sauté for a few seconds then add tomatoes
- Deglaze pan scraping bottom with wooden spoon to gather the browned bits
- Cook until thick
- Add vodka and reduce by half
- Stir in cream and cook another minute or two
- Stir in basil and remove from heat
- While making sauce cook pasta in pot of salted boiling water until al dente, drain well
- Toss sauce and pasta together
- Garnish with fresh basil

Serves 2-3
Wine Pairing: Pouilly-Fume, White Bordeaux or Chardonnay

SOLE MEUNIERE
Pronounced: men yare
2004

One of the first restaurants we chose when we moved to Sarasota was Divino's Italian on Main Street. I ordered this wonderful dish and have been making it at home ever since.

½ cup flour
4 sole or flounder fillets (3 ounces each)
Sea salt
Freshly ground pepper
Canola oil
2-4 tablespoons unsalted butter

1 teaspoon lemon zest
6 tablespoons fresh lemon juice (3 lemons)
1 tablespoon minced fresh parsley
Capers rinsed (optional)

- Rinse fish and pat dry
- Sprinkle fish with salt and pepper
- Dredge fish in flour
- Heat the oil in a skillet until hot
- Add half of the butter
- Cook fish until golden brown
- Turn fish and cook until golden
- Add 3 tablespoons lemon juice and ½ teaspoon lemon zest
- Remove fish to a warm platter and pour sauce over fish
- Add remaining butter and a little more oil to the skillet
- Repeat cooking process with the last two fish filets adding the remainder of lemon zest, lemon juice and optional capers at end of cooking
- Place fish on warm platter and pour remainder of sauce over fish
- Sprinkle with parsley and capers
- Salt and pepper as needed

Serves: 2
Wine Pairing: Chardonnay or Fume Blanc

MUSSELS
IN WHITE WINE
2005

- 3 pounds mussels
- ⅓ cup flour
- 2 tablespoons olive oil
- 1 cup chopped shallots
- 5-6 minced garlic cloves
- ½ cup chopped Italian tomatoes
- ½ teaspoon saffron threads (optional)
- ⅓ cup chopped Italian parsley
- 1 tablespoon fresh thyme leaves, minced
- 1 cup good white wine (Pinot Grigio for example)
- 2 teaspoons salt
- Freshly ground pepper to taste

- Clean mussels, put them in a large bowl with water and flour to cover
- Soak for 30 minutes so that the mussels disgorge sand
- Remove and brush under running water
- Discard mussels whose shells are not shut
- In large stockpot, heat the butter and oil
- Add the shallots and cook for 5 minutes
- Add the garlic and cook for 3 more minutes
- Add tomatoes, saffron, parsley, thyme, wine salt and pepper
- Bring to a boil
- Add the mussels, stir well, cover the pot and cook over medium heat for 8-10 minutes until the mussels are opened (discard any that do not open)
- With the lid on, shake the pot
- Pour the mussels and the sauce into large serving bowls
- Serve hot with toasted crostini

Serves: 2

BOB'S
SALMON
2002

Our neighbor at Gaston Lake made this dish for us one summer. It is an easy dish with lots of flavor.

4 pieces salmon filets
Olive oil
Minced garlic
½ cup breadcrumbs

4 tablespoons melted unsalted butter
Orange juice
Honey
Chopped pecans, toasted

- Preheat oven to 375°
- Toast pecans
- Preheat skillet
- Sauté garlic a bit
- Sauté salmon on each side
- Place in rectangle baking dish
- Sprinkle with bread crumbs mixed with melted butter, orange juice, honey
- Sprinkle chopped pecans over top
- Bake for 15 minutes

Serves: 4

SHRIMP AND GRITS
2008

My son-in-law, Spencer, fixed this dish during one of our family Christmases.

1 cup white grits
2 cups water
1 can chicken broth
¾ cup half and half
¾ teaspoon salt

¾ cup cheddar cheese shredded
¼ cup Parmesan cheese
2 tablespoons butter
½ teaspoon hot sauce and white pepper

- Boil water, broth and half and half then whisk in the grits. Cook according to package directions (20-25 minutes)
- Add cheeses, butter, hot sauce and white pepper and salt
- Fry bacon, crumble
- Fry shrimp in bacon grease until pink
- Add chopped bacon
- Spoon grits into bowl and add shrimp, mix and serve

CHICKEN AND SEAFOOD PAELLA
2009

- 1 tablespoon olive oil
- 4 ounces chorizo sausage sliced thick
- 1 onion chopped
- 1 red pepper, chopped
- 2 cloves garlic, chopped
- 1 tomato chopped or one ½ cup canned diced tomatoes
- 1 cup Spanish short grain rice or Arborio rice
- Good pinch of saffron threads
- 1½ cups chicken stock
- ¼ teaspoon paprika
- Salt and pepper
- 1 pound shrimp, shelled and deveined
- ¼ cup dry white wine
- 1 tablespoon fresh lemon juice
- 1 dozen littleneck clams, scrubbed and cleaned (can also use ½ pound of mussels)
- 1½ cups roasted chicken (at deli section of grocery store), skinned, shredded
- Cooked lobster tails
- ½ cup frozen baby peas thawed
- Coarse salt and freshly ground pepper to taste
- Flat leaf parsley chopped for garnish

- Preheat oven to 350°
- Heat oil in paella pan
- Sauté the chorizo until browned, remove and set aside
- Add the onion, red pepper and garlic and cook until softened
- Stir in the tomatoes, rice, saffron and 1½ cups of chicken broth
- Season with salt, pepper and paprika, bring to a boil, cover and simmer for 15 minutes
- In large skillet heat some oil
- Season the shrimp and cook over high heat until pink and cooked through
- Transfer the shrimp to the rice
- Wipe the skillet and pour in the wine and lemon juice, add the clams, cover and cook until they open (3minutes)-discard those that do not open
- Pour the cooked clams and their liquid over the rice
- Stir in the cooked chicken, the cooked lobster tails, and the thawed peas
- Cover and cook in the oven for 5-10 minutes to warm the paella
- Garnish with fresh parsley
- Drizzle with olive oil and serve

Serves: 6-8
Wine Pairing: Sauvignon Blanc

PRIME RIB ROAST
WITH AU JUS
2007

We served roasted or grilled Cornish hens for over 30 years for Christmas dinner while the children were growing up. When we moved to Florida I introduced this Christmas dinner option.

1 (4-rib) prime rib roast with ribs (have the butcher cut the roast away from the bone and tie the bones back on for easy carving)
Salt
Coarsely ground fresh pepper
1 cup red wine
2 cups rich beef stock
1 tablespoon fresh thyme finely chopped

- Let roast stand at room temperature for at least one hour
- Preheat oven to 450°
- Put oven rack in middle position
- Trim all but a thin layer of fat from the roast
- Rub the roast all over with salt and pepper
- Transfer to a rack set in a roasting pan
- Roast 20 minutes, then **reduce** oven to **350°** and roast until thermometer inserted registers 110 (about 1½ to 2 hours more)
- Transfer to large cutting board
- Let stand, uncovered, 30 minutes
- Prepare au jus while meat sits
- Place the roasting pan on top of the stove over 2 burners set on high heat
- Add the wine to the pan drippings in the pan and cook over high heat until reduced, scraping the bottom of the pan with a wooden spoon
- Add the stock and cook until reduced by half
- Whisk in the thyme and season with salt and pepper, to taste

Serve with traditional Yorkshire pudding or potatoes of choice

Wine Pairing: Pinot Noir, Merlot or Bordeaux

BRISKET
WITH PORTOBELLO MUSHROOMS AND DRIED CRANBERRIES
2006 Progressive Dinner Florida

4-pound trimmed flat-cut brisket
1 cup dry red wine
1 cup canned beef or chicken broth
½ cup frozen cranberry juice cocktail concentrate, thawed
¼ cup flour
1 large onion, sliced
4 cloves of garlic, chopped
1½ tablespoons chopped fresh rosemary
12 ounces medium Portobello mushrooms, dark gills scraped away, caps thinly sliced
1 cup dried cranberries (4 ounces)

- Preheat oven to 300°
- Whisk wine, broth, cranberry concentrate and flour in a medium bowl
- Pour into 15x10x2-inch roasting pan
- Mix in onion, garlic and rosemary
- Sprinkle brisket on all sides with salt and pepper
- Place brisket, fat side up, in pan
- Spoon some of wine mixture over
- Cover pan tightly with heavy-duty foil
- Bake brisket until very tender, about 4½ hours, basting with pan juices every hour
- Transfer brisket to plate
- Cool 1 hour at room temperature
- Thinly slice brisket across grain
- Arrange slices in pan with sauce, overlapping slices slightly

At this point Brisket can be prepared 2 days ahead. Cover and refrigerate.
OR proceed as follows

- Preheat oven to 350°
- Place mushrooms and cranberries in sauce around brisket
- Cover pan with foil
- Bake until mushrooms are tender and brisket is heated through (about 30 minutes if brisket is room temperature and 40 minutes if brisket has been refrigerated)
- Transfer sliced brisket and sauce to platter and serve

Serves: 8

Serve with vegetable of choice and creamy potato bake—and of course the wine

Wine pairing: Cabernet Sauvignon or Burgundy

ROAST PORK TENDERLOIN
2008

A simple way to roast a pork tenderloin.

1 teaspoon Dijon mustard
1 teaspoon grated ginger
1 garlic mashed with salt

- Smear mustard, garlic and salt over pork
- Refrigerate for one hour
- Preheat oven to 375°
- Roast with vegetables around base of roast at 375° until internal temperature is 145°

YORKSHIRE PUDDING

½ cup milk
½ cup flour
1 egg
¼ teaspoon salt
drippings from roast beef

- Combine milk, flour, egg and salt in food processor and mix well
- Cover and refrigerate for 1 hour
- Preheat oven to 400°
- Spoon 1½ teaspoons drippings into each of 4 custard cups
- Divide batter evenly
- Bake at 400° for 20 minutes
- Reduce oven to 350° and continue baking until pudding puffs and is golden (10-15 minutes)
- Serve as a side like a baked potato with the roast beef and/or roasted vegetables

APPLE AND PRUNE
STUFFED PORK LOIN
2012

	Extra virgin oil
4	slices bacon cut crosswise
1	small red onion diced
	Salt
2	granny smith apples, peeled, diced into ½ inch bits
½	cup prunes, quartered
2	sprigs fresh rosemary, chopped fine
½	cup brandy, Calvados
3-4	pound boneless pork loin
1	cup chicken stock

- Swirl some olive oil in a skillet.
- Add bacon and cook until the bacon is crispy.
- Add onions and salt, cook 5-6 minutes.
- Add the apples, prunes and half the rosemary.
- Cook until soft.
- Take pan off heat and add the brandy.
- Return to heat and flambé, let cool.
- Spoon the apple mixture onto a 24-inch sheet of plastic wrap. Make a log down the center that is about the same length as the pork loin.
- Roll tightly and twist ends. Place log in freezer and freeze solid.
- Insert a long thin knife into center of one end of pork loin, repeat at the other end.
- Wiggle the knife back and forth to create a space for the frozen log.
- Preheat oven to 375°.
- Slide the stuffing log into the pork loin through the space you created.
- Season the outside of the pork generously with salt and pepper and remaining rosemary. Coat a roasting pan with olive oil.
- On high heat sear pork on all sides until brown.
- Add chicken stock.
- Roast 25-35 minutes or until the internal temperature reads 140, turning halfway through cooking time.
- Remove from oven and cover with foil and let rest for 15 minutes.

Serves: 8
Wine Pairing: Sauvignon Blanc
Pouilly-Fume

OSSO BUCCO

2002

We served this dish at one of our Florida neighborhood progressive dinners.

    Olive oil
4 veal shanks tied in the middle with string
½ cup flour for dredging
    Bouquet garni (sprig of rosemary, sprig of thyme, 1 bay leaf)
    Salt (about 2 teaspoons)
    Freshly ground pepper
1 onion diced
1 carrot diced
1 stalk of celery diced
1 tablespoon tomato paste
2 tablespoons minced garlic
1½ cups dry white wine*
3-4 cups chicken stock*
¼ cup minced Italian parsley

- Heat oven to 350°
- Prepare Bouquet garni wrapping herbs together with twine
- Pat veal shanks with paper towel, secure with twine
- Season shanks with salt and pepper, then dredge in the flour
- Heat Dutch oven, add oil
- Brown the veal shanks on all sides, remove to platter
- Add the onion, carrot and celery to the pan and sauté for about 8 minutes until vegetables are soft
- Add the tomato paste and mix
- Add the shanks with the wine and reduce the liquid to about half
- Add the bouquet of garni, garlic and the chicken stock
- Bring to a boil, cover and put into the oven
- Cook for about 2½ hours or until the shanks are very tender
- Remove from oven, pour juices over shanks and garnish with parsley and a sprinkle of Parmesan cheese

Serves: 4
Wine pairing: Full bodied Pinot Noir, a light Chianti or Sangiovese
    Sides: Orzo, risotto or mashed potatoes
    *For a heartier flavor use a red wine and beef stock

POLLO AL LIMONE
2014

While visiting Albuquerque, New Mexico, we stopped at a local Italian restaurant and ordered this dish. The owner graciously shared the recipe with me.

- 3-4 pound chicken cut up or leg quarters
- 2 lemons
- 1 cup white wine
- ¼ cup olive oil
- 2 tablespoons olive oil
- 5 tablespoons fresh herbs minced (sage, thyme, rosemary, parsley and basil)
- 2 garlic cloves minced
- Salt and pepper to taste

- Wash and dry chicken
- Zest the lemons into a large bowl
- Squeeze the lemons
- Whisk in the wine, ¼ cup oil, herbs, garlic, salt and pepper
- Add the chicken turning to coat chicken with marinade
- Set aside covered in a cool plate to marinate OR refrigerate in the morning for about 8 hours
- Preheat the oven to 350°
- Heat 2 tablespoons olive oil in large skillet
- Drain the chicken (reserve the marinade)
- Sauté the chicken on medium heat until brown about 7 minutes
- Place the chicken in a long casserole dish (single layer)
- Pour reserved marinade into the skillet
- Boil and scrape the bits off the bottom of the skillet with a wooden spoon
- Pour over the chicken
- Bake for 35 minutes

Serves: 4

COQ AU VIN
2004

This classic dish takes some time to prepare, but well worth the effort.

10	slices of bacon cut into pieces
3-4	pounds of chicken rinsed and patted dry (I use about 8 chicken thighs and legs)
½	teaspoon salt
	Freshly ground pepper
1	onion, minced
½	cup shallots minced
20	pearl onions, peeled
	Several cloves of garlic peeled
1	pound of mushrooms quartered
¼	cup flour
2	teaspoons tomato paste
3	cups dry red wine
1½	cups chicken stock
6	sprigs thyme
1	bay leaf
	Chopped fresh Italian parsley

- Preheat oven to 350°
- Preheat a large Dutch oven and fry the bacon until crisp
- Transfer bacon to paper towels and reserve
- Season chicken with salt and pepper
- Brown in the hot bacon fat
- Transfer browned chicken to warm platter
- Remove some of bacon fat and add onion, pearl onions, shallots and garlic
- Cook until soft
- Add mushrooms and cook a few minutes
- Add flour and tomato paste and cook
- Slowly add the wine and the stock, stir well
- Add the thyme, bay leaf, bacon and chicken
- Bring to boil
- Cover pot and put in oven for about 1½ hours
- Transfer chicken to serving dish and cover
- Return pot to heat, skim off fat and cook the sauce until it has thickened a bit about 15 or so minutes
- Taste and adjust seasoning, return chicken to pot and heat through
- Garnish with parsley

Serve with egg noodles, wild rice mix, roasted vegetables or creamy mashed potatoes. I also serve with Green bean salad with Shitake mushrooms

Serves: 6
Wine pairing: Pinot Noir, Merlot, Cabernet Sauvignon or Chateauneuf-du-Pape

STUFFED CHICKEN MARSALA
2002

6 chicken breasts	Flour for dredging
Salt and pepper	Canola oil
Fresh thyme minced	10 ounces sliced fresh mushrooms
6 slices prosciutto sliced very thin	½ cup marsala wine
6 slices fontina cheese	2 cups chicken stock

- Cut pockets into chicken breasts
- Season pockets with salt, pepper and fresh thyme
- Stuff each breast with a slice of prosciutto and a piece of fontina cheese
- Fold in half and secure with pick
- Dip chicken breasts in flour
- Heat skillet; add oil to skillet
- Sauté chicken breasts until brown on both sides
- Remove browned chicken breasts from skillet
- Add more oil if necessary and add mushrooms to skillet and sauté on high heat until browned (mushroom liquid will start to deglaze the pan)
- Add marsala wine to skillet and reduce by half, about 5 minutes
- Add chicken stock to skillet
- Put chicken breasts back into the pan
- Simmer until chicken is cooked through, about 5-10 minutes
- Transfer chicken to platter and remove the picks
- Thicken sauce by making a Beurre Manie with the butter and the flour
- Whisk in until the sauce thickens

BEURRE MANIE:

a thickening agent made by kneading equal parts of unsalted butter and flour together into marble size chunks and added COLD to hot liquids. It is important not to boil for long periods of time. Simmer just enough to "cook" out the flour taste.

1 tablespoon unsalted butter
1 tablespoon flour

Serves 6
Wine pairing: Pinot Noir, Valpolicella, Merlot or Chianti Classico

WEIGHT WATCHERS
CHICKEN DISH
2005

My friend Jean Crouch shared this recipe.

4 chicken filets
2 cups mushrooms halved
3 tablespoons balsamic vinegar
2 teaspoons Dijon mustard
1 clove garlic
⅓ cup chicken stock

MARINADE:

2 tablespoons balsamic vinegar
2 teaspoons Dijon mustard
Garlic

- Marinate the chicken a few hours
- Sauté the mushrooms and set aside
- Sauté the chicken filets till done
- Return the mushrooms to pan and add the rest of the balsamic vinegar (1 tablespoon) and the ⅓-cup of chicken stock
- Deglaze with a wooden spoon and finish
- Serve with mashed cauliflower (pureed in processor with butter, salt and pepper)

Serves: 4

SPICY BOURBON GLAZED
SPARERIBS
2006

- 6-12 pounds baby back spareribs
- 4 tablespoons Worcestershire
- 4 tablespoons brown sugar
- 6 tablespoons bourbon
- ¼ cup chopped onion
- 2 tablespoons chili sauce
- 1 teaspoon cayenne pepper or to taste
- 2 tablespoons paprika
- 1 tablespoon chili powder
- ½ cup wine vinegar
- 4 cups tomato sauce
- 2 tablespoons dry mustard
- ½ teaspoon salt
- ½ cup molasses
- 1 cup favorite bottled barbeque sauce

- Combine all ingredients except ribs
- Simmer for 30 minutes to allow flavors to mingle
- Parboil ribs in 2 tablespoons Old Bay seasoning and 2 bay leaves for about 30 minutes
- Preheat oven to 325°
- Drain ribs
- Sprinkle ribs with salt and pepper
- Bake for 10 minutes
- Remove ribs and put ribs on aluminum foil
- Pour sauce over ribs and fold the foil closed
- Bake for 2 hours

If using a grill, oil grill first and preheat to 250-275° or medium low

- Place ribs on grill and cover with foil
- Turn every 20 minutes
- Baste with sauce twice during the last 20 minutes

Wine pairing: Zinfandel

SEABOURN BREADSTICKS
2011

While on our Seabourn cruise to the Baltics Chef Kurt Timmermans gave us a cooking demo making these wonderful breadsticks. They were served every night in the dining room. On our next Seabourn cruise I learned this is a Seabourn signature bread that all chefs on Seabourn cruises make for their guests.

- 3½ cups flour
- 1 package of yeast (3/4 ounce)
- 1 teaspoon salt
- 1 tablespoon sugar
- ¾ cup (14 tablespoons) unsalted butter softened
- ⅔ cup cold water
- 1 egg yolk with 1 tablespoon water beaten (to brush the breadsticks)
- Kosher salt

- Blend the butter, salt, yeast and flour in food processor
- Add the water and pulse
- Form the dough into a ball, flatten, wrap in plastic and refrigerate for several hours
- Take a small handful of dough and roll your pasta machine
- Using the fettuccini blade of the pasta machine, cut the dough into long strips
- On baking sheet arrange the individual "fettuccine" sticks in a straight line
- Make sure there is enough of a gap between each as they will puff up
- Brush with the egg wash
- Sprinkle with the salt
- Let sticks rise for 10-20 minutes in warm place
- Bake at 350° for about 10-12 minutes until crispy and golden brown

Makes: full recipe about 40 sticks

RECIPE FOR 10 STICKS:

- ¼ cup flour
- 1 tablespoon water
- 1¼ tablespoons butter softened
- ¼ teaspoon salt
- ½ teaspoon yeast
- ¼ teaspoon sugar
- 1 egg with 1 tablespoon water for egg wash

ALMOND MERINGUE
WITH MIXED BERRIES
2004

- ⅓ cup confectioners' sugar
- ⅓ to ½ cup sliced almonds, toasted and ground
- 4 large egg whites, room temperature
- ⅛ teaspoon cream of tartar
- ⅔ cup superfine granulated sugar
- ⅛ teaspoon almond extract
- 4 cups mixed berries
- 2 tablespoons sugar
- 1 tablespoon fresh lemon juice or orange liqueur
- ⅔ cup heavy cream
- 1 tablespoon confectioners' sugar
- ½-1 teaspoon vanilla or almond extract

- Toast almonds at 350° for 5 minutes; cool.
- Set oven to 300°.
- Make sure oven racks are in the center and the top third of oven.
- Grease a 10-inch pie pan.
- Put almonds and ⅓ cup confectioners' sugar in food processor and process until almonds are ground.
- Beat the egg whites and the cream of tartar until foamy.
- Add the almond extract then turn mixer on high.
- Begin adding sugar 1 tablespoon at a time until meringue is stiff and shiny.
- Fold almond mixture into meringue.
- Spread in pie pan.
- Bake in 300° oven for 20 minutes.
- Reduce oven to 250°.
- Bake until chewy about 30-40 minutes.
- Let cool in oven with the door ajar or on counter.
- Smash a few berries then mix with whole berries with sugar and lemon juice, cover and refrigerate for 1 hour or up to 8 hours.
- Whip the cream with the confectioners' sugar and extract in a chilled bowl with a chilled beater at high speed, refrigerate until ready to serve. Can be made up to one-day ahead, if it separates, whip it again.
- Spread the berries over the meringue and top with the whipped cream.
- Sprinkle with confectioners' sugar and serve.

Serves: 8

AUSTRALIAN PAVLOVA
WITH LEMON CURD AND BERRIES
2008

A puffy white meringue almost resembling a big marshmallow is referred to as the Pavlova.

MERINGUE FOR THE PAVLOVA:

1 cup superfine granulated sugar
1 tablespoon cornstarch
3 large egg whites room temperature
3 tablespoons cold water
1 teaspoon white vinegar

- Preheat the oven to 300°.
- Trace a 7-9 inch circle on a piece of parchment, then turn paper over and place on a cookie sheet.
- Whisk together sugar and cornstarch and set aside.
- In large mixing bowl beat egg whites with a pinch of salt until soft peaks form.
- Add water and continue beating until soft peaks form.
- On high speed beat in sugar mixture (1 tablespoon at a time) until all the sugar has been incorporated.
- Continue to beat an additional minute.
- Add vinegar and beat on HIGH for about 5 minutes. The meringue should be very glossy and has very stiff peaks.
- Spread meringue onto circle making sure the sides of the circle are higher than the middle in order to hold the lemon curd and berries.
- Bake in center of oven for about 45 minutes or until the meringue is lightly golden in color and has a crust.
- Turn the oven OFF, prop the door ajar, and cool in oven for an additional one hour.

This can be made ahead and frozen in plastic wrap. Thaw before using.

LEMON CURD FILLING:

1 jar prepared lemon curd
1 cup heavy cream chilled
4 cups blueberries or a combination of berries

- Chill beaters and bowl
- Beat heavy cream until it holds stiff peaks
- Fold in about ¼-½ cup of the whipped cream into the lemon curd
- Spoon curd filling into the Pavlova and top with berries
- Serve with an additional dollop of cream or pass cream

Serves: 6

CREAMY APPLE TART
Tartas de manzana individuales
2011

Our neighborhood has block parties that centers on food. I made this apple tart for our Spanish theme party. The tart is made deep-dish pie plate, but the recipe calls for four individual tart pans. This dessert is not very sweet.

3-4 Granny Smith apples	1 package (16-ounce) frozen puff pastry
2 tablespoons lemon juice	1 cup heavy cream
8 tablespoons sugar	1 egg
Cooking spray to coat pans	1 tablespoon cinnamon

- Remove puff pastry from freezer and set on platter to thaw while preparing apples.
- Preheat the oven to 300°.
- Prepare a pie plate with cooking spray or prepare four 5-inch round metal pans for individual tarts.
- Peel, core and slice the apples.
- Sprinkle the apples with lemon juice and toss.
- Unfold the pastry onto a lightly floured cutting board.
- Using pan to determine size cut a round to fit the bottom of pan, I just put the pastry into the pie plate and press it in place on bottom and sides.
- Cut narrow strips to line the sides of the pans, pressing into the sides.
- Prick the pastry with a fork.
- Place apple slices in a circle around the pan. Sprinkle 1 tablespoon sugar over the top of each individual tart or 4 tablespoons over a large tart.
- Place tarts on cookie sheet and place in oven on middle rack for 10 minutes or until apples are a bit browned.
- Remove from oven and place on counter.
- Turn oven up to 350°.
- Beat the egg, add the cream and 4 tablespoons sugar.
- Beat thoroughly.
- Pour the cream and egg mixture into each tart pan, covering the apples.
- Return to oven and bake for 45 minutes.
- If knife is inserted and comes out clean, it is done.

Serves: 4

JANICE'S
FRENCH APPLE TART
2009

This is one of my newer recipes handed down from my friend Janice. It is a no fail dessert that delights guests. She adapted this from Ina Garten. I altered the recipe using a different jelly.

PASTRY:

- 2 cups flour
- ½ teaspoon salt
- 1 tablespoon sugar
- 12 tablespoons (1½ sticks) cold unsalted butter, diced
- ½ cup iced water

APPLES:

- ½ cup sugar
- 4 Granny Smith apples
- ½ cup peach jelly or warm and sieved peach jam
- 2 tablespoons Calvados, rum or water: I use the Calvados and feel it makes the best tart

- Place flour and sugar in a food processor.
- Pulse for a few seconds, add butter and pulse 10-12 times or until the butter is in small bits about the size of peas.
- With the motor running, pour the water down the tube and pulse just until the dough starts to come together.
- Dump onto a floured board and knead quickly into a ball.
- Wrap in plastic and refrigerate for 1 hour.
- Preheat oven to 400°.
- Line a sheet pan with parchment paper.
- Roll the dough to slightly larger than 10x14 inches.
- Using a ruler and small knife, trim edges.
- Place dough on prepared sheet pan and refrigerate while you prepare the apples.
- Peel and core apples. Slice the apples crosswise into ¼ inch slices.
- Place overlapping slices of apples diagonally down the middle of the tart dough and continue making diagonal rows on both sides of the first row until the pastry is covered with apples.
- Sprinkle with the full ½ cup of sugar and dot with butter.
- Bake 45 minutes to 1 hour, until the pastry is browned and the edges of the apples start to brown.
- Rotate the pan once during cooking.
- If the pastry puffs up in one area, cut a little slit with a knife to let the air out.
- The apple juices will burn in the pan but the tart will be fine.
- When the tart is done, heat the jelly with the Calvados.
- Brush the apples and the pastry completely with the jelly mixture.
- Loosen the tart with a metal spatula so it does not stick to the paper.
- Allow to cool and transfer to a platter, serve warm or at room temperature.

JEAN'S
LEMON SOUFFLE
WITH RASPBERRY SAUCE
2012

My very dear friend, Jean Crouch, shared this recipe with me. In 2007 I had an idea to have several of our neighbors over for an Italian dinner. Jean offered to help me. She brought this delicious cake. No one can make this cake like Jean. It is a light dessert that complements any entrée.

- 2 packages soft lady fingers
- 2 cups powdered sugar
- 4½ tablespoon fresh lemon juice
- 4 teaspoons pure vanilla extract
- 16 ounces cream cheese
- 4 drops of yellow food coloring
- 1 pint heavy cream

- Line the bottom and sides of a spring form pan with ladyfingers
- In large bowl, blend cream cheese, lemon juice, vanilla, powdered sugar and food coloring
- In separate (chilled) bowl whip the cream until almost stiff
- Gently fold the whipped cream into the cheese mixture until well incorporated, but still a bit fluffy
- Spoon into the spring form pan and refrigerate until time to serve

RASPBERRY SAUCE:

- 4 cups frozen raspberries, strawberries or blueberries (you can use fresh berries)
- 2 teaspoons cornstarch thinned with cold water
- 3 teaspoons Grand Marnier

- Dissolve the cornstarch in the cold water and add to the berries
- Bring to a boil and allow to cool
- When thickened, stir in the Grand Marnier
- Place sauce over each individual serving

TIP: you can add a drop or two of red food coloring to the strawberries or raspberries for richer color.

Serves: 12

NEW YORK STYLE CHEESECAKE
2010

CRUST

2 cups graham cracker crumbs
¼ cup sugar
½ cup melted unsalted butter

FILLING

32 ounces cream cheese, room temperature
1 cup sugar
3 tablespoons flour
5 large eggs, room temperature
⅓ cup heavy whipping cream
1 tablespoon lemon zest
1 teaspoon pure vanilla extract

TOPPING

1 cup sour cream
2 tablespoons sugar
½ teaspoon vanilla

- Spray a 9-inch spring form pan with PAM
- Place the spring form pan on a baking sheet to catch any leakage
- Preheat oven to 350°
- Combine crumbs, sugar and melted butter
- Press crumbs evenly over the bottom and about 1-inch up sides of pan
- Refrigerate while you make the filling
- Using a good electric mixer, place the cream cheese, sugar and flour in bowl
- Beat mixture on medium speed for about 2 minutes, scraping down sides as needed
- Add the eggs, one at a time, beating well for about 30 seconds after each egg
- Scrape down sides of the bowl
- Add whipping cream, lemon zest and vanilla; beat well
- Pour into prepared crust
- Bake for 15 minutes at 350°

- Reduce the oven to 250° and bake for another 60-90 minutes or until firm and only the center of the cheesecake looks a little wet and wobbly
- Remove from oven and place on a wire rack
- In a small bowl, combine the sour cream, sugar and vanilla
- Spread the sour cream topping over the warm cake and return to oven for 15 minutes
- Remove from oven and carefully run a knife or spatula around the inside edge of pan to loosen the cake and prevent the surface from cracking
- Let cool completely before covering with plastic wrap
- Refrigerate several hours, preferably overnight
- Serve with fresh fruit sauces (see Sauce section)

Serve: 10-12

This cake can be frozen. Place cooled cake on a baking pan and freeze uncovered until firm. Then wrap in aluminum foil and place in freezer bag. Seal and freeze for several months. Thaw uncovered cake in the refrigerator overnight.

2014 Cumming, Georgia

FLORIDA KEY LIME PIE
2000

Florida is known for Key Lime Pie. Having lived in Florida over 10 years, I have sampled many recipes but this one is the best.

CRUST:

1 cup plus 2½ tablespoon graham cracker crumbs
5 tablespoons melted unsalted butter
⅓ cup sugar
½ cup ground pecans (optional)

- Preheat oven to 350°
- Butter a 9-inch pie pan
- Place in food processor and process to crumbs
- Add butter and sugar (pecans optional) and pulse until combined
- Press mixture into pie pan forming a neat border around the edge; I use a measuring cup to help spread and form the crust
- Bake until set and golden about 8 minutes; set aside

FILLING:

3 egg yolks
2 limes, zested with grater (about 1½ teaspoons of zest)
⅔ cup freshly squeezed lime juice (tiny Key limes have the best flavor) otherwise use regular limes
1 (14-ounce) can sweetened condensed milk

- In an electric mixer beat egg yolks and lime zest at high speed for about 5 minutes until very fluffy
- Gradually add the condensed milk and continue to beat until thick, 3-4 more minutes
- Lower the speed and slowly add the lime juice, mixing just until combined, no longer
- Pour mixture into the pie crust
- Bake for 10 minutes or until the filling has set (make sure pie is very cold before serving)

TOPPING:

1 cup heavy whipping cream chilled
3 tablespoons confectioners' sugar

- Whip the cream and sugar until stiff, spread over top of pie
- Garnish with extra zest and lime slices
- You can also make a meringue with 2 egg whites, 4 tablespoons sugar,
- Spread over pie
- Bake 20 minutes at 350° or until brown

GRILLING WITH STEVE

My husband's favorite time is when he is cooking on his grill. Over the years we have compiled some of his favorite recipes to share with you.

INTERNAL GRILLING TEMPERATURES

Steve always uses a cooking thermometer to judge the doneness of his meats and seafood's. He struggled with this for years until we developed this temperature map.

Temperatures are based on immediate removal from the grill area. Allow meats to sit for 5-10 minutes tented in foil before slicing or serving. This allows the meat to hold its juices.

Always preheat grill 10 minutes before cooking.

PORK TENDERLOIN:

- First brown over medium temperature turning often. Then grill until 140°. Transfer to cutting board TENT IN FOIL and rest or 10 minutes.

ALTERNATE METHOD:

- Brown the meat on the grill, then put into a foil pan with a cup of water, beer or wine
- Cook another 20 minutes or until temperature is 140°
- Take out of pan and let rest for 10 minutes tented in foil

PORK CHOPS: center cut bone in:

- Preheat grill to high, grill until slightly charred (4-6 minutes), turn over and reduce heat to medium.
- Grill until just cooked through (6-7) more minutes internal temperature: 140° medium rare, 150° well done.
- Insert thermometer on side of chop and push to center for best results

BEEF STEAKS:

- Brown first then grill till temperature of choice
    - Rare: 120-125°
    - Medium Rare: 130°
    - Medium: 140°
    - Medium Well: 150°
    - Well Done: 150-155°
- Transfer to cutting board
- Place alum foil over meat, let rest 10 minutes

BEEF HAMBURGERS: Grill to internal temperature of 165°

LEG OF LAMB: (bone in or boneless)

- Grill to 140°
- Remove from grill and rest 10 minutes

RACK OF LAMB:

- Grill to internal temperature of 125-130°
- Take off grill and rest covered in wrap for 10 minutes

LAMB CHOPS:

- Grill on high until lightly charred and crusty (3 minutes), turn over
- Reduce heat to medium, and grill just until cooked (2-3 minutes)
- Internal temp: 125° for rare, 125-130° for medium rare, 140° for medium and 150° for well done

TURKEY: 165° internal temperature of breast

FISH: Brush grill with oil before grilling

- Salmon: 125° on med/hi heat
- Tuna: 115° or below for rare
- Halibut: 130°

BONELESS CHICKEN BREAST:

- Brush grill with oil before, preheat grill 10 minutes or until at a medium high temperature
- Pound chicken breasts for even cooking
- Grill on medium heat 8-10 minutes per side to 160°
- Wrap in foil, rest 5-10 minutes

CHICKEN THIGHS AND DRUMSTICKS:

- Grill to temperature of 170° (8-12 minutes per side)

WHOLE CHICKEN:

- Put chicken on a stand with base to collect juices
- Cook until internal temperature reaches 160-165°
- Cover with foil and rest 10-15 minutes before slicing

CORNISH HENS: Grill to an internal temperature of 165°

BEER AND HONEY-HERB
GRILLED PORK
1990

- 3 pounds boneless pork tenderloin or pork loin roast
- 1 cup beer
- ½ cup honey
- ½ cup Dijon mustard
- ¼ cup oil
- 2 tablespoons onion powder
- 1½ teaspoons crushed rosemary
- 1 teaspoon salt
- 1 teaspoon garlic minced
- ¼ teaspoon pepper

- Place pork in plastic bag with ¾ of the marinade
- Marinate 1 hour
- Roast or grill to internal temperature of 140-145
- Serve with remaining marinade as a sauce

Yield: 8-10

GRILLED LAMB CHOPS
OR RACK OF LAMB
1990

Salt and freshly ground pepper
Garlic clove minced
Fresh rosemary, minced
Fresh lemon juice
Olive oil
Lamb chops or Rack of Lamb Frenched

- In a bowl whisk together all ingredients
- Marinate lamb a few hours before grilling
- Allow to stand for one hour at room temperature
- Grill to desired doneness (see internal temperature map)
- Cover with foil and let rest for 10 minutes before serving

GRILLED PORK CHOPS
WITH NECTARINE RELISH

Among his library of cookbooks, Bobby Flay is his favorite grill chef. We adapted this recipe from Bobby Flay. We have found peaches to work as well as nectarines.

- ⅓ cup pine nuts
- Four (6-ounce) center-cut bone-in or boneless pork chops about 1 inch thick
- Olive oil for brushing
- Salt and freshly ground pepper
- 4 firm nectarines or firm fresh peaches, halved and pitted
- 2 tablespoons balsamic vinegar
- 1 tablespoon honey
- ½ small red onion, thinly sliced
- 1 tablespoon shredded basil

- Light and preheat the grill
- In a skillet toast the pine nuts over high heat, stirring, until golden, about 4 minutes
- Transfer to bowl
- Brush the chops with olive oil, salt and pepper
- Grill the chops over HIGH HEAT, turning once, until cooked through 10-11 minutes or until the internal temperature is 140°
- Transfer to plate and let rest for 5 minutes
- Meanwhile, brush the nectarines with olive oil and grill cut side down until browned, about 3 minutes
- Turn and grill until charred and softened, about 2 minutes longer, cut into ½-inch pieces
- Put the nectarines in a bowl and stir in the vinegar and honey
- Add the onion, basil and pine nuts and season with salt and pepper
- Serve the pork chops topped with the relish

Serves: 4
Wine pairing: A fruity, flamboyant Australian red like Shiraz or Pinot Noir

GRILLED ARTICHOKES
WITH PARSLEY AND GARLIC
2008

- 6 fresh artichokes
- 2 lemons halved, plus ⅓ cup freshly squeezed lemon juice
- 3 tablespoons freshly chopped flat-leaf parsley
- 1 teaspoon minced garlic
- Salt and freshly ground pepper
- ½ cup extra-virgin olive oil

- Bring a large pot of salted water to a boil
- Trim the stem from each artichoke to 1-inch long
- Bend back and snap off the dark outer leaves
- Cut top inch of artichoke with serrated knife
- Using a vegetable peeler, peel dark green areas from stem and base of artichoke
- Quarter each artichoke
- Using a small sharp knife, remove the purple, prickly tipped leaves from the center of each wedge
- Place each finished artichoke in large bowl of cold water and squeeze 2 lemons into the water and stir
- Preheat grill to med-high heat
- Drain the artichokes and place into boiling water and cook until crisp-tender...about 12 minutes
- Drain the cooked chokes and place onto grill
- Cook until tender and lightly charred in spots, turning occasionally, about 10 minutes
- Meanwhile in a bowl, add remaining lemon juice (⅓ cup), parsley, garlic, salt and pepper to taste
- Gradually drizzle in the olive oil
- Toss or drizzle the grilled artichokes with the garlic/parsley/oil mixture and serve
- Excellent with grilled boneless chicken breasts

Yield: 6 servings

GRILLED CORN IN HUSKS

- Remove silk from corn
- Dip unhusked corn into ice water and let stand for 15 minutes
- Place corn on grill and cook until husks are blacken, about 10-20 minutes
- Turn frequently to cook evenly
- Using gloves, remove husks with quick, pulling motion
- Serve immediately with butter, salt and pepper

GRILLED SALMON
2013

1½ pounds salmon
Lemon pepper
Garlic minced
Salt to taste
⅓ cup soy sauce
⅓ cup brown sugar
⅓ cup water
¼ cup vegetable oil
Fresh ginger grated

- Season the filets with the lemon pepper and salt
- In small skillet sauté ginger and garlic
- In small bowl mix together remaining ingredients along with the garlic and ginger
- Place in bag and marinate for at least 2 hours
- Preheat grill
- Oil grill grate
- Grill salmon and discard the marinade
- Cook salmon for 6-8 minutes per side (125° internal temperature) or until fish flakes with a fork

Serves: 4 six-ounce portions

RED SNAPPER
ON CEDAR PLANK
2001

We also have used salmon. This recipe is adapted from Emeril Lagasse. We have changed some of his ingredients to suit our taste.

    Zest of 2 lemons
    Zest of 2 limes
2 slices of bacon, chopped fine
1¼ cups dried breadcrumbs
1 tablespoon olive oil
    Salt, pepper, Italian seasoning or Emeril original seasoning
4 red snapper filets-skin off

- Drizzle fish with oil
- Blanch zest in boiling salted water for a minute
- Render the bacon till crispy
- Put into a bowl with the zest and 1 tablespoon olive oil plus the seasonings
- Season the fish with seasoning
- Rub the plank with oil
- Place fish on planks
- Sprinkle the crust mix over the filets—place planks on grill
- Cook until crust is golden and fish is flaky (18 minutes)
- Drizzle with lemon butter sauce

LEMON BUTTER SAUCE:

¼ cup white wine
    Juice of two lemons
8 peppercorns
½ teaspoon chopped fresh thyme

¼ cup heavy cream
8 ounces cold butter cubed
    Salt and pepper

- In saucepan put wine, juice, peppercorns, bay leaf and thyme.
- Bring to boil and reduce to half
- Add cream and boil, reduce to half again
- Whisk in the butter one cube at a time, season with salt and pepper
- Strain sauce through fine sieve—keep warm

Serves: 8

APRICOT-LEMON
GRILLED CHICKEN
2006

6-8 boneless chicken breasts
1 envelope French onion soup mix
1 (10-ounce) jar apricot preserves
2 lemons, sliced and seeds removed

- Prick breasts with tines of fork and place in a large baggie
- Combine soup mix, preserves and lemon slices
- Pour over chicken breasts, cover and chill overnight
- Prepare grill (if using a gas grill always preheat for 10 minutes)
- Grill breasts over grill for 12-15 minutes for average size breasts and 15-20 minutes for larger breasts or internal temperature of 160°
- Baste periodically with additional apricot mixture

Serves: 6-8

HERB AND HONEY
BBQ CHICKEN
2005

Chicken parts for grilling (thighs & legs)
¼ cup finely chopped onion
1 clove minced garlic
¼ cup canola oil
12 ounces pear nectar
½ cup white wine vinegar
¼ cup honey
2 tablespoons Worcestershire sauce
1 teaspoon prepared horseradish
1 teaspoon dry mustard
1 teaspoon salt
½ teaspoon dried thyme leaves
¼ teaspoon dried rosemary leaves
¼ teaspoons ground black fresh pepper

Rub or use mortar and pestle with all dried herbs to bring out their natural flavor and zest

- Cook onion and garlic in hot oil until tender but not brown
- Add remaining ingredients; simmer uncovered for 5 minutes
- Use for marinating and basting poultry or shrimp
- Preheat grill
- Cook chicken to desired doneness (internal temperature 160°)
- Let stand 5-10 minutes before serving
- Steve uses this marinade for his favorite chicken on the grill

BABY BACK RIBS
RESTAURANT STYLE
2008

One full rack of Pork Baby-back ribs
Heavy Duty aluminum foil
Clear plastic wrap
Rib/Pork rub
BBQ sauce of your choice

- Thoroughly rinse and pat dry the ribs
- Remove the membrane of the back of the ribs (this is the most important step or the rub will not penetrate the ribs)
- Rub the ribs thoroughly with the rub
- Wrap the ribs in a high quality clear plastic wrap
- Wrap the ribs again in heavy-duty aluminum foil, completely sealing in the ribs
- Place the ribs in the refrigerator and allow to marinate overnight
- Preheat oven to 300°
- Take the ribs from the refrigerator and place on a cookie sheet, place on top rack of oven
- Cook for 2½ hours
- Remove from oven and let rest 15 minutes to absorb flavors
- Remove the wraps slowly, be aware of steam
- Place the ribs on the grill over high heat, let cook for 3 minutes, then turn the ribs over and cook for 3 more minutes
- Thoroughly brush the ribs with BBQ sauce and flip the ribs
- Coat the other side with sauce and cook 3 minutes
- Repeat this process twice
- Coat the top side one more time with sauce
- ENJOY

STEVE'S MARINATED AND GRILLED
LONDON BROIL

1967

1 (2½ -pound) London Broil

MARINADE:

- ½ cup Burgundy wine
- 1 teaspoon Worcestershire sauce
- 1 clove garlic, minced
- ½ cup canola oil
- 1 teaspoon sugar
- ½ teaspoon salt
- 1 tablespoon vinegar
- ½ teaspoon marjoram
- ½ teaspoon rosemary
- 2 tablespoons ketchup or tomato paste

- Thoroughly mix all the marinade ingredients together
- Place the London Broil in a large plastic bag
- Pour the marinade into the bag with the steak, seal and place inside a large baking dish to prevent possible spills
- Marinate in refrigerator for 24 hours or at least 6 hours
- Preheat gas grill to high heat
- Remove the steak from the marinade and pat dry with paper towels
- Place the steak on grill and cook to desired doneness, about 6 minutes per side for rare
    - Using a meat thermometer, Rare: 120° Medium rare: 130°
- Transfer the steak to a cutting board and let stand for 5-10 minutes
- Slice across the grain into thin diagonal slices
- Serve with or without the horseradish sauce

STEVE'S HORSERADISH SAUCE:

- 2 cups sour cream
- ¼ cup horseradish
- 1 teaspoon white vinegar
- 1 teaspoon salt
- Dash hot pepper sauce

Yield: 4 servings Use 4 pound London broil for 6 people

SAVORY STUFFED TENDERLOIN

1999

This is definitely an impressive dish. The tenderloin is stuffed with a spinach and fennel filling for enhanced juiciness and texture. Serves: 6-8

2½ pounds center-cut beef tenderloin section, with a pocket (see Technique Tip)

FENNEL RUB

- 2-3 garlic cloves
- 1½ teaspoons fennel seed
- 1½ teaspoons kosher salt
- 1 teaspoon whole black peppercorns
- ½ teaspoon crushed dried red chile flakes

- Cut a pocket in the meat. See Technique Tip below
- Prepare the rub 2½ hours or up to 12 hours before you plan to grill the meat
- With a mortar and pestle or small food processor, combine the rub ingredients and puree the mixture (it will be grainy in texture)
- Coat the tenderloin thoroughly with the rub, massaging it inside and out
- Wrap the meat in plastic and refrigerate

SPINACH-FENNEL FILLING

- 1 tablespoon olive oil
- 1 small fennel bulb, cut into thin matchsticks
- 3 tablespoons minced red bell pepper
- 3 tablespoons minced onion
- ¼ pound fresh spinach, chopped

- Warm the oil in a skillet over medium heat
- Add the fennel, pepper and onion; cook until softened (5-7 minutes)
- Stir in the spinach, cover and reduce heat
- Cook for 5 more minutes or until the vegetables are very tender and liquid evaporates
- The mixture should be moist but not wet
- Set aside to cool

ASSEMBLY

- Stuff the tenderloin with the spinach filling 30 minutes before grilling
- Preheat the grill to HIGH heat
- Grill the tenderloin with grill lid up over the HIGH heat for 4-5 minutes; rolling the meat frequently to sear
- Reduce the heat to medium and continue grilling for 9-11 more minutes for medium-rare doneness; continue rolling the meat to cook all sides all sides

- If you wish to cook with the cover down: Sear the meat on HIGH for 4-5 minutes; and finish cooking with the cover down on MED HEAT for 7-10 minutes, turning the tenderloin once midway
- Serve the tenderloin hot, sliced into thick medallions

TECHNIQUE TIP:

For this recipe you want a pocket sliced in the tenderloin, as opposed to a butterfly cut. You want a relatively small slit (about 2 inches) on the cavity for the stuffing. With a sharp knife, make a small horizontal cut in the center of one of the long sides. Slice deeply into but not through the meat. Turn the knifepoint toward one of the ends and carefully work the blade toward it, avoiding going all the way through. Repeat the cut in the *other direction*

BEEF SHISH KABOBS

Beef cubes, use tenderloin chunks or top sirloin
Fresh green peppers (blanched) cut into 1-inch pieces
Cherry tomatoes
Onion, blanched and cut into pieces
Fresh mushrooms

Sometimes he skewers the meat and vegetables separately on individual skewers for more even cooking.

BUTTERFLIED CHICKEN
GRILLED WITH A BRICK
2011

This grilling method creates a very crispy and moist chicken.

2 (3-pound) chickens, butterflied
2 teaspoons coarsely ground black pepper
Olive oil
Salt
Freshly ground pepper
Your favorite chicken seasoning
OR
A combination of fresh rosemary, thyme, oregano, garlic, and oil smashed in a mortar and pestle to make a rubbing paste
2 large bricks covered with foil or a large heavy cast iron skillet
Lemon wedges for garnish

- Remove the backbone of the chicken and flatten the breast so that the chicken lies flat and cooks evenly on the grill. Your butcher can do this for you
- Rub the entire chickens, inside and out with oil, then sprinkle with your favorite chicken seasoning or rub with your herb oil paste
- Wrap chickens in plastic wrap and refrigerate 4 hours or overnight
- Let stand to room temperature
- Heat your grill to medium-high
- Remove the chickens from refrigerator and sprinkle with salt and pepper
- Place skin side down on grill with brick on top of chickens
- Grill until the skin forms a crust and pulls away from the grate, 15 minutes
- Turn the chickens over, put brick on chickens, close the grill hood and cook for another 15 minutes or until juices run clear
- Remove the chickens to a cutting board and let rest for 10 minutes
- Transfer to a platter or serving plates, garnish with lemon wedges
- Serve immediately

Serves: 4

THANKSGIVING MENU

Thanksgiving is always the same menu. I tried many recipes and always come back to this menu with my tried and true recipes.   Generally I make regular mashed potatoes, but my recipes for special mashed potato casseroles also work well.

Spinach balls

Butternut Squash Soup

Roasted Turkey

Turkey Stuffing

Turkey Gravy

Mashed Potatoes

Recipes for special mashed potatoes

Golden Crumb Broccoli Casserole

Traditional Green Bean Casserole

Candied Yams

Variations of Yam Casseroles

Cranberry sauces

Cranberry Jell-O Mold

Not so Sweet Pecan Pie

Pumpkin Pie

Apple Pie

Whipped Cream

ROASTED TURKEY

I stuffed my turkey for many years but discovered roasting an unstuffed turkey creates a juicier turkey.

18 - pound turkey cleaned
Fresh herbs (thyme, parsley, rosemary)
¼ stick of butter

Cooking spray
Aluminum foil
Cooking twine to tie legs

- Preheat oven to 500°
- Clean turkey thoroughly and wipe inside and outside with paper towels
- Put giblets, neck and heart of turkey in saucepan filled with water to make your stock for gravy
- Tuck wings under bottom of turkey
- Loosely stuff the cavity of the turkey with an assortment of fresh herbs, celery and onion
- Secure the legs with twine
- Shape a piece of aluminum foil for a breast tent making sure you spray the underside of the foil with cooking spray
- Rub the entire bird with ¼ stick of butter (I use disposable gloves for this)
- Put turkey into hot oven
- Roast for 30 minutes
- Remove the turkey from the oven and place the prepared aluminum foil over the breast
- Set the thermometer for 161° and place the probe directly through the foil into the deepest part of the breast
- Reduce the oven to 350°
- Keep door closed during the duration of the roasting process
- An 18-pound turkey will need about 2 to 2½ hours more
- When the breast reaches 161°, and the thigh reaches 180°, remove the turkey from the oven and place on platter
- Cover the turkey with foil and let it rest for at least 30 minutes
- Carve and enjoy!

MASHED SWEET POTATO CASSEROLES
1975

CASSEROLE #1 (ROCKY MOUNT, NC)

- 2-3 cups sweet potatoes, cooked and mashed with mixer
- 1 cup sugar, granulated
- ½ stick melted butter
- 2 eggs beaten
- ¼ teaspoon salt
- 1 teaspoon vanilla
- ¼ teaspoon nutmeg
- ¼ teaspoon cinnamon
- 1 cup milk

TOPPING:

- ¾ cup brown sugar
- Butter
- Chopped pecans

- Preheat oven to 350°
- Grease a 13x9 casserole dish
- Mix ingredients until smooth and well blended
- Pour into casserole dish and top with brown sugar dotted with butter and chopped pecans
- **OR** omit the butter, sugar and pecan topping and place marshmallows on top the last 5 minutes of cooking
- Bake for 30 minutes

CASSEROLE #2

- 6 pounds yams
- ¾ cup firmly packed brown sugar
- ½ cup heavy cream
- 6 tablespoons butter at room temperature
- 1 teaspoon cinnamon
- ½ teaspoon ground allspice
- ½ teaspoon ground nutmeg

1 tablespoon vanilla
Salt to taste
½ cup chopped pecans
Miniature marshmallows

- Preheat oven to 325°
- Grease a 13x9 baking dish
- Cook and mash the yams; add sugar, cream butter, vanilla and spices
- Beat until smooth about 2 minutes
- Season to taste with salt
- Spoon into baking dish, smoothing the top
- Sprinkle pecans and marshmallows evenly over the top
- Bake until heated through, about 30 minutes

CASSEROLE # 3 SARASOTA, FL

2½ pounds sweet potatoes, peeled and cut into 1-inch cubes
¾ cup packed brown sugar
¼ cup softened butter
1½ teaspoons salt
½ teaspoon vanilla
½ cup finely chopped pecans, divided
Cooking spray
2 cups miniature marshmallows

- Preheat oven to 375°
- Spray a 13x9 casserole dish with cooking spray
- Place the sweet potatoes in large saucepan, cover with cold water and bring to a boil
- Reduce heat and simmer for 15 minutes or till tender
- Drain, cool slightly
- Place potatoes in large bowl, add sugar and next 3 ingredients through the vanilla
- Mash the potatoes, fold in ¼ cup pecans
- Spread potato mixture into prepared baking dish coated with cooking spray
- Sprinkle with remaining ¼ cup pecans
- Top with marshmallows
- Bake for 25 minutes or until golden brown

Each version serves 8-12

CHRISTMAS MENU

Christmas starts at our house in November with the baking of Christmas cookies and the preparing of Polish Pierogi. It is a wonderful time of year. Our children and grandchildren continue to enjoy this menu. Years past our Christmases dinners centered on Cornish Hens. When our daughters became adults they preferred Rib Roast.

CHRISTMAS EVE

Lobster Bisque

Seafood Ramekins

Spaghetti All 'olio E Aglio

Polish Pierogi

Grandma's Chocolate Italian Cookies

Grandma's Cherry Cookies

Grandma's Rosette Cookies

Mexican Wedding Cookies

Brown Sugar Pound Cake

Rum Balls

Mocha Truffles

CHRISTMAS MORNING

Mock Soufflé Egg Casserole

English Muffins

Apricot Daisy Coffeecake

Fresh Assorted Fruits

Coffee and Juice

CHRISTMAS DINNER

Mary's Liver Pate

Rock Cornish Hens

Prime Rib Roast with Au Jus

Grilled Asparagus or Broccoli Casserole

Rice Mingle

Chocolate Mousse Pie

SAUCES

Sauces augment foods. Their intense flavors bring all the components of a dish together into one delicious unity. I decided to include a few of the sauces I mentioned throughout this book and some additional basic sauces

BEURRE BLANC–BUTTER SAUCE

1 tablespoon chopped shallots
3 tablespoons white wine
2 tablespoons white wine vinegar
3 tablespoons heavy cream
6½ tablespoons cold unsalted butter cut into tiny pieces
Salt and pepper to taste
Cayenne pepper (optional)

- Put the shallots, white wine and vinegar into a saucepan
- Bring to boil and reduce to a syrupy consistency
- Add the cream, bring back to boil and whisk in the butter a few pieces at a time
- Season to taste
- Pass through a fine chinois or fine mesh sieve
- Keep at a warm temperature

DEMI GLACE FOR STEAKS

¼ pound mushrooms
¼ cup sherry
2 cups brown sauce
1 tablespoon beef extract

- Combine mushrooms and sherry in a saucepan
- Cook until sherry is reduced by half
- Add brown sauce and beef extract (I use Better than Bouillon stock paste)
- Bring to boil, reduce heat and cook for 15-20 minutes

BERNAISE SAUCE

BASIC FRENCH SAUCE

- ¼ cup tarragon vinegar
- ¼ cup dry white wine
- 2 tablespoons shallots, minced
- 1 crushed peppercorn
- 2 tablespoons fresh tarragon chopped
- 3 egg yolks
- 1 teaspoon salt

- In saucepan, combine tarragon vinegar, dry white wine, minced shallots, crushed peppercorn, and fresh tarragon.
- Boil, then simmer to reduce down to about 2-3 tablespoons (5 minutes), strain by pushing down the contents and cool.
- Melt 2 sticks unsalted butter, keep hot.
- In blender jar place 3 egg yolks, the reduced liquid and 1 teaspoon salt. Blend for a few seconds.
- With blender on, slowly pour the hot butter through the lid until smooth.
- Add 2 tablespoons tarragon and blend for a second or two.
- Add white wine or water if too thick.
- Keep in a water bath until ready to use or serve immediately.

If I am having a dinner party, I make my sauce and place in a small bowl and keep it warm in a water bath in my slow cooker on LOW.

LEMON BUTTER

- Melt ¼ cup butter
- Add 1-2 tablespoons lemon juice
- 2 tablespoons snipped parsley
- ½ teaspoon salt and dash of pepper

- Melt butter
- Add remaining ingredients
- Heat and serve over asparagus, broccoli or fish
- Add some fresh or dried herbs as a topper for grilled steaks or hot vegetables

QUICK BROWN SAUCE

1½ tablespoons butter
1½ tablespoons flour
2 cups rich brown stock or 1 can condensed beef broth plus water to make 2 cups

- For a more gourmet brown sauce, reduce the sauce to half by boiling and add ⅓ cup sherry
- Bring to a boil, remove from heat
- Serve hot with roast beef or veal, baked ham or chicken

BASIC BROWN SAUCE (Española)
Basic French Sauce

1 small carrot, coarsely chopped
1 medium onion, coarsely chopped
¼ cup unsalted butter
¼ cup flour
4 cups hot beef stock
¼ cup tomato puree
1 piece of celery coarsely chopped
2 large coarsely chopped garlic
½ teaspoon whole black peppercorns
1 bay leaf

- Cook carrot and onion in butter, add flour and cook this roux until brown
- Add hot stock whisking constantly to prevent lumps
- Add tomato puree, garlic, celery, peppercorns, and bay leaf
- Bring to boil, reduce to simmer and cook uncovered for 45 minutes
- Pass through mesh sieve

Yield: 4 cups

BROWN SAUCE
FOR STEAK OR CHATEAUBRIAND

This is an impressive sauce to serve over your favorite grilled steak or tenderloin. We serve it with Steve's Savory Stuffed Tenderloin. You can purchase demi glace in your grocery store.

- 8 ounces cremini or white mushrooms, cleaned and sliced
- 2 tablespoons canola or grape seed oil
- 2 teaspoons minced garlic
- ½ cup rich beef broth
- ½ cup red wine
- ¼ cup demi-glace
- 2 tablespoons butter
- Freshly ground pepper
- Touch of Cognac

- Sauté the mushrooms in the oil until soft
- Add garlic and sauté
- Add beef broth, wine and demi-glace
- Simmer the sauce until it is reduced by half (5-7 minutes)
- Add the butter and stir
- Add Cognac and pepper
- Serve over or under your steak

FONDUE SAUCES
Located under Fondue recipe

BASIC PAN SAUCE

The Basic pan sauce is created from the tidbits left at the bottom of a sauté pan after meat has been browned.

This sauce consists of only 4 ingredients:

1. **Fragrant ingredient:** shallots, garlic, onion, mushrooms, fresh ginger (about 1 tablespoon) less for garlic and ginger or other strong ingredients
2. **Liquid with a strong flavor:** wine, brandy, port, lemon juice, fruit juices or vinegars (about ¼ cup)
   Basic liquid: reduced-sodium broth or stock, fruit juices or cider (about ¾ cup)
3. **Flavor accents:** fresh herbs, capers, black olives, fresh fruit, Dijon mustard, soy sauce, or green peppercorns (about 1 teaspoon to 1 tablespoon depending on the strength of the flavor)
4. **Enrichment:** unsalted butter or cream or crème fraiche (about 1-4 tablespoons cream or 1-2 tablespoons butter)

METHOD:

- After browning meat in half oil and half butter, (dusting the meat with flour before browning will give the sauce a thicker consistency), set the meat aside and allow it to drain off juices that you will add to your basic liquid
- Pour off fat from the pan using a fat separator
- Add your **fragrant** ingredient (shallots, garlic, onion, mushrooms or fresh ginger) to the browned bits at the bottom of the pan, cook and stir for about 30 seconds
- Add your first **liquid**, (wine, brandy, port or vinegar)
- Reduce this liquid down to a spoonful or so
- Next add your basic **liquid** (meat stock, fruit juices) using the broth and the drained off juices from the meat
- Cook and reduce to ⅔ thirds of its original volume
- Add a **flavor accent** (herbs, capers, olives, fresh fruit, mustard, soy sauce)
- Add an **enrichment** (butter or cream)
- At this point you can strain the sauce or not
- Taste and adjust seasonings to suit your taste

MINT SAUCE

½ cup vinegar
¼ cup sugar
¼ cup water

Dash salt
Mint leaves finely chopped

- Boil, reduce heat, simmer uncovered for 5 minutes
- Pour immediately over ½ cup finely snipped mint leaves
- Let steep for 30 minutes
- Strain –can be used hot or cold

PERGUEUX SAUCE

1½ cups beef consommé or rich beef stock
1 tablespoon arrowroot
⅓ cup madeira wine
1¼ tablespoons butter

- Heat consommé or stock and the butter
- Add arrowroot mixed with wine
- Cook until thickened

CLASSIC MAYONNAISE

2 egg yolks
2 teaspoons white wine vinegar
¼ teaspoon Dijon mustard

Salt
1 -1¼ cups olive oil or canola oil
1 tablespoon fresh lemon juice

- Put yolks, vinegar, mustard and about ½ teaspoon salt in food processor
- Pulse until blended, scrape down sides
- With motor running add the oil in a very slow steady stream, stopping to scrap sides if necessary
- Whirl in the lemon juice a few drops of water, if sauce looks too thick
- Refrigerate up to

REMOULADE SAUCE

1¼ cups Mayonnaise
2 tablespoons grain mustard
2 tablespoons ketchup
1 tablespoon lemon juice
1 tablespoon Worcestershire sauce
¼ cup very finely chopped scallions
¼ cup very finely chopped celery
1 tablespoon chopped parsley
2 very finely minced garlic
2 teaspoons horseradish
1 teaspoon hot sauce

- Mix all together and chill. Goes well with crab cakes

HOMEMADE MUSHROOM SAUCE

3 tablespoons butter
½ pound mushrooms sliced
1 tablespoon flour
1 teaspoon soy sauce
¾ cup light cream

- Melt butter
- Add mushrooms, sprinkle with flour, toss
- Cook over medium heat, stirring occasionally 8-10 minutes
- Add soy sauce
- Slowly stir in cream
- Cook and stir until mixture bubbles and thickens
- Season to taste
- Serve with steak or on toast

CUMBERLAND SAUCE

½ cup currant jelly
2 tablespoons port wine
3 tablespoons lemon juice
¼ cup raisins
1 teaspoon dry mustard
1 teaspoon paprika
½ teaspoon ginger
3 tablespoons thinly slivered orange rind or grated rind

- Combine all ingredients in saucepan
- Cook down to make a sauce
- Use sauce with pork or combine ingredients and use to baste a pork roast one hour before it is done for a beautiful glaze

PAPRIKA SAUCE

2 shallots, chopped
1 clove garlic, minced
4 tablespoons butter
3 tablespoons flour
1 teaspoon paprika
2 cups chicken stock
⅓ cup dry white wine
2 tablespoons sour cream
1 teaspoon lemon juice

- Melt butter
- Sauté shallots and garlic (5 min), stir in flour and paprika to make a roux
- Cook a minute blending with whisk
- Add stock and wine stirring constantly
- Cook until thick, add sour cream and lemon juice

RAISIN SAUCE
1971

Great with ham.

¾ cup seedless raisins
4 whole cloves
¼ cup packed brown sugar
1 teaspoon cornstarch
1 teaspoon cider vinegar
1 tablespoon butter
Dash pepper

- Put raisins and cloves into a saucepan
- Cover with water
- Simmer until soft
- Remove cloves
- Mix sugar and cornstarch with the vinegar to form a paste
- Stir into raisin mixture
- Simmer 5 minutes
- Add butter and pepper, serve hot

Makes 1¼ cup

HOLLANDAISE SAUCE
Basic French Sauce

BLENDER METHOD:

3 egg yolks, room temperature
¼ teaspoon salt
Pinch of pepper or cayenne

2 tablespoons fresh lemon juice
½ cup unsalted butter

- Place the yolks, salt, pepper and 1 tablespoon juice in bottom of blender jar
- Cut the butter into pieces in small pan
- Heat butter until hot and foamy, remove foam from top
- Cover the blender jar and blend the yolk mixture for 2-3 seconds
- Uncover, while still blending immediately start pouring the hot melted butter in very thin stream s of droplets making sure to leave the bottom residue in the pan
- Taste the sauce and blend in more seasonings and juice to taste

STOVETOP METHOD:

1 tablespoon fresh lemon juice
2 tablespoons water
¼ teaspoon fresh pepper

¼ teaspoon salt
1½ sticks butter, softened

- Cook and reduce the juice, water, salt and pepper down to 2 Tablespoons (about 5 minutes)
- In saucepan, using a wire whisk, beat the egg yolks until thickened
- Add 1 tablespoon butter and beat into the egg yolks
- Cool the reduction mixture and add to the beaten egg yolks
- Over heat, carefully cook the egg and reduction mixture whisking constantly until the yolks foam on top (you may need to move off heat periodically and then return to heat as you are whisking)
- Add a tablespoon of butter at a time continually whisking
- When all butter has been incorporated taste for seasonings
- Add more juice or seasonings to taste

SAUCE TOMAT
Basic French Sauce

- 2 ounces salt pork
- 1 onion, chopped fine
- 1 stalk celery chopped fine
- 1 carrot chopped fine
- Olive oil
- 1 large can tomatoes, mashed
- 1 clove garlic, chopped
- Fresh herbs, salt, pepper and pinch of sugar

- Sauté salt pork in a bit of olive oil
- Add the Mirepoix (onion, celery, carrot) and sweat the vegetables
- Add a bit of flour and cook a bit
- Add the canned tomatoes, breaking up the tomatoes
- Add garlic and simmer 1½ hours
- Add a dab of butter or cream
- Use with mussels marinara, ratatouille, minestrone soup, or clam chowder

MORNAY SAUCE
Basic French Sauce

- 3 tablespoons unsalted butter
- 3 tablespoons flour
- 2¼ cups whole milk
- 1 cup grated extra-sharp cheddar cheese or Swiss cheese
- ¼ cup finely grated Parmigiano-Reggiano cheese
- ½ teaspoon salt
- ⅛ teaspoon fresh ground pepper
- Pinch of cayenne pepper
- Freshly grated nutmeg

- Melt butter in saucepan
- Whisk in flour to make a roux, cook a minute
- Add the milk, bring to a simmer whisking frequently
- Add the cheeses and seasonings
- Cook until cheese is melted and sauce is thickened

SOUTH AFRICAN SAUCE

This sauce is served over pap (ground and cooked maize) and accompanied with the famous Boerewors sausage. This sausage is made with a variety of meats ground together. We sampled both this sauce and sausage while in South Africa on safari.

Olive oil	Can of chopped tomatoes
2 chopped onions	2-3 teaspoons sugar
Salt and Chili powder (pinch)	3 tablespoons ketchup
2 tablespoons tomato paste	Can of baked beans
2-3 teaspoons paprika	

- Sauté vegetables and spices
- Add beans, simmer
- Cover and cook until thick

STIR FRY SAUCE

½ cup soy sauce
½ cup chicken broth
1 tablespoon cornstarch
1 tablespoon honey
1 teaspoon sesame seed oil
1 teaspoon rice vinegar
   2-inch piece ginger grated
2 garlic cloves grated

- Cook with stir fry vegetables 3 minutes

STEVE'S HORSERADISH SAUCE

- 2 cups sour cream
- ¼ cup horseradish
- 1 teaspoon white vinegar
- 1 teaspoon salt
- Dash hot pepper sauce

- Mix all together and serve with roast beef or steak or use as a fondue sauce

LEMON-BASIL PESTO
WITH PISTACHIOS

- 2 cups fresh basil leaves
- ¼ cup unsalted pistachios shelled
- 2 cloves crushed garlic
- 1 teaspoon lemon zest
- Salt
- ½ cup extra-virgin olive oil (or as needed)
- ¼ cup grated Parmesan cheese

- Place basil, nuts, garlic and zest in a food processor
- Process until a paste forms
- Add salt to taste; slowly drizzle in the oil until emulsified
- Stir in the cheese

Spread on slices of toasted crostini as an appetizer
Or thin with a few tablespoons of hot pasta water and toss with pasta
If not using immediately. Transfer to a bowl and top with a thin layer of olive oil, wrap tightly and refrigerate up to 2-3 weeks

Yield: 2 cups

VEGETABLE MARINADE
1988

Marinated vegetables add a nice touch to a tossed salad or served alone as a refreshing summer salad.

¼ cup lemon juice
½ cup vinegar
¼ cup water
2 tablespoons chopped onion
⅛ teaspoon pepper
1-2 tablespoons minced garlic

1 tablespoon fresh parsley roughly chopped
½ teaspoon salt
½ teaspoon sugar
⅛ teaspoon oregano

- Cook a variety of fresh vegetables
- Mix the marinade ingredients
- Add marinade to vegetables and mix well, refrigerate

BASIC BASIL PESTO
1990

Every year my basil plants overproduce and I make this pesto. It marries well with penne pasta.

2-3 cups packed fresh basil leaves
1-2 medium size cloves of garlic
½ cup extra virgin olive oil or as needed
Lemon zest
Kosher salt and fresh pepper to taste

¼ cups pine nuts or walnuts or mixture of the two
½ cup freshly grated Parmigiano-Reggiano cheese

- Wash and dry the basil well
- Place in processor with nuts and garlic
- Pulse several times until coarsely chopped
- Add ¼ cup of the oil and process until smooth, can use more oil as needed
- Season with salt and pepper
- If serving immediately add remaining oil and pulse again; transfer to bowl and add cheese and mix well
- This pesto is best served within the hour, but it can be refrigerated in an airtight container with plastic wrap pressed directly onto its surface for up to 3 days.

If freezing; transfer to freezer container and drizzle with remaining oil. Freeze for up to 3 months; thaw and stir in cheese.

Yield: 1 cup

BEEF MARINADE
1967

½ cup burgundy wine
1 teaspoon Worcestershire sauce
1 clove garlic
½ cup canola oil
½ teaspoon rosemary, minced

1 teaspoon sugar
½ teaspoon salt
1 tablespoon vinegar
½ teaspoon dried marjoram

LIGHT AND DARK ROUX
(ROUX BLOND ET ROUX BRUN)

LIGHT ROUX

4 tablespoons unsalted butter

5 tablespoons flour

- Melt butter in saucepan. Add flour and stir constantly until the roux starts foaming and whitens…no color
- Remove from heat, allow to cool and store until needed
- Use to thicken stock, milk or any liquid

DARK ROUX

Same as light roux but cook the mixture until it becomes brown

Chef's comments: When using roux to thicken a sauce, either stir **hot** liquid into **cold** roux or **cold** liquid in **hot** roux. Continue stirring until the liquid boils to avoid lumps

Roux can be cooked in a large quantity in moderate oven 250° for 1½ hours rather than over low heat.

BASIC CHICKEN STOCK

4 pound chicken (neck, wing tips, carcasses or legs and thighs)
2-3 carrots washed but unpeeled
1 large onion cut in half
3-4 garlic cloves in in half and unpeeled
2 leeks (washed thoroughly)
2-3 celery stalks

Bouquet garni (green leaves of the leeks, fresh thyme, bay leaves and stalks from parsley)
Whole peppercorns
Coarse salt
White pepper
3-4 quarts of water

- Cut chicken into small pieces
- Place in pan, cover with cold water
- Add just a handful of the salt
- Add vegetables and bouquet garni; bring to a boil
- Skim the foam off the top constantly
- When foam is completely gone add the peppercorns
- Simmer uncovered for 3 hours adding water if necessary to compensate for the reduction
- Pass through a chinois, do not press the solids
- Let cool in separate containers

VEAL STOCK

- Replace chicken with veal bones and simmer for 4-5 hours

PORK STOCK

- Brown pork neck bones in oil in a 400° oven until browned
- Sauté 6 cloves garlic smashed and unpeeled and cut in half, carrots, celery, and onion
- Add browned bones
- Deglaze the roasting pan with water, add to stock pot and cover with 2-3 cups water plus the deglazed water
- Add some cooked tomato paste and salt
- Add bouquet of garni (add fresh rosemary to bouquet)
- Add peppercorns, cook 3-4 hours, skim foam frequently

ROSEMARY MARINADE
FOR LAMB OR CHICKEN

- ¼ cup oil
- ¼ cup wine vinegar
- 2 teaspoons salt
- 2 teaspoons crushed dried rosemary, or minced fresh rosemary
- ½ teaspoon pepper
- ½ cup chopped onion
- 2 tablespoons ketchup or tomato paste

VARIATION

- ½ cup oil
- ¼ cup lemon juice
- 1 teaspoon salt
- 1 teaspoon marjoram
- 1 teaspoon thyme
- 1 clove garlic minced
- ½ cup chopped onion
- ¼ cup chopped parsley

BALSAMIC MARINADE

This marinade is perfect for pork tenderloin or London Broil. Roast the pork tenderloin basting with the marinade for about 1 hour. This will marinate up to 2 pounds of meat.

- 2 tablespoons of your favorite steak seasoning or rub
- ½ cup olive oil
- ½ balsamic vinegar

- Mix together and marinate meat 3 hours or overnight

TRUFFLE SAUCE

2 tablespoons butter
2 tablespoons fresh button mushrooms, chopped
2 tablespoons shallots grated
1 teaspoon peppercorns crushed
2 bay leaves
1 cup white wine (Pinot Grigio)
1 cup heavy cream
½ cup madeira wine
4 tablespoons finely chopped truffles
Salt and pepper to taste
2 cups chicken stock

- Melt the butter, add mushrooms, shallots, peppercorns and bay leaves
- Reduce liquid over high heat for about 2 minutes
- Add cream, bring the mixture to a boil, then reduce by one-third and until it is a smooth consistency, adjust the seasoning
- In another sauté pan, add wine to 3 tablespoons of truffles, reduce over high heat for 2-3 minutes
- Strain the cream sauce into the truffles and wine, and then reduce it to a smooth consistency
- Boil the noodles quickly, put pasta in pan with sauce, toss well

WHOLE CRANBERRY SAUCE

1 cup sugar
1 cup water
1 package rinsed fresh cranberries

- Mix sugar and water in saucepan; stir to dissolve sugar
- Bring to boil, add cranberries
- Return to boil, reduce heat
- Boil 10 minutes stirring occasionally
- Remove from heat
- Cool completely, then refrigerate

Yield: 2¼ cups

SAUCES FOR CHEESECAKES

STRAWBERRY TOPPING

1 pint fresh strawberries
⅓ cup sugar
1 teaspoon vanilla

- Chop strawberries and set aside ⅓ cup for later
- Add the berries to pan with sugar and vanilla; cook stirring occasionally until it thickens
- Puree the mixture with an immersion blender; add ⅓ cup of the uncooked berries
- Serve over cake
- Can add a drop of red food coloring to give it a richer color

BLUEBERRY TOPPING

½ cup of sugar
3 tablespoons cornstarch
1 pint fresh blueberries or frozen
2 tablespoons lemon juice
1 tablespoon butter

- Combine everything except the butter in saucepan
- Cook until it gets thick; add butter; let cool

RASPBERRY TOPPING

2 cups raspberries
1 cup sugar
1 tablespoon cornstarch

- Combine berries, sugar and some water
- Bring to boil; simmer 3 minutes
- In another bowl mix cornstarch and a bit of water
- Add to the berry mixture
- Cook stirring for 5 minutes or until thick

CHOCOLATE GANACHE

1 cup heavy cream
8 ounces semi-sweet chocolate

- Melt chocolate and cream over low heat
- Stir constantly until smooth and thick
- Pour it over a chilled cheesecake
- Spread quickly before it hardens
- Once the cake is covered with chocolate, return to the fridge to set
- Ganache can be stored in fridge, covered. To reuse, reheat gently

RASPBERRY SAUCE

Taken from Chicago cooking school. Decorate bottom of dessert plates with this lovely sauce.

*You can cook this sauce using the pectin, or omit the pectin and simply puree it and use the sauce the same day. If you cook the sauce, it loses its bright color, but stays longer in the refrigerator. You can add red food coloring to enhance the color.

½ cup raspberries
½ cup sugar
½ teaspoon pectin*

- Process in food processor
- Boil for 4 minutes* or use as is
- Put in squirt bottle

BASIC SABAYON SAUCE

This simple sauce can be whipped up in no time to serve over fresh or baked fruits, a brownie, or a piece of flourless cake.

- 4 egg yolks
- ¼ cup granulated sugar
- ⅓ cup sweet wine, marsala, madeira or port

- Pour water into a double boiler to a depth of 1-2 inches
- Put egg yolks and sugar in the top portion of the double boiler and whisk (about a minute)
- Add the wine and continue beating
- The yolks will thicken as the bowl heats up
- Beat for 8-10 minutes by hand and only 4-5 minutes if you use an electric beater
- It should become thick and frothy
- Remove from the heat and beat for 30 more seconds
- Serve immediately or pour into an airtight container
- Place plastic wrap on top of the sauce making sure the wrap completely covers the sauce
- Place lid on the container and refrigerate until ready to use

MY FAVORITE CHOCOLATE SAUCE

This sauce works well with baked Alaska, ice cream pies, or ice cream. My absolute favorite.

IN SAUCEPAN ADD:

- 1 stick butter
- 4 ounces dark chocolate (high quality chocolate such as Lindt)
- 1 cup sugar
- 1 large can evaporated milk
- 1 teaspoon vanilla

- Whisk carefully and bring to boil
- Simmer until desired consistency

CHOCOLATE SAUCE

1 cup milk
1 ounce cocoa
⅓ cup sugar
3 ounces bittersweet chocolate
1 tablespoon butter

- Boil milk, sugar and cocoa for 3 minutes
- Add the chocolate and boil for 4 minutes
- Whisk in 1 Tablespoons butter

ROMANOFF SAUCE

½ cup sour cream
3-4 tablespoons brown sugar
2 tablespoons Grand Marnier or Brandy
½ cup heavy cream
3 tablespoons sugar
Fresh mixed berries

- Chill the cream, bowl and beaters
- Mix sour cream, brown sugar, and liquor in bowl
- Whip the chilled cream until it just begins to thicken
- Add sugar and whip until thick
- Fold the sour cream mixture into the cream mixture
- Serve over berries

FRESH CRANBERRY ORANGE RELISH

1 package rinsed fresh cranberries
1 medium orange, washed
¼-1 cup sugar

- Slice unpeeled orange into eights; remove seeds
- Place half the cranberries and half the oranges into a food processor
- Process until evenly chopped
- Transfer to a bowl
- Place other half of cranberries and orange into food processor
- Process until evenly chopped
- Transfer to a bowl
- Add sugar and mix well
- Store in refrigerator or freezer

Yield: 2½ cups

CRANBERRY/APPLE RELISH

2 tablespoons butter
4 apples cut up
¼ teaspoon cardamom or allspice

1 bag fresh cranberries
¾ cup sugar

- In skillet melt butter and sauté apples with spices
- Cook for 10 minutes
- Increase heat to med/high and add cranberries
- Add sugar and 1¼ cups water
- Heat to boiling and simmer on low for 6-8 minutes or until cranberries pop
- Cool and refrigerate

SUGGESTED MENUS

I enjoy dinner parties. These are some meals I have arranged for both small and large dinners or for when family visits. Once I *plan the meal*, I make a shopping list and a "make ahead" list to keep me organized.

MENU # 1
Hot crab dip with crackers
Mozzarella/tomato/basil salad (*Caprese*)
Steve's grilled London Broil
Rice Mingle
Green beans with sautéed shallots
Raspberry-topped chocolate tarts with pecan crust
Wine Pairing: Cabernet or Merlot

MENU #2
Prosciutto-wrapped scallop salad over mixed greens or arugula
Veal Marsala
Zelda's fettuccini
Sautéed baby spinach with garlic
Bananas Foster
Wine Pairing: Pinot Noir

MENU #3
Classic crab and artichoke dip/crackers
Tossed garden salad
Grilled Cornish hens with currant glaze
Chateau potatoes
Elodie's Chocolate Cake
Wine Pairing: White Zinfandel

MENU #4

Assorted Cheese and olive tray with crackers
Green-bean salad with shitake mushrooms
Coq au vin
Mashed Potato Casserole
Blender Chocolate Mousse
Wine Pairing: Pinot Noir, Merlot, or White Zinfandel

MENU #5 SERVES: 8

Cheesy Nut Ball
Chilled asparagus soup with Timbale of Crab
Veal or Chicken Saltimbocca (double recipe)
Roasted potatoes
Spinach sautéed in garlic oil
Cherry Cheese Pie
Wine Pairing: Merlot or Sangiovese red Italian wine (veal)
Pinot Grigio, Merlot or Chianti Classico (chicken)

MENU # 6

Montrachet and Sun Dried Tomato Mold with crackers
Baby spinach salad with mandarin oranges and red onions
Pork Tenderloin with Cumberland glaze
Apple stuffing
Derby Pie with ice cream
Wine Pairing: Merlot, Beaujolais, Grenache

MENU #7

Olive Nut Spread with crackers
Asparagus with Lemon Herb Dressing
Grilled Pork Chops with Nectarine Relish
Baked Russet Potatoes on the grill
Green Baby Peas
Fudge Pie
Wine Pairing: Chardonnay, White Zinfandel

MENU #8

Assorted Cheese tray and crackers
Tomato, avocado, hearts of palm salad
Herb Crusted Roast Beef Tenderloin
Garlic mashed potatoes
Caramelized onions
Roasted Asparagus with Lemon zest
Mixed Fresh Berries with Romanoff Sauce
Wine Pairing: Bordeaux, Shiraz Malbec, Cabernet Sauvignon

MENU # 9

Baked Olives
Caprese Salad (Sliced Tomatoes, Fresh Mozzarella, Fresh Basil, Balsamic Vinaigrette
Stuffed Chicken Marsala
Steamed Broccoli
Roasted potatoes or Risotto Blanco
Grasshopper Pie
Wine Pairing: Valpollcella, Sangiovese, Merlot, Chianti Classico

MENU # 10

Cheese Krispies
Chilled Asparagus soup with Timbales of Crab
Grilled Pork Chops
Baked potato
Sautéed zucchini/mushrooms/tomatoes
Strawberry mousse
Wine Pairing: Zinfandel, Shiraz

MENU # 11

Crabmeat ball with crackers
Mixed spring greens with fresh Vinaigrette
Grilled Salmon
Basic Brown rice pilaf
Broccoli puff
Mile High Ice Cream Pie
Wine Pairing: Pinot Noir

MENU #12

Antipasto/Componata/crostini
Tossed salad with Pat's Homemade Salad Dressing
Spaghetti with Meatballs
Tiramisu
Wine Pairing: Chianti Classico

MENU # 13

Baked Artichoke Spread
Asparagus with Lemon Herb Dressing
Penne Five Cheese
Carrot loaf
Lemon Charlotte
Wine Pairing: Soave, Beaujolais, Chardonnay

MENU # 14

Champignons Farcis (Stuffed Mushrooms)
Apple and Prune Stuffed Pork Loin
Special Mashed Potatoes
Broccoli with Lemon Butter
Brandy Ice with Pirouettes
Wine Pairing: Pinot Noir, Chardonnay

MENU # 15

Crabmeat Ball with crackers
Basic Caesar Salad with croutons
Beef Brisket with Portobello Mushrooms and Dried Cranberries
Grilled Vegetables
Potato Casserole
Coffee Rum Cream with chocolate curls
Wine Pairing: Zinfandel, Beaujolais

MENU #16

Brie Cheese in puff pastry
Asparagus Soup with Crab and Caviar Timbales
Roast Port with Cumberland Glaze
Roasted Sweet and White Potatoes
Sautéed Green Beans
Baked Alaska
Wine Pairing: Pinot Noir, Chardonnay

MENU #17

PICNIC FOR WEARY TRAVELERS
Shrimp, Tomato and Olive Appetizer
Honey and Herb Grilled Chicken
Potato Salad
Overnight Salad
Corn Bread Sticks
Peach Cobbler

MENU #18

Beer Cheese with crackers
Hummus topped with Olive Oil
Lamb chops with rosemary, lemon olive oil marinade
Rice Pilaf with caramelized onions and sautéed mushrooms
Grilled Asparagus
Blender Chocolate Mousse
Wine Pairing: Pinot Noir

MENU #19

Spinach Balls
Bacon wrapped dates with blue cheese and almonds
Lobster Bisque
Stuffed Sole with Newburg Sauce
Green Beans Almandine
Corn Bread and Crusty Breads
Raspberry Topped Chocolate Tart with Pecan Crust
Wine Pairing: Meursault

MENU #20

Componata on Crostini
Asparagus Wrapped in Crisp Prosciutto
Chicken Cacciatore
Italian Style Greens
Penne Pasta
Zuppa Ingelese
Wine Pairing: Pinot Noir, Sangiovese Fattoria del Fe Isina

MENU #21

Smoked Salmon/Cream Cheese cups
Cheese crackers and olive tray
Grilled Filet Mignon with Béarnaise Sauce
Chateau Potatoes
Elegant Salad
Charlotte Russe
Wine Pairing: Cabernet Sauvignon, Bordeaux, or a hearty Pinot Noir

MENU #22

Artichoke Spread with crackers
Seafood Ramekins
Spaghetti All 'olio E Aglio
Elegant Salad
Asparagus with Lemon Zest
Pots de Crème
Wine Pairing: Pinot Grigio, Sauvignon Blanc

MENU #23

Bacon Wrapped Dates filled with Blue Cheese and Almonds
Mini Cheese Balls
Green Bean Salad with Shitake Mushrooms
Coq au vin
Mashed Potatoes Chantilly
Broccoli Spears
Roasted small Carrots
Lemon Meringue Pie
Wine Pairing: Red Burgundy, Beaujolais, or Pinot Noir

MENU # 24

Asparagus Wrapped in Prosciutto
Spaghetti and Meatballs
Sweet Italian Sausage with onions and peppers
Mixed Green Salad with Pat's Homemade Dressing
Cheesecake cubes with Strawberry Sauce
Chocolate covered Strawberries
Wine Pairing: Ruffino Classico Chianti

MENU #25

White Bean Puree with Baked Pita chips
Oven Dried Tomatoes and Eggplant Timbales
Veal Piccata
Angel Hair Parmigiano-Reggiano
Sautéed Broccoli Rabe
Crème Brulee
Wine Pairing: Chardonnay

DINNER PARTIES FOR 8-10

Hummus with pita points
Assorted Baked Olives
Marinated artichokes
Shrimp, olive and tomato salad
Mesclun Greens tossed with pears, almonds, walnuts, dried cranberries in Raspberry Vinaigrette
Rock Cornish Hens with Grapes
Sautéed green beans
Grasshopper pie
Wine: Pinot Noir

Bacon Wrapped Blue Cheese Stuffed Dates
Mini Brie baked in phyllo
Chilled Asparagus soup with crab timbales
Seafood ramekins
Spaghetti all' Olio
Green Bean Bundles
Brandy ice over bite-size pieces of fresh pound cake, fruit and shaved chocolate
Wine: 2006 Pouilly-Fuisse Laboure-Roe Chardonnay

Minced Oyster Bake
Beef Wellington with Perigueux Sauce
Crustless Spinach Quiche
Elegant Salad
Mississippi Mud Pie
Wine: Cabernet Sauvignon or Merlot

Brandied Shrimp Provencale
Elegant Salad
Grilled Filet Mignon
Béarnaise sauce
Chateau Potatoes
Almond Meringue with Mixed Berries
Wine: Merlot or Cabernet Sauvignon

ACKNOWLEDGEMENTS

Developing this book has been a long journey. It started nearly 10 years ago when my friend *Ann Milam* first put the idea into my mind. She has been my constant support. There were many times she would say, "Pat you have to get this book completed before I die. I am not getting any younger."

I am grateful to all of my family and friends who helped me along this journey.

To my dear husband Steve for putting up with many years of me sitting at my computer typing away. Without his daily encouragement and love I may have not made it to this point of completion. He is instrumental in photographing and scanning many of the pictures throughout the book as well as editing.

To my daughter, Mary Cerjan, for guiding me in the right direction with both the overall idea, and the format for this book. For her beautiful creative writing and editing skills that helped me develop the title and the introduction.

To my daughter, Janet Haney, for serving as Editor in Chief, and for her constant encouragement and patience when I pulled her husband away from her family to format the book.

To my granddaughters, Thia and Avery, for helping serve as Junior Editors.

To my sisters, Marie and Beverly, and all my incredible friends in Sarasota who have all supported and encouraged me to complete this project.

To my son-in-law, Spencer, who spent days wrestling with desktop publishing tasks and working with a professional printer to finalize the book.

To my son-in-law, Richard, who seems to have the patience to listen to my needs and always come up with a good solution.

To my brother, Ron, who has shared his love of cooking with me from childhood through our adult lives.

To John High who did sample sketches for me and encouraged me to insert live pictures. His idea of photos instead of sketches proved to be a better option.

To all my friends along my life's journey far and wide who shared recipes and cooking techniques that made me who I am today.

INDEX OF RECIPES

APPETIZERS AND SNACKS

BEVERAGES

PALATE CLEANSERS

BREAKFAST ITEMS, BREADS AND MUFFINS

SOUPS

SALADS AND SALAD DRESSINGS

VEGETABLES

COMFORT FOODS, CASSEROLES, QUICHES AND STEWS

PASTAS AND RICES

BEEF

PORK AND HAM

CHICKEN AND FOWL

VEAL AND LAMB

SEAFOOD

DESSERTS, CAKES, COOKIES, FROSTINGS AND CANDIES

INTERNATIONAL FOODS

    ITALIAN
    GERMAN/SWISS
    POLISH
    CHINESE
    CENTRAL AMERICAN
    SPANISH/MEXICAN
    FRENCH
    RUSSIAN
    ENGLISH
    SWISS

GRILLING WITH STEVE

SAUCES AND STOCKS

SUGGESTED MENUS

Appetizers

SNACKS
- HOMEMADE SNACK MIX 203
- HUMMUS 210
- PITA CHIPS 210

ASPARAGUS WRAPPED IN CRISP PROSCIUTTO 361
BACON-WRAPPED APPETIZERS 286
BAKED ARTICHOKE SPREAD 166
BAKED OLIVES 359
BARBECUED CHICKEN WINGS 236
BEER CHEESE DIP 211
BRANDIED SHRIMP PROVENCALE 233
BRIE CHEESE IN PUFF PASTRY 315
CAPONATA WITH VODKA 294
CARAMELIZED ONION AND ROQUEFORT TART 362
CHAMPIGNONS FARCIS 226
CHEESE BALL WRAPPED IN NUTS 211
CHEESE KRISPIES 286
CHEESE SPREAD 212
CHEESE STRAWS 207
CHEESY NUT BALL 235
CRAB PROFITEROLES 238
CRABMEAT BALL 198
CREAM CHEESE, PESTO AND SUNDRIED TOMATOES IN PUFF PASTRY 366
CROSTINI 223, 363, 374
HOT CRAB DIP 235
HOT CRAB RANGOON DIP 229
HOT CRABMEAT 123
HOT TACO DIP 236
LIVER PATE 313
MARINATED MUSHROOMS 234
MEXICAN CHEESECAKE 316
MINCED OYSTER APPETIZER 237
MINI CHEESE BALLS 207
MONTRACHET & SUN-DRIED TOMATO MOLD 228
MUSHROOM SPREAD 234
MUSHROOMS STUFFED WITH CRAB MEAT 227
MUSHROOMS STUFFED WITH SPINACH & ANCHOVIES 225
OLIVE NUT SPREAD 359
OVEN-DRIED TOMATO AND EGGPLANT TIMBALES WITH PESTO 317
PORK OR BEEF RIBLETS 237
POTATO SKINS 229
PROSCIUTTO WRAPPED SCALLOPS 364
QUICHE-LORRAINE SQUARES 284
ROASTED TOMATO AND RICOTTA CROSTINI 374
SALMON SPREAD IN FISH MOLD 224
SAUSAGE CHEESE BALLS 101
SEA LEGS DIABLE 223
SOMERSET POTTED CHEDDAR WITH WALNUTS 233

SPINACH BALLS	212
SPINACH-CHEESE SWIRLS	365
TAPENADE WITH SUN-DRIED TOMATOES	314
TOMATO OMBRE ON GRILLED RUSTIC BREAD	374

Beverages

CAPPUCCINO	134
CHAMPAGNE PUNCH	298
COFFEE PUNCH	278
MAY WINE	72
PLANTERS PUNCH	298
SOUTHERN PUNCH	298

Palate Cleansers

CHAMPAGNE SORBET	239
PALATE CLEANSERS	239
PINEAPPLE SORBET	240

Breakfast Items

ARIZONA GRANOLA	366
BANANA NUT BREAD	38
BELGUIM WAFFLES	105
BLUEBERRY MUFFINS	162, 164
BREAKFAST BACON ROLLUPS	279
BREAKFAST FRITTATA	368
CHEESY GRITS SOUFFLE	279
DOUBLE CHOCOLATE CHIP MUFFINS	163
EGG CASSEROLE WITH CANADIAN BACON	280
EGG ROYAL CASSEROLE	216
FRESH SCRAMBLED EGGS	12
HEARTY PANCAKES	367
HOMEMADE GRANOLA	202
MOCK SOUFFLE EGG CASSEROLE	280
MY FAVORITE PANCAKE RECIPE	96
OATMEAL AND WHEAT BLUEBERRY PANCAKES	367
POTATO FRITTATA	349
RAISIN BRAN MUFFINS	209
YOGURT BLUEBERRY MUFFINS	164

Breads

APRICOT DAISY COFFEECAKE	140
BANANA NUT BREAD	38
CHEESE BREAD	142
CORNBREAD STICKS OR MUFFINS	149
CRACKED WHEAT BREAD	141
CRANBERRY-ORANGE BREAD	288
CREAM CHEESE BRAIDS	290
CROSTINI	223, 363, 374
ENGLISH MUFFIN LOAVES	278
FRENCH BREAD	137

HONEY WHOLE WHEAT BREAD	143
HOT CROSS BUNS	146
ITALIAN BREAD STICKS	144
MARY'S SICILIAN PIZZA	129
MY ITALIAN BREAD	139
PAN ROLLS	145
PIZZA FRITTA	41
POLISH POPPY SEED COFFEE SWIRL	88
SALLY LUNN BREAD	147
SEABOURN BREADSTICKS	406
STROMBOLI	32
WHITE BREAD	138
YORKSHIRE PUDDING	398
ZUCCHINI WALNUT BREAD	206

Soups

BARNEY'S NAVY HAM AND BEAN SOUP	53
BARNEY'S OYSTER STEW	54
BLACK BEAN SOUP	346
BROCCOLI SOUP	157
BUTTERNUT SQUASH SOUP	309
CAULIFLOWER SOUP	240
CHILLED ASPARAGUS SOUP	310
FRENCH LENTIL SOUP	361
FRENCH ONION SOUP	241
ICED CUCUMBER SOUP	158
LOBSTER BISQUE	369
MANHATTAN CLAM CHOWDER	52
OLD FASHIONED SPLIT PEA SOUP	84
SUPER QUICK MINESTRONE	311
VERMOUNT BEER CHEESE SOUP	152

Salads

ASPARAGUS SALAD WITH LEMON HERB DRESSING	355
AVOCADO AND SHRIMP SALAD	312
BARNEY'S MACARONI SALAD	54
BASIC CAESAR SALAD	243
BROCCOLI SALAD	219
CHARITY BALL SALAD	198
CLASSIC VINAIGRETTE	371, 378
CRAB LOUIS SALAD	242
CRANBERRY JELL-O SALAD	217
CREAMY CAESAR SALAD WITH SPICY CROUTONS	372
CRISP APPLE AND ORANGE SALAD	376
CROUTONS	157, 372
ELEGANT SALAD	256
GARDEN MACARONI SALAD	219
GERMAN POTATO SALAD	79
GOURMET CHICKEN SALAD	221
LEMON MUSTARD DRESSING	256

LOUIS DRESSING	242, 360
MARINATED VEGETABLES	229
OIL AND LEMON SALAD DRESSING	370, 376
OVERNIGHT SALAD	218
PASTA SALAD	318
PATRICIA'S ITALIAN SALAD DRESSING	293
POTATO SALAD	56, 79
RICE AND VEGETABLE SALAD	220
ROASTED BEET SALAD	373
SALAD VINAIGRETTES	370
SHRIMP, OLIVE, AND TOMATO SALAD	360
SPINACH SALAD	265
WATERCRESS SALAD WITH DRIED FRUIT AND ALMONDS	377
WINTER GREENS SALAD WITH GOAT CHEESE	375

Vegetables

BAKED ZUCCHINI	384
BARNEY'S BAKED BEANS	57
BARNEY'S SCALLOPED POTATOES	55
BROCCOLI AND RICE CASSEROLE	184
BROCCOLI CASSEROLE	93, 159
BROCCOLI PUFF	245
BROCCOLI SUPREME CASSEROLE	160
BRUSSELS SPROUTS WITH PANCETTA	387
CANDIED YAMS	432
CARAMELIZED ONIONS	350
CARROT LOAF (TERRINE)	319
CHAMPIGNONS FARCIS	226
CHANTILLY POTATOES	190
CHATEAU POTATOES	246
CHEESY GRITS SOUFFLE	279
CORN PUDDING	100
CREAMY POTATO BAKE	191
EASY CAULIFLOWER GRATIN	379
EGGPLANT PARMIGIANO	30
FLUFFY POTATO CASSEROLE	187, 191
GOLDEN CRUMB BROCCOLI CASSEROLE	93
GRATIN DAUPHINOIS	302
GREEN BEAN BUNDLES	384
GREEN BEAN SALAD WITH SHITAKE MUSHROOMS	378
GREEN BEANS WITH ALMONDS	380
GRILLED ARTICHOKES WITH PARSLEY AND GARLIC	420
GRILLED GARDEN VEGETABLES	382
HAM AND SCALLOPED POTATOES SAUCE METHOD	167
ITALIAN SAUTÉED ESCAROLE GREENS	25
ITALIAN STUFFED ARTICHOKES	20
LEEK AND POTATO GRATIN WITH CREAM	379
LEEKS AU GRATIN	301
MARINATED VEGETABLES	229
MASHED POTATOES BAKED WITH THREE CHEESES	190

MASHED SWEET POTATO CASSEROLES	433
MICROWAVE SPAGHETTI SQUASH	331
MINT STUFFED MUSHROOMS	381
MUSHROOMS STUFFED WITH CRAB MEAT	227
MUSHROOMS STUFFED WITH SPINACH & ANCHOVIES	225
OVEN ROASTED VEGETABLES	382
PARLIAMENT POTATOES	246
PATRICIA'S BAKED BEANS	197
PICKLED BEETS	84
PIEDMONT ROASTED PEPPERS	383
POMMES ANNA	248
POTATO CHEESE CUPS	247
POTATO FRITTATA	349
POTATO SKINS	229
RATATOUILLE "KAGOOTS"	22
RED GERMAN CABBAGE (ROTKOHL)	73
ROASTED ASPARAGUS	350
ROASTED SQUASH	377
ROASTED SWEET POTATOES AND WHITE POTATOES	380
SAUTÉED APPLES, ONIONS, AND RAISINS	91
SAUTÉED ITALIAN SPINACH AND CANNELLINI BEANS	381
SAUTÉED MUSHROOMS	193
SAUTÉED MUSHROOMS WITH GARLIC, PARMESAN AND BREAD CRUMBS	193
SOUTHERN STYLE BLACK EYED PEAS	111
SPICY SWEET POTATOES	314
SPINACH SOUFFLE	244
STUFFED EGGPLANT	29
TOMATO VEGETABLE CASSEROLE	385
TRADITIONAL GREEN BEAN CASSEROLE	94
TWICE-BAKED POTATOES	192
VEGETARIAN CHILI	386
YELLOW SQUASH CASSEROLE	101

Comfort Foods

BEEF STEW	180, 181
CHILI CON CARNE	95
CORNED BEEF AND CABBAGE	179
DOUBLE CRUSTED CHICKEN POT PIE	176
MACARONI AND CHEESE	128
MEAT LOAF	110
POLISH GOLABKI	85
SLOW COOKER BEEF STEW	181
SUZANNE'S CHEESE ENCHILADAS	153
VEGETARIAN CHILI	386

Casseroles

BAKED LASAGNA	14
BROCCOLI AND RICE CASSEROLE	184
CHICKEN AND VEGETABLES WITH SUPREME SAUCE	178
CHICKEN FLORENTINE	388
HAM AND SCALLOPED POTATOES LAYERED METHOD	168
HOT CHICKEN SALAD	166
TACO CASSEROLE	169
TURKEY TETRAZZINI	173

Quiches

CRUSTLESS SPINACH QUICHE	253
QUICHE DE LANGOUSTE	230
QUICHE-LORRAINE SQUARES	284
SPINACH QUICHE	199, 253

Pastas

BAKED ZITI	320
CHEESE RAVIOLI	28
CHEESE STUFFED MANICOTTI OR PASTA SHELLS	23
FRESH SEAFOOD PASTA	327
GNOCCHI	47
LINGUINE WITH CLAM SAUCE	31
MACARONI AND CHEESE	128
PASTA WITH TRUFFLE SAUCE	390
PASTA WITH VODKA SAUCE	391
PENNE PASTA WITH FIVE CHEESES	321
POLENTA WITH SAUCE AND MEAT	49
RIGATONI WITH SQUASH AND SHRIMP	389
SPAGHETTI ALL'OLIO E AGLIO	15
ZELDA'S FETTUCCINI	249

Rices

BASIC LONG-GRAIN BROWN RICE PILAF	92
BASIC RISOTTO	322
FRENCH RICE	177
RISOTTO AND BEANS	323
ROCK CORNISH HENS WITH RICE MINGLE	89
SAVORY TURKISH LAMB PILAF	109

Beef

ARTHUR'S STUFFED FILET MIGNON	250
BEEF SHISH KABOBS	427
BEEF STEW	180, 181
BEEF STROGANOFF	108
BEEF WELLINGTON WITH PERIGUEUX SAUCE	252
BOEUF BOURGUIGNON	254
BRACIOLE	21
BRISKET WITH PORTOBELLO MUSHROOMS AND DRIED CRANBERRIES	397

CHILI CON CARNE	95
CORNED BEEF AND CABBAGE	179
FLANK STEAK WITH BRANDY CREAM SAUCE	264
HERB CRUSTED BEEF TENDERLOIN	348
ITALIAN MEATBALLS	18
MEAT LOAF	110
PRIME RIB ROAST WITH AU JUS	396
SAVORY STUFFED TENDERLOIN	426
SLOW COOKEER BEEF POT ROAST	182
SLOW COOKER BEEF STEW	181
STEAK DIANE	251
STEVE'S MARINATED AND GRILLED LONDON BROIL	425
STUFFED GREEN PEPPERS	170
STUFFED ROUND STEAK	186
SWISS STEAK	187

Pork

APPLE AND PRUNE STUFFED PORK LOIN	399
BABY BACK RIBS RESTAURANT STYLE	424
BEER AND HONEY-HERB GRILLED PORK	418
GRILLED PORK CHOPS WITH NECTARINE RELISH	419
PORK CHOPS WITH TOMATO, SHITAKE MUSHROOMS AND MARSALA	329
PORK CUTLETS WITH ORANGES	189
ROAST PORK TENDERLOIN	398
ROAST PORK WITH CUMBERLAND GLAZE	90
SPANISH PORK CHOPS	169
SPICY BOURBON GLAZED SPARERIBS	405
SWEET AND SOUR PORK	351

Chicken

APRICOT-LEMON GRILLED CHICKEN	423
BREAST OF CHICKEN PERIGOURDINE	258
BUTTERFLIED CHICKEN GRILLED WITH A BRICK	428
CHICKEN AND SEAFOOD PAELLA	395
CHICKEN AND VEGETABLES WITH SUPREME SAUCE	178
CHICKEN BREASTS SUPREME	194
CHICKEN CACCIATORE	26
CHICKEN DIVAN	172
CHICKEN FLORENTINE	388
CHICKEN MARBELLA	257
CHICKEN MARENGO	188
CHICKEN OR VEAL CORDON BLEU	74
CHICKEN POT PIE	174, 176
COQ AU VIN	402
CREAMY BAKED CHICKEN BREASTS WITH FRENCH RICE	177
DOUBLE CRUSTED CHICKEN POT PIE	176
HERB AND HONEY BBQ CHICKEN	423
HOT CHICKEN SALAD	166
ORIENTAL SKILLET CHICKEN	196
POLLO AL LIMONE	401

ROAST CHICKEN	305
STUFFED CHICKEN MARSALA	403
VEAL OR CHICKEN PARMESAN	33
VEAL OR CHICKEN SALTIMBOCCA	295
WEIGHT WATCHERS CHICKEN DISH	404

Fowl

DUCK A L'ORANGE	232
ROASTED TURKEY	430
ROCK CORNISH GAME HENS WITH GRAPES	259
ROCK CORNISH HENS WITH RICE MINGLE	89
TURKEY TETRAZZINI	173

Veal

CHICKEN OR VEAL CORDON BLEU	74
GRAHAM KERR'S VEAL SCALLOPINE DON QUIXOTE	135
OSSO BUCCO	400
VEAL MARSALA	326
VEAL OR CHICKEN PARMESAN	33
VEAL OR CHICKEN SALTIMBOCCA	295
VEAL PICCATA	324
WIENER SCHNITZEL	72

Lamb

GRILLED LAMB CHOPS OR RACK OF LAMB	418
LAMB WITH PINE NUTS, SPINACH AND SUN-DRIED TOMATOES	328
OVEN-ROASTED LEG OF LAMB	330
RACK OF LAMB	331, 417, 418
SHEPHERD'S PIE	185

Seafoods

BAKED STUFFED LOBSTERS	352
BAKED STUFFED SHRIMP	120
BOB'S SALMON	394
BRANDIED SHRIMP PROVENCALE	233
CLAMS CASINO	121
COQUILLES ST-JACQUES	231
FISH FILLETS A LA LUIS	354
FRESH SEAFOOD PASTA	327
HOT CRABMEAT	123
LINGUINE WITH CLAM SAUCE	31
LOBSTER BISQUE	369
MUSSELS IN WHITE WINE	393
PELICANO CORVINA	353
PROSCIUTTO WRAPPED SCALLOPS	364
RED SNAPPER ON CEDAR PLANK	422
RIGATONI WITH SQUASH AND SHRIMP	389
SAUTEED BASS WITH HERB BUTTER	304
SEAFOOD RAMEKINS	261

SEAFOOD STRUDEL	262
SHRIMP AND ARTICHOKE HEARTS CASSEROLE	171
SHRIMP AND GRITS	394
SHRIMP CANTONESE WITH RICE	196
SHRIMP CREOLE	183
SHRIMP DU JOUR	263
SOLE MEUNIERE	392
SPICY MARINARA SAUCE FOR SEAFOOD OR SNAILS	48
STUFFED QUAHOGS	122
STUFFED SOLE WITH SAUCE NEWBURG	260

Desserts

ALMOND MERINGUE WITH MIXED BERRIES	407
AUSTRALIAN PAVLOVA WITH LEMON CURD AND BERRIES	408
BANANAS FOSTER	267
BLENDER CHOCOLATE MOUSSE	291
BLITZ TORTE	104
BOSTON CRÈME CAKE	10
BRANDY ICE	266
CHOCOLATE CHARLOTTE RUSSE	273
CHOCOLATE FONDUE	78
CHOCOLATE MOUSSE GALLIANO	266
CHOCOLATE MOUSSE PIE	268
CHOCOLATE POTS DE CRÈME	342
CHOCOLATE SOUFFLES	334
COFFEE RUM CREAM	200
CREAM ANGLAISE	308, 445
CREAMY APPLE TART	409
CRÈME BRULÉE	308
CREPE SUZETTE	306
FLAN	357
FRANGIPANE	343
FRANGIPANE FRUIT TART	343
FRESH PEACH COBBLER	150
FRESH STRAWBERRY MOUSSE	291
GERMAN RUMTOPF (RUM POT)	82
HOMEMADE CHURNED ICE CREAM	118
JANICE CHOATE'S ICE CREAM PIE	271
JANICE'S FRENCH APPLE TART	410
JEAN'S LEMON SOUFFLE WITH RASPBERRY SAUCE	411
LEMON CHARLOTTE	276
MERINGUE TOPPING	60
MILE HIGH ICE CREAM PIE	213
MILLION DOLLAR FUDGE	12
MINUTE RICE PUDDING	42
MISSISSIPPI MUD PIE	272
MOM'S BASIC VANILLA CREAM	59
PATE SUCREE	132, 300
PEACH COBBLER	150
RASPBERRY-TOPPED CHOCOLATE TARTS WITH PECAN CRUST	332

RUM COFFEE ICE CREAM	267
SHERRIED ROCKY ROAD PUDDING	152
SOUFFLE GRAND MARNIER	307
TIRAMISU	296
WARM CHOCOLATE PUDDING CAKES	333
ZUPPA INGLESE	274

Cakes

ALMOND POUND CAKE	205
APPLE WALNUT SUPREME CAKE	131
BANANA BREAD WITH CHOCOLATE CHIPS AND WALNUTS	335
BANANA NUT CAKE WITH COCOA WHIPPED CREAM	102
BOSTON CRÈME CAKE	10
BROWN SUGAR POUND CAKE	282
CHOCOLATE CHIP CAKE	287
DELICIOUS BUNDT CAKE	204
ELODIE'S CHOCOLATE CAKE	270
FEATHERY FUDGE CAKE	124, 126
JEWISH COFFEE CAKE	289
LIME GOAT CHEESE CHEESECAKE	356
MARY'S OLD FASHIONED SOUTHERN POUND CAKE	99
MILK CHOCOLATE CHEESECAKE	336
MOM'S CHEESECAKE	39
MOM'S COFFEE CAKE	40
MY SECRETARY'S DELICIOUS CHOCOLATE CAKE	281
NEW YORK STYLE CHEESECAKE	412
ORIGINAL GERMAN BLACK FOREST CAKE	80
PECAN TOPPED COFFEE CAKE	283
PINEAPPLE UPSIDE-DOWN CAKE	36
PUMPKIN WALNUT CAKE	134
SUZANNE'S CHOCOLATE CAKE	154
TINY CHEESE CAKES	133

Cookies

ANISE-ALMOND BISCOTTI	37
BLOND BROWNIES	115
BUTTER PECAN TURTLE COOKIES	285
CHOCOLATE CHIP BROWNIES	113
CHOCOLATE CRINKLES	208
CHOCOLATE ITALIAN WEDDING COOKIE	46
CHOCOLATE PECAN BARS	214
CHOCOLATE SYRUP BROWNIES	112
COFFEE BROWNIES	117
ITALIAN ALMOND COOKIES	35
ITALIAN CHERRY COOKIES	44
ITALIAN PIGNOLI COOKIES	35
LEMON MERINGUE BARS	215
LITTLE MARY'S CHOCOLATE CHIP COOKIES	127
MAGIC COOKIE BARS	288
MARBLED BROWNIES	114

MEXICAN WEDDING COOKIES	107
NIEMAN-MARCUS $250 CHOCOLATE CHIP COOKIES	161
PINEAPPLE SQUARES	34
ROSETTE COOKIES	45
RUM BALLS	155
SAUCEPAN BROWNIES	116
SNICKERDOODLES	130
SPITZBUDEN URCHIN COOKIES	78

Frostings

BLENDER CHOCOLATE FROSTING	130
CHOCOLATE SATIN FROSTING	128

Candies

MOCHA TRUFFLES	156

Pies

APPLE CRUMBLE PIE WITH ALMONDS	341
APPLE PANCAKE PIE	123
APPLE PIE	64
ASSORTED CREAM PIES	62
BEST PECAN PIE BY MEL	340
BLUEBERRY PIE	65
CHERRY CHEESE PIE	132
CHERRY PIE	66
CHOCOLATE MOUSSE PIE	268
DERBY PIE	201
FLORIDA KEY LIME PIE	414
FRESH RHUBARB PIE	67
FUDGE PIE	200
GRAHAM CRACKER CREAM PIE	60
GRASSHOPPER PIE	103
JANICE CHOATE'S ICE CREAM PIE	271
LEMON CHESS PIE	106
LEMON MERINGUE PIE	63
MERINGUE TOPPING	60
MILE HIGH ICE CREAM PIE	213
MINCEMEAT PIE	66
MISSISSIPPI MUD PIE	272
MOM'S BASIC VANILLA CREAM	59
MOM'S CUSTARD PIE	69
MOM'S PECAN PIE	65
MOM'S PUMPKIN PIE	68
NOT SO SWEET PECAN PIE	97
PEACH PIE	67
PIE PASTRY FOOD PROCESSOR METHOD	338
PIE PASTRY FOOL PROOF DOUGH	339
PIE PASTRY MOM'S RECIPE	61
PIE PASTRY RICH CRUST	338
STRAWBERRY PIE	201

International Foods

CENTRAL AMERICAN
- ARROZ CON POLLO 345
- BLACK BEAN SOUP 346
- FISH FILLETS A LA LUIS 354
- FLAN 357
- GALLO PINTO 347
- PELICANO CORVINA 353

CHINESE
- CHOW MEIN OR CHOP SUEY 195
- ORIENTAL SKILLET CHICKEN 196
- SHRIMP CANTONESE WITH RICE 196

ENGLISH
- BEEF WELLINGTON WITH PERIGUEUX SAUCE 252
- YORKSHIRE PUDDING 398

FRENCH
- BOEUF BOURGUIGNON 254
- CHOCOLATE CHARLOTTE RUSSE 273
- CHOCOLATE POTS DE CRÈME 342
- CHOCOLATE SOUFFLES 334
- COQ AU VIN 402
- COQUILLES ST-JACQUES 231
- CREAM ANGLAISE 308, 445
- CRÈME BRULÉE 308
- CREPE SUZETTE 306
- DUCK A L'ORANGE 232
- GRATIN DAUPHINOIS 302
- LEMON CHARLOTTE 276
- SOLE MEUNIERE 392
- SOUFFLE GRAND MARNIER 307

GERMAN
- A TYPICAL GERMAN HOUSPLATTE 73
- CHICKEN OR VEAL CORDON BLEU 74
- GERMAN POTATO SALAD 79
- GERMAN RUMTOPF (RUM POT) 82
- MAY WINE 72
- ORIGINAL GERMAN BLACK FOREST CAKE 80
- RED GERMAN CABBAGE (ROTKOHL) 73
- SPAETZLES AND PAPRIKA SAUCE 83
- SPITZBUDEN URCHIN COOKIES 78
- WIENER SCHNITZEL 72

ITALIAN
- ANISE-ALMOND BISCOTTI 37
- BAKED LASAGNA 14
- BAKED ZITI 320
- BASIC RISOTTO 322
- BRACIOLE 21
- CAPONATA WITH VODKA 294
- CHEESE RAVIOLI 28

CHEESE STUFFED MANICOTTI OR PASTA SHELLS	23
CHICKEN CACCIATORE	26
CHOCOLATE ITALIAN WEDDING COOKIE	46
EGGPLANT PARMIGIANO	30
GNOCCHI	47
GRAHAM KERR'S VEAL SCALLOPINE DON QUIXOTE	135
ITALIAN ALMOND COOKIES	35
ITALIAN CHERRY COOKIES	44
ITALIAN MEATBALLS	18
ITALIAN PIGNOLI COOKIES	35
ITALIAN SAUSAGE AND PEPPERS	19
ITALIAN SAUTÉED ESCAROLE GREENS	25
ITALIAN SPAGHETTI SAUCE	16
ITALIAN STUFFED ARTICHOKES	20
LINGUINE WITH CLAM SAUCE	31
MARINARA SAUCE	24, 48, 320
MARY'S SICILIAN PIZZA	129
OSSO BUCCO	400
PIZZA FRITTA	41
POLENTA WITH SAUCE AND MEAT	49
POLLO AL LIMONE	401
RISOTTO AND BEANS	323
ROSETTE COOKIES	45
SPAGHETTI ALL'OLIO E AGLIO	15
SPICY MARINARA SAUCE FOR SEAFOOD OR SNAILS	48
STROMBOLI	32
STUFFED CHICKEN MARSALA	403
STUFFED EGGPLANT	29
TIRAMISU	296
VEAL MARSALA	326
VEAL OR CHICKEN PARMESAN	33
VEAL OR CHICKEN SALTIMBOCCA	295
VEAL PICCATA	324
ZUPPA INGLESE	274

MEXICAN

SUZANNE'S CHEESE ENCHILADAS	153

POLISH

POLISH GOLABKI	85
POLISH PIEROGI	86
POLISH POPPY SEED COFFEE SWIRL	88

RUSSIAN

BEEF STROGANOFF	108

SPANISH

CHICKEN AND SEAFOOD PAELLA	395
ROCK CORNISH GAME HENS WITH GRAPES	259

SWISS

CHEESE FONDUE	77
CHOCOLATE FONDUE	78
FONDUE	75, 76, 77, 78, 441
FONDUE SAUCES	76, 441

Grilling with Steve

APRICOT-LEMON GRILLED CHICKEN	423
BABY BACK RIBS RESTAURANT STYLE	424
BEEF SHISH KABOBS	427
BEER AND HONEY-HERB GRILLED PORK	418
BUTTERFLIED CHICKEN GRILLED WITH A BRICK	428
GRILLED ARTICHOKES WITH PARSLEY AND GARLIC	420
GRILLED CORN IN HUSKS	421
GRILLED LAMB CHOPS OR RACK OF LAMB	418
GRILLED PORK CHOPS WITH NECTARINE RELISH	419
GRILLED SALMON	421
HERB AND HONEY BBQ CHICKEN	423
INTERNAL GRILLING TEMPERATURES	416
RED SNAPPER ON CEDAR PLANK	422
SAVORY STUFFED TENDERLOIN	426
SPICY BOURBON GLAZED SPARERIBS	405
STEVE'S MARINATED AND GRILLED LONDON BROIL	425

Sauces

MARINADES
- BALSAMIC MARINADE 454
- BEEF MARINADE 452
- ROSEMARY MARINADE FOR LAMB OR CHICKEN 454
- VEGETABLE MARINADE 451

STOCKS
- BASIC CHICKEN STOCK 303, 453
- PORK STOCK 303, 453
- VEAL STOCK 303, 453

BASIC BASIL PESTO 451
BASIC BECHEMEL (WHITE) SAUCE 446
BASIC BROWN SAUCE (ESPAÑOLA) 439
BASIC PAN SAUCE 441
BASIC SABAYON SAUCE 458
BERNAISE SAUCE 438
BEURRE BLANC-BUTTER SAUCE 437
BROWN SAUCE FOR STEAK OR CHATEAUBRIAND 440
CHOCOLATE SAUCE 213, 458, 459
CLASSIC MAYONNAISE 442
CRANBERRY/APPLE RELISH 460
CREAM ANGLAISE 308, 445
CUMBERLAND SAUCE 443
DEMI GLACE FOR STEAKS 437
FONDUE SAUCES 76, 441
FRESH CRANBERRY ORANGE RELISH 460
HOLLANDAISE SAUCE 447
HOMEMADE MUSHROOM SAUCE 443
ITALIAN SPAGHETTI SAUCE 16
LEMON BUTTER 422, 438
LEMON-BASIL PESTO WITH PISTACHIOS 450

LIGHT AND DARK ROUX (ROUX BLOND ET ROUX BRUN)	302, 452
MARINARA SAUCE	24, 48, 320
MINT SAUCE	442
MORNAY SAUCE	448
MY FAVORITE CHOCOLATE SAUCE	458
PAPRIKA SAUCE	83, 444
PERGUEUX SAUCE	442
PONZU SAUCE	445
QUICK BROWN SAUCE	439
RAISIN SAUCE	444
RASPBERRY SAUCE	411, 457
REMOULADE SAUCE	443
ROMANOFF SAUCE	337, 459
SAUCE TOMAT	448
SAUCES FOR CHEESECAKES	456
SOUTH AFRICAN SAUCE	449
SPAETZLES AND PAPRIKA SAUCE	83
STEVE'S HORSERADISH SAUCE	450
STIR FRY SAUCE	449
TRUFFLE SAUCE	390, 455
TURKEY GRAVY	431
VELOUTE SAUCE	446
WHOLE CRANBERRY SAUCE	455

Menus

CHRISTMAS MENU	435
DINNER PARTIES FOR 8-10	468
MY TYPICAL ITALIAN DINNER PARTY	292
SUGGESTED MENUS	461
THANKSGIVING MENU	
CANDIED YAMS	432
MASHED SWEET POTATO CASSEROLES	433
ROASTED TURKEY	430
THANKSGIVING MENU	429
TURKEY GRAVY	431

P.S. Dearest Patricia, Dearest Mom ~

Congratulations on fulfilling your lifelong dream.
We are very, very proud of you.

Love ~ Mary, Janet, and Steve